ORDINARY WISDOM

ORDINARY WISDOM

Sakya Pandita's Treasury of Good Advice

....

Sakya Pandita

With a commentary entitled

A Hive Where Gather Bees of Clear Understanding

by Sakya Khenpo Sangyay Tenzin

Translated by John T. Davenport
with Sallie D. Davenport
and Losang Thonden

Foreword by His Holiness Sakya Trizin

WISDOM PUBLICATIONS • BOSTON

Wisdom Publications
199 Elm Street
Somerville MA 02144 USA

Library of Congress Cataloging-in-Publication Data
Sa-skya Paṇḍi-ta Kun-dga'-rgyal-mtshan, 1182–1251.
    [Subhāṣitaratnanidhi. English]
    Ordinary wisdom : Sakya Pandita's treasury of good advice / by Sakya
Pandita Kunga Gyaltsen ; with commentary entitled: a hive where gather
bees of clear understanding / by Sakya Khenpo Sangye Tenzin ; translated
by John T. Davenport, Sallie D. Davenport, and Losang Thonden.
      p. cm.
    Includes bibliographical references and index.
    ISBN 0-86171-161-0 (alk. paper)
    I. Davenport, John T. II. Davenport, Sallie D. III. Blo-bzaṅ-don-ldan,
Lha-sa-ba. IV. Sakya Khenpo Sangye Tenzin. Legs par bśad pa rin po che'i
gter gyi don 'grel blo gsal buṅ ba 'du ba'i bsti gnas. English. V. Title. VI. Series.
PL3748.S2 S813 1998
895.4'1—dc21   97-005275

ISBN 0-86171-161-0

04 03 02 01 00
6   5   4   3   2

Interior design by: Gopa Design
Cover design by: Melissa Kulig
Cover image: Sakya Pandita, artist unknown, Central Tibet, c. 1600–1699 © 1999 Shelley and
    Donald Rubin Foundation, courtesy of the Himalayan Art Project, www.tibetart.com

TABLE *of* CONTENTS

FOREWORD

The *Sakya Legshe* (*sa skya legs bshad*, or, more properly, *legs par bshad pa rin po che'i gter*), or *A Jewel Treasury of Good Advice*, is one of the most important literary works of Kunga Gyaltsen Pal Zangpo (kun dga rgyal mtshan dpal bzang po), or Sakya Pandita, the greatest of the five founding lamas of the Sakya tradition. A profound, down-to-earth, and practical guide to the art of living as a wise and good human being, from the time of its composition in the early thirteenth century to the present, the *Sakya Legshe* has been one of the most popular and widely read Tibetan books. Numerous Tibetans, common people as well as nobility, have drawn from it inspiration and guidance in the conduct of their lives. It has been extensively studied by scholars and was considered a model literary style. Together with a number of other works by Sakya Pandita it has come to be highly valued, not only within Sakya, but by all the Buddhist traditions of Tibet. When someone was judged to have expressed themselves eloquently, it was common in Tibet for it to be said that they must have studied the *Sakya Legshe*.

Written primarily for lay people, who generally did not have the time or resources for extensive study and consequently were not skilled in sophisticated philosophy, the *Sakya Legshe* presents concrete examples expressed in pithy parables and aphorisms. Sakya Pandita describes the method of teaching he uses in one of the book's concluding verses (immediately following verse 457):

> As the physician Kumāra Jīvaka cured the seriously ill
> By persuading them that medicine was food,
> So have I taught this sacred Dharma
> Through reference to the ways of the world.

This verse refers to the story of a wise and skilled physician who cured an ailing king, with a hereditary aversion to the appropriate medicine, by putting the medicine in beer for the king to drink. The Venerable Sakya Pandita says, "employing skillful means, my approach has been to talk about the various characteristics of the foolish and the wise. In fact this great treatise I have taught, *A Jewel Treasury of Good Advice*, provides for the needs of students according to the level of their mental abilities. It is the sublime Dharma whereby one can attain the state of high status and definite goodness."

The present translation of the *Sakya Legshe* is unique since it is not only a fresh new English translation of the complete text itself, but one that benefits from inclusion of a translation of a commentary by a contemporary scholar, the late abbot of Ghoom Monastery near Darjeeling in India, Sakya Khenpo Sangyay Tenzin (sa skya mkhan po sangs rgyas bstan 'dzin, 1904–90), entitled *A Hive of Bees of Clear Understanding*, which explains all 457 verses of the *Sakya Legshe*. This is an important feature since many of Sakya Pandita's verses are enigmatic without a commentary. Beyond mere elucidation, however, Sakya Khenpo Sangyay Tenzin has brought to the *Sakya Legshe* his own highly regarded wisdom and poetic imagery, filling out the text with an engaging vitality. This makes this classic work of Tibetan literature available to an English readership as has never before been possible. It will be of great interest to contemporary students of Tibetan history and culture, of Buddhist thought and practice, and of ethics in general. The voice of Sakya Pandita gives us a window through which to observe something of the outlook of ordinary people, of the climate of religious and philosophical opinion, and of the modes of literary expression in old Tibet.

But the work is not just of importance with regard to Sakya Pandita's audience of Tibetan citizenry in the thirteenth century. It addresses human life of every era, in all cultures. Perhaps what is of greatest importance and relevance to the world today is the contribution of timeless wisdom Sakya Pandita makes in the *Sakya Legshe* to our current struggle with the perennial problem of the human condition: How are we to live peaceably with ourselves and each other? Sakya Pandita's discourse touches on many topics related to human character—achievement and failure, anger and kindness, friends and enemies, death, deceit and desire, excellence and coarseness, generosity and greed, intelligence and foolishness, power, respect, shame, wealth, and wisdom, to name but a few.

To appreciate both the historical significance of the *Sakya Legshe* and its current application, one must understand something of the way its subject, ethical conduct, is the touchstone and in a profound sense the heart of Buddhist practice. From a Buddhist perspective, sentient beings are trapped within the imaginings of their own minds, creating for themselves a lifetime of tribulation, ranging from minor annoyances to extreme suffering. This entrapment is due not to some permanent defect in the ultimate nature of mind; rather, the mind is defiled by disturbing emotions, which are in fact removable. These disturbing emotions distort our perception, generating feelings and actions based on ignorance. In Buddhism, the concept of ignorance applies to a fundamental error in our perception of how all phenomena exist, in that we tend to assume that things are concrete, inherently real, and autonomous—existing in a way that they do not.

We especially do not perceive our own situation properly. All our actions are accompanied by an intentional activity of mind: good actions follow good intentions, and bad actions follow bad intentions, and in each case the respective tendencies are reinforced, generating more of the same—a perpetuating cycle of causes and effects. Our present state, then, is the complex expression of a long history of causes and effects from time immemorial to the present and on into the future. Whether we know better or not, we often ignore the relation between our actions and their consequences, preferring instead to regard external factors as the source of both our happiness and our difficulties. This mistaken perception leads us to act in ways contrary to our most fundamental interests.

In the *Sakya Legshe*, Sakya Pandita is trying to help us escape this pitfall with repeated advice to stop doing that which must be avoided (because it is a cause of suffering for oneself and others) and engage in that which should be practiced (because it is a cause of benefit for oneself and others). He often illustrates his points with captivating, and sometimes amusing, aphorisms. For example, to emphasize the self-destructive momentum of the mind trapped in disturbing emotions, in verse 208 he describes the dangers of arrogance this way:

> Excessive praise of an evil king's status
> Eventually will lead to his destruction.
> When an egg is thrown up into the sky,
> What else can happen than for it to break?

Buddhist practice enables liberation from this destructive cycle by encouraging one to live in ways that transform and purify these negative mental tendencies. This purification rids the mind of all the perceptual, emotional, and intentional activity based on the deluded belief in inherent existence; this is accomplished both by formal study and practice, and by how one lives everyday life in general. The *Sakya Legshe* is a definitive guide to ethical conduct in everyday life.

Conduct is considered ethical when one's motivation is free from the mental defilements of greed, hatred, and the delusion that all phenomena exist inherently, because the effects of actions arising out of such pure motivation are beneficial to all. The underlying principle, then, is our fundamental relatedness, our interdependence, and the responsibility that each individual bears for the impact of their actions. Awareness of these dynamic interconnections fosters a healthy sense of shame, that there are limits one cannot transgress and expect positive results either for oneself or others, which in turn encourages conscientiousness in one's behavior. In the commentary to verse 252 it is stated,

> It is said that to the extent one has a sense of shame,
> To that extent one has the supreme jewel of good qualities.

Sakya Pandita presumes shame to be a curb on excessive, negative human behavior. In the thirteenth century, with its viable small, rural, organic communities, one could not use the cloak of anonymity to avoid being held accountable for one's wrongdoing. The censure of family and personal acquaintances, and any immediate or long-term detrimental effects on the community as a whole, were keenly felt to be one's personal responsibility. In today's large, impersonal urban environments, under the pressures of industrialism, consumerism, and a growing and extremely mobile population, the individual often is dissociated from any meaningful community. This removes any sense of restraint, as well as any sense that one's actions are relevant to the concerns of others, or that the concerns of others are relevant to one's own short-term advantage. The impetus becomes competition and personal success, whatever the cost. Perhaps we can apply Sakya Pandita's advice as an imperative to strengthen our communities so that, among other things, a sense of shame can exert a greater influence in regulating civil society and its relationship to the planetary environment within which society is conducted.

In current Western psychology, unquestionably due at least in part to the alienating conditions described above, shame has taken on an additional dimension that is recognized as damaging, even disabling: the sense of shame is internalized, such that individuals perceive their very being, not just their behavior, as shameful. This concretized identity results in feelings of worthlessness, hopelessness, and isolation, and consequently spawns a host of destructive psychological and behavioral disorders. In contrast, Buddhism recognizes that every human life is an extraordinarily rare and precious opportunity. Regardless of the activities one might have engaged in, the qualities one might have developed, the assumptions one might have absorbed, one is never permanently stained. One always has the capacity to achieve authentic transformation and to generate beneficial effects for oneself and others. There is no implied external judge; by developing knowledge, discernment, and ethical conduct, the laws of causality will produce the results for oneself in the experience of well-being, the development of good personal qualities, and the eradication of those faults that obstruct one's liberation.

At all stages of the Buddhist path, then, ethical conduct is both a cause and result of purification. It is psychologically necessary for the mental clarity and concentration needed for study and practice. It is an integral and inseparable aspect of the process of liberation. Moreover, with the culmination of one's path in the realization of emptiness, the primordially clear, ultimate nature of mind emerges and spontaneously functions as wise and compassionate activity benefiting all sentient beings. This is the "definite goodness" described by Sakya Pandita in the *Sakya Legshe*.

His Holiness Sakya Trizin
Head of the Sakya Order of Tibetan Buddhism
Rajpur, U.P., India
January 2000

TRANSLATORS' PREFACE

THIS TRANSLATION OF the *Sakya Legshe* began as a reading exercise when I was working in Dharamsala (1988–91) as an advisor to the newly formed Planning Council of the exiled government of Tibet. Losang Thonden, resident scholar at the Library of Tibetan Works and Archives, kindly responded to my interest in exploring some secular literature during free time from my work responsibilities. We first read over the letter by the Fifth Dalai Lama (discussed on p. 12) and then moved on to Sakya Pandita's classic. For most of that time I was accompanied by my long-time partner and good friend, Sallie. As time passed and as our interest and knowledge of this work developed, the three of us realized that a formal translation of this work could be a significant contribution to the growing body of Tibetan literature that is now available to an English readership, most of which is of a distinctly religious genre, and much of that tending to the abstruse. The *Sakya Legshe* fills a gap at the beginner's end of the spectrum of this literature. It should appeal to ordinary people who are interested in learning something about Tibet and its form of Buddhism, yet who may not be prepared for the more complicated materials that are the usual options on the bookshelf.

The present work serves as a partial response to Kolmas's comment on Bosson's translation of the *Sakya Legshe* that "the only thing, in my view, that still remains to be done in this field is to peruse carefully the numerous commentaries to this famous didactic work of Tibet in order to explain many of the allusions and stories found in it."[1] A more complete response would look systematically at the full range of commentaries available, a task beyond the scope of this work. Toward that end this translation offers both an updated translation of the main text along with a verse-by-verse commentary. It has been made from Sakya Khenpo Sangyay Tenzin's 1972 commentary on all 457 verses of the *Sakya Legshe*.[2] Reference was also made to a thirteenth-century commentary on the forty-seven verses that includes stories.[3] This commentary was written by one of Sakya Pandita's direct disciples, Marton Chögyay (dmar ston chos rgyal). Assistance in the rendering of difficult terminology was obtained from Yangchen Gaway Lodro's (dbyangs can dga ba'i blo gros) glossary of unusual terms in this text.[4]

Sakya Pandita composed the *Sakya Legshe* in four-line verses with each line containing seven syllables.[5] It was impossible to replicate that traditional prosodic form, though effort was made to create some semblance of verse rhythm where possible. We tried to retain the original ordering of the lines of verse except in cases where differences between Tibetan and English syntax would have made the rendering of English too awkward.

The literary style of some Tibetan literature, such as the commentary, employs repetition of the same idea with different amounts of detail in each repetition, a literary device that fosters retention of the subject matter. The translators have taken the liberty of trimming from Sakya Khenpo Sangyay Tenzin's work some of this repetition, which becomes burdensome to an English reader. It is hoped that the repetition that remains will be useful in conveying the flavor and emphasis of the original work without being unduly tedious. Another alteration to the commentary is the occasional rearrangement of passages to enhance the flow of the argument in English. These are not indicated; however, occasionally clarifying words that do not appear in the original are added to Sakya Pandita's verses or the commentary and are placed in brackets.

Sakya Khenpo Sangyay Tenzin's commentary contains many references to other works such as the ever popular *Bodhisattvacaryāvatāra* by the eighth-century Indian master Śāntideva. Sometimes in order to clarify the meaning of a citation, we included additional lines from the cited verse, added in brackets. Wherever possible we have tried to identify the author and book title being cited, and these are found in the Subject Index. However, location of all the citations was beyond the scope of this work, especially those attributed to unidentified authors, referred to in the text as "some great masters."

Of central concern throughout the book is the subject of "yon tan," which we have translated in two ways, depending on the context. Often we use "good qualities," or "good personal qualities," and we also use "knowledge." At first glance, these may not appear to be equivalent terms in English, because our modern secularized notion of knowledge is usually that of acquired, practical, often career-oriented information or skills of one sort or another that enable us to perform some function such as to program computers, fix cars, practice medicine or law. We also recognize that someone might be knowledgeable about some subject as a result of study or experience—again, the notion of acquired information. The Tibetan term "yon tan," however, embraces a dynamic interrelationship between what is known, the knower, and the experience of knowing, and hence denotes that in the act or experience of knowing, the knower becomes characterized by qualities or attributes that are consistent with the nature of what is known. In the context of Indo-Tibetan Buddhist cultural heritage, knowledge most often refers to a penetrating inquiry into the nature of self and the manner of existence. Therefore, becoming learned would imply not merely acquiring information about a given subject, for example the six perfections, but would include becoming so deeply familiar with that knowledge through study, contemplation, and meditation that it becomes thoroughly internalized, allowing one gradually to acquire the "good qualities" of generosity, patience, enthusiastic perseverance, and so forth.

In translating the proper names that appear in the text, we have opted to use Sanskrit designations whenever possible, because they flow more easily from an English speaker's tongue than do transliterations of Tibetan names. Only where the Sanskrit was unknown or nonexistent did we resort to phonetic designations of Tibetan names. For the titles of books, we have applied the Wylie transliteration system. In verse 375, we used the English names only because they are so delightfully descriptive.

Some verses and segments of the commentary are obscure in meaning, and remain enigmatic to us. We have rendered them as faithfully as we are able and leave them for the reader, too, to puzzle over.

The text was translated by John Davenport. Sallie Davenport wrote the English, correcting translation errors and give the text a more flowing, contemporary style. Losang Thonden made the whole enterprise possible in the first place through his patient and careful translations of literary into colloquial Tibetan to make the meaning of the main text and its commentary more accessible to us.

The translators would like to express their appreciation to the following individuals for their help at various stages of this project: Mr. Gyatso Tshering, the Director of the Library of Tibetan Works and Archives in Dharamsala, India, where this project originated; Venerables Professor Geshe Lhundup Sopa of the University of Wisconsin and the Deer Park Buddhist Center in Oregon, Wisconsin, and Geshe Sonam Rinchen of the Library of Tibetan Works and Archives for their clear explanations of Tibetan Buddhism that have so greatly contributed to our understanding of this text; Venerables Yangsi Rinpoche of the Deer Park Buddhist Center and Khenpo Lobsang Donyo of Sera Jey Monastery in India for their assistance in locating several of the more obscure quotations in the commentary and for clarifying some difficult passages; Ruth Sonam especially, for her invaluable time and advice on the complexities and finer points of the ninth chapter; and Elizabeth Napper, Jeremy Russell, John Newman, Peter Schein, Cyrus Stearns, Tsetan Chonjore, Joanne Craig, Janice Giteck, Lauran Hartley, and Connie Walton.

A special nod of thanks is extended to Mr. Lobsang Lhalungpa of Santa Fe, New Mexico, who checked the entire translation, pointed out several errors as well as problems stemming from inaccuracies in the Tibetan text, and otherwise made numerous suggestions that have sharpened the meaning and improved the readability of this work considerably.

A most sincere expression of appreciation is made to Gene Smith, "bibliophile extraordinaire" and acquisitions editor at Wisdom Publications, for his thoughtful guidance in the final preparation of this work. He exemplifies perfectly the good editor who can turn a promising draft into a good book. His intimate knowledge of the *Sakya Legshe* and its commentaries, the Indian literature that preceded it, and the later Tibetan works that were inspired by it (to say nothing of his encyclopedic knowledge of the entire universe of Tibetan literature acquired through his years of work with the Library of Congress, for which all Tibetologists are eternally grateful) lies behind the preparation of the introduction, which provides a valuable context for understanding the significance of Sakya Pandita's classic. Thanks are also due to Samantha Kent, associate editor at Wisdom Publications, and Susanne Fairclough for their valuable editorial input.

John T. Davenport, Sallie D. Davenport, Losang Thonden
Seattle, Washington
January, 2000

INTRODUCTION

The *Sakya Legshe* occupies a unique position in Tibetan literature, being an unusual secular literary composition in a world that consists mainly of religious works. It was the first and an original Tibetan expression of the *subhāṣita* form of traditional Indian *nītiśāstra* literature—"eloquent sayings" about secular affairs in daily human life. As such, it played a substantial role in forging cultural and religious ties between India and Tibet that continue to this day. Its enduring popularity inspired several subsequent indigenous Tibetan subhāṣita literary works that were patterned after the *Sakya Legshe* and the Indian nītiśāstras from which Sakya Pandita drew for this work. That popularity continues today with the *Sakya Legshe* being incorporated into the modern education curricula of Tibet, India, and Bhutan. Its subject matter, the interweaving of the religious and worldly aspects of life, is representative of the life of its author, Sakya Pandita, a learned Buddhist cleric who, after a productive life as a monk and scholar, spent his last years in the royal court of the Mongol Empire forging ties between Tibet and Mongolia that survive today. To appreciate the significance of the *Sakya Legshe*, this introduction will examine first the life and work of Sakya Pandita, then the Indian nītiśāstra and subhāṣita literature upon which his composition is based, the subsequent works in Tibet that were inspired by the *Sakya Legshe*, and finally will close with a few remarks about previous English translations.

SAKYA PANDITA—HIS LIFE AND WORK

As a scholar, translator, teacher, author, and statesman of wide-ranging and unparalleled talents, Sakya Pandita was a unique figure in Tibetan political-religious history. By the time of his birth in 1182, more than three hundred years after the death of Lang Darma in 842, Tibet was in a state of decentralized control, divided into many smaller hegemonies often at odds with each other.[6] By the twelfth century, Buddhism had made a recovery after the persecutions of Lang Darma and many of these smaller hegemonies were established around monastic communities and centers of learning.[7] One such location was Sakya, situated on a tributary of the Tsangpo River to the southwest of Lhasa and directly north of the border between Nepal and Sikkim. This was the birthplace of Sakya Pandita.

The history of Sakya is woven around the history of the Khon ('khon) clan who originate in legend with the descent to earth in Tibet to the northwest of Sakya of three brothers of the God of Clear Light.[8] The Khon people enter Tibetan recorded history in the eighth century prior to the time of Lang Darma when a prominent member of the clan, Khon Palpoche ('khon dpal po che), became a minister of King Trisong Detsen (khri srong lde bstan, 754–797)[9] when Tibet was expansive and powerful. A subsequent descendent, Sakya Pandita's great grandfather Konchog Gyalpo (dkon mchog rgyal po, 1034–1102), is credited with establishing the first monastery at Sakya, an event that was indirectly foretold in a prediction of the famous Indian pandit, Atisha (982–1054), when he passed through the area in 1042. One of Konchog Gyalpo's sons, Sachen Kunga Nyingpo (sa chen kun dga' snying po), formulated the distinctive Sakya religious doctrine and brought into being the Sakya sect of Tibetan Buddhism. One of his four sons, Palchen Ohpa (dpal chen od pa), was Sakya Pandita's father while another, Jetsun Dragpa Gyaltsan (rje brtsun grags pa rgyal mtshan), was his uncle and first spiritual teacher.

As the eldest of two sons, Sakya Pandita was destined to carry on the family heritage of religious scholarship set by his uncles and grandfather, while his younger brother carried on the family name. According to the hagiographic style of Tibetan biographical sources, as a toddler Sakya Pandita is said to have drawn Indian letters in the dirt while playing and then carefully avoided crawling over them.[10] His early education began at ages five to six under the tutelage of his father and uncle. At age seventeen he had two auspicious dreams that presaged the major contribution he was to make to Tibetan scholarship in the area of logic and epistemology. The following year, 1200, he began four years of travel to other parts of Tibet to further his education, and it is during this period that his studies of logic commenced in earnest. Some of his earliest writings date back to this time.[11]

The renaissance of Buddhism in Tibet that began in the tenth century was marked by an interchange of scholars between India and Tibet that continued for about three centuries.[12] Tibetans such as Rinchen Zangpo (rin chen bzang po, 958–1055) would journey to India to learn Sanskrit and Buddhist teachings while Indian pandits such as Atisha would come to Tibet for long periods to teach. Sakya Pandita's life spanned the end of this period of fertile interchange. One year after the death of his father in 1203, he met one of the later Indian pandits to visit Tibet, the Kashmiri Śākyaśrībhadra (1127–1225), who was to be one of his most formative teachers. He studied for nine years with Śākyaśrībhadra and the other Indian scholars traveling with him, receiving full ordination from him in 1208. It was during this time that he acquired the mastery of Sanskrit and other subjects that was to earn him the title "Pandita," and enable him to translate several texts from Sanskrit into Tibetan.[13]

In 1216 Sakya Pandita's uncle passed away, leaving him to be the heir of the Sakya tradition and a religious teacher in his own right, thus marking the start of a twenty-eight-year period that was to be his most productive as a scholar. His compositions number over one hundred, with his primary interest being Buddhist logic and epistemology.[14] His longest, most detailed work was *A Treasury of Logic and Epistemology (tshad ma rigs pa'i gter)* composed in 1219, which, along with its autocommentary, summarizes the logical epistemological traditions of Dignāga and Dharmakīrti, the first attempt to do so.[15] The *Sakya Legshe* was his sixth longest book, a popular text for a wide audience that offers practical guidance for daily living. Though undated, recent scholarship suggests that it may have been composed shortly after *A Treasury of Logic and Epistemology.*[16] The range of his writing achievements is wide indeed, with compositions in such diverse areas as the Sanskrit language arts (grammar, prosody, poetics, synonymy, and lexicography), tantric works, commentaries, and biographies. His contributions to the development of Buddhist studies in Tibet are substantial, but have been overshadowed by his achievements as a statesman later in life.[17]

The beginning of the thirteenth century marked the rise of the Mongol Empire under the leadership of Genghis Khan (1167–1227). When Mongol troops took over Hsi-hsia, the Tangut Empire to the northeast of Tibet, the Tibetans sent tribute to the Mongols and avoided being invaded.[18] After the death of Genghis Khan, his son, Prince Godan, took control and the Tibetans ceased sending their tribute. In 1240 the Mongol army then did invade, pressing far south close to Lhasa, burning and killing as they proceeded. Having been identified as a learned lama, Sakya Pandita was summoned to the Mongol court by a letter from Godan in 1244.[19] Earlier in his life a prophecy had informed him that he would be invited by a "border race who wore hats like falcons and shoes like a hog's snout" to propagate the Dharma.[20] In 1244 he departed Tibet accompanied by his two young nephews, Lama Drogon Phakpa (bla ma 'gro mgon 'phags pa) and Chakna Dorji (phyag na rdo rje) and arrived in Mongolia three years later to spend what was to be the remainder of his life in service to the Mongol court, eventually passing away there (near the modern Chinese city of Lanzhou) in 1251.

In general, Sakya Pandita's role in Mongolia was twofold. He was charged with the religious task of teaching Buddhism to Prince Godan and helping him spread the Buddhist teachings in Mongolia, and with the temporal task of serving as "the Mongols' agent for achieving the submission of Tibet."[21] The first role had an enduring effect in that Buddhism remains the religion of Mongolia to this day. His second role was more complex. Initially Sakya Pandita was in the position of a vassal to a powerful lord wherein he essentially had to reconfirm Mongol authority over Tibet, which had earlier been achieved by Genghis Khan. However, this reconfirmation was achieved without the presence of Mongolian troops or administrators in Tibet. A letter from Sakya Pandita to Tibetan leaders written shortly before his death spells out the terms of this relationship between Tibet and Mongolia. In it he dwells at length on the piety of Godan and the importance of using this unique opportunity to spread Buddhism in Mongolia. But he also discusses the power differential between the two countries and how necessary it thus was for Tibetans to pay tribute to the Mongols to ensure their peaceful survival.[22]

This unique religious and temporal relationship between Godan and Sakya Pandita continued on into the next generation where it was formalized into the well-known *chö-yön* (priest-patron, *mchod yon*) relationship that evolved between Sakya Pandita's nephew, Phakpa, and Godan's successor, Kublai Khan. Eventually, as Mongol power weakened in the fourteenth century, the special relationship between the Mongol court and the Sakya sect in Tibet disappeared as power shifted to the noble house of Pamo Dru (phag mo dru) after their military defeated Sakya in 1350. The chö-yön relationship may have worked to a degree between Kublai and Phakpa due to their close personal relationship, but once they were gone it was no longer viable despite later Tibetan efforts to appeal to it as an instrument of foreign policy, especially in its relations with China.[23]

In summary it can be said that Sakya Pandita's life exemplified the ideal he explores in the *Sakya Legshe*, namely that people should strive to integrate the spiritual with the secular aspects of their lives. This ideal comes from a rich heritage of traditional Indian literature that was a formative influence on Sakya Pandita's intellectual and spiritual development.

NĪTIŚĀSTRA AND SUBHĀṢITA LITERATURE
AVAILABLE TO SAKYA PANDITA

In the seventh century a large-scale, rich intercultural exchange began between Tibet and India which was to draw to a close some decades after the death of Sakya Pandita. This exchange was primarily devoted to the transmission of India's Buddhist heritage to Tibet, but the interchange was not limited to religious ideas. The flow of wanderers, traders, and pilgrims, as well as monks and scholars, back and forth across the Himalayas involved human interactions "associated with folklore...folk customs, folk arts, folk songs, folk narratives, material folk culture, and folk wisdom."[24]

India has a long tradition of folk wisdom embedded in its oral traditions that predate its earliest literature, which appeared in the first millennium B.C.E. This wisdom was often expressed in short, easily memorized verses, originally circulating orally but later put into written form. Indians had a special fondness for didactic verse that offered people ethical guidance on the practicalities of daily living. This verse appears in a wide variety of literary genres.[25] Its subject matter is divided into three main categories: *dharma* (morality and duty), *artha* (profit or personal benefit), and *nīti* (common sense and judgment), with each expressed in its own *śāstras* (treatises).[26] Of particular interest in this study of the *Sakya Legshe* are the nītiśāstras, or those treatises that deal with "right or wise or moral conduct or behavior, prudence, policy, political wisdom or science."[27]

A subcategory of this Indian nītiśāstra literature is folk wisdom expressed as "wise sayings" that "contained not only beautiful thoughts but were also drawn and set down in beautiful language."[28] As such this subcategory is known as *subhāṣitas* (good or eloquent speech, witty saying, counsel).[29] Sakya Pandita elected to use this term in the Sanskrit title that he gave to the *Sakya Legshe*, the *Subhāṣitaratnanidhi*, thereby acknowledging the inspiration provided him by these Indian antecedents (although it was never composed in Sanskrit). Given the didactic quality of the subject matter, we have elected to gloss the term *subhāṣita* "good advice," hence the title in English: *A Jewel Treasury of Good Advice*.

As the extensive corpus of folk wisdom literature in India draws upon a common mass of oral tradition, it can be said to be authorless.[30] Indeed, while there are many texts attributed to various authors, the extant textual material is the result of a long period of scribes copying and recopying texts in response to demand and to keep ahead of the erosive climate of India, with each recopying subject to editorial omissions and additions reflecting the interests and judgment of each scribe. Without looking in detail at all of this material, it is sufficient here to note three sources of this folk wisdom that were available to Sakya Pandita when he composed the *Sakya Legshe*. These are the two different versions of the Jātaka stories,[31] the *Pañchatantra*,[32] and the nītiśāstras. The shorter version of the Jātaka stories, known as the *Jātakamālā*, as well as the nītiśāstras were translated into Tibetan and included in the section of the Tibetan Buddhist canon known as the Tangyur (bstan 'gyur). (Since the Jātaka stories, the *Pañchatantra*, and the *Hitopadeśa*, mentioned below, are commonly referred to by their Sanskrit titles, the English translations of those titles will not be used here.)

The Jātaka stories are a collection of accounts about the previous lives of the Buddha. Its longer version, the Jātaka, is included in the Pali canon and, as such, represents some of the oldest written folk wisdom of India, dating back to sometime between the death of the Buddha and the start of the Common era. These stories constitute a "running commentary of life, its perils, rewards, follies, virtues, and general unpredictability." The Jātaka was written in Pali,[33] a popular language accessible to ordinary people, whereas the *Jātakamālā* was written in Sanskrit, a specialist language of a small but sophisticated literary subculture of India. These tales express the long-time affinity between humans and animals found in Indian fables of the oral tradition that first took written form in the Upaniṣads.[34]

The *Sakya Legshe* draws upon the *Pañchatantra*, an important Indian text devoted to the subject of *nīti*. Its most popular later version, the *Hitopadeśa* was not compiled until the twelfth or thirteenth century in Bengal and may not have been available to Sakya Pandita. The *Pañchatantra* has been popular all over the world with two hundred versions existing in over sixty languages throughout the Middle East and Europe.[35] Even more than the Jātaka stories, this book offers animal fables in which animals impart timeless lessons. However, a divergent opinion is expressed by one student of this literature who cautions the modern reader against assuming these animal stories to be similar to the warm and fuzzy variety composed for children nowadays. Rather, he states that they focus on "management" in the sense of political manipulation for self-serving ends where there is a premium on duplicity, subterfuge, creating dissension, and so on. Further, he considers them less as moral exercises for the training of princes (as they are often described), than as "wisdom" appropriate to the trading community with its imperatives of success in the world of commerce.[36]

The nītiśāstras, or collections of wise sayings, were committed to writing beginning around the first century C.E. and by the tenth century had become a highly appreciated literary form for the development of literary ability and good taste, used "to teach cultured men right behavior."[37] In the cultural interchange between Tibet and India the scholars and monks from India brought not only their knowledge of Buddhism but also their individual appreciations of folk wisdom, perhaps stories and fables they had grown up with as well as knowledge of nītiśāstras they may have studied. The Tibetans also had an appreciation for these wise sayings and "Tibetan scholars felt interested in translating into Tibetan the Indian nītiśāstras to acquaint the common people of Tibet with the Indian views on practical life."[38] Altogether there are eight nītiśāstras translated into Tibetan during the ninth to eleventh centuries and included in the Tangyur. Translating the term "nītiśāstra" into English as "a treatise on temporal affairs," these are:[39]

A Treatise Called "A Hundred Verses of Wisdom"
(Prajñāśatakanāmaprakarana),

A Treatise on Temporal Affairs: The Staff of Wisdom
(Nītiśāstraprajñādandanāma), and

A Treatise on Temporal Affairs: The Drop that Nourishes People
(Nītiśāstrajanaposanabindunāma) by Nāgārjuna;

A Treatise on Temporal Affairs: A Treasury of Verses (Āryākosanāma)
by Ravigupta;

A Hundred Verses (Śatagāthā) by Vararuci;

A Precious Garland of Flawless Questions and Answers
(Vimalaprasnottararatnamālānāma) by Amoghavarsa;

King Cānakya's Treatise on Temporal Affairs (Cānakyarājanītiśāstra)
by Cānakya;

A Treatise on Temporal Affairs (Nītiśāstra) by Masūrāksa.

These translations generally follow the Sanskrit four-line verse form, usually with seven syllables per line, ranging in length from a short 22 verses *(A Precious Garland of Flawless Questions and Answers)* to the longest at 260 verses *(A Treatise on Temporal Affairs: The Staff of Wisdom).* For the most part, the authorship, while attributed, is unclear. The author of the first three, for instance, may not be the famous Mādhyamika philosopher who lived in the first century, C.E., but some other unknown Nāgārjuna.[40] Similarly, it is uncertain just which Masūrāksa may have written the last text. As for Cānakya, numerous collections of sayings have been attributed to him, with his fame accounting for more than he actually authored as other lesser known writers probably used his name in order to impart a cachet of prestige and authority to their own work. Moreover, the Tibetan translation of *King Cānakya's Treatise on Temporal Affairs* attributed to him does not match Sanskrit works by that name, but more closely matches portions of the large compendium known as the *Garudapurānam.*[41] Sternbach claims that the Sanskrit originals from which these translations were made have been lost, except for *A Treatise on Temporal Affairs: The Drop That Nourishes People.*[42]

Sakya Pandita likely borrowed stories from all of the nītiśāstras noted above, especially from *King Cānakya's Treatise on Temporal Affairs,* which itself was influenced by and contains material from the *Pañchatantra*[43]. One of his biographies states that he studied the *Cānakya* and *Masūrāksa* nītiśāstras as well as the *Pañchatantra* from his uncle, Jetsun Dragpa Gyaltsan.[44]

It is useful to recall that in Sakya Pandita's time books were all hand copied and thus comparatively rarer than in later times. Block printing was not introduced until early in the fifteenth century when the Tangyur was first printed in China. Though all eight of the nītiśāstras above are conveniently included in the Tangyur, that compendium was not available to Sakya Pandita. He would have had to possess individual copies of whatever books he studied. But given that he came from a prominent family, which was able to support a Sanskrit teacher for him for three years (1205–1207),[45] and that he had a personal library of three thousand books,[46] one can assume that he had all or most of the nītiśāstras, as well as the *Jātakamālā* and the *Pañchatantra*, in his possession when he composed the *Sakya Legshe*.

THE POPULARITY OF THE *SAKYA LEGSHE* AND ITS INFLUENCE ON LATER TIBETAN AND MONGOLIAN LITERATURE

Because the preponderance of literature in Tibet has been religious in nature, the *Sakya Legshe* belongs to a small minority of secular works. Tibet was a feudal society where literacy and education were not available to ordinary lay people but only to aristocratic ruling families and the literate segment of the monastic community. This body of secular literature is so small, for instance, that there is only one Tibetan novel, *The Tale of the Incomparable Prince*, an eighteenth-century tale of romantic adventure of a pattern echoing the *Rāmāyana* but recast into a Buddhist world view.[47] Like the *Sakya Legshe*, it draws some of its material from the Jātaka stories. The more common form of secular literature is the subhāṣita genre, collections of wise sayings patterned after the *Sakya Legshe* in particular and its Indian nītiśāstra antecedents in general.

The *Sakya Legshe* had widespread popular appeal and was the best known of Sakya Pandita's works. Its popularity is due not only to its subject matter, but also to its four-line heptasyllabic verse form, which is an excellent mnemonic device.[48] In a time when most people were illiterate and books were rare, texts such as this became popular through their memorization and oral transmission, story-telling being an important leisure activity of ordinary people. The literate ruling classes also appreciated this book. Sarat Chandra Das includes in an appendix of his grammar book on the Tibetan language a Tibetan marriage deed for a Sikkimese royal wedding, a document that contains several lines of the *Sakya Legshe* offered as advice to the newlyweds. A line from *SL*47 reminds them that the "the noble and ignoble are judged by their behavior" and "degeneracy ruins one's family lineage," and from *SL*121, "a good person is like a jewel, unchangeable in any situation."[49] While I was working as an advisor to the exiled government of Tibet in India during 1988–91, I was told that it was customary for government officials of old Tibet to have memorized part or all of the *Sakya Legshe*.

Sakya Pandita's prominent position in the Mongol court during the last stages of his life led to the *Sakya Legshe* being translated into Mongolian, perhaps during his lifetime, but certainly by the early fourteenth century. In this way it entered Mongolian folklore—for example, many of its aphorisms became part of a popular Mongolian folk song.[50] An appreciation for Indian nītiśāstra literature in Mongolia is probably due to the influence of Sakya Pandita. For example, *A Treatise on Temporal Affairs: The Drop that Nourishes People* was translated into Mongolian, and has a Mongolian commentary.[51] Another text in Mongolian inspired in part by Sakya Pandita (he is given homage in its colophon) is an expository[52] compendium of history and Buddhist metaphysics intended for pious laymen that was written by his nephew, Phakpa Lodro Gyaltsan, for a Prince Jin-gim who was a son of Kublai Khan.[53]

In Tibet a few subhāṣita compositions that were inspired by the *Sakya Legshe* are as follows:

1. *Virtuous Good Advice (dge ldan legs bshad)*, by Panchan Sonam Drakpa (pan chan bsod nams grags pa, 1478–1554),[54] was composed about 300 years after the *Sakya Legshe*. It consists of 125 verses that examine the differences between the wise and the foolish. All but a few of these verses are paired, with one presenting how a wise person deals with a certain situation, and the other showing a fool's approach. It draws heavily on the *Sakya Legshe*. At least a quarter of the verses used Sakya Pandita's material, in two cases entire verses nearly verbatim, in others using two lines, and the rest borrowing the imagery but rewording it in a different manner. (Compared to Western literary conventions, this was not considered plagiarism in Tibet, but a common literary technique expressing appreciation of the text used.) A typical approach would take a verse from the *Sakya Legshe* that deals with both the fool and the wise person, then expand that into two verses as noted above. An example of this can be noted in the way Panchan Sonam Drakpa treats verse 106 of the *Sakya Legshe*, which reads:[55]

SL106 Noble people, when angry, are mollified by apology,/ But coarse people become even more obstinate./ Solid gold and silver can be melted,/ But heating dog turds just creates a foul stench.

In *Virtuous Good Advice* this becomes:[56]

VGA102   Though the wise can express heartfelt anger,/ When properly respected they are pacified;/ Though gold and silver are very hard,/ See how they can be melted.

VGA103   Whether or not fools are angry,/ When properly respected they become obstinate;/ When a pile of dog turds is melted,/ See how only a foul stench arises.

About two hundred years after this book was written, a commentary on it was prepared by Yangchen Gaway Lodro (1740–1827). It has been reprinted in both Tibet and India.[57]

2. *A Treatise on Water and Trees (chu shing bstan bcos)* by Gung Thang Tenpay Dronmay (gung thang bstan pa'i sgron me, 1762–1823)[58] is actually two separate works that present advice on how to deal with daily affairs, one using the imagery of water and the other using that of trees. Each of these, in turn, is separated into two sections, one concerned with worldly matters and the other with Buddhist Dharma. The first of these, the treatise on trees, presents 35 verses on Dharma, followed by 71 verses on worldly matters. The treatise on water reverses this order by presenting first 81 verses on worldly matters, then 59 verses on Dharma.

Near the conclusion of the second treatise (*TWT*103) the author acknowledges his debt to Sakya Pandita by stating that he based his composition on the *Sakya Legshe*. However, unlike in *Virtuous Good Advice*, Gung Thang relies much less on actual borrowing of verses, lines, and imagery from the *Sakya Legshe* because his subject matter of water and trees limits what he can use from Sakya Pandita's work. The end result is that by contemporary standards it is more of an "original" work.

A typical example of Gung Thang's few parallels with the *Sakya Legshe* is shown in a comparison between two verses from the two works. Here Gung Thang and Sakya Pandita both liken a coarse person who becomes arrogant, whether by acquisition of knowledge (*SL*104) or wealth (*TWT*33), to the noisiness of tumbling stream water. But Sakya Pandita equates the silence of the open seas to that of the wise person, whereas Gung Thang selects the roar of the ocean waves on the coastline to exemplify the noisy character of a bad person.

SL104   Those with limited knowledge have great pride,/ But when they become wise, they are composed./ A small creek babbles incessantly,/ But what clamor does the ocean produce?

*TWT*33   A bad type of person can get a little wealth,/ But he becomes arrogant just like a king;/ A stream flowing through a narrow canyon/ Is noisy, just like the ocean's waves.[59]

More typical of Gung Thang's work is the following verse, remarkable for poetic imagery that does not echo anything in particular in the *Sakya Legshe:*

*TWT*6   The one who knows how to be impartial/ Will pick up the good qualities of others;/ A clean brook in a grassy meadow/ Gurgles along collecting flowers.[60]

There are several commentaries on *A Treatise on Water and Trees.* Gung Thang himself, in the colophon to the second of his compositions, *A Treatise on Water (bcu'i bstan bcos),* says that after writing *A Treatise on Trees (shing gi bstan bcos)* it became so popular he was urged to prepare a commentary for it. However, he felt that to do full justice to the subject he would have to draw from the nītiśāstras (he mentions seven of the eight listed above) and the *Sakya Legshe,* and such a commentary would become too "heavy." Instead, he complemented his treatise on trees with a treatise on water.

Later, in the twentieth century, a commentary on *A Treatise on Trees* was prepared by Zemay Tulku Losang Paldan (dze smad sprul sku blo bzang dpal ldan, 1927–).[61] In his introductory remarks the author says that Gung Thang wrote *A Treatise on Water* in a "meaning commentary" to *A Treatise on Trees.* Then, "just as trees grow when watered," Zemay Tulku Losang Paldan, in turn, based his "word commentary" to *A Treatise on Trees* on *A Treatise on Water.*[62]

A Treatise on Water and Trees is seen in modern times as an important work of literature for promoting cultural literacy in students of public school systems. This is the case with another twentieth-century commentary on the entire *A Treatise on Water and Trees* that appeared in Bhutan in 1984.[63] It was published by the Department of Education of the Royal Government of Bhutan under a cover letter from the king of Bhutan. The same appeal for cultural literacy in public schools appears in Zemay Tulku Losang Paldan's remarks in his commentary noted above. The Department of Education of the exiled government of Tibet also has come out with its edition of *A Treatise on Water and Trees* in 1984, and it has been reprinted many times and included in anthologies in Tibet where it is used as a text book for Tibetan literature.[64]

Finally, mention needs to be made of another early twentieth-century work that is patterned after *A Treatise on Water and Trees.* This is a two-part work by the sixth Panchen Lama, Chokyi Nyima (chos kyi nyi ma, 1883–1937), which uses the two themes of earth and water instead of water and trees.[65] Though not a commentary in the usual sense of the term, it is an original work patterned after and elaborating on the work of Gung Thang, especially in its extension of the metaphoric themes to include earth. Even though no reference to the work of Gung Thang appears in the colophon, acknowledgment is paid to the *Sakya Legshe*. The work consists of ninety-five verses on the topic of earth and ninety-four on water. A few have parallels with the *Sakya Legshe* but most display compositional originality.

3. *A Treatise on Kingship (rgyal po'i lugs kyi bstan bcos)* by Ju Mipham Gyatso ('ju mi pham rgya mtsho, 1846–1912)[66] is a classic example of a treatise on worldly advice prepared by a monk-scholar at the behest of a king. A recent study has been made of the socio-historical circumstances from which this text arose.[67] In this case the "king" was actually a prince who was contending with his older brother for the throne of the kingdom of Derge (sde dge) in eastern Tibet in the late nineteenth and early twentieth centuries. (His father, the real king, was being held in Chengtu by Manchu authorities. He died there shortly thereafter without returning to Derge.) Possibly in an attempt to substantiate his claim to the throne, in 1895 the prince, Jampal Rinchen ('jam dpal rin chen), asked a prominent monk, Ju Mipham Gyatso, for advice on how to be a proper king. In response Mipham composed this text, a rather long treatise of over 1,200 verses arranged in twenty-one chapters dealing with such subjects as attentiveness, the speech of oneself and others, acting with equanimity toward others, how to safeguard the peace of the kingdom, and so on. Among the sources drawn on in the composition of the text, the colophon cites the *Sakya Legshe* along with seven of the eight nītiśāstras listed above. There are a few borrowings from the *Sakya Legshe*, but mostly it is an original work. It places more emphasis on practical advice for the king (such as dealings with officials, taxation, and the treasury, and how to treat rural and urban areas) than in the *Sakya Legshe*. As with all this literature on spiritual and worldly affairs, the overall tone is that through ruling in accordance with the Dharma and acting in all situations in a noble manner, a leader will enjoy success.

4. The Fifth Dalai Lama, Ngawang Losang Gyatso (ngag dbang blo bzang rgya mtsho, 1617–1682), wrote two short compositions on worldly and spiritual matters. In a letter of advice to a petitioner,[68] a short text of seventy-five verses, the Fifth Dalai Lama follows a familiar pattern of setting forth worldly advice in the first thirty-four verses. Then, in effect, he says that such advice is all well and good, but what really is important is putting the Dharma into practice. Therefore he dedicates the remainder of the text to a short presen-

tation of the graduated path to enlightenment. This style is used by Sakya Pandita, who devotes the ninth and final chapter of the *Sakya Legshe* to an examination of the Dharma. The Fifth Dalai Lama cites Sakya Pandita specifically in footnotes to verses five, seven, and thirty, in two cases quoting directly from the *Sakya Legshe*.

The second text consists of two separate documents containing precepts on religion and politics.[69] The first consists of twenty-six versified paragraphs containing advice to a leader on a variety of topics such as how to interact with others and the consequences of so doing. Though this first document is not in the subhāṣita verse form, the second document displays that format in part, especially the fourth chapter. Here a series of quatrains contrasts the qualities of the wise/fools, noble/ignoble, good/bad, and so on. One verse contains a reference to the story of the foolish rabbit who was scared by a falling branch (*SL117*) and another the example of digging a brackish water well (*SL399*).[70]

EXAMPLES OF TEXTUAL PARALLELS

Some additional examples of textual parallels are presented here to show how subject matter flowed from the Indian sources to the *Sakya Legshe*, and then from there to the later subhāṣitas in Tibet. The first example derives from a Jātaka story[71] that relates how a certain rabbit, sleeping beneath a vilva tree, was startled at the sound of a vilva fruit falling upon a leaf. He jumped up and ran off telling all he met that the world was coming to an end, thus causing them all to become frightened also and to run as he was doing. The misunderstanding was brought to an end by a wise bodhisattva lion (a former incarnation of the Buddha) who halted the stampede with a roar and got them all to think clearly about what they were doing, thus saving them from rushing to their destruction.

The *Sakya Legshe* verse in question here, *SL117*, does not mention the rabbit, but an old dog that barks without any reason represents fools who cannot reason things out:

SL117   The wise can investigate things for themselves,/ But fools chase after whatever is popular./ When an old dog yelps,/ Other dogs run without reason.

However, the rabbit story does appear in the explanation of this verse in the first commentary to the *Sakya Legshe* by Marton Chögyay, so one can presume that Sakya Pandita may have referred to this Jātaka story in his oral teachings on the *Sakya Legshe*. In any event, the story here changes to a rabbit being scared by the fall of a branch in water, as shown in its later appearance in *A Treatise on Water and Trees*:

TWT27   The wise investigate what is true or false,/ Fools chase after whatever is popular./ Because a branch fell into the river,/ Just about all of the animals fled.[72]

and twice in the Fifth Dalai Lama's letter:

5DL5   Undertaking things by carefully investigating at length and in detail/ With the vast wisdom that differentiates among countless/ Misunderstandings about spiritual and worldly affairs/ Is the general approach of the analytical ones.
[A footnote is added at the point of "carefully investigated" that reads, "Like the story of the rabbit and the branch that deceived the animals."][73]

5DL25   With no prior specific knowledge of a person/ And merely a brief fleeting impression of their good or bad qualities,/ A superficial judgment perceives them as friend or foe;/ That is reason for oneself to fall into an ocean of regret.
[A footnote is added at the point of "superficial judgment" that refers to SL117.][74]

A second example, which appears in the *Pañchatantra*,[75] tells of another rabbit, this time a wise one, who takes on a menacing lion that is killing the animals of the forest by compelling them to send themselves one by one each day for the lion's meal. When the rabbit's turn comes he institutes a clever ruse, telling the lion that there is another lion who is threatening his sovereignty in the forest. So the first lion, puffed with pride, demands to be taken to him, whereupon the rabbit leads him to a well and tells him to look in. Upon seeing his reflection in the well, the angry lion jumps in and is killed.

The story next appears in *A Treatise on Temporal Affairs: The Staff of Wisdom*:

TSW85   Whoever has intelligence has power./ Without intelligence, what use is power?/ A certain lion who was powerful/ Lost his life because of the rabbit.[76]

Then Sakya Pandita employs it in the *Sakya Legshe* (and Marton Chögyay elaborates the story in his commentary):

SL25   One may be weak, but if one has wisdom,/ What can a powerful enemy do?/ Although the king of beasts was strong,/ He was put to death by a clever rabbit.

Panchen Sonam Dragpa included it in *Virtuous Good Advice:*

VGA21   Though the wise may have little bodily strength/ Through masterful judgment they defeat an enemy./ There is a well-known tale about an intelligent rabbit/ Who killed a lion, king of the beasts.[77]

as did Gung Thang in *A Treatise on Water and Trees:*

TWT59   Taking a dare out of stupidity/ Is ruinous to oneself, not heroic;/ Like jumping at his reflection in water/ Led a lion to his death.[78]

Similar examples can be shown: (a) of the story of the blue fox as it crops up in the *Pañchatantra*, *A Treatise on Temporal Affairs: The Staff of Wisdom*, *A Treatise on Temporal Affairs: The Drop That Nourishes Beings*, the *Sakya Legshe*, and the *Virtuous Good Advice;*[79] and (b) of Ruru the deer as it wanders from the Jātaka, to the *Sakya Legshe*, the *Virtuous Good Advice*, and to Mipham's *A Treatise on Kingship*.[80]

Another kind of textual parallel concerns verbatim borrowing of verses. Generally speaking the wording of the *Sakya Legshe* indicates that Sakya Pandita had borrowed ideas but the compositions were truly his own. In one example, SL328, he appears to borrow from Masūrākṣa's *A Treatise on Temporal Affairs*, ATTA6.15, changes the wording slightly, mostly by the use of synonyms, and ends up with a nearly identical meaning:[81]

SL328   Gentleness will pacify the temperate/ And even quell the uncouth./ Because gentleness can accomplish anything,/ The wise say, "Gentleness itself is sharp!"

ATTA6.15 Flexibility destroys the inflexible/ Gentleness overcomes the coarse./ There is nothing untamed by flexibility,/ So flexibility is very sharp.

Another example shows Sakya Pandita again borrowing from Masūrākṣa's *A Treatise on Temporal Affairs*, ATTA3.3, in the creation of SL192, modifying it somewhat to illustrate bad situations that naturally worsen if left unattended:

ATTA3.3   Like unsettled debt and undoused fires,/ Enmity that is left unresolved/ Grows more troublesome over time,/ So do not leave these untended.[82]

SL192   Unsettled debt, the root of enmity,/ Bad laws, bad speech,/ A bad lineage, and bad conduct—/ Though unintended, these things naturally worsen.

The interesting feature of this example is that in the commentary to SL185 Sakya Khenpo Sangyay Tenzin also uses ATTA3.3 along with 3.1 and 3.2 to develop further the ideas in this verse. In this case he cites Masūrākṣa verbatim. Such nearly verbatim borrowing of verses also extends from the *Sakya Legshe* to some of the later texts. For example, SL23 and SL134 appear in the *Virtuous Good Advice* as VGA25 and VGA60 respectively.[83]

The last example shows how Sakya Pandita uses an anthill as a simile for things that accumulate slowly through regular effort. This idea is expressed in both Masūrākṣa's *A Treatise on Temporal Affairs*, ATTA4.3,[84] as well as in *A Treatise on Temporal Affairs: The Staff of Wisdom*, TSW28 and TSW29.[85] In both cases the idea is expressed in a simpler form than the image Sakya Pandita creates in his compositions, first to the collection of taxes, and second to the acquisition of knowledge.

ATTA4.3   Just as an eye potion appears to wears off when used, and anthills accumulate, so the wise make their accumulations little by little.

TSW28   Through accumulation anthills grow larger, through use eye potions wear off; so also what is created over time diminishes —that in itself is the thing to know.

TSW29   Anthills and honey, the waxing moon, the wealth of kings and beggars—little by little these grow by accumulation.

SL323   For adequate revenue, the royal vault is filled/ With small taxes, not excessive ones;/ Little by little, anthills, beehives,/ And the waxing moon become full.

*SL*449 Each day one should take to heart a few words/ Of the scriptural advice that one needs;/ Before very long one will become wise,/ Like ant hills are built or honey is made.

ENGLISH TRANSLATIONS OF THE *SAKYA LEGSHE*

The *Sakya Legshe* was one of the first Tibetan books to be translated, in part, into English. In 1819 a quiet, humble eastern European scholar, Alexander Csoma de Körös (1784–1842), departed on a two-year foot journey from his native Hungary to India in search of the "origin to his nation."[86] He spent the rest of his life living in the Himalayas with various Tibetan scholars, mastering their language and studying their literature, never to return to his homeland. His work represents perhaps the first substantive Western scholarship in Tibetan studies. One of these works was a partial translation (234 of the 457 verses) of the *Sakya Legshe* into English that was completed in 1833 but not published until twenty years later.[87]

Over the next century the *Sakya Legshe* was translated into other European languages, but it wasn't until 1965 that a complete English translation became available with the dissertation of Bosson, later published as a monograph by Indiana University. This work actually consisted of two translations, one from a Mongolian text and one from a Tibetan text.[88] Though praised for setting a standard as a "travail critique," this work was prepared without access to any of the commentaries to the *Sakya Legshe* that explain many of the enigmatic references in the verses.[89] The availability of this work to a wider readership also was limited because of its publication as a university monograph.

In 1977 the next English-language publication of the *Sakya Legshe* became available from Dharma Publishing, thus improving its availability to the public.[90] Though not so attributed, a little sleuthing reveals this is not an original work, but essentially a reprint: it includes the 1925 translation of *A Treatise on Temporal Affairs: The Staff of Wisdom* by Campbell,[91] and the verses of the *Sakya Legshe* translated by Alexander Csoma de Körös and published posthumously in 1855–56. This book is lacking in that the compilers perpetuate the original deficiencies by making very few alterations to the wording found in the earlier versions.[92]

Finally, a brief excerpt from the present translation of the *Sakya Legshe* and its commentary appeared in the Year of Tibet issue of *Chö-Yang*.[93]

A JEWEL TREASURY
of GOOD ADVICE
with Commentary

. . . .

This Commentary, *A Hive Where Gather Bees
   of Clear Understanding,*
Is a Mirror Elucidating the Wonderful *Good Advice,*
A *Jewel* Satisfying All Desires for Well-being,
A Sacred *Treasury* Pacifying Cyclic Existence.

INTRODUCTORY VERSES OF PRAISE

Oṃ Svāsti

Praises to the leader of the Śākyas, master of temporal and spiritual
   wonders;
To the feet of Srongtsan Gampo who exemplified the Buddha's
   ethical conduct;
And to the great Sakya Pandita, the master who kindly presented again
The message that temporal and spiritual affairs are complementary.

Whatever one does, wherever one goes or stays,
Whether in the company of the high or the low, the weak or the strong,
Engaging in any kind of activity with body, speech, or mind,
This superior method treats temporal and spiritual affairs
   as complementary.

Therefore, as assistance especially in these times,
I will explain, strictly in accordance with the teachings
   of credible masters,
A Jewel Treasury of Good Advice, which demonstrates clearly
How to ensure that temporal and spiritual affairs are complementary.

Having made the above promise as an expression of worship, I shall here
explain the very nectar of the Dharma to students who aspire to excellence

and are committed to liberation and a mastery of all knowledge. Known as *A Jewel Treasury of Good Advice*, this is a timely teaching, which clarifies the difference between what are the ways of the world and what are not. Among the unimaginably detailed teachings of the distinguished Venerable Master Sakya Pandita Kunga Gyaltsen, this text is one of three most extraordinary. The other two are *An Explanation of the Three Vows (sdom pa gsum gyi rab tu dbye ba)*, which explores various doctrinal issues in Tibetan Buddhism, and *The Treasury of Logic and Epistemology (tshad ma rigs pa'i gter)*—his classic study of Buddhist epistemology, an exposition on Indian Buddhist logic, especially the works of Dharmakīrti.

Part I

CORRESPONDENCE *of the* TITLE
of the TEXT WITH SANSKRIT

THE TITLE IN SANSKRIT is *Subhāṣitaratnanidhi*. In Tibetan it is *legs par bshad pa rin po che'i gter* [English: *A Jewel Treasury of Good Advice*]. Translating the title from Sanskrit into the language of Tibet, the Land of the Snows, we have in both languages [and English]:

subhāṣita	legs par bshad pa	[Good Advice]
ratna	rin po che	[Jewel]
nidhi	gter	[Treasury]

In accordance with the tradition among all accomplished scholars of India, this text exemplifies the special qualities of its author, Sakya Pandita: the highest being his direct perception of the true nature of all phenomena; the middle, his being a tantric adept; and the lowest, his being a scholar who mastered the five major Buddhist sciences.

Additionally, in conformity with the translation salutation, I respectfully prostrate to the youthful Ārya Mañjuśrī.

Although this is not a Sanskrit translation, it is presented in this way to show that it is a part of the Abhidharma teachings.

Part II

THE CONTENT *of the* TEXT

SALUTATION TO THE BUDDHA

> The supreme gods, the *nāga* kings, adepts, knowledge holders,
> The great ascetics Akshapāda and Valmiki, and so forth,
> All paid homage with pleasing bejeweled crown ornaments;
> So also we prostrate to the omniscient leader of sentient beings.

Regarding the last line, the ones who are prostrating are the composer of the text, the Venerable Sakya Pandita Kunga Gyaltsen, together with his followers. The recipient of their prostration is the fully accomplished omniscient Buddha, the leader of all celestial and other sentient beings. He is worthy of prostration because all of the following made offerings with crown jewel ornaments, even to the dust upon his feet: the most prominent among the gods, such as Brahma and Indra, who are praised, exhorted, and eulogized in this world; the nāga kings such as Gapo and Nyerka; the accomplished knowledge holders such as the universal monarch Trinshon; the ascetic Netsopa, who was a fully accomplished teacher; Akshapāda of Trogmokhar, who through practice became a great accomplished ascetic; the nine-headed Valmiki Dragpa who so cherished his moral principles that he kept his eyes cast down below his armpits toward the bottoms of his feet, stealing no glances (he was retained as a guard for Umā, wife of the great Śiva, and had he looked at her he would have felt desire); as well as the famous Five Great Ascetics, including Dupa, Nejok and Rabga. Thus, Sakya Pandita says, "I also prostrate to him."

PROMISE TO COMPOSE THE COMMENTARY
BY EXPLAINING THE MEANING OF THE TITLE

> When analysis is done right, gaining excellence
> Through all temporal deeds and proper spiritual methods

Corresponds to how the sages practice;
This teaching is *A Jewel Treasury of Good Advice.*

This verse defines the text by showing that it is like a treasury of jewels that are flawless as determined by the threefold test. Indeed, such good advice is like a mound of jewels, a source for achieving all one's desires; that is, a method taught for those who wish to train in the sages' practice of knowing just what to engage in and what to avoid. Therefore, follow the instructions of this text. When one's analysis employs reasoning and scriptural authority, one will accomplish well all unmistaken sublime spiritual practices and faultless worldly activities. Nāgārjuna says,

If worldly activities are done right,
The celestial realms are not far off.
If the worldly and spiritual stairway is climbed,
Then even liberation is at hand.

As Āryadeva says in *The Four Hundred (Catuḥśataka),*

Various temporal conventions,
Are designated "spiritual practices."
Thus it appears as if worldly affairs
Are more powerful than the spiritual.

As Śāntideva says in *Engaging in the Bodhisattva Deeds (Bodhisattvacaryāvatāra),*

Anything that could erode the trust of others
Should be looked into, inquired about, then abandoned.

The sages say,

Without deceit, spiritual and temporal affairs are one;
With deceit, spiritual and temporal affairs are different.

And,

The Buddha did not proclaim
Skillful means as to be deceitful.

Chapter 1 ~

AN EXAMINATION *of the* WISE

1   The wise who nourish a treasury of good qualities
       Gather to themselves precious good advice.
       The great ocean is a treasury of rivers
       To which all running waters descend.

People who have become wise are a treasury of many good qualities. They have gathered and gladly adhered to good advice, so that a wealth of benefits comes naturally to them. The great ocean is a treasury of water; it does not need to intentionally collect the rivers that flow into it.

Once upon a time in the land of Śrāvastī there lived a householder named Pindada and his daughter Sumagadhā. In the southern land was another householder who repeatedly asked to marry the daughter, but Pindada refused. The rejected householder then presented his case to the Buddha, who told him to make his requests for the daughter again. This time she was given.

Sumagadhā was very gloomy when she went to her husband's home. People asked her, "Whatever is making you so unhappy?" and each time she replied, "There are no fields."[94]

The southern householder protested, "But there are several fields! And to cross each of them requires a journey of several days!"

"These are not the fields I mean. There are no fields of charity!"

"We have those fields also," he responded, "fields having many great sages."

"What is so wonderful about that?" retorted his wife. "The most excellent field is the perfect omniscient Buddha. He is the teacher of all sentient beings and comprehends all knowledge."

There ensued much discussion, and the householder agreed he would approach the Buddha in order to console Sumagadhā. "We shall invite your teacher," he promised.

"If that is the case, then prepare the necessary foods, suitable for the Buddha and his retinue," she instructed.

Her husband and the others laughed. "They still need a month to travel from there to here. We have plenty of time to make the preparations."

But Sumagadhā insisted, "Because my teacher need have no regard for ordinary time, you must get ready now!" So arrangements were made. Sumagadhā went to the rooftop and offered fragrant incense, praying:

> Master of all sentient beings,
> Who has vanquished the inexhaustible army of demons,
> Having fully comprehended all manifest phenomena—
> Victorious One and your retinue, please come stay here.

Due to the blessings of the Buddha that enabled the monks of Śrāvastī to hear clearly, they all discerned the words of this invitational prayer. Turning to Ānanda the Buddha said, "The monks with miraculous powers must take up their discipline sticks[95] and fly. Those without powers should go by land."

Accordingly, one learned pandit reached for his discipline stick. "You don't have miraculous powers!" the others challenged.

"But I have attained the wisdom that relinquishes whatever must be abandoned, so I can acquire such abilities straightaway," he replied. "Please, sit for just a while."

Then through meditation he at once achieved miraculous powers. By this demonstration all were inspired to have faith in him and to generate their own realizations.

So the Buddha and his retinue went to the southern land. Some disciples rode on the elephant named Son of the Protector, some sailed on clouds, some rode the mountain of fragrant incense, some were borne by pheasants.[96] As each of the disciples with miraculous powers arrived, with apprehensive reverence everyone inquired of Sumagadhā, "Is this your teacher?"

"This one is not," she answered. "This is Śāriputra, the chief of the wise Hearer disciples of the Buddha. This is the great son, Maudgalyāyana, the greatest of the miraculous ones." She went on, identifying each one.

At last, with the gods of desire below him, the gods of form above, the bodhisattvas on his right and left, surrounded by an inconceivable array of spiritual and worldly offerings, the Buddha arrived. Only then did Sumagadhā proclaim, "*This* is my teacher."

Her husband and the crowd of people prostrated with tremendous faith. Because the Dharma was shown to them, all were set upon the path of liberation.

Even wise people must discard their pride and exert themselves in acquiring good qualities that others possess.

2   People may or may not be knowledgeable, but
The wise are judicious in what to do and what to avoid.
A magnetic stone is able to extract
Iron filings that are mixed in with dust.

It is important to have discriminating intelligence that perceives long-term advantages and disadvantages, but is unconcerned about minor, short-term benefit or harm. One can tell who has or lacks knowledge of temporal and spiritual matters when decisions must be made concerning what to avoid and what to put into practice. Those with the sense to make such determinations on the basis of long-term rather than short-term results are wise and praise-worthy. Only a magnet can separate iron filings from dust.

Once upon a time in the southern region there was a master of deception, a king called Bhojadeva, who was very skilled in the essential points of the Magic Wheel. Many tall wooden sentries guarded his kingdom; they cast intruders into the Magic Wheel, beat them with hammers, and so on. The king's bodyguard was a sword-wielding monkey.

A Brahmin of that land, having squandered his wealth at gambling, went as a thief to the palace of the king in order to recoup his losses. As he hid in the shadows of the king's quarters, he saw a snake above where the king was sleeping. The unwise monkey was about to strike the snake with his sword. The would-be thief wisely thought to himself, "This coincidental harm to the king would be unbearable. The welfare of the country depends on this leader of men; if he is killed it will be tragic for all. But what would it matter if I, an ordinary person, were killed?" Thus inspired, he sprang forth and seized the sword of the monkey.

The ensuing commotion awoke the king. "What is the reason for this?" he exclaimed. When told what had happened he was very pleased, and said:

> The wise are good even if they are your enemies,
> But not so the fools who are your friends.
> See how the Brahmin thief prevented
> The monkey from killing the king.

The king rewarded the Brahmin with a warm reception and gladly gave him whatever he wished. Therefore, strive to acquire such discerning intelligence.

3   Skilled in good advice, the wise know,
But foolish people do not.
When the radiance of the sun appears,
Owls become blind.

In order to correctly understand good advice, we need to develop the skills to analyze its essential meaning. Untrained foolish people cannot grasp the significance of sage counsel. When the sun rises, its brilliance causes owls to become blind, because they cannot tolerate sunlight.

Once upon a time there was an intelligent king named Brahmadatta who assembled a group of scholars. The king was so impressed with the debating skill of the great scholar Brahmin Vararuci that he offered his daughter Suvarnottama in marriage. "If he is the most learned of all," Suvarnottama declared, "then I shall marry him. But if he is not, then I will be the most learned."

Brahmin Vararuci took offense, thinking to himself, "If she is averse to one so scholarly as I, then I must deceive this girl."

The Brahmin went searching everywhere. In a remote place he discovered a handsome cowherd perched on a tree limb, sawing away. Since he was cutting the limb on the tree trunk side of where he was sitting, the Brahmin concluded that this cowherd must be quite stupid. "I shall present him as my very wise master, and offer him as an object of veneration to the king. Then I shall marry the daughter," he resolved as he led the cowherd away.

The Brahmin sat the cowherd down in the shade of a tree and massaged him with milk, while teaching him to say the prayer, "Oṃ Svāsti." Then he clothed him in the garb of a pandit, and seated him amid a gathering of many people. "When the king and his retinue seat themselves on their thrones," the Brahmin instructed, "place a flower on the top of the king's head, recite 'Oṃ Svāsti' and say nothing to anyone else."

But the cowherd forgot the "Oṃ Svāsti" he had been taught, so as the king was sitting down, he said, "Oṃ Sentur" and tossed the flower. Because this was understood as the lewd words "the long tongue of the vagina" when translated, all the people were embarrassed and astonished.

The Brahmin quickly explained, "This pandit is actually very wise. Of the various ways in which the syllables 'Oṃ,' 'Sen,' and 'Tur' can be pronounced, the method used here subdues pride."

Then the daughter addressed the pandit (who was actually the masquerading cowherd), "When 'Atikasa Chitta Bagvisha' is translated, is it understood as some special language of the āryas?"

The cowherd gave no reply. Again the Brahmin interrupted, "How can this great learned teacher of mine respond to a woman?" The same question was put to the king's subjects, and none of them could answer.

In order to investigate the matter further, they escorted the cowherd to the temple. He showed no interest in any of the statues representing the body, speech, and mind of the tathāgathas. As they were leaving, however, near the temple entrance he noticed the animal realms depicted in the painting of the Wheel of Life.⁹⁷ This activated his negative predispositions to cow-herding and he pointed his finger, saying, "These are buffalo," and so on.

At this the daughter was convinced that the Brahmin Vararuci was deceiving them. She resolved to make the cowherd even more clever than the Brahmin. Since he could not become intelligent by studying grammar and logic, she had him engage in lengthy devotional practices to Sarasvatī, the goddess of learning. He achieved nothing.

Finally one evening she instructed her servant Kalika, "Go sit behind the clay statue of Sarasvatī in the temple. In the early morning say to the cowherd, 'Do you not desire spiritual attainments?' and gently give him a sweet."

So the servant slipped into that place and waited. When the time came she said to the cowherd, "Take this spiritual attainment," and held out her hand to give him a sweet from the mouth of the statue. The cowherd had acquired such devotion that he beheld a vision of Sarasvatī herself giving him a sweet, and at the moment of eating it he became very wise. He even answered the daughter's earlier questions, and became famous in the world as the pandit Kālidāsa who composed the poetic treatise called *The Emergence of Youth*.

At that same time the king, who was also wise, composed a half-verse in order to test the scholars. It asked a question:

> The lotus in the water
> Quivers for what reason?

He dispatched a notice with this half-verse to all public places where people gathered—monasteries, taverns, and so forth—promising a great reward for anyone who could compose a response. Though many interested people submitted answers, the king was not satisfied.

One day Kālidāsa was in a tavern and that popular topic was being discussed by the patrons. He realized that a bee might enter a lotus for its tasty nectar just as the sun was setting and the lotus closed. Wanting to fly away, the bee would beat its wings, causing the lotus to quiver. Kālidāsa said,

> A bee enters, the sun sets:
> Wings of trapped desire vibrate.

Thus he provided the answer to the half-verse, completing both question and answer with one verse.

A barmaid who coveted the award then killed the pandit and hid his body. When presented with the completed verse, the king was very pleased.

"Who understood how to solve this?" he asked.

"I did," the barmaid replied, but when the king examined her further, he could see she was incapable. Again he asked about the author, but no answer was forthcoming.

A search for the pandit ended when his body was found buried under a house. The great Śiva brought him back to life.

> Therefore, it is said, the Gods
> Look after those who are very wise.

4   The wise can eradicate faults,
       But the foolish cannot.
       The *garuḍa* can kill poisonous snakes,
       But crows cannot.

Wisdom arising from contemplation enables us to eliminate our most immediate shortcomings, fulfill our desires, and attain virtuous qualities. But foolish people lacking analytical skills are unable to shed their principal weaknesses, let alone attain what they need. The soaring garuḍa can slay a poisonous snake, but not so the useless crows.

Once upon a time a king was seeking a suitable minister. He bade a youth named Mahausadhi to take care of one of the royal mules. After some time the king sent another fellow to steal the mule, and he was successful. Mahausadhi was left wondering, "When the king comes to retrieve his mule, whatever am I going to do?"

Pondering the fix he was in, a plan occurred to him. When he saw the king approaching, Mahausadhi climbed upon his father's back and rode him about, appearing to beat him.

"Why are you behaving so terribly?" the king exclaimed.

"I am taming my father," the youth replied.

"Hey!" commanded the king, "In this world, the lamas, the Three Jewels, and one's own parents are those whom one should respect! You must cease such bad behavior!"

"Oh Your Majesty," whined the youth, "don't speak like that. The son is the worthy one. Of what use are parents?" So the king spoke extensively on the great kindness of parents, because they give us our bodies and minds, care for us when we are helpless infants, and so on.

Then Mahausadhi said, "Your Majesty, if that is the case, are only my parents good, or are all parents besides mine also good?"

"In this world, all parents whatsoever are better than their children and are worthy of respect," the king answered.

"If that is so," said Mahausadhi, "I will confess that the king's mule is lost. But is this not the father of the mule? Here, oh master of men, please take this," and he presented a donkey to the king.

The king was so pleased with the youth's intelligence he appointed him minister.

5   When the very wise become destitute
          Their intelligence grows even stronger.
          When the king of beasts becomes hungry
          It swiftly attacks the elephant's head.

Even when met by poverty, truly intelligent people will still achieve their objectives. Like the minister Vikṛiti, the force of their intellect intensifies. A lion is able to kill a powerful elephant, even when weakened by hunger.

Once upon a time an evil fishmonger named Rutol was appointed minister by King Dharmapāla of Magadha. Having thus acquired great power, Rutol soon forgot the kindness that the king had originally bestowed on him. One day he killed the monarch, seized absolute control of the kingdom, and banished the two princes, Rāmapāla and Pāla.

To Dharmapāla's official, Pandit Vikṛiti, he declared, "I have spared your life. Now you must serve as my minister."

But Vikṛiti indignantly replied, "You are the one who killed my king! I shall not become your minister!" This made Rutol so angry that he put Vikṛiti in a pit and gave him very little to eat.

Vikṛiti lingered there, subsisting on merely a three-finger measure of barley flour and a like amount of water daily. Three months later, the fishmonger's ministers noticed that the pandit's entire body had become hairy. They took him out of the pit and again asked him to assume duties, but Vikṛiti's resolve had strengthened all the more, and his reply was the same.

The evil king thought, "Because of his great intelligence, I am reluctant to kill him, but because he is an enemy, it is unsuitable to keep him here. I must expel him!" So upon the king's order, Vikṛiti was sent into exile.

Pandit Vikṛiti then went searching for the sons of King Dharmapāla and found them among a group of children. Calling them all together, he played the role of a Brahmin minister. He seated himself in meditative posture, as if on a lion throne, and drew Ramapāla into his lap. The rest of the children took the parts of ministers, generals, and other members of the court. Rāmapāla ruled over them all.

Years later, they fixed a time to wage war on Rutol and assembled an army. Poised to attack, the fishmonger king covered his elephants' faces with golden nets. The elephants were confused and angered by these nets, so when they were removed during battle the sight of the enemy upset them completely. They wheeled around and stampeded back into the fishmonger's ranks, destroying the entire army. Rāmapāla was then installed as ruler of the kingdom.

Therefore, one should endeavor to acquire not just intelligence alone, but intelligence conjoined with power.

6   Until the learned are thoroughly questioned,
        Their depth cannot be assessed.
        Until a drum is beaten by drumsticks,
        Its distinction from other drums is unknown.

Although certain people may be renowned as scholars or experts, they may not truly understand what wisdom is. Consequently, we should not look to outer appearances and chase after the famous. Many large drums look alike; others have nicely painted designs and distinctive shapes. However, until a drum is beaten with a drumstick it cannot be known whether it differs from a common wooden milk cask. Since we cannot distinguish the wise from the foolish until they have been fully scrutinized, we should not be followers of nonsense.

7   Even if one is to die the next morning, today one must study.
        Though one may not become a sage in this life,
        Knowledge is safely deposited for future lives,
        Just as riches safely deposited can later be reclaimed.

Studying the Dharma is necessary not only for those who desire to accumulate wisdom over time; even people about to die must continue to learn. If one deposits gold and silver with a reliable person, one has the right to repossess and use it later as needed. However, if nothing has been previously stored, then there is nothing from which one can freely draw. Similarly, without the predispositions established by previous study and meditation practice, one will later be born as an ignorant fool. So all people—old, young, and in between—must study diligently.

8   When a person possesses good qualities,
        Others spontaneously gather around.
        The fragrant flower may be distant,
        But bees are drawn like gathering clouds.

A teacher must be accomplished in the virtuous qualities of learnedness, respectability, and goodness, and have the attitude of being helpful to others. This is the root of well-being for oneself and others. Students who aspire to follow such an example will assemble of their own accord. Though fragrant flowers may be far away, bees desiring their nectar come not at the flower's behest but, like clouds in the sky, gather naturally from all directions.

9 A single wise person who has fully developed
 All good qualities illumines the earth.
 But the mean-spirited, like stars,
 Even when numerous, cannot illuminate.

Spiritual progress benefits all beings. It can be achieved by a discerning individual whose thoughts are focused on the Dharma and who has thoroughly mastered all its subjects beyond mere "study" and "understanding" in name alone. Such a person, like the rising sun, has the power to clarify all activities in the world. Others may acquire a little knowledge, but have not earnestly developed their intelligence in some areas, such as their actions and effects. No matter how numerous, these people cannot bring light to beneficial worldly endeavors. They are like the stars: no matter how many are in the sky, they are unable to shed much brightness upon the earth.

10 Although the wise have immeasurable learning,
 They still embrace the lesser knowledge of others.
 By means of continuously practicing thus,
 They quickly proceed to omniscience.

Having engaged in study, contemplation, and meditation, learned people acquire limitless good qualities. However, to attain the state of a fully omniscient Buddha, it is necessary to fully comprehend all things; therefore the wise will respectfully consider and take on even the lesser knowledge of others, not to mention the greater. In this way their wisdom becomes not merely a fleeting appearance; they quickly attain the ultimate state. Therefore, we need to rid ourselves of pride in empty talk and achieve the inner purpose that assuredly benefits this and future lives.

11 Though enemies are numerous, when the wise
 Are protected by wisdom, how can they be harmed?
 Single-handedly, the Brahmin boy of Ujjayinī
 Triumphed over an entire assembly of foes.

Wise people are skilled in developing their good qualities and eradicating faults. Such discriminating wisdom is their protection; their enemies, however many, will be inferior and cannot cause them harm.

Once upon a time in southern India, in the great city of Ujjayinī there was a rich little thief called Khavara. Not far away lived a wise Brahmin boy named Śikhīn; with him stayed an old woman. Śikhīn's wealth amounted to nothing more than a single goat. Since he had no belongings to sell, he could not do business. As he was unable to work, he was always trying to think of a way to earn his livelihood.

Seeing Khavara one day, it occurred to him he that could deceive this thief. He borrowed some jewelry and fine clothes and sat down contentedly for a picnic near the thief's house. Khavara concluded that Śikhīn was actually very wealthy and set about to rob him. The Brahmin boy cleverly expected this, so he situated the old woman in their house and told her not to say a word.

The thief began digging an opening in the wall of the house. Śikhīn found an empty box, weighted it down with rocks, and placed it inside just in line with the thief's tunneling. Then he dropped a key into the box, making a clinking sound. Khavara, under the impression that Śikhīn was rich, assumed the container was filled with coins and reached inside. Śikhīn then seized him, exclaiming, "Because of all the trouble you've been causing everyone I'll take you before the king!"

"What you say is true," admitted Khavara, "but if you will refrain from taking me before the king, I'll give you whatever you want." So Śikhīn accepted five hundred *tamka* coins from the thief and sent him away.

"That evil fellow will come later to kill us," Śikhīn thought, so they decided to go to Pataliputa. Before they left he wrapped the five hundred tamkas in leaves and fed them to his goat.

The three were trudging along the road when they met a rich landlord. Śikhīn requested that he let them sleep at his house, and the landlord agreed. After some time the canny youth punched his goat's stomach. The goat vomited up a coin. Śikhīn handed it to the landlord.

"What is this?" asked the landlord.

The boy replied, "This is a wish-fulfilling goat, the source of all kinds of precious things."

"Sell this goat to me!" the landlord demanded.

"I can't sell it," cried the boy. "This goat is the source of livelihood for my elderly mother and me."

But the landlord persisted. "Do not refuse me!" he urged. Finally the goat was sold for ten thousand gold tamkas.

"Give just the right amount of water and grass to the goat," Śikhīn instructed the landlord. "To get a tamka you punch its stomach and what you desire will appear. Oh, and one more thing—at first take the coins slowly, then later you can get more and more." Having carefully advised the landlord in this technique, he fed a few more tamkas to the goat and carried the rest off for himself. Being fearful of bandits, Śikhīn sent the old woman on one road and he traveled by another, the junction of the two being Vārāṇasī.

The rich landlord punched the goat's stomach and was able to get a few tamkas. He was very pleased. Later, when no more coins appeared, he dealt so many blows he killed the goat. He realized then that he had been fooled.

As for the boy, after a long while he came face to face with a dangerous bear in a dense forest. There was no alternative but to fight. He grabbed the bear's two ears and they battled hour after hour to the point of exhaustion. The bag of tamkas tore open, and the coins spilled out all over the ground.

A young prince, out for a pleasure ride from the city of Mathurā, came upon them. He was splendidly dressed in fine clothes and jewelry, and his horse was well bred. Seeing all the commotion, he called out, "Whatever is going on here?"

Śikhīn could only manage a gesture and grunt, "Um! Um!"

"I am the son of the king! Speak clearly!" demanded the prince.

"Sa Ha Lo!" the boy responded. The prince repeated his question. "You are really interrupting me," said Śikhīn irritably. "I am seeking the powers of the god of wealth. If you must ask what is happening, this is a geni[98] with a bear's body, and therefore I am obtaining spiritual powers. If you must ask what these spiritual attainments are, does Your Highness not see that it is like a rain of gold?"

"Indeed, it is so," agreed the prince. All that was taking place was so very amazing to him that he ordered Śikhīn, "Hand it over to me!"

The boy said, "In all the world there is no method of propitiation as excellent as this. It is even more valuable than one's life. Therefore, Your Highness, do not even make such a request!"

"Take my horse, my clothes, my jewels—I insist you give this to me!" entreated the prince.

"For all that it would be difficult to get even one hundred thousand gold coins," replied the boy. "Since I get this kind of wealth every day I am reluctant to part with it. However, because you are the prince, you take on the spiritual powers of this deity. Since I can acquire another, it is all right." By lifting one hand at a time he passed the two ears of the bear to the prince, instructing him to hold on tightly. Then he told the prince to recite the prayer requesting the attainment of spiritual powers "Om Drim Kab Tshol Kye Ma Re Tshar! In the future I'll come and hold your ears! Then you'll understand! Hung Hung Hung Svaha!" and so guided him in recitation, visualization, and practice.

Śikhīn gathered up the scattered tamkas and proceeded on to Vārāṇasī, taking with him the prince's horse, clothes, and jewels. In the city were merchants from the same district as the rich landlord that the boy had deceived.

They recognized Śikhīn, and promptly informed the landlord, who present-ed his case to the king.

"Hand that scoundrel over to the landlord," the king commanded, and this was done.

The landlord tied the boy up in a gunny sack to throw him into the Ganges, and Śikhīn was carried off by two bearers. Upon nearing the river, the boy urinated. It streamed down the bearers' heads. "Again you're behaving like this!" they exclaimed, and left the sack with a cowherd while they went off to wash.

In the meantime the cowherd asked Śikhīn what was going on. "This has happened because I am the son of a king and don't want my kingdom. They won't allow me to go off and practice Dharma," the boy explained.

"You should be glad to be the king," the cowherd said. "You ought to do as they request."

The boy replied, "It would be pleasing to be king, but because I am mindful of death I want to practice the Dharma. If you so desire, you become the king."

"Oh, I couldn't do that!" exclaimed the cowherd.

"But you must!" insisted the boy. "Now you get into the bag. Don't open it until you've reached the jeweled throne. Once the bag is placed on the throne, you will definitely be king."

The cowherd, delighted, got into the bag while Śikhīn hid in the top of a tree. After finishing their bath, the bearers returned and carried off their load.

One of them said, "What is this load? It has become light!" Another replied, "Of course it has become light. We stopped to rest and drink, so it natural-ly seems lighter once we start to go again." Without inspecting the contents, they went to the bank of the Ganges and threw the bag into the river, recount-ing tales of Śikhīn's trickery.

Then the Brahmin boy, with his horse, clothing, and jewels, went to the rich landlord's door and called for him. The landlord came out of his house, aston-ished. "What is this! Where did you come from? Didn't you die?" he asked.

Śikhīn replied, "I am alive, very well, and happy. Look at my horse, clothes, and jewels. Because you were so kind to me, I have come to you in gratitude." He presented the landlord with many precious gifts.

"Why are you doing this?" demanded the landlord.

"Because you threw me into the river, I received empowerment to the throne of a ruling deity who died last year," said the boy. "That deity was the lord of an inconceivable number of river-dwelling deities."

"Is such empowerment available only to you, or to others also?" asked the landlord.

The boy replied, "It is available to anyone who goes there. Even such king-doms as the one I have taken are plentiful these days."

"Well then, I shall go there, too," announced the landlord.

"The best way is exactly as was done before," said the boy. He tied up the landlord in a gunny sack and threw him into the Ganges.

Then Śikhin remembered the animosity of the Vārāṇasī king who hadn't protected him from the landlord. He took the horse, clothing, and jewelry of the prince killed by the bear and went to see the prince's father, the king of Mathurā.

"Where has your son gone?" the boy asked.

"He is on a jeweled throne," answered the king.

"Do not be so sure," said Śikhin. "I saw your enemy, the king of Vārāṇasī, kill him."

"That's not true!" said the king.

"It is true, just as I say!" insisted the boy, who then showed the king the prince's horse, clothing, and jewelry.

"It must be true!" acknowledged the king. "The king of Vārāṇasī must be killed!"

Then the wise boy promised, "Give me what is needed and I shall conscientiously do the deed for you."

The king agreed and Śikhin went off to the king of Vārāṇasī. "Do you want your enemy the king of Mathurā killed?" he asked. "If so, then you should know that he is friendly with me."

"What is the significance of that?" asked the king.

"The king of Mathurā has fine jewelry that I can take," said Śikhin.

"Well then," said the king of Vārāṇasī, "take his crown jewel."

The boy conveyed that instruction to the king of Mathurā, and he continued in all these many ways to be deceitful. Finally he led the king of Vārāṇasī with a small retinue to Mathurā. After they entered the door was secured; a signal was given, the troops of Mathurā killed the king of Vārāṇasī and his retinue, and stole all their jewels. Then the kingdom of Vārāṇasī was given to the Brahmin boy Śikhin, and the period of his rule was known as Protection by the One of Wisdom.

12   When offensive talk from small minds creates quarrels,
       The wise skillfully restore harmony.
       The river's turbulence muddies the water,
       But the sparkling water-jewel purifies it.

Wisdom that exercises good judgment is necessary to bring resolution to our objectives. The small-minded quarrel back and forth, saying, "It's not my fault! It's your fault!" Intelligent people restore peace by deciding what to do and what to avoid; they clarify everyone's doubts using words that accord with the Dharma. As Śāntideva says in *Engaging in the Bodhisattva Deeds,*

> If a problem has a remedy
> Why worry about it?
> If it has no remedy
> What is the use of worrying?

Rivers that are otherwise beneficial become so agitated by summer rains and wind that they are not suitable for people's use. But if a *ketaka* jewel is dropped into a container of muddy water, the water becomes pure and clear.

13   Howsoever the wise become destitute,
        They do not take the path of fools.
        Even if thirsty, birds who crave rain[99]
        Will not drink water fallen to the ground.

Learned, unconfused individuals working to achieve well-being and an understanding of what is and is not the Dharma rarely become destitute. However, if through the mighty power of karma they should happen to fall into privation, still they do not have mistaken thoughts, act badly, or follow a path that induces foolish acts of wrongdoing for the sake of reward in just this life. Cuckoos like to drink the rainwater on leaves. Even if they are so thirsty that they can only utter a distressed cry, they will not drink the life-giving water that has fallen to the ground.

So even if others are happily preoccupied with things that contradict the Dharma, leave them aside! Those who knowingly engage in immorality lose their happiness, discover misery, and are more stupid than cattle.

14   Even if the wise are deceived,
        They are not confused about what they do.
        Although ants are sightless,
        They are speedier than creatures with eyes.

Those having the wisdom that carefully analyzes both appearances and actual conditions are not confused about the things they must do in a timely way, even when fooled by the lies and swindling of others. They are astute like the Brahmin's daughter, and fulfill without difficulty the purpose of their work. Ants may be sightless and fragile, but they are faster and more efficient than other creatures with eyes and strong bodies.

Once upon a time in the land of Mo Jig, there lived a king Lubdhin who did not look after his subjects and was concerned only about his own wealth.

In that region was a rich Brahmin who, due to his previous merit, had at his house a well from which came whatever he desired.

"I must render honor to the king," the Brahmin declared one day.

His daughter objected, "That would be unwise. This king is so covetous and shameless he will come and appropriate our well."

"Don't be so suspicious," said the Brahmin, and he proceeded to show the king great courtesy.

When the king arrived back at his palace, evil thoughts spawned in his mind. He sent a messenger to the Brahmin saying, "Ah! I have heard you have this well at your house. You must send it on loan to my palace for a few days. It will not be good for you if you do not comply."

Upon hearing this message, the Brahmin was horrified and regretted what he had done. "Alas," he mourned, "these unreasonable words from the king surely mean that my wealth will be seized." He pondered his family's assets, utterly disheartened and cringing in fear.

The Brahmin's daughter, who had the perspicacity to assess the situation, said to him, "Whatever has made you so depressed?"

Her father told all that had happened. The daughter laughed tenderly and said, "But father, you have mastered the three kinds of knowledge. How can you be bewildered by such talk?"

"Truly, such threats to us are unprecedented!" exclaimed her father.

"It doesn't matter," said the daughter. "You can promise that you will offer the well. But tell him that the well itself, though offered, does not desire to go; it says, 'If I must go to the court of the king, I must have an envoy to lead me there. If one is not made available, I won't go!'" Then the daughter wrote a message to send to the king:

> Wealth is attracted by wealth
> As elephants are by elephants.
> O powerful king—please send us one well,
> Then our well will come to you.

Her father conveyed this verse to the king's messenger. Upon receiving it the king assembled his ministers. "Send a courier! Send him to obtain the Brahmin's well!" he ordered. "If you do not your heads will be cut off!"

The ministers conferred with each other and said, "This king doesn't investigate things. He utters such nonsense, saying a well must be sent to him as if it can be led around like a cow. If this troublemaker isn't killed, he will utter yet more such inanities." So the ministers killed the king.

Thus the wise Brahmin daughter was clear-headed, and her father was saved from hardship.

15   When two wise people engage in discussion,
        Further worthy wisdom can arise.
        By mixing turmeric with borax,
        Another color is produced.

When two intelligent individuals, who are straightforward and conduct them-
selves according to the Dharma, question and debate with each other and have
discussions, it is possible for them both to have excellent new insights supe-
rior to their previous ideas. One person alone has access only to his own
knowledge, but when two wise people get together is like discovering the
wonderful colors that result from mixing borax and turmeric.

16   The noble wise ones who have gathered merit
        Will be victorious over all, even if they stand alone.
        The lion, king of beasts, and universal monarchs
        Have no need of allies for their rule.

Some individuals, outwardly genuine and inwardly very wise, have accumu-
lated truly meaningful merit. Even if they are alone and without any assis-
tants, they surmount all obstacles and effortlessly attain what they need. The
objectives of ourselves and others—wonderful accomplishments and the
enjoyment of a full life span—all depend on merit, so we must exert ourselves
accordingly, with body and mind. Some great masters have said, "One must
proceed in accordance with the lines on one's forehead."[100]
      The lion, king of beasts, needs no helper to reign carefree and victorious
over all animals. Likewise, sovereigns who have no need for allies triumph over
all opposition; their wishes are spontaneously and effortlessly fulfilled because
they have the seven precious possessions of a universal monarch, which arise
from previously accumulated merit.

17   When skilled in method, why should it be hard
        To employ even the great as servants?
        The garuḍa, though very powerful,
        Is ridden by the golden-clad one.

When one has skillful means that befit the circumstances, how can it be diffi-
cult to enlist not just the lowly, but great people as well? The golden-clad
Viṣṇu, by his cunning, came to ride upon the back of the mighty garuḍa who
soars in the heavens.
      Once upon a time Viṣṇu and the garuḍa were engaged in battle. Viṣṇu was
unable to subdue the great strength of his opponent. Seeking to prevail over

the situation, he said to the garuḍa, "How it pleases me that you conquer your foes! Never before have I fought with one such as you. Now, ask me for something wonderful, and I shall give it to you."

"How shall the eminent make requests to someone of lower status? You must ask me for something wonderful, and I shall grant it to you," replied the garuḍa arrogantly.

Viṣṇu entreated the garuḍa three times in the same way, but each time received the same reply. Finally he said, "If that is the case, then since you are very fast and powerful, please let me ride on you."

Thus Viṣṇu tricked the garuḍa, and ever since the garuḍa has been known as Viṣṇu's mount.

18   Wisdom is what achieves happiness
       In both this and future lives.
       Prince Candra's wisdom protected King Sudāsa
       In his lifetime and in those to come.

The way to achieve good fortune for oneself and all others, both now and in future lives, is to be motivated by great compassion and develop the wisdom that conjoins skillful means with altruistic intent. The bodhisattva Prince Candra, by way of love, compassion, and the enlightened attitude, protected King Siṁha Sudāsa's one thousand sons from suffering and brought happiness to all.

Once upon a time there lived a boy named Candra, the son of a royal family of the famous lineage of Rucaka. He was respectful toward teachers and elderly people, loved those who were inferior and miserable, and was adorned by many naturally virtuous qualities, such as the twelve branches of learning.

Some years before, a king of the south named Sudāsa had gone into the forest for his studies. His presence attracted a lusty lioness. She accosted him, dragged him away, and forced him to copulate with her. Eleven months later, the lioness gave birth to a son who had the handsome body of his father and his mother's multi-colored fur, as well as her love for meat, power, and savagery. He was known as Kalmasapāda, or Siṁha Sudāsa.

When he came of age, he was given his father's kingdom. He acquired many queens, of which two were most favored. One day he instructed them, "Tomorrow, come where I go walking in the garden. I shall make love with whichever of you I meet first, but not with the one who arrives later."

The two queens put on their fine clothing and jewelry and left the palace at the same time. One dismounted at a small temple on the road to say her prayers. She fell behind during that short time, so the other arrived first and made love with the king.

Because she had not received the king's affection, the later queen became angry and cried to the deity in the temple, "O, you deity! Because of my devotions I was detained and couldn't be the most favored queen of the king. If you are at all powerful, you should help me!" Then in a fit she destroyed the temple.

The deity was outraged and, in turn, went off to the entrance of the palace intending to harm the king. There the deity saw one of the king's clerics, a sage, departing to beg for alms. This sage was one who was honored with the three types of white food: yogurt, milk, and butter. The deity, seeing an opportunity, manifested himself as the sage, went into the kitchen, and ordered the cook, "From now on, serve meat to me." The cook said that he would have to ask the king and hastened to do so.

The king replied, "Oh my! How astonishing that the sage is now eating meat! Nonetheless, serve him as he wishes; there is no other choice!" So the cook offered meat, which the impostor ate and then left.

The next morning the real sage came for alms and was presented with meat. Aghast, he demanded, "Who has said that I should be served meat?"

The king admitted giving the order. The furious sage cursed the king, "You shall eat human flesh for twelve years!" and disappeared.

One day thereafter the kitchen servant was unable to buy meat because an alms-begging monk had given a vow of fasting to the townspeople. There being no other solution, he went to the cemetery and found the body of a child who had just died. Secretly he cut it up and took it home, and this meat was served to the king. The time of the sage's curse had come to pass.

Finding it very delicious, the king asked the servant, "What kind of meat is this?"

The servant was terrified and said nothing. But the king insisted, "You must tell me, there will be no punishment!"

"It is the flesh of a child since I could find no other meat," confessed the servant.

"From now on serve me this kind only," ordered the king. "Since it will not be available everyday, you must go to the village and steal it."

The servant did as he was instructed, and many children of the village disappeared. People began to talk. One day, concealing themselves along the road, they ambushed the villain who had carried off their children and took him before the king. But their ruler jeered, "I myself authorized him to do this, so you have nothing to say in the matter!"

The king's ministers and the townspeople discussed the situation. "This king who says such despicable things must be killed!" they declared.

Around the palace a large army assembled. Finding no escape route through the royal gate, the king ascended to the roof. Poised at the edge, he swore this oath: "By the power of any meritorious predispositions that there may be in my consciousness, may I become a human-flesh-eating demon with the power to fly!"

Instantly he soared into the sky and flew to a cliff fortress, where he made his dwelling in a cemetery. There he became notorious as the cannibal King Kalmasapāda, who lived outside the law, killing and devouring many people. Moreover, he imprisoned the one thousand princes who had been his sons.

One day the bodhisattva Prince Candra and his entourage came near to the dwelling of Kalmasapāda. A Brahmin from another land happened to approach and requested the kindness of a donation. He pleased the bodhisattva by reciting four verses he had composed.

Prince Candra noticed that all the people who had assembled were distressed, and he wondered what was going on. Then he saw Kalmasapāda, wearing a filthy shirt, wielding sword and shield, wreaking havoc and destruction. He called to the demon, "Hey! Do not be in such a rage—I am the son named Candra." But because Kalmasapāda was very irate and hungry, he slung the bodhisattva across his shoulders and went off to his dwelling.

Arriving there, his amazement grew at the bodhisattva's distinctive beauty and brightness. He put Candra down in front of him and sat there, examining the prince carefully.

The bodhisattva's heart was sad. "Oh!" he thought, "I cannot satisfy the wishes of the Brahmin who offered me the well-composed verses." Tears came to his eyes.

When Kalmasapāda saw that, he laughed and said, "Indeed you should be crying now that I have you in my hands."

The bodhisattva replied, "I have discarded countless bodies since beginningless time, so why should I fear being in your grip? It is another thought that prompts my tears. Release me just for a moment—first I must go satisfy the request of the Brahmin sage; then I shall return to make you happy."

Kalmasapāda answered scornfully, "Are you sincere about that? What chance do you have for escape anyway when you are in the mouth of the Lord of Death?"

The bodhisattva prince said, "You are one who is evil by nature. But because I am the son named Candra, as a matter of principle I speak only the truth."

Kalmasapāda could endure no more and thought to himself, "If I judge correctly, he will probably come back. If he doesn't, it hardly matters since I already have a thousand sons." Accordingly he said, "Go, and come back quickly. Meanwhile, I shall make a fire to roast you."

So the bodhisattva returned to his kingdom. He met the Brahmin sage and said to him, "If one could put a price on these elegant verses, even giving a kingdom for each line would be insufficient." He then offered one thousand golden coins for each line.

As he started back to Kalmasapāda's lair, his father and ministers urgently tried to dissuade him, but the bodhisattva said, "Please don't try to change my mind. It is true that Kalmasapāda has no kindness for me. But even though you are fearful that I will suffer, you must not seek to alter the situation." He ignored all the insistent pleading of the ministers and many others, and set out alone on the road to the great cemetery.

Kalmasapāda was filled with wonder to see the bodhisattva coming. A qualm arose in him, but he kept on preparing his great fire. When the bodhisattva arrived, Kalmasapāda asked, "What are the special virtuous qualities of that person to whom you ordered offerings be presented? Explain this to me."

The bodhisattva replied, "What is the need of such wise advice for someone as inherently evil as you? Right now your one desire is to eat me."

"I'll eat in my own good time!" Kalmasapāda snapped. "The fireplace is still smoky. When meat is roasted over a smokeless fire, it really is delicious, so I shall listen awhile to your wise advice." Kalmasapāda requested two or three times more. Each time the bodhisattva cut him off, but still he insisted.

The bodhisattva saw that the moment was ripe to subdue Kalmasapāda. "You need to listen to the Dharma in the proper manner," he stated.

"What manner is that?" asked Kalmasapāda. The bodhisattva prince explained:

> Sit on your seat very humbly,
> And fill your heart with disciplined courage.
> Look with eyes of pleasure,
> As if drinking the nectar of words.
> Generate single-pointed devotion and reverence
> With a stainless mind of great faith.
> Respectfully listen to the Dharma
> As one listens to a doctor's advice.

Kalmasapāda took off his filthy shirt, spread it on a large flat rock, and the bodhisattva sat down. Kalmasapāda gazed at him and said, "O noble one, now please speak." The bodhisattva then uttered these profound and sweet words,

> It is appropriate to be in the company of
> Great masters as long as one wishes.
> One relies upon them totally
> Without needing to ask them never to part.

Kalmasapāda was exhilarated and repeatedly implored, "O great sage, please continue. Please say more." The bodhisattva continued his discourse for sixteen verses, concluding in this way:

> Greater than the distance between earth and sky,
> Greater than traveling from here across the ocean,
> Greater than the distance between the east and west mountains,
> Is the distance between ordinary life and the sacred Dharma.

Kalmasapāda was amazed and developed much faith. "O sage!" he exclaimed, "I offer you four sacred oaths for this wise advice. I pray that you accept."

"Who would ask anything good from one as shameless as you?" the bodhisattva marveled.

Kalmasapāda bowed his head and said, "I am offering. Please accept without any hesitation." Then the bodhisattva said:

> Adopt truthful principles, abandon killing beings,
> Release all those you are holding in prison;
> And you, fierce one, must give up eating human flesh.
> Of all the supreme things one can do, abandoning
> these four is best.

Kalmasapāda responded:

> The first three sacred oaths I present to you.
> As for the fourth—please give me another.
> I do not eat that which is not human flesh.
> Did you not understand this before?

To that Prince Candra replied:

> This meat-eating will corrupt
> Spiritual and temporal happiness and reputation.
> For what reason are you reluctant
> To discard the very source of your degeneration?

He reproached Kalmasapāda for myriad reasons and succeeded in reforming him. The princes were released from prison and reinstated in their domains. Kalmasapāda returned to his ancestral lands and for the time being the kingdom was peaceful. By faultlessly adhering to the ordained lay man's vows, he achieved a state of ceaseless happiness and became famous as Siṁha Sudāsa, the one who protected himself in both this and future lifetimes.

19   Though people may be very brave and strong,
      Without wisdom they cannot become heroes.
      Though people may become wealthy,
      Without virtues how can their wealth endure?

Because worldly might and valor eventually decline, it is important to have enduring knowledge. By gaining wisdom through hearing, contemplating, and meditating on the topics presented in the sutras and tantras, one will become like the celebrated scholar Vasubandhu, who acquired supreme power and fortitude, not just in this life but in future lives as well.

On the other hand, there may be fools who are famous and influential because they possess power derived from battlefield bravery or the ability to overwhelm others with their splendor. But they do not attain the essence of courage, for they will surely grow old and their karma and virtue will decline. Parents may acquire unlimited wealth—gold and silver, silken clothing, horses, *dzos*,[101] and mules—but how will such riches last without a basis of previously accumulated merit? It is impossible! It may be observed that their children become destitute beggars.

20   Distinct good and bad are clear to all,
      But the wise distinguish them when mixed.
      Anyone can take milk from the cow,
      But swans separate milk from water.

Anyone, no matter how foolish or learned, can point out the differences between good and bad qualities when they are exclusive of each other. The wise, however, are able to distinguish good from bad qualities when they are mixed together because they apply the analytical ability that arises through contemplation. Anyone can get pure milk from cows, but only swans are able to separate the milk from a blend of milk and water.

These days negative karma is causing the entire environment to be filled with evil, and individuals are preoccupied with unwholesome influences. This produces deceptively attractive situations that are a mixture of good and bad, where words and actions contradict each other. Be careful, because appearances are difficult for most people to analyze.

21   When they are commanded,
      Even animals can understand.
      Those who know what to do
      Without being directed are wise.

People who achieve things only through the prompting of others are like animals, prone to fear and being killed. They have to be ordered, "You must do these things! Do it like this!" and be urged on and on with a pointed finger. When trained by their masters, even parrots and dogs will speak, respond, and carry things around. On the other hand, there are people who accomplish things with their own intelligence, doing whatever is necessary to achieve present and future well-being for themselves and others as if it were their own special responsibility. When they perform such acts through analysis or intuition, they especially distinguish themselves from animals and even among humans are counted as wise.

22   If one has wisdom, one can understand others
      From just their demeanor, even if they say nothing.
      Even without eating a crab apple[102]
      One can tell its taste by its color.

When one has analytical intelligence, the innermost thoughts of others can be understood even in the absence of clairvoyance or anything actually being said. This is done by assessing external appearances, just as the presence of fire is deduced from the evidence of smoke. Even without tasting every crab apple, one can infer whether they are sweet or sour by whether they are yellow or green.

23   The wise command more respect in other lands
      Than they do in their homeland.
      How could a jewel, readily sold in other regions,
      Be prized on the ocean isle where jewels abound?

The wise, trained in textual systems that fully explain worldly and spiritual affairs, get little respect in their own country. Their learning is not appreciated because they are not seen as different from others. But if they leave their homeland and go abroad they are widely perceived as very kind and unusual individuals, and are honored as "the wise ones of such and such a place." Wherever wise people go, their inspiring activities and virtuous deeds flourish. On an island in the ocean where wish-fulfilling gems are plentiful in the surrounding waters, they cannot be sold for a good price, but if taken to other lands they will be highly valued as rare and precious.

The remarkable biographies of the learned masters of India and Tibet describe their journeys throughout Tibet and China, where they engaged in meritorious deeds as extensive as the heavens. One should conduct oneself in accordance with their example!

24   Learning entails hardship;
        Living at ease, one cannot become wise.
        Due to attachment to small pleasures
        One cannot attain great happiness.

If one has little tolerance and is enthralled by delicious food and attractive bodies, achieving the genuine happiness of the wise is impossible. But such happiness is the sole basis of one's own and others' fulfillment; therefore, one should abandon comfortable living and work hard for well-being in future lives. First, one must forswear attachment to food, clothing, reputation, and one's homeland (a source of attachment, anger, and ignorance), pay respects to learned teachers, and endure hardship to seek their teachings. Then, one must diligently apply the logical reasoning developed from contemplation and discussion with scholars as vigorously as one washes clothes through and through by beating them on rocks and rinsing them with water. Finally, one must patiently accomplish great happiness by being willing to tolerate adversity in one's studies, such as the difficulty of putting into practice what one has been investigating.

Slothful people who are attached to the minor pleasures of this life and who do not apply themselves for the sake of future lives have no possibility of ever achieving the great happiness of the wise. Therefore, get rid of attachments, the cause of suffering. To achieve omniscience without studying is also impossible, a topic that will be taught later.

25   One may be weak, but if one has wisdom,
        What can a powerful enemy do?
        Although the king of beasts was strong,
        He was put to death by a clever rabbit.

If one is able to discriminate between effective and ineffective action, then no matter how much stronger one's enemies might be, they can be defeated.

Once upon a time a mighty lion and an intelligent rabbit had been living continuously in each other's company. The lion, having an arrogant nature, was always tyrannizing the humble rabbit. Eventually the rabbit tired of this and began thinking of ways to remedy his predicament. Carefully and thoroughly analyzing the situation, the rabbit discovered a solution.

"O Master," he said, "I have unbearable news! There is another beast who looks just like you! He says if you fight with him, you will lose and will have to be his servant."

"Where is he?" growled the lion, swelling with pomposity. "I'll fight with him now!"

"Come, I'll show you," cried the rabbit excitedly, and led him to a very deep well. "He is in there," said the rabbit.

The lion peered down into the well, and saw his own reflection staring back at him. Due to his stupidity and pride, he assumed it was his enemy. He bared his fangs and shook his mane. The lion at the bottom of the well also bared his fangs and shook his mane. He snarled. The lion in the well snarled. Every time he postured his reflection did the same. The lion grew so incensed that he thoughtlessly lunged at his reflection, fell into the well and died, and that clever rabbit became renowned as the conqueror of the powerful enemy.

26   When one is able to behave harmoniously
       With other beings, then one is wise.
       Do animals not also abide compatibly
       In groups of their own kind?

Wise people abandon any proclivity to take pleasure in competitiveness, pride, jealousy, desire, hatred, or ignorance. They do not violate temporal and spiritual conventions, but act straightforwardly and in harmony with all sentient beings, especially those who enjoy life as fully free and fortunate humans. The wise realize wrong livelihood is unsuitable; they know that general welfare relies on practicing skillful means—conduct that is pleasing to others. Is it not also seen among the animals, such as horses and oxen, that they remain most agreeable in groups of their own kind? Those who do not act harmoniously with others, whether or not they know how to do so, are lower even than animals.

27   Know the difference between wise people and fools:
       The wise investigate a situation carefully
       Before taking action on what needs to be done;
       A fool's approach is to act before thinking.

Wise people commence a required task by assessing its size and difficulty, and what is necessary to accomplish it. Then they actually do what they can and avoid saying they will do what they cannot. Because they carry out their work with limited expectations, others will have a favorable impression of their efforts whatever the outcome, even if results are less than anticipated. But fools pursue their objectives with much vacuous blather, expecting the best results, as if an entire country could be governed simply in their imaginations. "Ultimately, if great hopes go unrealized, whatever one does is accompanied with regret"—this saying characterizes the pattern of foolish people. Therefore, it is important to understand that the way to achieve things is through careful examination from the outset.

28   When one knows what the wise investigate
        One is counted among the wise.
        A fool may be skilled in assessing a cow's age
        But that is not so valuable an attainment.

Anything one might happen to know is not necessarily worthwhile knowledge. But scholars who have mastered both temporal and spiritual doctrines are considered learned, praiseworthy, and wise. With reasoning and scriptural authority, they have thoroughly investigated non-Buddhist systems of knowledge, as well as the Buddhist Tripiṭaka and tantric texts. A fool, on the other hand, might be highly proficient in assessing the age of animals like horses and cattle by examining their teeth, horns, and tails, but such knowledge does not lead to enlightenment.

29   As the ocean is not filled up by rivers,
        The king's treasury is not sated by wealth,
        Sense desires are not quenched through indulgence,
        And the wise are never slaked with good advice.

All the rains and rivers flow into the great ocean, yet it is never overfilled by them and can still collect more water. The riches of gold, silver, and coral are not sufficient for a king's treasure house, in which he hoards absolutely everything. And no matter how much one enjoys the desirable sensations generated by form, sound, smell, taste, and touch, one is never satisfied but grows increasingly attached to such pleasures.

Similarly the wise, having experienced the taste of knowledge, avoid prideful arrogance and petty-minded complacency. Their thirst cannot be quenched by the texts that explain correctly the foundation of well-being for oneself and others. Like āryas who have attained the stages of the path, they cross the fire pits of the three thousand world realms in search of learning. So long as they have not fully grasped all aspects of the treatises of good advice, they remain dissatisfied and continue to practice.

30   Wise people fully accept good advice
        Even if it comes from children.
        For fragrant perfumes to be produced,
        Musk is taken from the scent gland of deer.

Since good advice is the basis for present and future well-being, it should be accepted from anyone.

Uneducated ordinary people usually crave the best of everything and chase after the latest fad, propelled by their previously accumulated merit. However, thoroughly learned, wise people do not mindlessly follow whatever is currently popular. They courteously accept good advice not only from the most knowledgeable āryas, but even from lowly impoverished children if they fully understand the meaning of the treatises. The finest perfumes are made not only with white sandalwood gathered in nice clean places, but also with the musk gland taken from the genitalia of deer.

Chapter 2 ~
AN EXAMINATION *of the* NOBLE

31   The good qualities of noble people
          Are always acclaimed by the wise.
          The fragrance of white sandalwood is spread
          Throughout the ten directions by the wind.

For those who have esteemed traits of character, there is no need to announce it; such fine qualities will become widely recognized in a spontaneous and natural way. Impartial observers who witness their superior deeds and the celestial beings who guard over the realm of virtue will proclaim their reputations. It is unnecessary to declare the distinction of white sandalwood; since the wind carries its fragrance to the ten directions, it is highly valued and extensively traded.

32   When sages are installed as rulers,
          There will be achievements and happiness.
          If a jewel is offered to the victory banner's tip,
          The wise say virtue then reigns over the land.

When people with good special qualities are installed as rulers, whether temporal or spiritual, their attitude to be of help to all sentient beings fulfills everyone's aspirations. They avoid wrongdoing and engage in wholesome activities, and thereby achieve both present and future happiness. It is said that wherever a precious wish-fulfilling jewel is offered and installed atop the banner of victory adorning the temple roof, sickness, ignorance and strife will diminish, while virtue and good fortune will prosper. The wise understand this special interrelationship; they proclaim it and put it into practice.

33   Once hurt by a despotic ruler,
          People fondly recall the Dharma king.

> A person stricken by a bout of fever
> Thinks only of the water from melting snow.

When wicked rulers who lack compassion and the attitude to help others are in power, times become mired in wrongdoing, suffering, and unprincipled behavior. A deep yearning arises in remembrance of the trustworthy Dharma kings, bringing tears to one's eyes, as in the proverb "Intense compassion arises for water, seeing it locked up as ice." People afflicted with feverish diseases can think of nothing but the cool water from melted snow.

34   For those harmed by unprincipled rulers,
        The manner of Dharma kings is especially protective.
        Those afflicted by evil spirits
        Are protected by tantric adepts.

Unprincipled rulers who lack compassion, love, and shame are no different from cattle; they dominate the land by tormenting and persecuting others. But when those with the bad karma to have suffered such oppression are treated well by the scrupulous behavior of a Dharma king, it is like the reign of King Srongtsan Gampo, who governed with integrity, according to laws he codified in his *Ten Moral Principles and Sixteen Rules of Public Conduct.*[103] Similarly, those afflicted by evil spirits must be treated by none other than tantric adepts, who possess the highest powers of all.

   In these times it is important for leaders to treat lowly, ordinary people according to the principles of Dharma.

35   Noble people abstain from even minor wrongdoings,
        But coarse people fail to avoid even major ones.
        Minuscule dust particles are removed from yogurt,
        But grains of yeast are specially added to beer.

Intelligent, self-reliant people cannot tolerate the sufferings of unfortunate states of existence, so they rid themselves of even small wrongful actions (to say nothing of large ones) by being discreet and conscientious. Conversely, coarse people brazenly refuse to avoid even major transgressions (let alone minor ones) and engage in no respectable behavior at all. Even the minutest specks of dust are plucked out of yogurt; on the other hand, not only is dust not removed from beer, yeast is deliberately added.

36   Even when noble people become impoverished,
        Their behavior remains distinctly honorable.

Even if a firebrand is pointed downward,
One sees the flames continue to blaze upward.

Excellent people seek refuge in reliable spiritual guides, tutelary deities, and
the Three Jewels, turn their inmost thoughts toward the sublime Dharma,
and avoid useless arrogant talk. By so doing they assume a humble demeanor
and therefore need not experience bad fortune. At times the imperatives of
previous karma may cause them to become impoverished for awhile; nonethe-
less their physical and verbal conduct shines, devoid of all vulgarity. These
are the natural characteristics of their excellence. Even when a lighted piece
of kindling is inverted, the flames keep burning upward due to the natural
characteristics of fire.

37   Noble people, even when living far away,
      Care for their friends by helping from a distance.
      The buildup of great heavy clouds in the sky
      Makes the earth's crops yield a rich harvest.

Benevolent people do not just take care of their students and supporters when
residing nearby. Even when they are far away and appear to neglect their fol-
lowers, they correct their own and other's mistakes. With a helpful attitude
they attend others, offering advice about what to adopt and what to reject.
Massive clouds high in the sky grow dense and release rain, inducing the
crops, fruit of the humble earth, to become especially bountiful.

38   One's reputation brings pleasure while one is alive;
      Merit brings happiness in future lives.
      Mere riches that do not include these two
      Are unable to gladden the wise.

Because it is the main condition for acquiring followers and worldly things,
a reputation for being learned in all spiritual and temporal matters brings
happiness in this life, which can last but a short while. However, happiness
in future lives depends on merit produced from causes created in previous
lifetimes. Thus it is better to accumulate positive energy in order to com-
plete the collection of merit and wisdom and to cleanse the two types of
obscurations. The wise who know the laws of cause and effect will not find
delight in what is generally recognized in the world as wealth, which lacks
these two causes of happiness. Śāntideva says in *Engaging the Bodhisattva Deeds*,

Know that the hassles of amassing, protecting, and losing it
Constitute the endless anguish of wealth.

Because this brief life has little happiness or suffering of real significance and
the desire for gratification leads one to misery, one must understand that last-
ing joy in future lifetimes is most important.

39   Those who can see far into the future,
        Have great forbearance and conscientiousness,
        Tremendous perseverance and competence—
        They can become leaders even if they are servants.

There are three special qualities of leadership: first, the ability to accurately
foresee events far into the future; second, physical, verbal, and mental con-
scientiousness that prevents one from engaging in wrongdoing, together with
great forbearance not to harm others by such means as bad language or bad
conduct in which others engage; and third, dependable competence con-
joined with enthusiastic perseverance that delights in working for the gener-
al welfare. Now anyone of stature who has these qualities can gain a position
of leadership without difficulty, of course, but the same is true of lowly ser-
vants.

40   Those who delight in always being charitable
        Have reputations that rise like the wind;
        More numerous than beggars who gather around
        Are those who wish to give offerings.

Charity, the absence of avarice, ranges from its highest expression of spiritu-
al offerings to the Three Jewels, to a lesser one of kindheartedness and gen-
erosity to all who are destitute. Individuals who rejoice in such charity gain
renown that spreads everywhere like the strong autumn winds of Tibet. Poor
beggars as abundant as clouds assemble near them; but even greater in num-
ber are others wanting to give bountifully to them. Later in the text, how to
increase wealth is discussed.

41   Willingly accepting contempt from the mean-spirited
        To whom they have given good advice that goes unpracticed
        And not forgetting even small favors bestowed on them
        Are superb distinguishing features of extraordinary people.

Truly great individuals understand the characteristics of cyclic existence, so they accommodate with compassion and courage even the contempt of ill-mannered persons to whom they have given good advice but who stubbornly refuse to implement it. Regarding this, Maitreya says in *The Ornament for Sutra (Sūtra Alaṃkāra)*,

> Have love for everybody—the incompetent,
> The quarrelsome, and the unscrupulous.

42 The good qualities of the noble, though hidden,
    Are apparent to everyone in the world.
    Even when the jasmine flower[104] is well covered
    Its fragrance permeates everywhere.

Good personal qualities like learnedness, respectability, and kindness degenerate when proclaimed. Therefore, excellent people learn to conceal themselves and understate their wisdom instead of showing off. Nonetheless, like subterranean gold deposits that radiate their presence into the sky,[105] such special qualities, because of their great power, become clearly evident to everyone. Even if jasmine flowers are covered well with earth, the atmosphere is still suffused with their exquisite perfume.

43 A king is great merely in his own country,
    But sages are respected wherever they go.
    Usually a flower is decoration only for a day,
    But crown ornaments are venerated universally.

Since the king of a particular country governs the subjects of that land only, his importance in terms of the respect and offerings he receives is confined to just those places. Elsewhere he is no different from ordinary people. But people of excellent character are honored as distinguished visitors wherever they travel because of their superb personal qualities. A flower is a pretty adornment for only a day or two and has no enduring splendor. Crown ornaments, however, can be precious offerings at any time, in any place.

44 Plentiful fruit indicates a matured tree,
    Beautiful tail feathers indicate a tamed peacock,
    Swift journeys indicate a fine tamed horse,
    And a noble person's calm manner indicates wisdom.

A bountiful yield of fruit in autumn is the sign that an excellent orchard has been well managed with fertilizer and other amendments. Beautiful tail feathers are a sign that a peacock has been domesticated with strong potions. Swiftness and steadiness when traveling signal that a good horse has been properly broken in by a skillful rider. Similarly, the presence of gentleness and conscientiousness in the words and behavior of good people is a sign of their inner wisdom.

Even if one is called wise, without gentleness and conscientiousness it is not genuine wisdom. Some great masters of the past say,

> Serenity is the sign of wisdom;
> A lack of delusion is the sign of meditation.

45   Noble and ordinary people may receive help equally,
        But their gratitude in response is not the same.
        Seeds make no difference to the fields,
        Yet there are vast differences in crops.

One may be even-handed in offering help and respect to ordinary people and to wise individuals of excellent character, but the gratitude they give in return is unequal. This is because the wise heed closely the three excellences during the preparation, actual, and concluding stages of all their actions. Identical seeds can be planted in many fields, but innumerable differences are noted in the resulting plants. This is because there are variations in the power of the respective farmers' merit.

46   When assistance is given to extraordinary people,
        There are fruitful results even if help is slight.
        One who gave a single sour fruit to the king
        Was regarded as equal to the king's son.

Truly great masters refrain from acting in their own interests and act primarily for the sake of others. When one assists and respects them even in small ways, numerous special consequences will later arise, including the eventual result of great enlightenment. This is illustrated by the exceptional circumstances that resulted when a young man gave a single myrobalan[106] fruit to a majestic person and became equal in stature to the son of a Dharma king.

Once upon a time a father lay dying, and he gave this advice to his son: "My last will is that whomever you rely upon and befriend should not have an evil nature or little wisdom. Associate with the opposite of such people."

The young man decided to test whether his father's advice was true or false. Accordingly he put his trust in an evil king, sought an evil spouse as his companion, and settled down with her.

One day the young man and the king went to the forest. Unexpectedly, the king encountered a man-eating tiger and was about to be killed when the lad charged the tiger, stabbed it in the neck, and saved both of their lives. The king, much impressed, said appreciatively, "Today you were very kind and saved my life." They returned happily to the palace.

Later the young man stole the dancing peacock that entertained the king and secretly left it with his friend for safekeeping. Then he caught another peacock in the forest and took it to his house.

He said to his wife, "I saved the king's life just as a tiger was about to kill him. But since I have received no gratitude from the king for that act, I shall kill his peacock and eat it." Then both he and his wife dined on peacock meat.

The king, wanting to recover his lost peacock, sent a messenger to announce a royal pledge that whoever found the bird would be granted whatever they desired. Greedy for this reward, the young man's own wife went and informed the king.

"Why did he kill the peacock when I was pleased with him?" asked the king. The woman related what her husband had told her.

"Summon him here!" the king ordered.

The young man appeared before the king. "Is it true that you killed my peacock? If so, why?" asked the king.

The lad related his reason, to which the king responded, "How can I favorably consider requests made by those who should serve the king?"

The young man, realizing then the evil nature of both his wife and the king, sent for the dancing peacock and returned it to the king. He separated from his wife and went off alone.

In time he sought out a woman companion of bad character but found a kind king, and he settled down. One day he and the king went into a thick forest. It was an extremely hot summer and the king became exceptionally thirsty. The young man said, "If Your Majesty is able to eat, I have these three small myrobalan fruits for you."

The king was overjoyed. "You have saved my life!" he declared. They returned happily to the palace.

Then one day the young man led the king's son away and hid him. He entrusted the prince's clothing and ornaments to his girlfriend, instructing her not to say a word to anyone. The king then announced to all that whoever found his son would be rewarded with whatever he or she desired. The lad's evil girlfriend, seizing her opportunity, informed the king.

"This cannot be true!" exclaimed the king.

"It is true!" she insisted, "Here are his clothing and ornaments." She showed him the articles.

The king believed her then and summoned the young man to the palace.

"Is it true that you killed my son?" demanded the king. The lad replied that it was true.

"Well then," ordered the king, "today you are to be killed!"

"Has the king forgotten the kindness I showed him?" asked the young man.

"What kindness?" snapped the king.

The young man reminded the king about the episode in the forest.

"What you say is true," said the king, recalling the incident. "Therefore, although I have great regret for my son, for the kindness of the first small myrobalan fruit you gave me your life will be spared; for the kindness of the second, I give you my daughter in marriage; and for the kindness of the third, I give you half my kingdom. This is my promise."

The lad was convinced then that his father's advice was true. This gladdened him, as did his understanding of the king's true nature.

"How can I take the king's rewards?" he entreated. "How could I have killed your precious son?" He returned the prince to the king and promised to do whatever the king asked of him.

This historical account clarifies the meaning of verse 45, which reads,

> Noble and ordinary people may receive help equally,
> But their gratitude in response is not the same.

47   Good ancestral lineage is protected by proper conduct,
       But when behavior degenerates, ancestry is irrelevant.
       People appreciate the fragrance of white sandalwood,
       But who is interested in its ashes?

When one's conduct degenerates into actions as reckless as a mad elephant, others will question one's lineage even though one's predecessors were highly regarded. It is then meaningless to mention, "How good my ancestry is!" Even people from good families can become faithless and irresolute, so it is essential to maintain respectable deportment.

People are very fond of the fragrant Malaya[107] white sandalwood that comes from South India. Even finding a small amount is highly valued. But who takes any interest in the ashes of burnt sandalwood? Nobody!

48   Though great people may be impoverished for awhile,
       They need not experience any anguish in that.
       The moon may be briefly eclipsed,
       But an instant later it is released.

Accomplished people, learned in both temporal and spiritual matters and enjoying the results of their previous meritorious actions, are protected by such knowledge and merit and are therefore rarely indigent. But even if the imperatives of karma deplete their resources temporarily, they need not suffer. Like the son of the king of Vārāṇasī, they can regain their position through their merit and helping others. The moon in the heavens can be eclipsed by the planet Rāhu, but after a moment or two it is freed.

Once upon a time a learned king of Vārāṇasī called Mahārāja had twenty thousand queens but no sons. He made continuous propitiations to the deities and in time two of his queens—one highly ranked and one of only middling status—gave birth to sons. The preeminent queen had virtuous qualities, being a conscientious, peaceful woman, while the lesser queen was just the opposite. On this basis, a Brahmin priest christened the two sons Subhartha and Papartha respectively. By age twelve, it was evident to the parents that the two sons were developing just as predictive signs had indicated.[108] In particular, Papartha behaved jealously toward his elder brother.

Some years later, Subhartha became acutely aware of the difficult lives led by the people who tilled the fields, and of the violence done to goats, sheep, buffalo and other beasts. An intense compassion grew in him, and eventually he found their suffering unbearable. He approached his father.

"There is something on my mind," he said. "Will you allow me to speak?"

"Please do," answered the king.

The prince spoke of all the misery he had witnessed, then made his request: "Please distribute the royal treasury among these poor people." His father consented and they proceeded throughout the land, giving away the royal riches.

The ministers then assembled to discuss what now could be done to replenish the treasury, since the kingdom depended on its wealth. They determined they would need to undertake the production and sale of goods, the cultivation of crops, and nomadic herding. In addition, they recommended collecting precious gemstones from the ocean.

"If this is the case," Subharta declared, "I want to go to the ocean myself." His parents refused him permission, but he insisted.

His mother then suggested that the king let him go. "It is possible for our son to return from the journey," she said, "and even if he doesn't, he will not die." At last the king agreed and Subhartha departed along with five hundred merchants.

The king then contacted a counselor in Vārāṇasī who was knowledgeable about the ocean. "Please accompany my son," the king requested.

But the counselor was afraid. "Those who go to sea and then return home again are very few in number," he said anxiously. "O, my king, why do you ask me to go to the ocean?"

The king mournfully replied, "My son has gone. I was unable to refuse his request."

"Ah," said the counselor. "All right then, if that is the situation I will go."

Meanwhile, the quarrelsome Papartha got it into his head that he also wanted to acquire some precious gems. "It would be unsuitable were I not to get some of those jewels," he thought, and joined the group.

Once they were all in the boat, the counselor warned, "If any of you are unhappy about going on this trip, you had better leave now." He repeated his announcement each day until the winds became favorable, and then they departed. The power of Subhartha's merit and compassion enabled them to reach the ocean swiftly.

At that point the counselor instructed, "Collect jewels only when the boat is in shallow waters and can be easily handled. If the water becomes very deep, the boat will sink and your efforts will all have been in vain."

When they had filled the boats, Subhartha said to the others, "You should all make a safe return. I will proceed in search of the wish-fulfilling jewel."

He and the counselor traveled on, sailing through water just above their knees. After seven days they came upon gold and silver sands.

The counselor sighed. "I have grown weary and must return to our country," he said. "Go on seven nights from here and you will encounter a golden mountain; from there after seven more days you will find rubies; from there after seven more days, a field of poppies; and beyond that, a palace of seven treasures. There lives the king of the nāgas who has the wish-fulfilling jewel in his left ear. Request it from him." With these directions, the counselor departed.

Subhartha did as he was instructed and journeyed alone to the land of the nāgas. He glimpsed a poisonous snake lurking beneath a lotus; the prince meditated on love and the snake crawled into view on top of the flower. He passed on and approached the gate of the nāga king's palace. Announcing his arrival, he entered.

Just at the front door he saw two crystal girls spinning crystal thread. "Who are you?" he asked.

"We are the servants who guard the outer door of the king of the nāgas," they replied. He continued through a passageway, discovering four intermediate doors of silver and eight inner doors of gold.

The prince of Vārāṇasī then knocked on one last door. Within, the nāga king sat on his throne. "Anyone who reaches the land of the nāgas cannot be considered an ordinary person," he thought to himself, and invited the prince into his chamber. "Why have you come here?" he asked.

"I have come to request the wish-fulfilling jewel because I care for the beings of the world," the prince responded. "I do this for those who have become destitute, in order to shelter them from the misery of poverty."

"This jewel is very difficult to find," said the nāga king thoughtfully. "However, I will give it to you because you are working very hard for the welfare of others."

Subhartha wrapped the jewel in his coat and flew off under its power, arriving instantaneously at the seashore. There he met his younger brother Papartha.

"Where have all your friends gone?" Subhartha asked.

"The boat sank and they all drowned," Papartha related. "I nearly died but escaped by grabbing hold of a corpse."

"That is fortunate!" exclaimed Subhartha. "The most precious jewel in the world is this human body."

His younger brother replied, "Things are easy if one is rich and dies, but what is the use of being alive and poor?"

Subhartha then revealed the news of his success. "I have the jewel," he said.

"Where is it? Show it to me!" his brother demanded.

"It is in this bag," said Subhartha, handing it to his younger brother. "When you are tired, I will guard the jewel, and when I am tired, you must guard it. Now I am going to rest, so it is in your hands."

As his parents had long ago had reason to believe, Papartha had a cruel nature. Once Subhartha had fallen asleep, Papartha put out Subhartha's eyes, left him with a cowherd, and took off with the jewel.

Time passed. One day Subhartha said to the cowherd, "Take me where there are some people," and they traveled to the town of Raja. There Subhartha began to recite many fascinating poems, legends, and stories. His eloquence prompted the townspeople to offer him abundant food and drink and gifts, which he in turn used to care for five hundred beggars.

One day the townspeople asked him, "Could you guard the fruit trees inside this fence?"

"But I am sightless!" he protested. "How can I guard anything?"

"We'll tie a bell to one tree," they explained, "and then by pulling on the string occasionally, you will protect all of them."

"All right then," he agreed, "we'll do it that way." So he pulled the bell string, again and again.

Soon he began playing music with small cymbals. Many people assembled, including the king's daughter. The girl took a liking to him and finally she asked him, "Who are you?"

"I am a blind man," he answered simply.

She stayed with him for a long time and wouldn't go home even when she was called to eat. "Bring my food here and I shall eat with him," she said to her family.

Eventually the girl beseeched her father, "Please help my blind man."

"Have you become possessed by an evil spirit?" asked the king in dismay. "I have already betrothed you to Prince Subhartha, and now you are chasing after a beggar!" But the king listened as the girl told him that she had promised to become the beggar's wife. Realizing he had no alternative, the king allowed his daughter and the beggar-prince to settle in the palace.

Three months later, when the time seemed opportune, Subhartha said to the girl, "Some time ago, you committed the transgression of seeing another man."

His words deeply offended her. She became woefully depressed and swore to restore sight to one of the prince's eyes as a measure of her purity. "I have not wrongly been seeing another man!" She declared. "May these words of truth bring forth sight to one of your eyes!"

Immediately, one eye was restored. But the girl was still angry with the prince.

"Do you know who I am?" he asked.

"You are a beggar!" she cried.

"I am not a beggar," he said, "I am Subhartha, son of the king of Vārāṇasī!"

"But he went to the ocean. You are not he!" she argued.

"If I am in fact Prince Subhartha," he vowed, "may these words of truth bring back the sight of my other eye!" In an instant his other eye was restored.

The girl then confronted her father with the evidence that the beggar was actually Subhartha. "This cannot be so!" he growled.

"But it is! Look!"

The king then carefully observed Subhartha and was convinced. He humbly requested forgiveness.

Subhartha replied, "I have no need of anything. Instead please pay your respects to this cowherd." So the king bestowed upon the cowherd seven kinds of precious jewels, which pleased the cowherd immensely.

Meanwhile, in Subhartha's own land, his parents gently caught a white duck that had been their son's pet. They tied a note around its neck and released it to search for the prince. It wandered everywhere and at last alighted in front of Subhartha, who recognized his pet and took the note from its neck. He then wrote a message relating all that had happened and bid the duck return home. His parents were overjoyed to receive word from him, but upon learning of his younger brother's wickedness, they bound Papartha in chains and threw him into a dungeon.

The king gave his daughter in marriage to Subhartha and sent them to the palace of the king of Vārāṇasī. There they received a magnificent reception. The prince greeted his parents, told them his happy tale, and asked where Papartha was.

"He has done such evil things!" they exclaimed.

But Subhartha persisted, "Father, I want to meet with him." Papartha was brought from the dungeon and his chains were removed. He, in turn, took the wish-fulfilling jewel from an underground hiding place and presented it to his older brother.

On the fifteenth day of the month everyone bathed, donned new clothes, and made extensive offerings in gratitude for obtaining the wish-fulfilling jewel. On that day a rain of maize flooded the land up to their knees. Similarly, each day all sentient beings of the world were made happy with clothing, gold, silver, and other such things. The mother and father of Prince Subhartha and their attendants became very famous as the ones who spread peace and happiness far and wide.

This legend also clarifies the meaning of verse 118 in the fourth chapter:

> Even when the wise become very poor,
> They please others with their good advice.

and verse 209 in the sixth chapter:

> As a rule, people are harmed
> By others of their own kind.

49   When great ones bestow love on their enemies,
Those enemies come under their sway.
Widely respected, they care for everyone;
Such a ruler commands the allegiance of all.

Distinguished rulers who serve the populace treat everyone equally, showing no partiality or malice. In particular, when with skillful kindness they wish happiness even for those perceived to be somewhat antagonistic, they are able to govern not only their friends but their enemies as well. By so doing they are regarded with loyalty and admired as leaders by all.

Once upon a time during the first eon, there was a kind of maize that needed no cultivation.[109] Even if the supply was depleted during the daytime, it would quickly grow again in the night. Whenever it was needed, it could be harvested. Then some lazy people began gathering the next day's food the day before. Thinking that to be a good approach, they soon started taking several days' worth of food in one day. The share of maize each person took for their family piled higher and higher. Moreover, some people began stealing from others, fomenting greed and general disharmony.

Finally they all discussed the situation and appointed a person of good

character as their leader, under whom administrators of justice systematical-
ly provided assistance, meted out punishment, and exercised appropriate
authority. The leader and administrators were supported by a tax amounting
to one-sixth of the harvest. The people invested the leader with sovereign
authority for the farmers. He became famous as King Mahāsammata, the
foremost of kings.

Rulers who govern without bias are essential in these degenerate times. In
the text entitled *A Classification of People (skyes bu rnam 'byed)*, Sakya Pandita
says,[110]

> Persons of serene character and extensive wisdom
> Whose equanimity to all is like the rays of the sun,
> And who care for their subjects impartially:
> These are the truly great ones.

50   No matter how impoverished the sages become,
      They will not eat food tainted with wrongdoing.
      Even though a lion is hungry,
      It will not consume what is disgusting and unclean.

Excellent people skillfully avoid partiality and maintain an attitude to be
helpful to others. By whatever circumstances they may seem to have become
destitute, they never take alcohol, garlic,[111] or tobacco, nor do they ever eat
food obtained from wrong livelihood. Those who do not bother to care for
themselves in this way are as vulgar as street dogs who crave filthy food. The
lion, king of beasts, even when famished, will never eat anything spoiled.

51   Even when the lives of sages are endangered,
      How could they abandon their superb character?
      Even testing gold nuggets by burning or cutting
      Does not diminish their golden color.

The basis of well-being for oneself and others is an altruistic attitude. Excel-
lent people consistently embark on their activities with this perspective, assess-
ing whether or not the consequences of their actions will be good. When
serious, even life-threatening, dangers befall them, they willingly retain their
equanimity and discriminate between what to do and what to avoid. Like
mountains unmoved by the wind, they are unaffected by others' slander or
discord. How could such integrity possibly be upset by cunning or flattery?
No matter to what extent gold is melted, cut, or rubbed, its golden color
remains unchanged.

52   Although coarse people get angry with them,
        How could noble people retaliate in anger?
        Even though the jackal[112] barks arrogantly,
        The king of beasts responds with compassion.

People of exceptional character have developed the comprehensive wisdom eye of clear mindfulness and can discriminate right from wrong. Even when they are irascibly attacked with foul language and ugly looks from petty, inconsiderate people who delight in base behavior, how could they ever respond in anger? Realizing such ways are intrinsic characteristics of degenerate individuals, they always treat them with special love and compassion. Jackals bark raucously because they are so proud to have found a little morsel of food like the corpse of a dog; even so, the lion kindly remains silent.

53   People seek defects in extraordinary people,
        But not in coarse individuals.
        People examine the flaws of gems carefully,
        But who would so scrutinize a fire brand?

Benevolent individuals who shoulder great responsibility for the welfare of many sentient beings are masterful at engaging in wholesome deeds and avoiding the unwholesome. They generally lack the slightest negative tendency to seek failings in others. Yet people of disreputable character, unreliable as friends and unable to distinguish good from evil, look for ways to project their own defective attitudes and actions on admirable individuals. Do not look for faults in others, nor blindly follow without investigation what is said by ill-mannered coarse people who lack regard even for prestige and wealth, whether in this or future lives. The good and bad qualities of a valuable jewel are carefully analyzed, but no one bothers to examine a firebrand in that way.

54   Not to be pleased by praise,
        Nor displeased by criticism,
        And to maintain properly their good qualities:
        These are characteristics of noble people.

Truly excellent individuals, recognizing that generally in this world there are friends, enemies, and neutral people, are unaffected by praise since they realize there are those who will surely criticize them. They are also unaffected when criticized, since they know there are yet others who will praise them. Knowing that particular words of acclaim and condemnation are merely melodious echoes, they focus on the Three Jewels, monitor their mental activity, are captivated by the Dharma, and properly abide in the three trainings. It is important to be able to restrain oneself from chasing after the seductions of approval and rejection.

55   Genuine wealth is not obtained
        By coercion or wrongdoing.
        Dogs and cats gorging themselves with food
        Is a classic case of shamelessness.

Gold, silver, silks, cattle, houses, land, and so forth acquired through ill deeds such as killing, poison, or alcohol, or by coercive means such as robbery or duress, are discreditable riches. Forsaking one's vows for wealth is lunacy and leads to misery in the unfortunate states of rebirth. Who could possibly tolerate the sufferings of the lower realms? No matter how much dogs and cats stuff themselves with food, such gluttony through killing, thievery, or eating filth is the classic example of shamelessness.

56   When prosperity comes to their subjects,
        That is the sign of the greatness of kings.
        Does not a decorative harness adorning a horse
        Also make handsome the rider herself?

Some rulers are conscientious in deed, word, and thought. They extend high regard to others without deceit, governing all their subjects, good and bad alike, with a kind heart that distinguishes truth from falsehood. Because ruler and ruled treat each other properly, the people become strong and prosperous. When the citizenry gains good fortune, both spiritual and temporal leaders develop the special qualities of greatness. Thus one can see the importance of being able to implement good policies. When a horse with a good canter is decorated with fine ornaments, doesn't that also beautify the rider? Of course!

57   To whatever extent rulers endeavor
        To govern their subjects with kindness,
        To that extent the citizenry strives
        To fulfill their civic duties.

Some rulers reign benevolently and achieve the aims of both themselves and their people. With clear intelligence, using suitable spiritual and temporal means, they give assistance without favoritism in any way they can. In such cases the citizens will also make every effort to do anything for their rulers, night or day, using whatever means they have at their disposal, without concern for life or limb.

58   In places where extraordinary people reside,
          Who would consider others as wise?
          When the sun rises in the sky,
          The stars are many but none are seen.

Great benevolent individuals have by nature a clear, fathomless intelligence and do not cloak themselves in hypocrisy. They have eradicated all self-centeredness and show no prejudice. Like the sun, they emanate rays of beneficence for sentient beings. Where they reside, what honest and dependable person would care in the least about other so-called "wise ones" who crave attention—those with hidden agendas, like seeking only their next meal, wanting to be famous scholars, or otherwise showing off in public because they are ignorant frauds? Nobody pays any attention to them! When the sun is not visible at night, the stars shine in their glory. But when the sun rises to the heavens and its brilliant rays illuminate all things equally, the stars will not be seen no matter how bright or numerous.

Because one really helps oneself when helping others, it is clearly important to dedicate oneself to altruism, the kind of activities the truly benevolent pursue.

Chapter 3 ~
AN EXAMINATION *of the* FOOLISH

59   Bad people can acquire wealth, but then
      Their behavior truly degenerates.
      No matter how one tries to reverse a waterfall,
      It is well known it can only flow downward.

Usually it is quite difficult for bad people to get rich. However, if through wrongdoing they acquire a little wealth, the slight enjoyment it provides makes them particularly arrogant. Being totally ignorant, attacking everyone, and using very forceful but crude language, they are compelled by their bad natures to engage only in decadent conduct like drinking and gambling. Try as one might to make a cascade of water flow uphill, it is obvious that its natural tendency is only to descend.

60   Good conduct may occur in coarse people,
      But it is an instance of artificiality.
      Glass may be colored to look like a jewel,
      But when it touches water, its true color shows.

Just as bad smells emanate from filth, usually nothing but bad behavior comes from coarse people. Even something good they might do is insincere deception. The nature of their impulsive behavior becomes obvious when they meet good people. Someone might be fooled by a piece of colored glass, thinking it a real gem, but contact with water will reveal its actual quality. So be careful! Artificiality is commonplace nowadays.

61   Although a fool may do something good,
      It's a lucky coincidence, not deliberate.
      The silk thread from a silkworm's saliva
      Does not come about through skill.

Usually it is difficult for fools who lack the intelligence to assess good and bad consequences when accomplishing anything constructive. But even should they do something temporarily beneficial, it is the result of good fortune or karma rather than discernment and careful study. Silk thread spun from saliva is due not to the silkworm's knowledge of thread-making, but to fate or karma. Do not admire such ways of accomplishing things.

62   Things that the great achieve with effort,
       Bad people destroy in an instant.
       Crops for which farmers toil months and years,
       Hailstorms destroy in an instant.

Admirable individuals who have mastered the distinction between right and wrong labor hard at their good works, spending many days carefully analyzing potential outcomes. But then degenerate people, ignorant of such discrimination, gather in meetings and give disruptive speeches that are impassioned, partial, verbose, and rude, destroying in an instant any accomplishments and wasting all the effort underlying them. Farmers may labor for months, then just as they are about to harvest, a hailstorm can suddenly decimate their crops, nullifying all their efforts.

63   Bad people usually attribute to others
       Any faults they themselves possess.
       Crows smear their filth-eating beaks
       Vigorously over other clean places.

Be careful with bad-natured, greedy, and shameless people because they inflict their example on others like an infectious disease. Their degenerate character makes them project their own deficiencies, such as vulgar thoughts and crude behavior, upon faultless individuals. Ugly, foul-mouthed crows exuberantly wipe their dirty, smelly, offal-eating beaks upon such clean places as lotus flowers.

64   When responsibilities are given to a fool,
       Things deteriorate, then get even worse.
       It is said that because a fox was appointed king,
       He tormented his followers and was himself killed.

Inexperienced fools, unskilled in any spiritual or worldly matters, are sometimes delegated to eradicate faults and achieve the well-being of themselves and others. Forget about them meeting these goals! Because they have no means to accomplish their purpose, not only will the situation degenerate, they will ruin themselves as well. In a well-known story a stupid fox was instated as king of the carnivores. This not only brought misery down upon his fellow foxes, but ultimately cost him his life.

Once upon a time a fox was wandering around looking for food. He came upon a dye-master mixing dye in a copper pot. The inquisitive fox fell into the pot. After floundering about he escaped, but the tips of his fur had become the color of blue sesame flowers.

At that time all the animals were assembling to designate a king. The fox was such a nice color that some asked, "Who are you?"

"I am the jewel of sentient beings, king of the carnivores!" replied the fox.

With his beautiful fur and subdued manner he convinced the animals that he was a suitable king, so they installed him on the throne. He selected a lion as his minister, and when they went on tour, the fox rode on the lion's back.

Although the fox was highly respected, he became antagonistic toward most of his subjects, especially his fellow foxes. Unable to tolerate such abuse, all the foxes gathered together to discuss the situation.

"Even though this king is of our own kind, he is hostile and harmful only to us," they complained. After further deliberation they came up with a plan. "On the fifteenth of the month[113] we shall all howl. If he is truly one of us, he will also howl and expose his true colors."

At the appointed time they all joined in as planned. The king sneaked off into a corner and he also howled. All the animals quickly convened to reprimand him.

"So this is what has been going on!" exclaimed the lion, and he killed the fox on the spot.

65   While the ignorant are wishing for happiness,
      Their deeds bring them only suffering.
      Some people possessed by evil spirits
      Are seen to commit suicide to ease their pain.

Ignorant fools are noted for incongruity between their outer activities and inner desires. They want to be happy, but lack firm belief in the relationship between cause and effect. Their talk of actions and results is merely hollow; accordingly, they fail to protect themselves. This deficiency leads them to kill, steal, and do other things motivated by greed, anger, and confusion, which only brings them more misery. Śāntideva says in *Engaging in the Bodhisattva Deeds,*

> Though we desire to be happy, in our ignorance
> We destroy happiness as if we were our own enemy.

For example, some individuals are actually seen to resort to suicide by fire, drowning, or jumping off cliffs, in order to relieve the misery caused by their being in the grip of malignant spirits.

66   Some straightforward dull people ruin themselves,
     And some bring destruction to others.
     Straight trees in the forest are sought out and cut,
     And straight arrows are used to kill others.

Directness is not always a good quality. Some people know when to extend themselves and when to hold back, and take care that "measured action is like a proverb and measured speech is like an ornament." But those of poor intelligence may be unable to discern the likely consequences of their actions and thus bring much misfortune to themselves and others. They are like "those who pour water on their own heads"; they injure and ruin themselves and do whatever they can to make trouble for others. Straight trees in the forest are sought out and cut down; likewise, straightforwardness can bring misfortune to oneself. Straight arrows are use to kill others; likewise, straightforwardness can bring misfortune to others.

67   Always ignoring the interests of others
     Is to behave in the same way as cattle.
     Is it not possible even for animals
     Merely to acquire food and drink?

Those whose physical, verbal, and mental actions are directed solely to procuring their own sustenance and clothing and who lack any thought of the general welfare of others are no different than animals. Such actions do not fulfill the purpose of obtaining a human rebirth—one sees cattle and deer living this way! It is necessary to make effort on behalf of others.

68   Those oblivious to what helps or harms,
     Who do not think carefully or listen to others,
     And aspire only to a full stomach—
     They are nothing but hairless pigs.

Some people fail to examine carefully what will affect their own and others' vital interests in this and future lifetimes. Having acquired no knowledge to clear away stupidity and develop their intelligence, they do not perceive the gifts of learned, respectable, excellent spiritual masters and wise elders who practice Dharma. Aspiring only to a full stomach in this life, they are useless swine—nothing more than mean-spirited, hairless creatures, the lowest of beasts, who will eat anything, dirty or clean. Make sure your precious human life does not degenerate into a porcine existence.

69   Those who are delighted and amused amid fools,
       But intimidated and shy with the wise,
       Though lacking a hump or dewlap,
       Are actually cattle with upper teeth.[114]

Some individuals, when in the company only of unlearned fools, are pleased and playful because of their education and fame, and lounge around like smart-alec showoffs. But in an assembly of wise people who have special knowledge and ability in spiritual and temporal affairs, they feel bashful, diffident, and go off to hide in a corner, unable to hold up their heads. They may lack the distinctive hump and dewlap, but their true behavior is equivalent to cattle with canine teeth. Take care that your special human circumstances do not degenerate into a bovine existence.

70   Those who run around seeking food and drink
       Yet flee when assigned important duties,
       Even if they can tell stories and joke around,
       They are just old dogs without tails.

Prompted by greed, some people are insensible to problems and just go around to wherever there is eating and drinking. They fail to carry out not only the responsibilities they have willingly assumed, but tasks others have sincerely entrusted to them as well; then they vanish. By not applying a correct attitude, they achieve nothing. They can amuse others with mimicry and tell silly stories, but they do not recognize their obligations and merely pursue the satisfaction of their bellies. But for their lack of tails, such people have the characteristics of old dogs. Work hard to transcend canine behavior and become a fully free and fortunate human being.

71   Hoof prints are easily filled with water,
       Small treasuries are easily filled with wealth,
       Small fields are easily planted with seeds, and
       Small minds are easily contented with knowledge.

One can easily fill a bull's hoof print with only one or two handfuls of water. A small storeroom is readily filled with a few measures of wheat or rice. To sow a small field is easy with only a pouch or two of seeds. Likewise, it is easy to impress people of dull intellect with just a little knowledge. They appear convinced by mere shreds of understanding that repudiate others, and make extensive use of their own fanciful notions devoid of any real evidence, credible scriptural citations, or instructions from experienced spiritual masters. To develop firm conviction, one must rely on sound reasoning, as do the very wise.

72   Even if he is important, an arrogant fool
      Who makes promises is disastrous.
      By giving away a one-step measure of land,
      Bāli lost the three realms.

Insolent fools who make commitments but do not have the intelligence to examine the virtues and faults of a situation can easily ruin things even if they are ordinary people, not to mention if they are somebody important! Bāli, king of the *asuras*, gave away a single-step measure of land carelessly and hence lost his entire kingdom consisting of the three realms of the universe. He was left with no alternative than to slink away and disappear underground.

Once upon a time Bāli ruled above, below, and on the earth, inflicting misery on all sentient beings. The subduer Viṣṇu was extremely angry with his uncle Bāli and so turned his mind to deception. Transforming himself into a dwarf, he went to his uncle and said, "I must make an offering to the deities. Since you are very generous, please give me a secluded piece of land that can be measured off by a single pace." With no careful inquiry, Bāli promised, "I can give you three such measures of land." Viṣṇu then placed one leg atop the golden base of the mandala of the universe and the other leg on top of Mount Sumeru, thus encompassing the entire cosmos.

"This is the first one-step measure of land. Now give me the second and third measures!" Viṣṇu declared.

Bāli was utterly humiliated and withdrew into the depths of the earth. In *The Especially Exalted Praise (Viśeṣastava)*, Udbhaṭasiddhasvāmin says,

> By transforming himself into a dwarf's body
> Viṣṇu deceived his uncle with illusory ways.

This also clarifies verse 381 below, which begins:

> Since swindlers use deceit in their words,
> The honest must check them out carefully.

73   Small-minded people with malice in their hearts
        Signal their intent before giving harm.
        Even vicious dogs, upon seeing an enemy,
        Emit a growl before biting.

A sign of the stupidity of spiteful people is that they physically and verbally indicate their intentions prior to actually setting upon and harming their enemy. They are like some old dogs who do not attack at the moment of seeing a thief, but bark first and give the thief a signal to escape. Conduct yourself as intelligent people do: maintain a mild countenance and try to achieve your desired objectives when the time is right.

74   Fools know the hassle of amassing wealth
        But not the enjoyment of putting it to use.
        Time and again they wander around seeking riches;
        In their avarice they are just like mice.

Fools with no merit from previous lives care nothing for the wrongs they commit, the misery they endure, nor the bad things said of them while they amass gold, silver, barley, and rice. But it is not in their destiny to experience the pleasures of affluence. Contrary to their wishes, one day the riches they compulsively pursued will be appropriated and enjoyed by others, just like stashes of wheat that busy mice garner yet are powerless to prevent others from stealing.

75   Amid fools, a man with a leashed monkey
        Is much more respected than the wise.
        The organ grinder is honored with money and food,
        But the wise person leaves empty-handed.

Someone with a monkey on a leash is just looking for a meal, whereas a wise person is the foundation of all well-being. Undiscriminating fools, enchanted by fleeting laughter and dance, will judge the organ grinder important, and will generously give him food, money, and respect. But toward the wise they will remain rude, contemptuous, and miserly.

76   People devoid of good personal qualities
        Are particularly hostile to those who have them.
        A crop grown in winter in a snowy land
        Is proclaimed to be a bad omen.

It is inappropriate for untrained people, deficient in knowledge or ability, to harbor special hatred toward others who are honest, sincere, and competent in spiritual and temporal affairs. Attempts to grow crops in the frozen earth during the winter are said to be inauspicious because of the incongruity with time and place.

77   Poorly trained people have special disdain
        For those who are properly schooled.
        On some islands, those without goiters
        Are criticized for stunted limbs.

Some people, though much admired and said to be "truly wonderful and learned," are just scholars for show, liars skilled in the eight worldly obsessions, who spout nonsense irrelevant to the path of liberation. They despise the genuinely wise who are trained in the flawless sutras and tantras, saying, "if they don't even know how to find their food, how can they know anything about the great treatises?" Such disrespect exposes the inferior merit of demented individuals who "confuse those who should be honored with those who should do the honoring."[115] On certain islands everyone has a goiter, so when goiterless people arrive, the inhabitants judge them as having incomplete, atrophied limbs.

78   Those who do their work defectively
        Disparage others who complete their tasks.
        When they venture to the land of the one-legged ones,
        Two-legged people are not considered human.

Some people do things poorly, failing to fully prepare for, implement, and conclude their duties. Yet saying, "Oh! You do so much needless work!" they ridicule others who accomplish their work in accordance with the instructions of the old masters of India and Tibet. In the land of one-legged people, those with two legs are not deemed human. To censure two-legged people as non-human is inappropriate. In this way, the wise must make careful distinctions.

79   Some who perform their work improperly
        Rebuke those who do their tasks well.
        Dog-headed people mock the honorable
        By calling them insulting names.

People who do flawless work are criticized by those whose work is offensive and deceitful and who seek their wealth by fraud. Such criticism only reveals ignorance of how to properly engage in spiritual and temporal matters. Dog-headed people view the praiseworthy with disdain and scorn them with derogatory remarks.

80   Those who gain food and riches from wrong livelihood
    Criticize those who are wise but poor.
    Old monkeys, when they behold human beings,
    Burst out laughing and say, "They have no tails!"

Motivated by greed, hatred, and ignorance, reckless fools acquire their food and wealth by wrong livelihood, engaging in acts of hypocrisy and flattery. Shamelessly they despise those who are wise but poor, saying of them, "Even for just this life they are incapable of providing for themselves!" Yet the wise realize the positive results of thinking, "I might die today, but it is better than surviving by wrong livelihood as do those who forsake future lives for this one." Fools are like old monkeys who grasp a human being's hand and brazenly exclaim, "This creature doesn't even have a tail!"

Śāntideva says in *Engaging in the Bodhisattva Deeds,*

    Even if I die today it is superior to living
    For a long time by wrong livelihood.

81   If oppressed by karma, a wise person
    May wander among fools.
    The sweet and fragrant *mallikā* flower,[116]
    Borne by the wind, is trampled into rubbish.

Usually, wise people who understand the law of actions and their effect do not unscrupulously engage in wrongdoing since they would rather die than survive by wrong livelihood. But some, due to their wayward conduct, end up roaming aimlessly among fools, drinking, gambling, beating up enemies, defending friends, doing business, and farming.[117] Impelled by the force of karma, they have no choice. Like the fragrant mallikā flower, they are helplessly blown by the wind into the refuse of the streets and crushed. Do not scorn mindfulness, nor deliberately act in this way; it is essential to diligently cleanse one's karmic obscurations.

82   Zealously clinging to their faults
    Yet never retaining any exemplary qualities,
    Bad people, like strainers,
    Catch debris and let pass what is pure.

Even though learned masters advise ridding oneself of the ten nonvirtuous actions and the five boundless transgressions, some people tenaciously hang on to these shortcomings. The masters also counsel the development of special qualities that lead to higher rebirth and definite goodness, important in both spiritual and temporal matters. But it is characteristic of bad people that they refuse to heed this advice. They are like sieves that retain spent tea leaves but pass on the clear tea liquor.

83   Those with no sense to tell right from wrong
        Stand outside the ranks of the wise.
        Those absorbed in talk of food and riches
        Are referred to as two-legged cows.

The wise discern clearly and intelligently. Excluded from such standing are people who lack the intelligence ever to distinguish right from wrong, whether in the short or long term. Their physical, verbal, and mental energies are consumed by their quest for gratification; then life is over and they die. They may appear to be humans with two legs, but their actual behavior is essentially bovine.

84   Even when many small minds gather together,
        They can achieve nothing important.
        Even when many twigs are bound together,
        They cannot support a house beam.

Incompetent, small-minded people lack the capacity to envision what a course of action will likely yield. Even many of them working hard together fail to accomplish anything useful because they do not have the intelligence to analyze strategies and procedures. Bundles of small twigs will not be able to brace a house beam.

85   Things may be achieved without investigation,
        But who would consider that wise?
        Insects leave tracks that look like letters,
        But they themselves are not literate.

Small-minded people are said to lack the sense to differentiate between good and bad. It may appear that they have achieved something in spite of their inability to investigate things intelligently, but their accomplishments are trivial and happen by chance. No sensible person would consider them wise. Insect tracks might include marks that appear to be one or two letters, but insects can hardly be considered literate.

86   Sensual talk of the weak-minded,
           Magnificent but dull-witted horses,
           Swords that fall on the battleground:
           It is unsure whose allies these will be.

Ordinary people of languid mind mostly chatter about their own desires, not realizing how this affects themselves or others. Similarly, there are grand but stupid horses that know not the difference between victory and defeat, and there are swords that drop to the ground in the midst of the battle. It is uncertain whether these three will be helpful allies or harmful foes.

One should avoid getting caught up in careless, passionate conversation. Rather, one must develop good intelligence so one's speech will be truly beneficial to oneself and one's friends, and detrimental to one's enemies.

87   Even if ignorant fools are numerous,
           They succumb to the power of their foes.
           A large herd of many strong elephants
           Was tamed by a single wise rabbit.

Fools lack both inborn and acquired wisdom. They may assemble in force but no matter what their number, when an entire group consists of nothing but dense-minded individuals they will in the end fall under the control of the enemy. A single lowly but intelligent rabbit once skillfully subdued a herd of mighty elephants and banished them to another land.

Once upon a time there were a multitude of rabbits living in a dense forest near a pond, where they went every day to drink water. A large band of thirsty elephants, threatened by the springtime heat, came and thrashed in the water. The smart rabbits were driven away and left without access to their pond. They all assembled to discuss what should be done.

"I have a plan," one rabbit announced.

"What is it? What is it?" the rest clamored.

"Lift me up to the top of a tall tree and I'll show you," he replied. So they all did as he requested and perched him in the highest tree.

Soon the elephants gathered by the tree. The rabbit called loudly and clearly from the treetop, "You herd of elephants! Sit down and listen to me!" They all looked upward. "Who are you?" they asked.

"I am the messenger of the moon of good fortune," the rabbit answered.[118]

"Why were you sent here?" asked the elephants in wonder.

"The moon says that if these intelligent rabbits who dwell in his stomach are driven out of their land, it will radiate down upon you the hot rays of the sun," the rabbit declared. "Until the fourteenth of the month the moon will remain behind a bank of swirling clouds, but after that it will bring harm to you. So if you want happiness, listen to my words!"

The elephants deliberated over this message, and then said, "The moon of good fortune has not harmed us as yet, and furthermore what harm can you, the moon's messenger, bring to us?"

The rabbit replied, "I will fall down on your heads!"

"Go ahead and do that," the elephants laughed, and the rabbit tumbled down upon them in a rain of branches and leaves.

Just at that moment the moon appeared from behind the clouds. The rabbit demanded, "Let the rabbits stay here and you go away peacefully." The elephants retreated in fear, and the resourceful rabbits lived happily as they had in the past.

88 Though the ignorant may have wealth,
   They generally gain little benefit from it.
   Though the wish-fulfilling cow has milk,
   There is not much for its calf to drink.

Short-term well-being is to eliminate the suffering of accumulating and protecting what is temporary. Long-term well-being refers to the profound spiritual attainment of higher rebirth and definite goodness. Some people lack the perception to investigate these two kinds of propitiousness. They may get rich by the power of merit amassed in former lifetimes or by negative actions in their present life; but since they have created the cause to lack wisdom, their wealth is usually of little use. They may appear to be somewhat helpful to others, but mostly they are preoccupied with wrongdoing. The udder of the wish-fulfilling cow does yield milk, but its own calf can drink and enjoy very little of it.

It is important for those who have amassed a little wealth to focus on developing the wisdom that discerns those achievements that are truly beneficial for this and future lives.

89 It is uncertain whether or not
   Even the wise would be honored by fools.
   When the bright sun shines
   Do evil spirits not flee?

Fools do not bother to educate themselves and have no decent friends. They fail to respect and learn from not only ordinary, intelligent people, but also from the exemplary wise who uphold, protect, and propagate the precious Buddha's teachings, source of all well-being. Bright, warm sun rays are a fitting source of happiness for all sentient beings, yet harmful demons and evil spirits, active at night, hastily retreat from the merest gleam of the morning sun.

Seek the knowledge of wise spiritual teachers. They enable one to attain the most worthwhile objectives from now until reaching the fully completed state of a buddha.

90   When do fools who have accumulated wealth
        Ever think of their friends and relatives?
        Solely absorbed in wrongdoing and cursing,
        They get rich and then die, just like mice.

When fools with poor merit, knowledge, and ability amass large amounts of grain and silver, do they have noble thoughts of security for their allies, help for their friends and relatives, or good relationships with spiritual teachers? Such possibilities never enter their minds! They talk badly with no shame and commit evil deeds like killing and stealing—suffering heat, cold, hunger, and thirst. This makes them rich but ultimately they die at the end of a pointless life. Greedy mice labor intensively to hoard quantities of grain, then die with no freedom to enjoy their riches.

People who accumulate a little wealth can put it to good use if they work at creating merit that benefits both present and future lives. The bodhisattva Thogmay Zangpo says,

      Rejoice in whatever wealth you have;
      It can really enable meritorious virtuous deeds.
      Whatever well-being is yours, present and future,
      Is certain to be the fruit of merit.

91   How can those with special qualities
        Be respected in a group of bad people?
        Even lamplight does not shine forth
        In places where poisonous snakes live.

Although the wise are deemed to have special qualities, how could they ever be highly regarded among vulgar people who are arrogant, jealous, and competitive? This is not a possibility because their characters are incompatible. Since the nature of a bright shining lamp is incompatible with that of a poisonous snake, lamps cannot illuminate areas where snakes dwell.

The wise must stay in the supportive company of other wise people in order to do good work.

92   Though greedy people may have wealth,
        Their bad karma renders them powerless to enjoy it.
        In the season when grapes are ripe for eating,
        The *didi* bird's mouth is always sore.

No matter how much wealth some people have, it simply causes unhappiness in this life and unfortunate states of rebirth later. This is because it was greedily accumulated through the power of negative karma, and thus becomes of no use whatsoever to themselves or others. Due to its pitiful karma and merit, the didi bird always gets a sore mouth when the grapes hang plump and sweet.

93   Those who must always be helped by others
        Someday will certainly land in trouble,
        As in the well-known story of the turtle
        Who was carried off by crows, and then fell to earth.

Arrogant people unable to fend for themselves require the compassion and kindness of others for protection and care. They can live in this carefree way for awhile, but one day the limits to others' kindness coupled with their own arrogance will surely land them in trouble. There is a classic account of a helpless turtle who was skillfully carried aloft by crows but met his end because of his own stupidity.

Once upon a time a turtle from the ocean came inland up a canal that farmers used for irrigation. When the water stopped flowing the turtle was stranded in a field. He grew very weak and had no idea what to do.

A crow came by. "What is the matter?" she asked. The turtle told her what had happened.

"Why are you so upset? You can still get back home," commented the crow.

But the turtle complained, "Look at my predicament! I can't move!"

"I have a way to help you," said the crow. She summoned a crow friend and with their beaks they each took hold of either end of a small stick. The turtle bit down on the middle of the stick with his mouth.

"Hold tight!" instructed the crow. "We two will carry you off to the ocean," and they flew away.

Some villagers saw them. "Look at those two smart crows up there!" they exclaimed.

The helpless, arrogant turtle heard that and was about to say to them, "I am the smart one here!" But as soon as he opened his mouth, he let go of the stick, fell to the earth, and died.

Rid yourself of pride and diligently cultivate self-reliance.

94   The marks of a fool are: not knowing good from bad,
           Ingratitude, indifference to inspiring biographies,
           Understanding things yet persisting with questions,
           Cowardice, and blindly following others.

The following traits are characteristic of fools:

- an inability to tell the difference between good things (knowing what to do, not harming others, having gratitude, respect, and honesty) and bad things (accepting others' help but harming them in return, being wasteful, and despising the lowly);
- ingratitude for spiritual and temporal help received from others;
- disinterest in the marvelous accounts of the lives of the buddhas, bodhisattvas, and spiritual masters;
- directly perceiving the true nature of ordinary things like pillars and vases, yet persisting in asking pointless questions about them; and
- wandering off into misery after carelessly following tricksters who contrive nice talk and gentle actions with evil intent to do harm.

Recognizing these and similar qualities of fools, strive to develop the antidotes that give rise to discriminating wisdom.

95   Cowards talk about subduing enemies
           And shout loudly seeing them at a distance
           But fold their palms when confronting them in battle,
           Then speak boastfully after returning home.

The following behavior indicates insecure cowardice of the lowest sort:

- talking at length of how to subdue enemies by various means without any certainty at all about their disposition;
- shouting bravely at enemies when seeing them from a distance;
- rather than defeating enemies in actual confrontation on the battlefield, instead surrendering weapons to them, supplicating them with bowed head and folded palms, and begging their protection; and then
- speaking proudly of all one's exploits in battle after returning home.

Therefore, prior to battle first thwart an enemy's confidence, then endeavor to conquer him at once.

96   At the time of discussion, cowards are dauntless;
        When assigned duties they reckon their costs;
        When it is time to go to work they become ill;
        And in battle they shout and give orders from afar.

At first during discussions lowly cowards seem brave, always volunteering,
"I'll go! I can do it!" When individual work assignments are delegated at
taxation time, they calculate the costs they must bear.[119] When they finally
need to carry out their responsibilities, they become sick and make excuses
like "I'll slip on the grass or trip over a hummock." In combat they yell,
"Fight! Kill!" from a distance, but when they actually come face to face
with the enemy on the battlefield, they fold their palms in supplication as
described above.

97   The small-minded boast of some small victory;
        Then when they lose they blame their friends.
        In discussion they create dissension
        And reveal secrets to others.

Unlike people of good character who find no need to boast of trivial matters,
loud-mouthed, dull-witted people cannot achieve major objectives, but are
proud when they attain minor ones. When their own ineptitude brings them
defeat, instead of admitting their faults they become irate and accuse their
friends and relatives, "You didn't do such and such!"
    When discussions are being held, instead of realizing the purpose of the
meeting and speaking honestly, the small-minded stir up conflict, being pre-
occupied with their own long-range, selfish interests. When secret talks occur
one should respect confidentiality and neither speak with others nor be deceit-
ful. But they don't do this. They whisper to everyone, "Don't tell this to any-
body! Don't speak a word to them!" In this way they spread the secret
throughout the land.

98   They clean their ornamental gear on the battlefield
        And hide when the enemy confronts them;
        When charging, they terrify ally instead of foe,
        And toss their weapons into the enemy's hand.

During battle bad people assess the situation in terms of their own survival,
avoid fighting, and preoccupy themselves with shining their swords and
firearms. When they actually do meet with their opponents, they keep their
loyalties secret and hide. Then when it is crucial to go united into battle,

their own allies are the first to be frightened instead of the enemy. In the end they scatter their weapons within reach of the enemy's hands and flee in all directions.

99   When troops go off to battle, he moves in the rear;
         When they return home, he is in the lead;
         When he sees food and drink, he partakes enthusiastically;
         And when he sees hard work, he avoids it cleverly.

Some people are doubly shameless, having neither a sense of personal shame nor any regard for what others may think of them. Recognize the following misdeeds as indicators of bad people:

* when soldiers march off to the battlefield, they lag behind with the alibi that they have more important things to do;
* on returning home they are at the head of the troops, showing off and boasting of their exploits;
* when they learn where refreshments are available, they arrive before others and eagerly help themselves; and
* when they hear about or see difficult work, they avoid it with clever excuses and do absolutely nothing at all.

100   Although many things can be said
         About the characteristics of bad people,
         Who would draw water from a filthy well?
         What wise person wants to taste vomit?

Due to widespread degeneracy nowadays there is an immense amount that can be said about different kinds of coarse behavior—physical, verbal, and mental—as noted above. However, what sensible person would knowingly draw water from a thoroughly filthy well? One can engage in such debased conduct, but what wise person would? Discriminating individuals consider it easy to understand the deportment of fools in accordance with what has been explained here, so cast aside behaviors such as deliberately belittling and deceiving others.

101   Giving a signal by moving one's lips,
         Winking when talking about others,
         Groaning loudly when stories are being told—
         It is a sign of coarseness when such things happen.

Anyone who does the following is branded as the worst kind of bad person:

◆ signaling to others in a crowd by moving one's lips to show one needs to say something;
◆ winking an eye when talking about others to indicate whether something more should be said or not; and
◆ uttering noises of complaint when interesting accounts of other people's lives are being related.

Foolish people lack the knowledge, ability, and intelligence to investigate the various issues explained above. Know well the nature of fools' faulty conduct, and take care to distinguish between what needs to be done and what must be avoided.

Chapter 4

AN EXAMINATION *of*
BOTH *the* WISE *and* FOOLISH

102   Though coarse people acquire great wealth,
    They are still overshadowed by the noble.
    As the hungry tiger roars,
    The monkey falls from the treetop.

Ignorant, coarse people can become temporarily affluent. But superior people of good lineage, even if briefly impoverished, overawe them with magnificence because of their excellent innate and acquired knowledge and their estimable conduct. This is like the monkey that was stunned by a tiger's splendor. Hungry and thirsty, the tiger emitted a great roar that frightened the monkey so that it fell from a tree and ended up as the tiger's dinner.

    Forsake the ambition to acquire wealth; it is devoid of real essence anyway. Maintain instead respectable qualities of ancestry and conduct.

103   A fool's knowledge shows on the surface,
    But a wise person's knowledge is hidden within.
    A straw floats on top of the water;
    A jewel sinks even when placed on the surface.

Fools with little understanding of temporal and spiritual matters do not assimilate what they learn into their physical, verbal, and mental activity, yet they prance around showing off what they know like a dog with a yak-skin butter sack in its mouth. The wise, on the other hand, integrate their experience into their deeds. At appropriate times they draw from scriptural authority, logic, and their own experience to give thoughtful instruction on the collections of merit and wisdom; when circumstances are unsuitable they keep their knowledge hidden within rather than display it openly. Practiced in maintaining a positive view of things, they live in harmony with others.

A straw, light and hollow like a fool lacking the weight of experience, floats on top of the water. The heavy wish-fulfilling jewel, like a wise person weighted by the capacity to grant what is needed and desired, settles into the depths even if carefully placed on the surface.

104   Those with limited knowledge have great pride,
        But when they become wise, they are composed.
        A small creek babbles incessantly,
        But what clamor does the ocean produce?

Some people may gain a little knowledge from being educated in general worldly affairs, but because their learning is neither internalized nor serves as an antidote for mental coarseness, they become arrogant. However, once they fully assimilate their learning, they regard the fine qualities in others as superior to themselves and maintain a temperate demeanor free of pride. Fast-flowing little creeks tumble noisily downhill, but large accumulations of water like the great ocean, whose undulations are unpretentious, do not rush around with a lot of hullabaloo.

105   Coarse people disparage the noble,
        But noble people do not belittle anyone.
        Though lions treat the foxes well,
        The foxes quarrel among themselves.

Because of their bad attitudes, ill-mannered people show their contempt for those of noble character through offensive behavior. But good people are impartial, belittling no one and holding a benevolent attitude toward all. As king of beasts, the lion is protective of other animals like foxes. But foxes are competitive and contentious creatures, and create more woe among themselves than for anyone else.

All beings want only happiness and wish to avoid suffering, so cultivate the temperament of fine people who make themselves and others happy at no expense to others.

106   Noble people, when angry, are mollified by apology,
        But coarse people become even more obstinate.
        Solid gold and silver can be melted,
        But heating dog turds just creates a foul stench.

Good people usually will not become angry because they analyze and understand the causes of a situation. If for some reason they do get rankled, as soon as others apologize they calm down, in keeping with their excellent character. However, coarse people get angry if they fail to achieve the slightest objective. Apologies make them yet more irate because the issue appears so important. Gold and silver are hard by nature, yet become fluid when subjected to heat; but when dog excrement is put into a fire, the only result is a repulsive smell that offends everyone.

107   The wise possess all virtuous qualities,
        While fools have only shortcomings.
        From precious jewels comes whatever one needs;
        Poisonous snakes bring only misfortune.

The truly wise continuously possess all the finest attributes such as learnedness, nobility, and kindness—the consummate marks of those who serve both sentient beings and the Buddha's teachings. Conversely, foolish people who lack these good qualities have only deficiencies, like jealousy and competitiveness. As a consequence, not only are they of no help to others, they end up ruining themselves and others. A wish-fulfilling jewel will provide all the gold, silver, and fine silk clothing one desires, but only the misfortune of sickness and death ensues from a poisonous snake. Therefore, do not follow fools; rely instead on the accomplished ones whose purpose goes beyond mere talk.

108   Even in the forest malicious people deteriorate,
        Even in the city noble people remain serene.
        One sees that forest animals are wild and ferocious,
        But the best horses are well-disciplined in town.

Degenerate behavior among ill-mannered fools with undisciplined minds is not solely caused by unfavorable external conditions; it is also due to their own mental delusions. Merely dwelling in a mountain hermitage free of desire and competitiveness does not ensure that one will develop seclusion of the inner mind. Decent people integrate the Dharma into their lives, and because of their good character their conduct never deteriorates, whether they stay in isolated places or in cities amid many people. Leopards and other wild animals in the deep forest are vicious by nature for no apparent reason. But a superb horse with a fine canter, even in the city among mules, will remain steady and disciplined.

109   The excellent observe their own faults,
        While the coarse seek faults in others.
        Peacocks attend to their own form,
        While owls hoot bad omens to others.

Wise people investigate situations differently than fools do. Well-trained to uphold the glorious spiritual and worldly traditions, the wise realize that because of their faults they cannot achieve their own objectives, let alone benefit others. By looking within they try to eliminate weaknesses of body, speech, and mind, and to strengthen their good qualities. Coarse, ignoble people, however, do not analyze themselves but instead look outward, seeking imperfections in the ways good people do things. Peacocks examine their form and their way of moving, and notice how their shadows are cast by the sun so they can improve what is good and lessen what is bad. But owls land on top of a house, cry out, and send forth bad omens.

Since nothing worthwhile is accomplished for either oneself or others when one has shortcomings, it is always good to practice as the wise do. Some great masters have said,

> To hide the body—live alone on a remote mountain;
> To hide speech—resolve not to talk too much;
> To hide the mind—focus only on your own shortcomings:
> One who does this is certainly called a hidden yogi!

110　Noble people gently care for themselves and others;
　　　Bad people stubbornly torment themselves and others.
　　　A fruit-laden tree shelters itself and others;
　　　A dry, brittle tree incinerates itself and others.

Because they have calmed their own minds, good people are like the bird that dwells on the golden mountain: skillfully knowing what to do and what to avoid, they protect not just themselves but also their dependents. But fools whose minds are estranged from the Dharma are like birds living on a mountain of poison. Their obstinacy brings misery not just to themselves but to their associates as well. The tree that bears fine fruit not only protects itself from being cut down, it nourishes others with its abundant yield. But dead, dry trees will not merely catch fire themselves; the whole forest goes up in smoke.

111　When one is wealthy, all are friends,
　　　But if one is poor, all are enemies.
　　　People come from afar to the jeweled isle,
　　　But everyone avoids a dried-up lake.

The support of wealth is only a temporary advantage. When people benefit from the results of merit and get rich, then others from all walks of life naturally congregate and are friendly. But when merit is exhausted and one enters into poverty, antagonists, friends, and even relatives become enemies. People will spend months and years traveling great distances to meet on the island of jewels, but even ducks will abandon a lake parched by drought.

Wealth devoid of merit does not endure, so it is critical for those who enjoy some prosperity to exert themselves in accumulating merit. The bodhisattva Thogmay Zangpo says:

> Rejoice in whatever wealth you have:
> It can really enable meritorious virtuous deeds.
> Whatever well-being is yours, now and in the future,
> Is certain to be the fruit of merit.

112   Fools are happy when acquiring wealth;
       Noble people find happiness in giving it all away.
       Lepers feel better when they scratch their sores,
       But note how the wise dread leprosy.

There are long-range advantages that depend on wealth. When greedy fools gain a little prosperity they remain conceited in their pleasures, oblivious to the miseries of amassing and guarding wealth. But truly good people recognize its virtues and faults, both short and long term. They take but the essence of illusory wealth, and delight in giving it away because this enables them to achieve their immediate and future objectives. Candrakīrti says in his *Supplement to (Nāgārjuna's) "Treatise on the Middle" (Madhyamakāvatāra)*,

> Since the degree of pleasure felt by bodhisattvas
> Upon hearing and pondering the word "Give!"
> Is not felt by foe destroyers abiding in peace,
> Is there need to mention the joy of giving all away?

Although lepers draw blood when they scratch their lesions, they feel relief and keep doing it. But the wise who know how to reason are terrified of the disease itself, to say nothing of scratching lesions.

113   Toward those individuals who persecute them,
       The great are friendly, but the coarse are abusive.
       Though wind fans the blaze of a forest fire,
       It will extinguish the flame of a small lamp.

The force of merit differs from that of ordinary facilitating factors. Great people empowered with merit may be endangered by menacing enemies but they befriend them, thereby achieving the two excellent collections of merit and wisdom for this and future lives. But when some small misfortune befalls base people with no merit, they cannot acquire even their immediate needs for food and clothing, leave aside the collections of merit and wisdom. When fire burns a large forest, a gust of wind instantly fans the flames and they burn all the more intensely; the same wind will snuff out a small lamp.

Once upon a time in the land of Mo Jig, there lived a king called Candraprabha who ruled the southern continent. After deliberating over the causes he had created in the past, he assembled his family and ministers and pledged to give all his possessions to everyone in his kingdom. All the poor people gathered and enjoyed whatever riches their hearts desired.

Hearing of that virtuous act, the arrogant king Bhīmasena became thoroughly agitated with jealousy. He went to a Brahmin guru who had long been granting his wishes. After paying his respects he said, "I am depressed and miserable and cannot sleep. You must think of a way to relieve this problem."

"Whatever is the cause of this?" the Brahmin asked.

"King Candraprabha has ruined my name," Bhīmasena declared.

The Brahmin said, "King Candraprabha has become like a mother to all. I cannot harm him." Then, without a care for his immediate needs, he departed.

Bhīmasena was thoroughly perturbed. "To whosoever is able to cut off the head of King Candraprabha, I shall give half of my kingdom," he vowed.

Another Brahmin named Leu Ducha heard of the king's pledge and presented himself to Bhīmasena. "I can carry out this task," the Brahmin promised, and after a week of repeating magic incantations, he departed.

In time, epidemics swept the land. An earthquake occurred, and the night heavens were bright with lightning and shooting stars. Cries of distress were everywhere. There was the sound of drums and the rulers of 84,000 small kingdoms dreamed that the golden roof ornament of victory had shattered. In particular, the minister Mahācandra dreamed that a large preta had stolen the crown of the king. Everyone was beset with misery. The palace guards recognized the bad omens and would not admit Brahmin Leu Ducha when he arrived at the palace.

A short while later the gods of the pure realm, knowing King Candraprabha's generosity would this time complete his perfection of generosity, promised him in a dream, "You will give the most wonderful gift of all."

Just then, Leu Ducha came to the palace door again. The king awoke, summoned Mahācandra, and requested him to go open the door. The minister went and spoke to the guards.

"Isn't it true that there are many bad omens?" he asked fearfully.

"It is true," they replied, "but we cannot disobey the king's orders." Leu Ducha was invited inside.

Mahācandra set out five hundred heads made of the seven precious jewels to try to dissuade Leu Ducha, but the Brahmin desired only the head of the king himself. He proceeded directly to the king and asked for it. The king was pleased and agreed to comply with his request.

"When can I take it?" asked Leu Ducha.

"After one week," replied the king.

King Candraprabha rode on an elephant for one thousand miles, then summoned all the gods and humans of the land. All his subjects, his ten thousand ministers, his twenty thousand queens, his five hundred sons, pleaded with him but he would not listen. "First you must pray," he instructed them, "and then I shall give away my head."

"I cannot cut off your head here," complained the Brahmin. "If you are really going to do this, we must go off to a secluded grove."

So the king and the Brahmin went into the remote forest. At last they reached a particular grove and the Brahmin said, "Your head must be tied to a tree trunk."

"That is not right," the king objected. "I wish to attain enlightenment, so you must hold it in your hand like a proper offering."

A tree goddess tried to halt these proceedings, but the king said, "Just look! Here at the root of this tree in previous lifetimes I have given my head nine hundred ninety-nine times. Today it shall be one thousand. Do not create obstacles to my attaining enlightenment!"

With that, he placed his head in Leu Ducha's hand and the sacrifice was completed. Immediately thereupon the earth trembled with an earthquake that radiated in all directions.

The moment he heard that King Candraprabha had completed the perfection of generosity by sacrificing his life, King Bhīmasena had a heart attack and died. Brahmin Leu Ducha was just delivering the head when he heard that King Bhīmasena had perished. He tossed the head away, vomited blood, and also died. They both then went to the hell realms.

According to the sutras, King Candraprabha was Buddha Śākyamuni in a former lifetime, Bhīmasena was Māra, the Brahmin Leu Ducha was Devadatta, the tree goddess was Maudgalyāyana, and the minister was Śāriputra.

In verse 336 it says,

> If one wishes to harm an enemy,
> One must possess good personal qualities.
> They will exasperate the enemy
> And increase one's own stock of merit.

Elsewhere it is said,

> Inability to tolerate
> The good fortune of others
> Destroys one's own good fortune;
> Therefore, eradicate jealous feelings.

114   Saying, "These are my friends, those are my foes,"
      People of small intelligence pigeonhole others.
      The wise love everybody equally,
      Since it is hard to ascertain who is helpful.

Weak-minded, ignorant people categorize their acquaintances, saying, "This person is dear to me and a helpful friend, but that one is an enemy who harms my body and mind." They make distinctions, holding some close and keeping others distant. But intelligent people are impartial; they cherish everybody—the important, the lowly, and the ordinary—wishing all to be happy. Consequently, there is no way to be certain whether one person is truly supportive to them, or another injurious.

    Labeling people as either friends or foes in this lifetime is creating an unreal phenomenon, like a drawing of a butter lamp. Develop the nature of the wise who are equitable toward all.

115   Accomplished people are attracted to knowledge,
      But ignorant people are not.
      Honey-gathering bees are attracted to flowers,
      But ordinary houseflies are not.

Being educated themselves, knowledgeable people value others who are learned and respectfully stay in their company. Uneducated people, out of ignorance, have no special preferences at all, like dogs who spy tasty food. Honey bees seek out flowers because of the excellent nectar they provide; houseflies have no such interest.

116   The wise shine among the wise,
      But how can fools recognize them?
      As for sandalwood which is dearer than gold,
      Look how fools turn it into charcoal!

The wise who have mastered the great scriptures are quite distinguished when among other learned people. But fools do not comprehend the distinctive qualities of wisdom, so how will they ever recognize who is wise or not? Because of this, they cannot accomplish anything skillfully.

Once upon a time a foolish fellow had some premium quality sandalwood. He went everywhere trying to sell it but found no buyers.

One night he went to sleep in a vacant house. There he met another person who was peddling charcoal. They struck up a conversation. "There is nobody around here who will buy my goods," the sandalwood peddler complained.

The next morning they went off separately to sell their wares. When they returned to the house that evening the charcoal peddler had sold all his charcoal and went to sleep peacefully. Seeing this, the fool thought to himself, "Ah me! I need to find a special way of selling my goods like he did." So he turned his priceless sandalwood into charcoal. This was the fool's notion of making a profit.

Therefore, shun the company of fools who, even if they have some slight appreciation for knowledge, do not grasp true excellence. Be like the wise, who either dwell alone in a peaceful forest or live with respect among other wise people.

117   The wise can investigate things for themselves,
        But fools chase after whatever is popular.
        When an old dog yelps,
        Other dogs run without reason.

Nowadays most people are fascinated by novelty and tend to be fickle, treacherous, and probe into others' affairs with broad smiles and slick talk. Wise people, well-trained in all fields of knowledge, question others and analyze things carefully. They distinguish between what should be done and what should be avoided. Fools, however, lack analytical wisdom, so they chase pointlessly after whatever is popular and talked about, and never know the right thing to do. A dog will bark at some minor provocation, prompting other dogs to chase after it for no apparent reason. Then they all end up being hurt by people throwing sticks and stones at them.

Once upon a time a rabbit was sound asleep on a riverbank. Suddenly a nearby tree branch fell into the water. The great splash scared the rabbit so much he bolted into the forest, running smack into a friend.

"What happened?" the friend asked the breathless rabbit.

"A splashing noise!" sputtered the rabbit, and the two of them took off lickety-split.

The same exchange took place with a fox, a jackal, a wolf, a tiger, a leopard, a bear, and a giant ape. They all ran away in a panic.

Eventually they met a lion. The rabbit delivered the same dreadful news and started off, but the lion called, "Wait! What was this splashing noise?"

"I'll show you," said the rabbit, and led them all back to the place from which he had earlier fled. In the water was nothing but the branch of a tree.

"This is it," admitted the rabbit. They all looked, and all were astonished.

118   Even when the wise become very poor,
    They please others with their good advice.
    Even when fools become wealthy,
    They consume themselves and others with dispute.

Because their practice of Dharma is strong, the wise and purposeful rarely become destitute. They may at times seem wretched and poverty-stricken due to strong karma created in previous lifetimes, but this extinguishes their negative potential for misery and exhausts it for others as well. Their lives are meaningful, and they please others with eloquent advice based on the Dharma like the story about the caravan leader, Mitra.

It is difficult for ignorant fools to gain wealth naturally, though they may succeed through the power of ill deeds. Even then their own pride and other peoples' jealousies make them competitive, leading to nothing but bickering back and forth with others. Hence, they bring themselves and others to ruin as if incinerated by fire.

119   Some are known to achieve things through talking;
    Others silently pursue their objectives.
    A mean dog barks at the enemy;
    Cats and herons[120] silently ambush their prey.

Some people are skilled talkers and achieve their objectives primarily by giving thorough and critical explanations of things. Others think excessive talk that ignores whether something said is helpful or harmful brings trouble swarming like a cloud of enemies. They try to meet their goals with minimal discussion. When vicious dogs see thieves or other enemies, they proudly guard their riches by raising a great ruckus. But cats, herons, and robbers get their quarry by waiting motionless in ambush. Śāntideva says in *Engaging in the Bodhisattva Deeds*,

    Herons, cats, and robbers
    Clearly attain their objectives
    By moving silently and stealthily;
    That is how the Buddha always functions.

Though limits should be put on speech, if the time is appropriate one should say a few words, rather than just sit mutely.

120   Even when attacked, noble people help others;
       Even when befriended, bad people inflict harm;
       Even when angry, the gods protect sentient beings;
       And even when smiling, the Lord of Death kills.

People of good character do not retaliate even when they are attacked; instead they try skillfully to gain some positive outcome from the situation. People of bad character, even if they seem to be affable companions, are harmful because their friendship is fickle, their honesty fleeting. Although the wrathful deities look savage, gritting their teeth, brandishing swords and spears, their compassionate nature protects sentient beings from misfortune and guards those engaged in wholesome deeds. But the Lord of Death, even as he smiles, grips in his fangs the three worlds—above, below, and upon the earth—and always tries to claim the living by engulfing them with his army.

121   Like precious jewels, noble people
       Remain unchangeable in every respect.
       Like a balance scale, bad people
       Feel elated or dejected at the slightest change.

Whatever temporary conditions, such as wealth or poverty, befall good people, they maintain their excellent character and do not change; they never become arrogant or degenerate in any way. They are like precious gold, whose yellow color never alters irrespective of being subjected to any of the four elements, such as being thrust in water or burnt in fire. But bad people, like the pans of a balance scale that move simply at the addition of a tiny grain of rice, have dispositions that fluctuate up or down merely by getting some small bit of food or drink, or hearing a single coarse or nice word.

122   Though friends live far away, they are supportive;
       Though unfriendly people live nearby, they are remote.
       Though growing in mud, the lotus remains unsoiled
       And is always nurtured by the sun.

Like-minded associates such as spiritual teachers, parents, relatives, and friends strive to be helpful directly and indirectly, not just when they are close at hand but even if they live far away. Disagreeable people, however, unknowingly make trouble for each other even if living far apart, so when in close proximity, they should remain separate in order not to torment each other. The lotus grows in mud, yet its flower is completely distinct from the mud and not soiled by it. Rather, the blossom opens, nurtured by supportive rays from the sun that rises in the distant sky.

123   As long as one maintains a sense of shame,
         One's personal qualities are like the finest jewels;
         But when shame is eclipsed, these qualities
         Become partial, and one's speech coarsens.

Insofar as physical, verbal, and mental conduct that breaches propriety causes one to feel shameful and afraid of disgrace in the presence of others, to that extent whatever positive worldly and spiritual qualities one may have gained through study, contemplation, and meditation thereby become supreme ornaments of one's body, speech, and mind. But people who have no concern for personal embarrassment and care not what others say have few good qualities. They act out of prejudice or pretense and their coarse speech spreads everywhere.

The glorious Maitreya says:

> Bodhisattvas clad in the understanding of shame,
> Even undressed have no offensive defilements.

124   Good people give sound advice even if not requested;
         Bad people are misleading even when asked for help.
         Bodhisattvas are compassionate even if abused;
         The Lord of Death kills even when paid tribute.

Even if good people are not asked for advice about this and future lives, they give sound counsel and are adept in inspiring others about what to do and what to avoid. As Śāntideva says in *Engaging in the Bodhisattva Deeds*,

> The words of those who deftly counsel others
> And, though unsolicited, instruct well,
> Should be respectfully accepted.

But the nature of bad people is different. Even when it is appropriate to answer a proper question, it is their nature to be silent or even to respond misleadingly.

When bodhisattvas are disrespectfully maligned, it is as Āryadeva says in *The Four Hundred*,

As a mother extends love especially
To her child stricken with illness,
So is the bodhisattva's compassion
Especially extended to those who are inferior.

The bodhisattvas are eminently loving, as Maitreya says:

Have love for everybody—the incompetent,
The quarrelsome, and the unscrupulous.

One may bribe the Lord of Death with offerings of gold and silver in an
attempt to be spared, but he ruthlessly takes one's life nonetheless.

125   It is possible that what helps one
      May cause harm to another.
      At moonrise, the water lily[121] blossoms,
      But the lotus flower closes.

One must consider the existing circumstances to determine what will benefit
others. For example, for one person the delusion of attachment might be
temporarily quelled by the antidote of focusing on unpleasant qualities. In
this case such a concentration is helpful; but for somebody else it might give
rise to another delusion like anger, thereby increasing their hostility and caus-
ing harm.

Being a flower that favors cool conditions, the water lily opens up once the
moonlight begins to shine. But the lotus flower closes since the warm con-
ditions it prefers have disappeared.

126   Although a goal may be achieved through wrongdoing,
      Why would the wise admire it?
      Although something done right may go wrong,
      The wise may not feel ashamed.

It is often difficult for anything good to come from ill deeds since wrongful
actions lead to harmful effects. But even if, through the power of karma,
wrongdoing does produce temporarily useful results, no real good comes from
this. Wise people who have the intelligence to understand this causal rela-
tionship would never seek such achievements!

Conversely, sometimes despite applying fully competent physical, verbal,
and mental activity to achieve something good, ultimately the exact opposite
happens and trouble arises because of previous karma or other extenuating

circumstances. In such cases, wise people see no basis for criticism if one's efforts do not turn out well.

127   Some discoveries are profitable,
          Others turn out adverse.
          A pregnant mare increases one's wealth,
          But when a mule becomes pregnant, it dies.

Discovered riches may or may not be beneficial. That which comes from merit is of long-term benefit to oneself and others. But wealth derived mainly from the power of nonvirtuous deeds becomes pernicious in two ways: in this life, anger and jealousy generate hatred and strife as one tries to subjugate others; in future lives, it brings rebirth in the three unfortunate realms. A mare that becomes pregnant adds another horse to one's wealth, so it is an excellent discovery. But if a mule becomes pregnant, forget about increasing one's wealth; the mule itself will die.

128   Noble people are hard to alienate and easy to reunite;
          Coarse people are easy to estrange and hard to reunite.
          See the difference between cutting trees to make charcoal
          And trying to reconstitute trees from charcoal.

Good people, steadfast as mountains against the winds of flattery, remain unaffected by others' slander and discord. Their disposition makes it difficult to incite rifts between them. First, they fully investigate all circumstances to see whether or not they should disassociate, and they may appear to do so. But after some discussion they are easily reconciled, having no long-range impediments to their spiritual progress; they realize mere words are empty.

     Ignorant, bad people are different. When dissension is created by others, they simply go along with whatever is said, not knowing how to analyze the situation. Easily alienated from each other, as soon as they feel anger they talk about one another's shortcomings. When friends try constructively to mediate among them, they give lots of excuses and make many demands, showing just how difficult it is for them to come to terms.

     It is easy to grow a fruit tree and cut it down to make charcoal, but quite another matter to recreate a tree from charcoal.

129   Even the strong have trouble defeating
          Those who are weak but cautious.
          Even the weak often defeat
          Those who are strong but careless.

Lowly people, born of humble surroundings and poorly educated in spiritual and worldly matters, can take care to avoid bad conduct by paying strict attention to actions and their results. They then meet their goals and even the rich and clever have difficulty dominating them because they cannot be accused of anything. But when otherwise respected, learned, and important people carry out their intentions by blithely assuming that whatever they say is a command, and are careless about honesty and responsibility, there soon comes a time when they can be totally defeated, not just by other influential people but by the lowly as well.

130 Having wealth, one's power increases;
   Without wealth, one's power diminishes.
   The rich mouse's mastery of pilferage waned
   Because his precious jewel was stolen.

Wealth is of two kinds: external wealth, which is useful and valuable, and internal wealth derived from past meritorious activities. If one has wealth, one's influence over property and people increases unhindered; without it, one's command of resources naturally dwindles. Wealth has great potential and worth; be careful with it, and make effort in the ways of accumulating merit.

Once upon a time in a faraway land, lived a mouse who owned a priceless jewel. The significant feature of that jewel was that whoever held it could steal the riches of others.

One day the mouse robbed a local Brahmin. "This is a very powerful mouse," mused the Brahmin. "It seems he cannot be caught by anyone or repelled by any force. In my estimation, he surely must have in his possession a particularly valuable jewel."

A well-known thief named Parivrājaka was nearby, and he overheard what the Brahmin said. He kept a close eye on the mouse and his activities. Finally an opportunity arose and he snatched the mouse's jewel.

Later, the mouse returned to his house and discovered that he had been robbed. He was terribly depressed. Others asked him why he was sad and he told them what had happened. From then on he could not even guard his own food, let alone steal from others. As it is said in Masūrākṣa's *A Treatise on Temporal Affairs:*[122]

   Wealth is the friend of the worldly.
   It enables one to attain high status,
   Friends and relatives,
   Previously unseen, pay respects;
   But when status and wealth are lost,
   Even one's own people become unfriendly.

Finding himself in just such a situation, the mouse abandoned his home and went off into the forest.

131   Upon those who cultivate virtues, wealth falls like rain,
        Even when it is given away.
        Wealth can be amassed in the absence of virtues,
        But think, who will put it to use?

Wealth that comes from the magnificent power of merit has the special advantage of not diminishing. There are people who enjoy merit as the result of past generosity; they offer respect to the Three Jewels and give aid to the poor. Upon them, inexhaustible riches will pour down like rain. Nāgārjuna says in his *Precious Garland of Advice for a King (Rājaparikathā-ratnāvalī)*,

     Generosity creates wealth and morality brings about happiness.

Other people have done nothing in this or previous lifetimes to gain merit, yet still get rich through miserliness or other wrongdoing. However their affluence may have been acquired, just imagine who will one day enjoy it! Inevitably it again will lead to more corruption. Remember death! Everybody knows there is no use for wealth then. One must understand that the place to deposit wealth for the future is in the meritorious actions of generosity and offerings.

132   Noble people may decline for awhile,
        But later prosper like the waxing moon.
        If coarse people decline just once,
        They sputter out like a butter lamp.

Good people work to improve their knowledge and accumulate merit. For one reason or another they occasionally get into trouble, failing in their aspirations or even hurting themselves. But such situations are only temporary and the strength of their merit and wisdom enables them to soon recover. The moon declines during its waning stages, but then shortly afterwards it increases again and is full on the fifteenth of the month.

However, when other people of deficient good karma and merit fail, they remain stuck in their predicament due to their ignorance, inability, and unsupportive merit. Once a lamp has used up its oil, it goes out and cannot restore its light.

133   By extending patience to an enemy,
      The wise bring them under their influence.
      By responding to an enemy's challenge,
      The inexperienced meet continuous difficulties.

Those who possess both wisdom and skillful means will spend a long time
being attentive to their antagonists, overt and clandestine alike, eventually
subduing and befriending them. But helpless, hesitant, weak-minded indi-
viduals immediately sass their opponents and point out their faults, provok-
ing them to retaliate. One reply becomes two, two replies become three, and
so on, until there is a whole tree of worthless words without one leaf of mean-
ing. Such people encounter endless trouble. So even when angry, try to pacify
enemies with a kind expression and gentle words.

134   When the wise avoid dangerous situations,
      It is an indication of courage.
      When the lion is out to slay a bull,
      Would avoiding the horns be cowardly?

It is the mark of a skilled hero to take action only after assessing its impact.
Wise people clearly distinguish right from wrong and come to firm conclu-
sions about the consequences of their actions. This enables them, even when
personally threatened, confidently to disregard troubling situations during
times when the well-being of the Dharma or sentient beings is at stake. When
the king of beasts sets out to kill the greatest of bulls, where is his cowardice
if he deliberately steers clear of the horns? That indicates not timidity, but
bravery! Develop the special courage to ignore annoying but irrelevant mat-
ters when undertaking anything important.

135   Leaping at foes impetuously
      Is the telltale sign of a fool.
      By fighting with the butter lamp
      Does a fly become a hero?

Determine what to do and what to avoid by first estimating the possible
future advantages or disadvantages for each situation. Succumbing to the
power of one's pride and then rapaciously leaping at an enemy without inves-
tigating all circumstances in advance is the act of insistent fools, leading to
destruction for both themselves and others. Some great masters have said,

      Defeat is certain when confronting an unbeatable enemy.

Does a fly become a hero simply because it jumps and flies round the butter lamp at night and dies? Hardly!

136   Evil people oppress those who depend on them,
          But noble people protect those who depend on them.
          The silkworm eats away the leaf that bears it,
          But the lion protects the land and its inhabitants.

Shameless people harbor a sinister, tyrannical attitude in their hearts and expect everyone to follow their orders. The rights and wealth of those who rely on them are slated for ruin by such hypocrisy. But good people care for all their dependents as a parent protects a child by teaching it what is acceptable and what is not. With utter indifference the silkworm eats away the very leaf upon which it is seated, yet the lion gives protection by looking after its territory and all who live there.

137   Coarse people conceal insignificant things,
          Yet divulge important secrets for no reason at all.
          Noble people do not contrive secrets pointlessly,
          Yet guard confidential matters with their lives.

Ignorant people pompously make secrets of inconsequential affairs without knowing why. Then they turn around and openly divulge important confidential information for no reason at all. Good people with proper judgment do not make special secrets out of trivial things that require no containment. Yet critical matters that do need to be kept quiet they shelter closely in their hearts, not revealing them to others even at risk to their lives.

138   When coarse people get rich, it makes them arrogant;
          When noble people get rich, it makes them refined.
          When the fox is satiated, it barks with pride;
          When the lion is satiated, it sleeps peacefully.

When coarse people without any intelligence, ability, or honesty have a little wealth, they become ostentatious and conceited, and are plunged into misery because of their lawlessness and contemptuous talk. But when good people are affluent their physical, verbal, and mental activities become particularly subdued. They only engage in what is truly beneficial because they understand wealth to be a source of endless trouble; they carefully extract only the essence of its illusory nature. When the fox has had enough to eat, it barks imperiously at everything. But when the lion is full, it sleeps peacefully with no concern for anything.

Think about the disadvantages of wealth! The best way to enjoy it is to be without attachment or pride, and to strive to put it to its highest use.

139   The behavior of both noble and coarse people
      Acquires strength through habituation.
      Why bother training a bee to seek flowers,
      Or a duck to enter into the water?

The proper conduct of noble people and the improper conduct of coarse people can be attributed to temporary conditions like the influence of friends, but it arises primarily from the force of habit exerted on one's character by previous karmic actions. The natural way ducks take to lotus ponds and honeybees seek fresh nectar-bearing flowers is due in both cases to the power of familiarization, requiring no training by others.

140   When evil kings confront an enemy
      They end up punishing their own subjects.
      Some fools who fail in their objectives
      Commit suicide by hanging themselves.

The influence poor merit exerts on their karma and aspirations sometimes means that citizens end up with evil rulers. Even when faced with an outside enemy, these leaders will discharge a rain of vituperation on their own subjects and punish them severely for trivial reasons.

Also, there are fools who do not bear in mind the subtleties of right and wrong action, and cannot achieve their goals. Due to poor judgment and violent anger they destroy themselves. Were they to be open-minded, they would examine things properly and find it pointless to get upset. Generally their case is like the earlier quotation in verse 12 from Śāntideva:

    If a problem has a remedy,
    Why worry about it?
    If it has no remedy,
    What is the use of worrying?

141   When Dharma kings encounter an enemy,
      They become even kinder to their subjects.
      A mother feels special concern
      Toward a child stricken with illness.

Universal monarchs rule according to the Dharma. When facing cruel, barbaric enemies, they govern with special benevolence out of fear that their subjects will be oppressed by despotism. Though a mother cares affectionately for all her children, if one among them is sick, she is greatly worried and gives it special care for fear it will die.

Present and future happiness for all will be increased by relying on good rulers who govern their subjects with compassion and kindness.

142   Noble people can become very degenerate
When in the company of bad people.
The gratifying water of the Ganges
Becomes saltwater when it reaches the ocean.

Some good people are compelled by the strength of their karma to linger in the company of evil characters. The influence of such associates can cause every aspect of their conduct to decline. Water from the River Ganges is essentially delicious, but when it meets and mixes with the great ocean it becomes unpalatable saltwater.

Long-term, honorable relationships with trustworthy companions are very important; to bear antagonism toward good people and friendliness toward the depraved is to court corruption.

143   When bad people are close to good people,
They assimilate their excellent behavior.
Notice how those daubed with musk scent
Become very fragrant.

When greedy and shameless individuals stay in the company of good people such as spiritual teachers, they develop intelligence, skill, and good conduct due to the positive influence. Usually people do not have a pleasant odor when they are not wearing perfume, but a dab of aromatic musk oil makes them smell very nice.

144   Like a mountain that absolutely nothing can move,
Extraordinary people maintain consummate stability.
Like small wisps of cotton wafting about,
Coarse people behave unduly erratically.

As the highest mountain stands firm against any wind or storm, so truly great people remain steady, unprovoked by discord, slander, attachment to their desires, or flattery. But the notions of bad people are very changeable, like fluffy cotton carried here and there by a puff of wind.

Nowadays the conduct of most people is erratic and unreliable because they are primarily preoccupied with novelty. Whatever your status or wealth, do not be influenced by empty gossip. Practice the excellent deeds of bodhisattvas, whose dependability is trusted by others.

Chapter 5 ~
AN EXAMINATION *of* BAD CONDUCT

145   The sweet talk of deceitful people
      Is due to self-interest, not respect.
      The pleasant, laughing cry of the owl
      Is an evil omen, not a sign of happiness.

Manipulative, dishonest people are always testing others. Their sweet words and polite smiles are strictly self-serving, intended to deceive rather than to show respect. The cry of an owl sounds like pleasing laughter, but it is not a genuine laugh welling from a happy disposition; it is meant to cast bad omens on a place.

The inauspicious owl once alighted on a tower of Indra's palace in the Heaven of Thirty-three. It gave forth its laughing call, and the younger gods said, "Such utterance is a bad omen! Kill that owl!"

But the owl protested, "I am the one with profoundly wonderful advice. Let me live awhile longer." It then proceeded to fool them with this verse of nonsense,

> The sounds of the words—"I" and "precious spiritual teacher,"
> A gentle voice, a trilling voice,
> A soft, smooth voice, and a roaring voice—
> These are the six melodious sounds of the world.

Then it gave a laugh and left.

146   Bad people first mislead others with their words,
      And if that goes well they later swindle them.
      Notice how fishermen catch and kill fish
      By baiting their hooks with food.

Bad people with no sense of shame mislead others by first drawing their attention with nice actions and beguiling words, or even offering a little food or drink. If that approach works they later defraud them outright, leaving them in a regretful state. They are like fishermen. See how they first disguise a hook with a little bit of meat or bread, then later land the fish on the beach and kill it. Smart people sense others' intentions, but the stupid cannot, so analyze situations thoroughly and do not be misled by mere sweet words and little morsels of food.

147   As long as coarse people remain helpless
       They maintain a good disposition.
       As long as the poisonous thorn is immature
       It cannot prick others.

As long as dull-witted people are unable to harm others, they give a good impression, seeming to be of good character and doing what is asked of them. But their true nature is hard to ascertain while their abilities are stifled, so careful examination is necessary. Poisonous thorns that are still soft and unformed cannot injure anyone.

148   Some people keep one idea in their minds,
       But convey something else with their words.
       They are known as "deceivers,"
       Fools pretending to be wise.

Some people outwardly seem impartial, likable, and honest while discussing the importance of the general welfare, but inwardly they think only about achieving their own ambitions. These people are renowned as "frauds who always test others, keeping their personal intentions hidden." In fact, they should be called "those who make weak-minded fools appear wise." Do not err when formulating judgments about such people, and try to promote the refreshing new idea of helping others.

149   When deception is carried too far,
       It may work for a while but later brings downfall.
       The donkey wearing a leopard skin
       Ate the crops, but later was killed.

Activities that deceive others for personal gain may succeed for a while by gaining others' confidence and misleading them. But when deception is insensitive to practical limits and becomes extreme, in the end there is no possibility other than ruin. It is like the well-known story of the donkey who was disguised in a leopard skin.

Once upon a time a disreputable householder had a donkey. At that time, forage for livestock was in very short supply. One day, the householder was gathering firewood in the forest when he came upon a leopard skin. He carried the skin home and put it on his donkey, then sent the donkey off into the countryside to look for grass.

"There's a leopard in the fields!" the villagers exclaimed.

The donkey did much damage to the fields, and before long all the people banded together and killed it.

Another famous legend is about a fool who was walking along and came upon a radiant treasure vase filled with gold that had been hidden by King Bhikramatita. The fool carried the vase home, and later he took a little gold out of it and went to see a clever friend of his.

"What is this stuff?" asked the fool.

"It's gold!" his friend replied in astonishment.

"I see," said the fool, "there is even more of this gold."

"Excellent," said his friend encouragingly. "We should share it together."

So the two of them hid the vase at the base of a tree trunk, and whenever they needed gold they would both go to the tree and take some.

One day the clever fellow got a notion to deceive the fool. He took the vase and hid it in another place. Later he called the fool and they went to the tree. As soon as they saw the vase was not there, the clever fellow accused the fool, "You have stolen the vase!"

The fool replied, "You accuse me of being a thief. If that were so, why would I be sharing the vase with you, since I had possession of it in the first place?"

The clever one refused to listen. "I know what I'm talking about here!" he insisted. "There is nobody but you who could steal the vase!"

So he took the fool before the king, related what had taken place and demanded that he be punished. But the king said, "We must investigate this matter further."

"Then we should consult with the forest deity who lives where the gold was stashed," the clever fellow suggested.

"That is a good idea," consented the king, and a date was fixed.

Meanwhile the clever fellow advised his elderly father about how the fool had stolen the golden vase. On the appointed day he concealed the old man inside the decayed hollow trunk of the tree. Soon the king came with his entourage to make offerings to the forest deity and request the truth of the situation. The king asked for details of what had happened. The old man, masquerading as the deity, related the events as his son had instructed.

A debate began, but the king declared, "Look here! This account is true and correct."

The fool replied, "If all you say is true, and since I am also correct, then if anyone is wrong it must be the tree deity. First I shall burn down the deity tree and then you can kill me."

But the clever fellow protested, "Since this is a deity tree it is not right to burn it down. If the tree is destroyed, misfortune will befall you."

"I am about to die now anyway," said the fool. "There is nothing worse that can happen to me." Everyone agreed.

So he piled up sticks at the base of the tree and ignited it. The old man, overcome by the smoke, tumbled out of the tree. The fool asked why the clever fellow's father had been in there, to which the old man responded,

> The very clever one is not so clever;
> The very foolish one is not so foolish.
> When the clever one is excessively clever,
> There is danger smoke will kill the old man.

Hearing this the king had the clever fellow killed and the old man punished, and the golden vase was awarded to the fool.

Restrain yourself from engaging in bad deeds by remembering where they will lead.

150   If one is wise, one is able
       To deceive others with blatant lies.
       Because the thieves called it a dog,
       The Brahmin boy lost his goat.

People who have discriminating awareness can use outright lies to deceive others and achieve their objectives with no need for any other trickery. It is like the story of the wise thieves who were openly able to acquire a goat through the sheer audacity of calling the goat a dog.

Once upon a time there was a young Brahmin boy who went out searching for a goat to offer the gods. Having found one, he was leading it along the road when five wise thieves saw him and agreed among themselves, "We must take away his goat."

One of the thieves walked down the road at a suitable moment and ran into the Brahmin. "Oh my!" said the thief. "Of all the things to see in this world, here is a Brahmin leading a dog!"

A little question arose in the Brahmin boy's mind. Then a second thief came along, said the same thing, and the boy became even more doubtful.

Meeting the third thief, who gave the same observation, the boy was now quite perplexed. He glanced back at his goat, then went on his way. Then a fourth thief made the same comments, yet again. The boy stopped to double-check that he really did have a goat and not a dog. He examined its horns, its beard, its hooves, and so on, then continued on his way.

Finally the fifth thief came along and said the same as the other four. The Brahmin boy panicked. "A real demon in the form of a goat has come to eat this offering of mine," he thought, "and furthermore, it appears as a dog to everyone else." So the Brahmin boy abandoned his goat and ran away, and the five thieves carried off their prize.

151   Even while indulging in harmful deeds,
     Manipulative people deceive others with words.
     Mahādeva, while crying out helplessly,
     Proclaimed the truth of suffering.

Everyone can see that significant wrongful deeds, like the ten nonvirtuous actions and the five boundless transgressions, are destructive. But just as harmful and notably prevalent are the cunning distortions that charlatans use to deceive the innocent. Recalling the many grave ill deeds he had committed, the monk Mahādeva wailed with uncontrollable regret, but to mislead others he declared, "I have seen the truth of suffering!"

Once upon a time in the great city of Varuṇa in southern India, there was a rich householder. Because he had no son, he prayed to the gods. Ten months later his wife gave birth to a boy, whom they named Mahādeva. Wishing to hold a feast in honor of this wonderful event, the father embarked on a journey to the ocean to get some jewels. For twelve years he was away. During that time Mahādeva grew very big, matured into a youth, and committed incest with his mother.

"Son," the mother instructed the lad, "I like your company and want to continue our relationship, but the time is nearing when your father will return from the ocean. You must wait on the roadside and kill him."

Mahādeva did as he was told and killed his father on a small back road. But some time later, his mother befriended another man. In a rage, Mahādeva killed his mother. Then one day he sat listening to various Dharma teachings from his spiritual teacher, a foe destroyer. Suddenly fearing that the teacher, through his omniscience, would discover the despicable crimes he had committed and would inform others, Mahādeva murdered him as well.

At last, disgusted with his misdeeds and no longer wishing to stay in his home, he gave away all his belongings and traveled to a nearby country. There was great famine in that land. As a lay man he was unable to find any nourishment, but he saw he could get food easily if he dressed as a monk. He found some monk's robes in a graveyard and, seeing no abbots or spiritual masters around, he administered the monk's vows to himself and went off to live in a distant region. For food, he went alms-begging in town. Because of his previous wrongdoing, he lived unhappily and always looked angry.

One by one the local shepherds who tended the buffalo, goats, and sheep noticed the monk and came to see him. Mahādeva had acquired a little learning, so he taught the Dharma to the shepherds, using good explanations and sweet-sounding words. By describing the odious nature of cyclic existence, he instructed them in how to transform their minds.

"This great practitioner is a good being who meditates on the misery of the land and practices the Dharma sincerely," the shepherds agreed. He was very much liked and his reputation, though based on pretense, became widespread, drawing the townspeople to him. Initially, it was the women and children who paid him respect, but gradually nearly everyone assembled and a great alms-giving took place. On that occasion Mahādeva collected donations from the wealthy, stockpiled everything, then gave it all away to the poor without reservation. In this way a great redistribution of wealth occurred.

Because he was so adept in dealing with others, praising them and respecting their opinions, the people said, "This great teacher exemplifies mastery in both worldly and spiritual matters. As someone with great compassion, he is much more exalted than even the foe destroyers."

With fervent affection and aspiration, they offered to him whatever they had. Even the rich opened up stores of treasures they had inherited from their parents. He, in turn, gave them necessities such as food, clothing, and places to live. "I am a foe destroyer!" he proclaimed, "I have exhausted all my misery! I can do anything!" Though really not accomplished, his deft management of all interactions enabled him to pose as a spiritual teacher rather than the lay person he in fact was.

Everyone thought Mahādeva was totally genuine, so there were many who requested ordination from him—some because they had generated faith, but most did so in order to acquire essentials for daily living. He ordained many monks and nuns, enabling them to assemble together. Monks from elsewhere also left their teachers and gathered around him to avail themselves of his generosity. Eventually he was surrounded by an entourage of many hundreds of thousands. It is commonly known that the number of followers of Buddha Śākyamuni after his passing on to nirvāṇa was not greater than Mahādeva's adherents.

One day, in the early morning hours while teaching the Dharma to his followers, he began thinking to himself, "First I had sexual relations with my mother. Because of that I killed my father, then later my mother. Due to that I murdered a foe destroyer. Then I ordained myself as a monk, and squandered the faith and offerings given me. Now I am a dishonest lama, speaking about worldly matters and deceiving many people."

Pondering the nature of these heinous deeds and the terrible consequences of having to take rebirth in the hell realms, he spontaneously cried out three times, "Oh misery! Misery!"

His cries were heard by some disciples in nearby huts. Later, during their morning prostrations they asked their abbot, Mahādeva, "Why did you cry out in distress this morning? Did you transcend suffering?"

"What are you talking about?" Mahādeva demanded.

They repeated his words exactly. "But didn't you hear what else I said?" he asked them.

"No, we didn't," they replied.

"I proclaimed the Four Noble Truths: The Misery! Its Cause! Its Cessation! and The Path! You did not hear the other three?"

Mahādeva almost deceived his disciples with this, but the look on his face caused one of them to venture doubtfully, "Abbot, if you are a foe destroyer, why did you not understand our question about the Dharma?"

"Besides myself, there are hearers and solitary realizers like Śāriputra, messenger of the Buddha, who have had similar lapses of understanding. Only the Buddha has passed beyond doubt," Mahādeva replied.

Then they all gathered and requested that he show them some magic.

"My foe destroyer powers were destroyed this morning, so I have no magic," he claimed.

"Such powers can be destroyed?" they asked.

"Yes, very much so," he said. "The deterioration of foe destroyer powers is one of the acts of a spiritual practitioner. Another such act, as noted earlier, is for a foe destroyer to lack understanding. Similarly, spiritual practitioners should not only completely care for people, but should also deceive them." He tried to persuade them in this way, but his followers were displeased.

Nowadays there are some corruptions found in the sutras, such as these irreverent deeds of Mahādeva. It is said that he died and was reborn as a being in the Great Hell.

152   Deceivers, well-mannered and smooth talking,
        Should not be trusted until scrutinized.
        Peacocks have lovely forms and pleasing calls,
        But their food is extremely poisonous.

The beautiful, well-groomed appearance of those who deceive others is pleasing simply to behold. One is enchanted upon hearing their suave words. But they are not to be trusted until they have been thoroughly investigated; they must be identified as cunning, bad-natured people, always sizing up others. The peacock possesses a beautiful rainbow-hued body and a very sweet voice, but its food is a powerful poison found in dangerous, precipitous places.

153   Deceitful people first put on a good front,
        Then later cheat to achieve their objectives.
        By exhibiting the tail of a deer,
        One shameless fellow sold his donkey meat.

Initially, deceitful people are sincere with everybody, consistently appearing modest and good-natured. But once they have others' confidence, they completely abandon any pretense of decency, and betray them in pursuit of their own interests.

Once upon a time a shameless man was trying to sell the meat of a donkey, but nobody anywhere would buy it. One day he found the tail of a deer. He took it with him and again began asking, "Do you want to buy some meat?"

"What kind of meat is it?" people inquired.

He showed them the tail. Brazenly he said, "It comes from this kind of animal." The customers were fooled and bought the meat at once.

Thinking this ruse to be an ideal way to sell, he used it on market days in the bazaar from then on.

154   People of little shame use others' wealth
        To show off how important they are.
        By displaying a friend's garments for visitors,
        They demonstrate their own status.

Sometimes people with little or no shame are stingy and will not use their own wealth, so instead they use someone else's to create a favorable impression on others. When visitors suddenly arrive, they borrow clothing and other items from a friend and exhibit them in order to enhance their own appearance and ensure that they will be highly regarded.

Avoid this kind of behavior! Develop that sense of shame that is the adornment of good personal qualities.

155   Because of their abysmal degeneracy,
        The shameless boast of their own wrongdoing.
        In some royal families of the land of Kañci
        The royal drum is beaten when the father is slain.

Utterly shameless people boastfully assert their heroism, saying, "I did such and such!" They carry on about their evil thoughts and despicably crude conduct, offensive matters that are perpetually destructive and should be kept to themselves. Some royal families in South India commit patricide, then boast audaciously and beat the royal drums.

Once upon a time there was a ruler known as the king of Natamtima. According to the law of the land, when a prince reaches the age of twenty, he is placed before his father in an iron cage. He can go nowhere, and in that spot he is taught such subjects as the treatises on temporal affairs. When the father dies, whoever is the oldest son becomes the new king.

In those days there was a king who had an eight-year-old son. This boy had one particularly fine set of clothing, and he said to his mother, "Please store these clothes away. When I gain rule of the country I shall wear them."

"You can't become king," his mother told him, "You have older brothers."

"What can be done about that?" asked her son.

"If you kill your father and beat the royal drum, then you can become king," answered his mother.

"That's what I'll do then!" declared the boy.

His mother gave him a sharp knife, and the boy went before the king, who was seated on his throne. Using diversions of amusement and mirth, he came close to his father and stabbed him in the stomach with the knife, killing him.

"From today onward I am the king!" he announced, and he beat the royal drum.

The people proclaimed, "Since he was able to do these things, he is a great hero!" and they gave him the rule over the land.

One should set aside one's pride in wrongful conduct, and acknowledge with strong regret previously committed harmful deeds.

156   Sometimes help from the weak-minded
        Can be extremely harmful.
        The magpie chick plucks out its mother's feathers
        Thinking it is expressing gratitude.

Dim-witted people do not know the difference between what is helpful and what is harmful. What they think serves others really ends up being detrimental because their notions of help do not correspond to others' needs. For example, fledgling magpies pluck out all of their mother's feathers assuming this is a helpful way to repay her kindness to them, but in fact they are actually hurting her.

157   Brazen people think what comes from others' kindness
        Is entirely due to their own importance.
        Farmers believe themselves magnificent
        When rain falls due to the nāgas' efforts.

That which results from the benevolence and efforts of others is considered
by utterly shameless people to be produced by the great power of their own
merit. The powerful king of the nāgas causes the rain to fall, yielding rich har-
vests, yet farmers reckon the strength of their own labors is what produces
the crops.

158   Conceited people think the benefits of karma
        Are due to their own efforts.
        Thinking blood from its own punctured palate
        To be the bone's marrow, the dog keeps gnawing.

Weak-minded individuals enjoy the fully matured results of karma accumu-
lated long in the past and think it derives from their own immediate efforts.
One must develop wisdom that does not confuse the results of previous karma
with what comes about through one's present activities. When a dog chews
on a bone and pierces its upper palate, it keeps gnawing, thinking its own
blood flowing from the wound is the bone's marrow.

159   The ignorant are seen to destroy their allies
        And then take good care of strangers.
        Docking a peacock's head tuft to grace its tail is ludicrous;
        Who but a madman would do such a thing?

Ignorant people confuse proper and improper ways of doing things. They ruin
their close associates whom they ought to protect, then are seen caring for
enemies or other non-allies, giving them whatever they need, like food and
clothing.
    One eccentric fellow had a dancing peacock. He couldn't bear it when the
peacock lost a tail feather, so he cut off its crown tuft feathers and stuck them
on its tail—a useless, inane gesture. No intelligent person would even think
to do such a thing!

160   Fools do not contribute where there is need,
        But are very generous where there is none.
        A poor spring flows in summer,
        But is dry in springtime when needed most.

Fools are confused by causes and their effects, both those that have already taken place and those yet to occur. They are inordinately stingy with decent, frugal, poor people but lavishly generous with drinkers, gamblers, and other nonvirtuous characters with no real needs. A deficient spring will flow freely during the summer monsoon season, but will cease altogether come spring-time when water is scant and much in demand.

161   Bad people are especially harmful
       Toward peaceful, good people.
       The tree trunk that produces resin
       Catches fire, while others do not.

Usually it is pointless to harm good people of gentle disposition who never abuse others. Yet malicious people have strong negative karma that induces them to single out these honorable ones for persecution. Resin-bearing trees are particularly vulnerable to fire, whereas other trees are not so threatened.

Once upon a time in a dense forest, there lived a magnificent buffalo named Varada, who protected everyone with its subdued behavior. On top of the buffalo often sat a wild monkey. This monkey was a terrible nuisance and always teased the buffalo. Of their dispositions it was said that,

> To the very compassionate and gentle buffalo
> The wild monkey was arrogant and disrespectful.
> But seeing there was nothing to fear,
> The buffalo remained very happy.

Sometimes the monkey rode on the buffalo, sometimes he sat on its head and covered its eyes, and sometimes he blocked the road by running between its legs. But the bodhisattva buffalo was always patient and never wearied of the monkey. Once some local demon spirits urged the buffalo,

> The vajra tip of your horns is so strong,
> It can even destroy the rocky mountain.
> So if you angrily beat your four feet,
> Even the rocky mountain peak will sink into the swamp.

The bodhisattva replied,

> Force is an unsuitable remedy;
> What would result from employing it?
> Being patient and acting in a peaceful, virtuous manner:
> What else is necessary?

The demon spirits saw it was wrong to do harm. The buffalo gently took the monkey off its back and did not hurt him at all.

162   Rough people are tamed by roughness;
        How can they be peacefully subdued?
        Boils are removed by burning and cutting;
        Mild treatment just makes them worse.

Some coarse individuals are thoroughly evil and cannot be overcome peacefully. They can, however, be constrained with a wrathful approach thoroughly grounded in spiritual and worldly affairs motivated by great love and compassion. Virulent afflictions such as boils must be surgically removed; treating them delicately simply renders them more pernicious.

163   Failing to rule according to the Dharma
        Is the sign of a declining king.
        When the sun fails to dispel the darkness,
        It is the sign of a solar eclipse.

Dharma kings, the guardians of peace, rule the land according to Dharma in both temporal and spiritual affairs. But when this is not the case, the silken knot of temporal and spiritual matters comes untied, the cord that binds the sheaf of temporal and spiritual matters is severed, the golden yoke of royal law is broken, and, especially, the ocean of good counsel dries up. Vulgar conduct prevails; people direct their attention to evil and pursue ignorance. Preference for these ways should be recognized as evidence that the king has weakened. The sun itself is free of clouds; it dispels darkness naturally when it rises. Should darkness not be cleared away, it indicates that the sun has been eclipsed by the planet Rāhu.

164   A despot who has been appointed ruler,
        A house with a damaged top floor,
        And a mountain crest that is very unstable—
        Living under such conditions is always fearsome.

To live in a place of no Dharma is to live in woe. Some great masters have said,

        When one relies on uncompassionate rulers, misery prevails.

Similarly, people who live in unsafe environments, be they cruel despotic rulers, collapsing houses, or unstable mountain slopes, must endure a state of trepidation with no opportunity to rest comfortably, free from anxiety.

165   Somebody may be knowledgeable,
       But avoid him if his character is bad.
       A poisonous snake may be crowned with a jewel,
       But what wise person would place it in his lap?

Though it is usually hard for bad people to become well educated, should favorable conditions result in their acquiring some learning, they still must always be avoided due to their faulty intentions. A wish-fulfilling jewel might adorn the head of a poisonous snake, but no person of good judgment would even consider taking such a snake onto his lap!

166   Obeying ambitious rulers is difficult,
       Disobeying usually makes them unkind,
       And doing neither is risky—
       Some rulers are like raging fires.

There are rulers who particularly covet a reputation of being accomplished in worldly and spiritual affairs. Some subjects willingly obey them, but find it very difficult to follow their wishes exactly. Others do the opposite and ignore their instructions. They are rarely well treated since they are in conflict with the ruler's interests. Still others take a middle stance, neither completely agreeing with nor completely opposing the ruler, and thus are threatened by never knowing for sure what will happen. One should know that no matter what one does, some rulers act like great fires and will always be malevolent enemies.

According to Sakya Pandita in *A Classification of People,*

    Kings who rule the land benevolently say,
    "Even if my subjects have committed some errors,
    Yet say nothing and hide their misdeeds,
    Whatever happens, good or bad, is my responsibility."

167   Who would depend on a bad spouse,
       A bad friend, or a bad king?
       Would sensible people continuously live
       In a thick forest of dangerous carnivores?

Nobody of sane mind would rely on these three things: wicked spouses who are lazy, like to eat, know nothing, are preoccupied with their own appearance,

and run around with others; despicable friends who are shameless, change-
able, untrustworthy, deceptive, and oblivious to their own shortcomings; and
dreadful kings of unstable nature, unlearned, aggressive, unjust toward all, and
bereft of love and compassion. Dense forests inhabited by vicious carnivores
like tigers and leopards are quiet and peaceful, but do sensible people choose
to live there permanently? Of course not!

168   Good personal qualities are ruined by pride;
One's sense of shame is ruined by desire.
When he always criticize his subjects,
The ruler has gone to ruin.

Śāntideva says,

> To be devoid of arrogance
> Is the greatest of all good qualities.

If arrogance causes one to boast about one's own good qualities, then those
attributes will degenerate. Likewise, attachment to desires will destroy that
which supports all good qualities: one's sense of shame in the presence of
others. When subjects are always being oppressed by their rulers' incompe-
tence, ingratitude, unhelpfulness, cruelty, and bad laws, then ultimately the
rulers themselves are left isolated and fall into decline.

169   Rare are those who say helpful things;
Rarer still are those who listen.
Skillful doctors are hard to find,
But fewer are those who heed their advice.

Because these troublesome times are plagued by the five degeneracies, those
who speak up with the highest of intentions, free of deceit and hypocrisy, to
say, "I will help," are as rare as a daytime star. But while those who speak of
helping others are scarce, even scarcer are those who carefully listen, think cor-
rectly about what is said, and then suitably put the advice into practice. Heal-
ing physicians who are competent and kind-hearted are hard to find in this
world; doctors of total proficiency are only a faint possibility. But if the odds
of finding such a skilled physician are merely one in a hundred, fewer still are
those who follow their instructions. Some great masters have said,

> Those clad in spiritual garb are rare in this world,
> But those with spiritual hearts are rarer still.

Once upon a time when the Buddha was residing in Śrāvastī, he and all the monks became ill with a bad case of the flu. At that time the king of physicians, Kumāra Jīvaka, instructed them to prepare a butter medicine with sixty-four ingredients. He counseled Ānanda, "Because the Buddha has a vajra body, is strong, steady, and doesn't harm others, give him twelve measures of the butter medicine. To the other monks give no more than one measure." Ānanda did as he was told.

But Devadatta protested. "Give me two measures," he demanded. "Aren't Gautama and I of equal caste?"

He was given two measures, which he took. Unable to digest it properly, he nearly died. Ānanda called for Kumāra Jīvaka.

"Alas, there is no cure for undigested medicine that has turned into poison," the doctor replied.

Kumāra Jīvaka left and Ānanda turned to the Buddha for help. Placing his right hand on Devadatta's head, the Buddha said, "If I have equanimity toward both Rāhula who is the son born of my flesh and Devadatta who has the attitude of an enemy, may these words of truth cure the Venerable Devadatta's illness."

Devadatta was thereby relieved of disease and became well again. Expressing his thanks, Devadatta declared, "This monk Gautama is known to be a skillful physician. He will not die even when he is a starving, emaciated old man." With these true but insulting and contemptible words, he departed.

170 When one is very arrogant,
  One is continuously beset with misery.
  Due to the lion's great conceit,
  The fox induced him to carry the load.

When an uncontrollable urge to be important makes people arrogant, they create their own misery. They assume responsibilities that they cannot discharge and are defenseless against an endless rain of trouble. The story is told of a lion who, because of his excessive pride, had to bear the load that a lowly fox put on his back.

Once upon a time there was a fox who had long been dining on deer meat together with his friend, the lion who killed the deer. One day the lion killed an elephant and said to the fox, "You have to carry this meat. Otherwise, there is no chance you will ever eat meat with me again."

The fox thought to himself, "I can't possibly carry this much, but it will not do at all to give up eating the lion's meat." So he concocted a plan.

"O Master!" he called to the lion, "Since I can't do two things at once, I will do one and you do the other."

"What are the two tasks?" asked the lion.

"Carrying the elephant and walking behind grunting," the fox replied. "According to worldly conventions, when one is struggling to carry the load of a big animal, somebody is needed to take up the rear and grunt."

The lion thought to himself, "I am the king of beasts! How could I ever walk in the rear making such noises!" So he went in front carrying the meat while the fox followed behind, grunting away happily.

Indeed, one should rid oneself of pride and exercise self-control.

171   Things hidden by crows,
        Assistance given to bad people,
        And seeds planted in bad fields
        Represent lots of hope but are of little use.

Crows find little morsels of food and, hoping to enjoy them later, hide them in the ground. Then they mark the place using the position of clouds as reference points. Help can be given to shameless people with the hope that they will repay the favor, and seeds can be planted in bad fields like those prone to frost and hail, with the hope to reap a good harvest. One can have high expectations of such things, yet they yield little satisfaction if one lacks the support of merit.

172   Until someone has been carefully examined,
        They should not be trusted nor spoken to candidly.
        From carelessness arises trouble;
        Conversation often creates enemies.

One should not believe or confide in anybody without first applying prudent scrutiny. Nowadays most people are hypocritical and are fascinated with new acquaintances. Such carelessness brings them ruin in both this and future lifetimes. One should speak honestly in meetings where various viewpoints are examined, but before saying anything, the effect that one's words might have should first be considered. To speak recklessly can be offensive and create many enemies.

Once upon a time a man who had lost his cows was searching everywhere for them. He got his directions mixed up and lost his way, wandering far and wide. Eventually, emaciated by thirst and hunger, dizzy with exhaustion, and mentally tormented by the heat, he collapsed under a tree. There he spied some *tintu* fruits that had ripened to a tempting yellow.[123] He tasted them. They were delicious and satisfying, so he looked around for more.

On the edge of a steep cliff, he saw another tintu tree with its branches bent low and heavy with fruit. He climbed along the cliff and up the tree, then picked the fruit one by one from the branches that were hanging out over the edge. When he reached the top, the last branch was small and over-stressed by his weight. It broke with a loud snap! as surely as if cut by an ax. Man and branch plummeted down together.

The abyss into which he fell was surrounded on all sides by rock, much like a well. He landed on water atop the leafy branch, so he was only slightly hurt. He crawled to the bank and looked all around, but no way to escape was apparent. The man grew depressed, thinking he would surely die. Tearful over his hopeless situation, he sat, crying out in distress again and again,

> This gloomy forest solitude is so inaccessible
> That there are no other travelers at all.
> I am fallen down into this abyss,
> There is no escaping death, though I have looked everywhere.

Now, in this forest there lived a bodhisattva monkey, who at that moment was looking for food. He came to the edge of the abyss and heard from below the cries of woe. Looking down he saw a skinny, ugly person with eyes full of misery.

"Oh, you in the abyss from which there is no escape!" the monkey called out to him, "Why did you come here? Who are you? Tell me all that happened."

The man bowed to the monkey and told his story:

> O venerable god! I am but a man
> Who went wandering in the forest,
> Searching all over for the fruit of this tree.
> That is how I got into this predicament.

The bodhisattva monkey's great compassion could not bear such misery, and he longed to free the man. First he found another tintu fruit and gave it to him. Then he conditioned himself for the rescue by carrying around a rock that weighed as much as the man. When he was confident he could do the task, he dropped into the abyss and said,

> Come here and get on my back,
> And I'll carry you out of the abyss.
> Hold on to me tight with all your might
> Until we get to the top.

The man bowed again to the monkey and did as he was told. The monkey was small and the man was heavy, so it required heroic determination and endurance; in this way he got the man safely out of the abyss. Pleased at having been able to help a human, the monkey relaxed and said to the man,

> In this place surrounded by good forests,
> Full-grown carnivores can come unhindered.
> Although it is possible I might awaken,
> I will sleep for awhile and you keep watch,
> Guarding over both of us.

The man, who in fact was a deceptive and evil character, promised to protect him, so the bodhisattva monkey fell fast asleep on a flat blue rock.

"Forget any kindness this monkey bestowed on me earlier," the man thought to himself. "If I kill him and eat his flesh, I can see to my own body's needs now; later I can purify my evil actions after returning to my land." Thus he abandoned compassion, the foundation of Dharma, and with not a shred of shame grabbed a big stone and threw it at the monkey's head. But the rock missed its target, only grazing the monkey's ear.

Awakened by the sound of the rock, the monkey jumped aside and checked around to see what was happening. He saw no wild animals about. Then he noticed that the evil man was hanging his head, his face perspiring, obviously in disgrace. The monkey could not abide the man's lack of gratitude, and so counseled him with many verses such as,

> My friend, even though you are a human being,
> You have committed such an act as this.
> I rescued you from the abyss—
> From the very mouth of the Lord of Death—
> And saved you from the next world,
> But now, in future lives you will fall into unfortunate rebirths.

The monkey, deeply saddened, showed the man a path that led to a nearby town. "Go peacefully now to your land and give up all wrongdoing. Exert yourself in purifying your past negative actions," the monkey instructed. Then he disappeared back into the forest.

Tormented by a fire of intolerable regret over his ill deeds, the man became afflicted with a severe case of leprosy. He was a dreadful sight with his body covered in sores. He stayed near the town but was unable to enter it.

One day the king was out chasing wild game and saw him. Not believing it was a human body before him, the king said,

Who are you? A preta, an evil spirit,
A body of evilness, a rotten-bodied specter,
A mass of many diseases?
How did you become so diseased?

The man prostrated three times to the king and said to him thrice, "O, great king, I am a man!"

"How ever did you get into such a state?" asked the king. The man replied,

In accordance with negative actions I have committed,
I am experiencing these results for awhile.
Even more unbearable results than this
Are those I must experience in future lives.

With these words he confirmed the visible results of his wrongdoing. Then, in order to reveal the fully ripened results of his evil actions that would occur in future lives, at that moment great cracks appeared in the earth. He became famous as "the one who plunged headfirst and took rebirth in the Great Hell without first abandoning his body."

173   Though there are many fearsome things in the world,
       Nothing is worse than evil people.
       Other bad things can be remedied,
       But trying to reform evil people just worsens them.

In this world there are many frightful things, such as sickness, poison, and weapons, but nothing is more perilous than bad people. Like enemies, they delight in wrongdoing, are inconsiderate, and have no sense of shame. Other terrible things can be remedied by various means, peaceful as well as wrathful, but if one attempts to reform bad people, it merely exacerbates their baseness, since they care only about themselves and nothing else.

174   One can never satisfy evil people
       Even by helping them in a hundred excellent ways.
       They become hostile when someone serves them:
       This is their special characteristic.

It is difficult to reform ill-mannered people. Their attitude is always malevolent and they are never pleased, even when one draws upon the vast knowledge of the wise. As much as one attends to them with genuine respect, to that extent they become even more abusive and intolerable.

175 Try as one might to reform bad people,
   They simply do not become good-natured.
   Even if one vigorously washes coal,
   It simply cannot be made white.

As noted above, no matter how one tries in countless ways to reform bad people, their evil nature makes it impossible for them ever to be recognized as someone of good character. They are just like coal—no matter how much effort is exerted to scrub it clean, it never becomes white since its natural color is black.

One should not associate with people of bad character, but rather cultivate in oneself the good behavior of respectable, decent people who never forget the kindness others extend to them.

176 In places dominated by evil people,
   Even if sages are seen they are shunned.
   In places where harm is inflicted by snakes,
   People flee even from golden chains.

Noble people are a source of merit and wisdom for both this and future lives. Even if they are seen residing in a place where one is always criticized by bad individuals consumed by jealousy and stubbornness, one thinks only of the faults of those evil ones and shuns any attachment to such a place. Where poisonous snakes are a danger, if someone sees even the golden chain of a balance scale lying on the ground, they will flee in fear.

177 One should bestow honor upon noble people;
   If the coarse are honored, trouble will arise.
   Milk is ambrosia for humans;
   If given to snakes, their poison gets stronger.

When giving respect and offerings to someone, bear in mind that they should always be people of excellence who are intelligent, skillful in means, and helpful to others. Discord may result from making offerings to coarse people, because a little dispute can arise and they will bear a grudge in their hearts, thus completely wasting the gesture. When humans drink milk, it turns into a nectar that makes them strong and glorious. But milk creates trouble when given to snakes because it intensifies their poison, making them more harmful.

178 However hard they strive to acquire it,
   Evil people can hardly assimilate kindness.

No matter how one tries to remedy death,[124]
It is impossible to remain fearless.

Evil people, whose nature is dark as coal, may try every way, direct and indirect, to mix with and serve good people, whose nature is fair as a conch shell. How can they can ever succeed? It is impossible because their qualities are totally opposite! No matter how much every sort of transient material means is used to cure death, the type of impermanence unique to living beings,[125] it is never possible to abide carefree, eluding death's inevitability.

179   Those always seeking to instigate disunity
       Will split apart even the closest of friends.
       When continually worn away by water,
       Will cracks not occur even in rock?

Vindictive, biased people constantly try to provoke dissension among others. Their skill at sowing discord enables them to separate even people who have been the closest of friends. Cracks will appear in even the hardest rock if it is constantly exposed to the soft, erosive properties of water. One must always guard against being led into spiteful and partial friendships under the influence of destructive companions.

180   Some say they have deceived and acted wrongly
       And relate the faults of abbots, teachers, and friends.
       When false, such liars cannot be trusted;
       When truthful, they arouse apprehension.

Some shameless individuals say, "I deceived so and so great person in such and such a place," or "I thwarted someone's ambitions and harmed them against their wishes." Or they mention, "The abbot from whom you received spiritual vows, your teachers who show you what to practice and what to avoid, and your friends who think as you do, these people all have thus and such faults of thought, word, and deed." If what they say is thoroughly examined and found to be false there is no need for concern because they are liars, and from then on they should be considered unreliable. But when they actually do speak the truth, one must be particularly on guard against such perfidy.

181   Who would mention in the presence of others
       Matters that should remain private?
       Whether such things be true or false,
       Beware of people so adroit.

When a person says something inappropriate at an unfavorable time in the presence of others, it matters not whether the utterance is true or false; the untimeliness of such remarks indicates an ulterior motive. Wise, incisive people must always be cautious, and pay careful attention in such instances to what is being said.

182   Untrustworthy people greedy for wealth,
        Even when friends, should not be trusted;
        Taking bribes from friends,
        Many powerful people are ruined.

There are shameless people who lack respect for the laws of this and future lives and are very attached to wealth. They might be intimate friends, but one definitely should not place confidence in them. Using bribes to cozy up to high officials creates much deception and wreckage in the world.

Once upon a time, near Vārāṇasī in a thick forest where people usually could not travel, there lived a deer named Ruru who was exceptionally clear-minded. Although she had the body of an animal, she seemed to be a mound of jewels that knew how to walk. It was said,

        The magnificence of both her body and mind
        Is adorned with her skill in all activities.
        To someone like that, so helpful to me,
        Who would not pay their deepest respect?

One day a man living in a village near that learned, wild creature was caught in a great flood. He cried out,

        Swept away by this fierce raging river,
        There is no one to save me, not even a boat.
        O, free me from misery and distress—
        Run fast and grab me with care for my plight!

Ruru saw him, sprang to his aid and pulled him to safety. Her genuine concern made the man very happy. The man asked Ruru, "Since you saved my life, please come to my village. I must give you an offering."

Ruru replied, "What makes people happy is one thing and what pleases us deer is something else again. Please do not reveal to others how I live. That is the offering I request." With that, Ruru went back into the forest.

One night the queen of Vārāṇasī had a great vision in her dreams. She saw an especially magnificent deer with a glorious body and splendid face sitting on a lion throne giving a discourse on the Dharma. She related this to the king who announced to all the people of the land that he would give a great reward to anyone who could find such a deer. Everyone set out eagerly to search. Before long, the man began thinking,

> Alas! Which is more important—
> My gratitude for help or my own self-interest?
> Should I treat others the way the sages do,
> Or cater to my own great ambitions?
> Do I act in the interests of all the world,
> Or in pursuit of my own immediate happiness?

Now, this man was long accustomed to unwholesome conduct and attached to his own habits of self-interest. So he went before the king and said, "I have seen this deer."

"Show me," the king replied, and together they departed, accompanied by the king's army. Soldiers spread out all across the land.

Ruru heard a great clamor. "Oh!" she thought, "some very greedy people are coming this way." She started to run but then saw that the troops were everywhere. She stopped still.

Just then the wicked, shameless man spotted Ruru and called out to the king, "What you are seeking is there!" He pointed with his finger to where the deer stood.

At the very instant he revealed Ruru, his hand broke off at the wrist and fell to the ground. The king quickly drew his bow, aimed his arrow, and was about to release it when the bodhisattva spoke these respectful words in a human voice, "O leader of men, please sit down for awhile. From whom did you learn that I would be here?"

"From him," the king said, pointing with his bow to the man Ruru had saved from the river. Ruru gazed at him and exclaimed,

> Alas! As a well-known true quotation says,
> "Rescuing a branch would have been simpler"
> Than helping this shameless fellow
> Who was carried off by the raging flood.
> Does his ingratitude for my effort
> Not make this fellow truly a fool?

Hearing this the king was shocked and saddened. He said to Ruru, "I would like to hear more, so that this situation can be clarified."

Ruru related in detail what had happened before. The king glared at the man. "Well then!" he challenged, "is what she says true or not?" The man admitted it was true.

The king scolded the man severely, his displeasure so great he was about to shoot him with his bow and arrow, but Ruru intervened. "Oh leader of men," she cried, "please do not do that! I beg you not to kill this man. He admits his mistakes. Furthermore, he was able to achieve everything you asked of him. Thus it would be fitting for you to give him the reward you promised, without further punishment."

The king remembered that the man had in fact led him to Ruru, which made him feel very grateful and pleased, so he did as the bodhisattva said.

Ruru was then invited to the kingdom and installed upon a lion throne. She taught the Dharma so pleasingly and gave such lucid explanations that the people of the land were very happy and enjoyed peace of mind.

183   It is easy to destroy enemies
       Who clearly show signs of malevolence,
       But how is one to overcome enemies
       Who give false signs of being helpful?

Certain enemies are easily recognized because they explicitly reveal their animosity; they are easy to overpower since one can prudently respond to them according to what they say. Other enemies are a little difficult to overcome no matter how one tries to do so. They exhibit misleading outer indications of being supportive, yet harbor malicious inner intentions toward others. Do not cling to angry, injurious thoughts about enemies; let such thoughts vanish into thin air. Rather than return harm for trouble, cultivate love and compassion.

184   Some words spoken skillfully can be valid,
       But obnoxious words cannot succeed.
       Because the crow once humiliated the owl
       They have remained antagonistic for eons.

Do not speak abusively in meetings. Even if some improper things are said in conversation with others, one can still set matters right by skillfully talking things over. But using truly obnoxious speech makes it impossible to achieve one's objective.

Once upon a time when all the birds gathered together to search for a king, one among them said, "Let us consider the owl—here in this assembly, he is magnificent! When he travels at night, his vision is very acute. He even has feather horns on his head, so surely he is the king of birds."

But the crow protested, "What are you talking about? His feet are like those of a servant, they are so cracked and calloused! He once stole meat from Ama Yarmo, so she poured meat broth on him and his eyes became greasy yellow! His voice is unpleasant! And when he gives his owl call in front of all the owls, his feather horns pop up on the top of his owl head—this is a bad omen! Count me out!" With that, he flew away.

The other birds chattered, "What the crow said is absolutely convincing," and they all scattered, leaving the owl sitting there alone.

One must weigh carefully the impact of one's words, and not recklessly blurt out whatever comes to mind.

185   "Hold malice firmly in your heart,
        But outwardly speak pleasant words."
        This is the advice of evil masters;
        It contradicts the ways of noble people.

"Inwardly, cling resolutely to your hatred and think, 'People like this are my enemies.' Outwardly, always speak nicely. Then one day when the time is right, completely crush your opponent!" Such counsel by the wicked, hermit sages of old must be rejected, as it contradicts the customs of good people. The following citations from the texts of ancient non-Buddhist sages Ahtrotala and Masūrākṣa illustrate this:[126]

        For as long as the time is not ripe,
        Tote an enemy on your shoulder;
        When the timing becomes opportune,[127]
        Crush him as rocks do clay pots.

And,

        Though down and crying for mercy,
        The enemy should not be given quarter.
        Do not be compassionate with them;
        Destroy those who were harmful before.[128]

And,

        Like unsettled debt and undoused fires,
        Enmity that is left unresolved
        Grows more troublesome over time,
        So do not leave these untended.

On the other hand, an example of proper advice from non-Buddhist traditions:

> Be pleasant toward good people,
> Do not befriend troublesome people,
> Do not trust unsuitable people,
> And be respectful toward spiritual masters.

Again, the bad kind of advice is:

> Confuse all who are unconfused;
> The perplexed can always be deceived.

This kind of guidance runs counter to the traditions of excellence and should be avoided. In verse 316 below is a verse to bear in mind:

> "While strength is partial respect foes;
> Once you have become fully capable
> Take whatever approach works best."
> Some treatises offer this advice.[129]

186   "Just as one unearths the roots of poisonous plants,
One should sunder enemies at their root."
Though this appears in the *Rājanītiśāstra,*[130]
Enemies act like sons when treated as sons.

Advice found in the *Rājanītiśāstra* says, "In the same way that one must extract the root of a poisonous plant to totally destroy its toxin, in order to eradicate completely a malevolent enemy, one must eliminate not just him alone, but his entire clan as well." However, Sakya Pandita advises here that if one cares for enemies as kind fathers care for their sons, then enemies will act like kind sons caring for their fathers.

187   Who could befriend those people
That act only in self-interest?
In fields where one works hard growing crops
There is little chance for other gardening.

Some people do things solely out of self-interest because they see no other way to satisfy their personal desires. What honest person is able to make friends with someone like that? Farmers primarily toil to grow crops like wheat and barley, so they rarely have an opportunity to cultivate flowers and other plants.

    When helping others, one actually helps oneself as well, so one should do whatever is possible to benefit others, and be minimally preoccupied with personal concerns.

188   How could one ever befriend
        Ungracious individuals?
        What farmer would cultivate fields
        Where even hard work isn't fruitful?

Kindness extended to those who do not understand gratitude is wasted. Some people fail to keep in mind the considerate things others once did for them. How is it possible ever to help or befriend them again? It would be pointless! Why would any knowledgeable farmer cultivate a field where staple crops never ripen no matter how hard they labor? Such effort would be meaningless and fraught with distress.

189   On account of their deceptive behavior
        The impetuous quickly deteriorate.
        Does the obstinate wild ox
        Not quickly break its tether?

Thick-headed, impetuous conduct makes shameless people quickly become degenerate. Restrain yourself from acting like a brash and stubborn, untrained ox; practice conduct of body, speech, and mind that is both conscientious and ethical.

190   No matter how much one gives to the coarse,
        What do they repay when oneself has needs?
        A pincers always seizes other things,
        But can a round, iron ball grip it in return?

To have expectations of bad people is pointless, a formula for disputes. No matter how much charity like food or clothing is donated to unprincipled individuals, their utter lack of shame means they give nothing in return when the benefactors themselves are in need. A pincers can always grasp things effectively, but can a round iron ball hold on to anything? Of course not!

191   Pretentiously claiming, "I will help others,"
        Bad people engage in wrongdoing.
        What wise person would destroy herself
        Doing what merely seems to help others?

Bad people, corrupted by self-deception, mouth altruistic words, "I am of great service to others!" In fact, they are just expressing self-interest and trying to get rich. In so doing they harm both themselves and others; debased, superficial altruism benefits no one. The wise have the wisdom eye of much learning, are eminently intelligent, and are truly enriched by the jewels of renunciation, love, and compassion. They avoid helping others simply for the sake of impression.

192   Unsettled debt, the root of enmity,
      Bad statues, bad language,
      A bad lineage, and bad conduct—
      Though unintended, these things naturally worsen.

The balance of a loan that a poor person cannot repay is the foundation of acrimony. So also, bad laws harm everybody, and bad speech offends the ear. Engaging only in wrongful actions due to bad lineage contradicts the norms of proper behavior, and bad conduct violates spiritual and temporal customs. Even if such things are not intentionally propagated, they naturally spread and flourish of their own accord.

Chapter 6 ~
AN EXAMINATION
of NATURAL TENDENCIES

193   When named to a high position,
       One rarely knows what to do.
       Though one has eyes to see others,
       A mirror is required to see oneself.

For without experience in both temporal and spiritual matters, simply being appointed to an important office seldom means one will know how to discharge the duties of that office. Pretending to be a skilled strategist, in fact one simply becomes preoccupied with scolding others and criticizing their work; one rarely knows what one should or should not be doing in order to lead and care for the citizenry.

When engaging in plans to help others, it is imperative first to understand one's own limitations. One uses one's own eyes to look at somebody else's face, but a mirror is needed to examine one's own.

194   Those who have one-sided wisdom
       Find it hard to be skillful in everything.
       Although the eyes see very clearly,
       They are incapable of hearing sounds.

Through the practice of spiritual and temporal activities like explanation, debate, and composition, some individuals develop mastery in a single area of knowledge. However they find it difficult to be thoroughly adept because they are not learned in whatever they have not studied. Eyes are sharp enough to see a fine hair, but they cannot hear sound since the object of perception is incompatible with the perceiving faculty. Some great masters have said,

When well educated but inept in explanation,
One is like a skillful doctor without medicine.
When accomplished in debate but unlearned in composition,
One is stupid even if able to speak many tongues.
When proficient in composition but poor in handwriting,
One is like a very brave hero with a clubbed fist.
When one's composition violates grammatical rules,
Be careful because scholars will greatly disapprove.
When one is lettered but lacking in poetic talent,
One is like a beautiful but unclad woman.
Thus, one must be learned in all that should be known.

195   It is possible for honest speech to be faulty
And for dishonest speech to be constructive.
Some direct routes can ruin one's wealth,
While the white conch shell twists to the right.

That which is partially true and partially false cannot be strictly judged either way. Straightforward, honest speech can be wrong, and convoluted, dishonest speech, where words diverge from intentions, can have positive attributes. Direct, fast roads sometimes present a threat to both people and their wealth due to thieves and wild animals, whereas conch shells that spiral to the right are considered auspicious.

196   People with some learning but no merit
Destroy themselves with their knowledge.
Oysters forfeit their lives
Because of the pearls to which they cling.

One might have a little special knowledge of spiritual and temporal matters, but deficient karma and merit renders that knowledge useless and may even bring about one's ruin. Oysters shelter their precious pearls, but then are gathered and killed by those who desire the pearls.

The point, as explained in verse 16, is to "proceed in accordance with the lines on one's forehead." One should strive to accumulate merit without flaunting what little knowledge one has.

197   When too dependent on someone, even if learned,
It is frequently possible to have regrets.
Even though sugar cane is tasty,
When always served, it is often refused.

Dependency has its limits, even dependency on knowledgeable people. Those upon whom one relies may have countless wonderful qualities, but one must recognize the limitations of one's own understanding, ability, trust, and aspirations. Depending on another too much for too long will most likely give rise to regrets once incompatibilities are understood. Sugarcane is very tasty, and just the right amount is good. But if eaten continuously, most people get tired of it and throw it away.

198   Even those who are good-natured
        Will grow malicious when continually abused.
        Though sandalwood sticks are cool by nature,
        When rubbed together they burst into flames.

It is not right constantly to find fault with good-natured people. Even someone with a good disposition, who is pleasant looking and mild mannered, when subjected to continuous aggravation and abuse will become rancorous and intolerant. Sandalwood usually has a cooling quality, but when two pieces are rubbed together, they ignite into a hot flame.

199   Although rulers are quite numerous,
        Only a few govern according to the Dharma.
        Although heavenly abodes of the gods are many,
        None shine as brightly as the sun and moon.

One sees and hears of many leaders reigning over their lands and peoples. But among them, those who rule in accordance with the Dharma—the foundation of happiness for the citizenry—are as few as stars that shine in the daytime. Although there are many gleaming places where celestial beings reside in the heavens, none are so radiant as the sun and the moon, which illuminate the entire world.

    Nowadays troubles like sickness, ignorance, fighting, and controversy spread in the world because the principles of Dharma are ignored. Realizing this deplorable situation, make an effort to request leaders to govern in harmony with the Dharma.

200   Anyone with the power to be harmful
        Is also able to be helpful.
        A king with the power to cut off one's head
        Is also able to govern justly.

There is a difference between kings with great authority and those with a minimum of influence. Rulers who can inflict terrible harm can also initiate benefit; those with the authority to execute someone also have the power to rule the land equitably. It is important to understand this distinction and to rely properly on effective leaders.

201   The high official who is honest and intelligent
        Achieves all objectives of the king and the people.
        When a straight arrow is skillfully shot,
        Whatever is aimed at is hit.

Some high officials are intelligent, skillful, have good memories, and are particularly honest in their dealings with the king. This enables them to accomplish all the objectives of both the king and the people. When a skilled archer shoots a straight arrow, it strikes with certainty, whatever the target. High officials must strive to implement policies based on these special leadership qualities.

202   When the king himself is disrespectful,
        Not even the omniscient will honor him.
        Even if a lifeless human corpse is attractive,
        Who would want such a thing?

High officials like those noted earlier may be learned in spiritual and temporal matters, but when the king of the land himself acts respectfully, then everyone's objectives are met, and their good, useful qualities emerge. However, if rulers abuse and disrespect their subjects, they only invite contempt, whether from semi-literate people or omniscient masters, and they will not achieve their goals. When the life force departs, the body is barren and the sense faculties inactive. Who wants a human corpse, even if it is good-looking? Nobody will have anything to do with such an utterly useless thing!

203   When many are of the same opinion,
        Even the weak can achieve great things.
        Through the united force of many ants
        A lion cub was slain, it is said.

When great objectives are to be achieved, not only must great minds agree with each other, but ordinary people must be united in opinion as well. With consensus, great achievements are actually possible even when people are lowly and feeble; what need is there to mention if they are important and wise? There is a well-known story about fragile ants who assembled in great number and, with singularity of purpose, were able to kill the cub of a lion, mighty king of the beasts, by sucking out its blood.

With this understanding, strive to be unified in common goals without chasing after the sounds of empty echoes.

204   Timid people who shun spirited effort
       Will deteriorate even if they are strong.
       Although the elephant is very powerful,
       It is enslaved by a slender mahout.

The timid and weak-minded think they cannot accomplish anything significant, so they abandon all physical and verbal enthusiasm and put off doing things until tomorrow or the next day. Before long such immature people will fall into decline even if at the moment they appear strong and flawless in every way. Elephants are very powerful and have massive, strong bodies, yet one scrawny elephant handler can control them and make them do whatever is desired. Thus it is said,

    When the courageous undertake something,
    There is nothing they cannot achieve.

It is essential to apply oneself with unyielding perseverance since achievement of one's purpose depends on the strength of one's efforts.

205   When one generates self-confidence and enthusiasm,
       One's brilliance intimidates even the great.
       Although the white conch is small,
       It is the great crocodile's executioner.[131]

Unflinching courage is needed to accomplish important objectives. When one strives eagerly to persevere, believing with self-confidence, "I can do anything whatsoever!" such radiant dignity renders powerless not only minor adversaries but primary ones as well, and significant achievements are made. A white conch, though very small and delicate, can put to death a monstrous crocodile.

206   The great need not be arrogant;
       For coarse people, what is the use?
       Precious gems need no advertising,
       But who would purchase trinkets?

Arrogance is an affectation to be completely avoided. Great people with every asset—high social status, power, knowledge, and wealth—do not need to be arrogant because they are already superior. But for others, deficient in both knowledge and experience concerning temporal and spiritual matters, how would it serve them to display conceit when they lack the ability, learning, and ambition to warrant such behavior? The good qualities of precious jewels like diamonds need no glorification, but no matter the extent to which ordinary cheap baubles are promoted, what sensible person would buy them? They are worthless!

Everyone, whatever their influence or social position, must strive to eradicate that mound of arrogance upon which the waters of good qualities cannot accumulate.

207   The wealth of the truly great endures,
        That of the coarse is at risk.
        The sun endlessly radiates light,
        But the moon waxes, then wanes.

Due to their especially good qualities, magnificent people engaged solely on behalf of others have wealth and power that remains intact without decreasing. Conversely, bad people of deficient merit are concerned only with their own interests. Today they might enjoy marvelous and plentiful wealth and power, but without supportive merit it will not last and their ruin is near at hand. The sun is complete in all respects: it shines continuously, has magnificent radiance, and remains intact without deteriorating. But the moon is in a state of fullness only on the fifteenth of the month, then gradually wanes until on the thirtieth it is a new moon.

The principal cause of undiminishing good fortune depends on having totally pure merit; therefore, work diligently at suitable ways of accumulating the two collections of merit and wisdom.

208   Excessive praise of an evil king's status
        Eventually will lead to his destruction.
        When an egg is thrown up into the sky,
        What else can happen than for it to break?

When one excessively praises the position of an evil king who harms others in many harsh ways, there is no alternative but for his weak understanding and shamelessness to bring about his downfall. The ultimate outcome of tossing an egg up in the air is obvious!

Maintain equanimity toward bad kings and high officials, because they can be extremely arrogant.

209   As a rule, people are harmed
        By others of their own kind.
        When sun rays begin to dawn
        Other light sources vanish.

One should be cautious; nowadays it is common for people to be very harmful to those with whom they share similar ancestral lineage, behavior, and attitudes. Driven by attachment and anger, refusing to examine their own shortcomings, they injure and aggravate others, exposing their weaknesses, and so forth. When the sun rises, its bright rays overwhelm the luminosity of the moon and stars, rendering them invisible.

One should nonetheless maintain an attitude to be helpful to others, because this is the remedy for one's concealed malice.

210   Rely on the helpful even if they are enemies;
        Abandon the harmful even if they are friends.
        Buy jewels from the ocean because they are dear;
        Remove inner aches and pains with medicine.

Anybody who is helpful, directly or indirectly, should be totally relied upon, certainly if they are friends, but even if they are enemies. On the other hand, when bad attitudes and coarse, mean behavior prompt people to be harmful in all kinds of ways, they must be avoided like the plague even if they happen to be relatives or close associates like parents, friends, or teachers. The distant ocean is an excellent source of precious jewels, and these should be purchased with no concern whatsoever for the cost, whereas one's own internal organs, if afflicted with disease, must be removed by the treatment of a skilled physician. Recognize what is helpful and what is harmful, then adopt the former and avoid the latter.

211   With the inner thought, "I'm rather rich,"
        An outward expression of smugness is shown.
        When clouds are completely laden with moisture,
        They swirl and roll with thunder.

Most people, when thinking to themselves that they have acquired a bit of wealth in the glorious knowledge of temporal and spiritual matters, outwardly become puffed-up and conceited in their demeanor. Clouds in the sky show they are thoroughly saturated when they roil about, resounding with thunder.

Be alert to discrepancies between outer appearances and inner intentions.

212   Those with all good qualities are rare,
       So also those with none at all.
       Rather than a mix of good and bad,
       The wise mainly rely on good qualities.

In these times of strife, individuals who are free of all faults and have acquired all good qualities are extremely rare, perhaps only one in a hundred. Similarly, individuals having nothing but faults and lacking any good qualities whatsoever are also rare. For that reason the wise who aspire to excellence place their trust in people who possess predominately good qualities, rather than those whose attributes are a mixed bag. Therefore, one must investigate spiritual masters on whom one might rely to determine their shortcomings and their virtuous qualities, then rule out the deficient and place confidence in the qualified.

213   At the outset it is uncertain
       Who is a friend, who is an enemy.
       Undigested food turns into poison,
       But even poison cures if understood.

Initially it is unclear whether one individual is a harmful enemy or another a helpful friend, because an enemy can turn into a friend for the slightest reason. As Śāntideva says in *Engaging in the Bodhisattva Deeds*,

       One moment someone is a friend,
       And in the next instant, an enemy.

Even excellent nourishing food, if not digested, becomes toxic; similarly, if one knows how to prepare harmful poisons, they can be transformed into medicines that are effective against disease.

       Remember, it is not always reliable to brand someone "enemy" or "friend." Instead, one should eradicate anger and attachment.

214   Those with favorable karma are rich;
       Those lacking such karma are poor.
       Ducks, though put in a house, do not stay there;
       Though flushed from a lake, they circle and return.

Everyone—parents, relatives, masters, and dependents—residing for a time in household and hamlet will enjoy an increase of all outer and inner wealth in places where they have the causes and conditions of supportive karma and merit from previous lifetimes. But for those who lack such a base of support, inner and outer goals are not attained and all wealth dissipates wherever they may live. It is as Candrakīrti says in his *Supplement to (Nāgārjuna's) "Treatise on the Middle,"*

> Dependent origination is a distinguishing feature
> Of all things that are composite phenomena.

Even if somebody carefully tries to keeps a duck in their house, it will not stay there. Conversely, even if they try to chase a duck away from its pond, it flies off and circles around for awhile, then returns.

215   The wise will pay to better their knowledge,
       But fools discard what they've already learned.
       Most people take medicine when sick,
       But some commit suicide when healthy.

The wise know how to achieve both present and future well-being: they please their teachers by offering them suitable gifts like gold and silver, then endure great difficulty to master the necessary subjects. But fools are oblivious to the difference between benefit and harm. They carefully learn about compassion and altruism, then abandon these good qualities even though they understand them well. When intelligent people suffer from diseases like wind or bile disorders, fear of death prompts them to take curative medicines for which they must pay. Conversely, some ignorant people, although vital and healthy, will take their own lives by fire, drowning, or jumping off cliffs.

Renounce foolish conduct; follow instead the ways of wise and accomplished bodhisattvas and generate enthusiasm to willingly take on the difficulties of learning what needs to be known.

216   All who have independence are happy;
       All under others' control know grief.
       A mixture of both brings controversy;
       Commitments impose constraints.

Those who abide without any attachments and have no need to depend on others are happy because they are self-reliant. But people who are totally under the power of others, and required to give heed to their concerns and do whatever they say, are miserable because they have no autonomy. Moreover, a straddled situation of being neither wholly free nor wholly dominated by others is troublesome because things are uncertain. Generally, commitments limit one's independence; in particular, a pledge one cannot fulfill engenders a state of foolish exasperation. Try to develop self-confidence, free of anger and attachment, desiring neither profit nor fame, nor to be spoken of favorably by others.

217   One who internally has all good qualities
       Yet is outwardly unkempt is scorned by all.
       It is said that even though bats are wise,
       Their baldness makes all birds spurn them.

Some people may possess internally the special qualities that bring about for both themselves and others the excellent collections of high status and definite goodness. But if externally their behavior offends others and violates both temporal and spiritual conventions, they will be scorned by everyone. As Śāntideva says in *Engaging in the Bodhisattva Deeds,*

    Through careful observance and inquiry,
    Avoid those things of which the world disapproves.

It is well known that bats have sharp intelligence and skillful knowledge. Yet they are left alone and friendless, rejected by all the birds because their bodies have no feathers and their appearance is ugly.

Once upon a time the birds set about searching for a leader. "Whoever is so clear-sighted as to be the first to see the sun rise will be made leader," they decided.

All the birds settled down and looked toward the east. The bat and the pigeon, however, were looking at a mountain peak off to the west, so they saw the sun first.[132] The bat tried to win by deceiving the pigeon, but was not awarded the victory.

Another contest was held to see which bird could fly the highest. The bat crawled in among the vulture's feathers and sat very still. Ultimately the vulture surpassed all the other birds.

"I am the one who can touch the sky!" declared the vulture when it returned, and it spread out its wings. The bat then emerged from among the vulture's feathers and cried, "I am also one who can touch the sky!" and flew away.

All the birds then protested, "That ugly creature is as bald as a goat's horn! How could it be acceptable? Forget about its being king, it must not even be allowed to remain in the company of ordinary birds!"

One should understand that sages completely avoid situations where people act hypocritically in order to deprecate and harass others.

218   When unsuitable people speak too honestly,
        They destroy both themselves and others.
        An arrow will either kill someone
        Or will itself be shattered.

There are problems when the ignorant are too straightforward. Unfit people who lack understanding and analytical ability ruin themselves or others—or both!—because they cannot discern right from wrong, even though they are very honest. A straight arrow can fatally strike a person or an animal, but it can also splinter from its own impact. One must strive to be judiciously honest and to understand what is advantageous and what is not.

219   Rain and rivers flow to the ocean;
        Intelligence and knowledge adhere to the wise.
        Wealth and subjects are gathered by the king;
        Forests grow in warm, damp places.

Abundant summer rain and perennial rivers all flow down to the ocean and accumulate there. Discerning intelligence and powerful knowledge surround and characterize the wise. Kings who rule over the land accumulate and retain riches and intelligent people. All kinds of forests will grow in warm seasons and moist places.

    Put effort into those activities that are worthwhile.

220   Springs that flow in summer, fires of grass,
        The sun or full moon peeking between the clouds,
        Friends with poor knowledge and low intelligence:
        At the time of need, their appearance is uncertain.

People who lack merit are unhelpful in times of need, though they may have some minor flashes of goodness. They are like springs that flow during the rainy season, but not in springtime when water is scarce;[133] like fires in small tufts of grass that burn quickly, and are dead when needed later; or like illumination from the sun or moon shining between clouds, a fleeting phenomenon not at all helpful when it is necessary to travel somewhere. There is no certainty that friends who lack a sense of shame will help out in confrontations with enemies or other emergencies.

    So also for knowledge acquired through a weak mentality absorbed in self-interest, devoid of any concern for others, and lacking the support of merit accumulated in previous lifetimes: it is unclear whether or not such knowledge will be of any use when one is really pressed. Whatever intelligence one has will be beneficial to both self and others if attachment to personal concerns is severed and one thinks solely of others' interests.

221   It is nice when fools seldom speak;
       It is nice when kings stay out of sight;
       It is nice when magic shows are rarely seen;
       When jewels are rare their price is high.

The talk of uneducated fools is uninformed about what is helpful and what is harmful, so if they do not say much in gatherings, they cannot be faulted and conversation remains congenial. When kings who are greatly respected in their lands remain secluded inside their palaces, not going where everyone can see them, that is proper and they are revered by all. It is considered enjoyable and amazing when conjurers' magic shows can be seen only now and then. If precious jewels such as diamonds are rare in the land, they are very costly because of the common perception that they are extraordinary.

222   When love is lavished excessively,
       That in itself generates hostility.
       Most of the disputes in this world
       Derive from close relationships.

Very familiar relationships are ultimately a cause of trouble. If associations with friends and relatives are overly loving and affectionate, eventually they lead to broken promises and hostility. In this world the majority of arguments between people arise from each one's knowledge of the other's personal affairs, because from the outset the individuals were too confiding with each other. As Śāntideva says in *Engaging in the Bodhisattva Deeds*,

       Such dependencies between oneself and others
       Will only beget tribulation.

And,

       Transitory friends and relatives
       Destroy even the eternal Dharma.

And,

       When meeting them, one should be pleasant,
       Without becoming overly familiar;
       Act properly in an ordinary way.

It is important to be aware of limits in relationships, which means to interact modestly with others, without the excessive familiarity that breeds contempt.

223   It is possible for heated arguments
To result in close friendships.
Usually following controversy
Reconciliation is observed.

Sometimes huge quarrels develop because people say to each other "I am right! I did a lot!" Yet in the end, the disputants become the closest of friends who cannot bear to be separated from each other. In this world, the majority of altercations are seen to conclude in harmonious agreement. Śāntideva says in *Engaging in the Bodhisattva Deeds,*

One moment someone is a friend,
And in the next instant an enemy.

224   The wealth of the greedy,
The friends of the jealous,
The lore of evil minds:
These exist, but cannot bring joy.

That which is inherently flawed may seem wonderful, but does not bring about happiness. Greedy people with passionate desires and an inability to enjoy things may have wealth, but they cannot put their riches to good use. Unbearably jealous people may have friends, but they take no pleasure in others' good fortune. Intelligent but bad people, trained in the nefarious ways of corrupt teachers or corrupt traditions, may have knowledge, but that knowledge is devoid of scriptural and evidential credibility and does not cultivate thorough analysis. All these things may exist, but they are unrewarding because they are of no use to anybody.

Because reliance on an excellent path that truly does benefit both oneself and others is so important, strive to reject what must be rejected and adopt what must be adopted.

225   The greedy are delighted by wealth;
The arrogant are pleased by praise;
The foolish are amused by other fools;
Good people are gladdened by words of truth.

People excessively attached to wealth are made happy only by more wealth.

Those who take great pride in their ancestral lineage and such rejoice when they are complimented. Shameless fools are entertained by drinking and gambling with other fools just like themselves. Lastly, good people are pleased to rid themselves of coarse dishonesty and to speak the truth, which makes everyone happy and benefits both this and future lifetimes.

226   The qualities of coarse people,
       The knowledge of weak braggarts,
       And the gratitude of evil rulers:
       The chance that these will benefit others is slim.

Consider the personal character of coarse-natured people who despise the lowly and scorn their efforts, the knowledge of weak but boastful people who have deficient merit and little charisma, and the thoughtfulness of evil rulers who abruptly issue punishments and rain down abusive scolding upon those who make just a few mistakes. There is little likelihood that any of these will be of any help to anyone. Rather, one's mind should be saturated with the enlightened perspective of wanting to benefit others.

227   What a wealthy person says is considered charming,
       But the words of the poor are rejected, even when true.
       Even wood from ordinary trees is quite costly
       When it comes from the land of white sandalwood.

Among those who have merit, rich people can say anything and it is regarded by others as wonderful and trustworthy. Conversely, poor people lack the resources that are the fruits of charity, and whatever they have to say is utterly repudiated, even if it is unquestionably true. The places where white sandalwood comes from are as treasured as riches that result from merit. Even ordinary logs in that vicinity are very valuable, to say nothing of sandalwood itself. Make effort to create the causes for acquiring the kind of wealth that those who have merit possess.

228   Talking too much gets one into difficulty;
       Silence is the way to stay out of trouble.
       Parrots are put in cages because they speak;
       The muteness of other birds allows them happiness.

Some people are blind to what is going on around them and fail to understand the relative importance of things. They generate difficulties with their profuse but pointless sweet talk, which harms both themselves and others. But other people adopt the manner of one who is speechless, using the excuse that they can neither see nor understand, in order to avoid trouble. Because parrots speak like humans, with dulcet tongue and skillful words, though they understand nothing at all, they are caught by people and thrown helplessly into cages. Other birds who do not know how to talk are not troubled with this misfortune and fly around happily under their own power. Therefore, one should adopt the style of those who say little; as stated in verse 221, "It is nice when fools seldom speak."

229   Whenever anyone in an undeceitful way
       Gives assistance to an enemy,
       And the enemy is straightforward in return,
       Such mutual respect is true greatness.

Thoughtful people who realize what is important will always use any appropriate means, material or spiritual, to give genuine help to hostile enemies. In return, their enemies will be pleased and honestly respect them. Such mutual esteem is truly noble in nature.

Giving kind-hearted assistance to anyone, be they friend, foe, or neutral stranger, is the supreme way to avoid having enemies. Try hard to practice this approach.

230   What use is there for the weak to get angry?
       What need is there for the strong to get angry?
       Therefore, no matter what one is doing,
       Pointless anger is a self-consuming fire.

What is known as anger is flawed and meaningless by nature. What purpose is served when those lacking both power and ability exercise anger to try to accomplish something important, since they are incompetent anyway? Moreover, why should it be necessary for powerful people to use anger in achieving goals that can be naturally realized? Anger is irrelevant in attaining one's objectives. According to Śāntideva in *Engaging in the Bodhisattva Deeds,* anger sets one's mind on fire:

> When harboring painful angry feelings,
> One's mind experiences no peace,
> One attains no joy or happiness,
> One is restless and cannot sleep.

Śāntideva goes on to say,

> Those who are careful and quell their anger
> Are happy in this and future lives.

Anger brings unhappiness in the present and for lifetimes to come. Therefore, one should disentangle oneself from anger and try to achieve worthy objectives.

231 Even foes gather for charity,
     But without it, even friends stay away.
     When the cow's milk has dried up,
     Though restrained, the calf tries to flee.

When someone freely distributes their wealth, everyone considers it worthwhile to gather from far and wide for gifts. As if powerless to do otherwise, even enemies (to say nothing of friends) naturally congregate. But when wealth is not generously shared, even friends (to say nothing of enemies) keep their distance. When a cow's milk is spent, there is no more reason to come and drink; no matter how much one tries to keep cow and calf together, the calf wants to run away.

Giving away material things is the most important of the four ways of gathering disciples, so take single-pointed delight in opening wide the door of generosity.

232 Just because one is skilled in some areas
     Does not mean they can do other things.
     The swan, which can separate milk from water,
     Imagines some things it sees to be food.

A person may be skilled in certain areas of general knowledge, but that is no guarantee they will be learned in other areas such as the Buddhist sciences contained in the sutras and tantras. One is proficient only in that which one has studied. Swans have one special ability, to separate milk from a mixture of milk and water, but then they mistake a piece of grass shaped like a bug for food and run after it. One must work hard to acquire training in all areas of knowledge and should not be proud that one happens to know something about only a few subjects.

233 When leaders always treat people kindly,
     It is easy for them to find followers.

Ducks need not be called to lotus ponds;
They gather there naturally.

Leaders with a genuine concern for others, wanting everyone to be situated
in as pleasant circumstances as their own, will have no trouble finding sup-
porters to carry out their wishes. Without being specially lured, ducks are
naturally attracted to lakes ornamented with enchanting lotuses because they
find them so pleasing.

One must take care of people in considerate ways that make them happy.
Great leaders, wanting to gather advocates, treat everyone kindly and impar-
tially. This point is very important, so please bear it in mind!

234   Proper use of wealth by the rich,
       Self-discipline after becoming learned,
       And good care of the lowly by the great—
       These three bring joy to others and help oneself.

Temporary well-being for others and lasting benefit for oneself come about
in the following ways: being rich obliges one to use one's wealth in suitable
ways without being wasteful; after being trained primarily in the Buddhist
treatises and becoming truly wise, one should maintain disciplined physical,
verbal, and mental behavior; and attainment of a prestigious position means
that one should care more for the disadvantaged than oneself.

On the other hand, some wealthy people are miserable, unable to put their
riches to good use; and those who make fraudulent claims of improving their
physical, verbal, and mental behavior become as faulty as the most contempt-
ible of enemies.

235   Things achieved through the strength of merit,
       Like the light of the sun, depend on nothing else.
       Things achieved through the strength of effort,
       Like the light of a butter lamp, depend on everything else.

There is a difference between how things are accomplished by those with
merit compared to those who lack it. Previously accumulated merit enables
one to achieve future goals for oneself and others naturally with no reference
to any other conditions, just as the sun's radiance shines everywhere inde-
pendent of all other factors. On the other hand, a lack of merit means that
one has to muster forceful physical and verbal effort, relying on oneself, assis-
tants, and others to achieve future goals. For the light of a butter lamp to
dispel the darkness, there is total reliance on other conditions. Supportive

factors like wicks and oil must be present, while impediments like wind must be absent.

236 When they rely on the great,
   Even the lowly achieve greatness.
   See how a vine that clings to a tall tree
   Climbs all the way up to the top.

With a firm understanding of the infallibility of the law of cause and effect, anybody can quickly attain a state of greatness if they rely on exceptional individuals of superb character, who have equanimity for all and are skilled in being compassionate and helping others. Even well-behaved, lowly people can attain such excellence due to the quality of those whom they trust. By themselves, vines grow coiled up on the ground, but when they attach to tall trees, one can see how they climb up to the crown where the sky is blue.

237 Those who admire good qualities should depend on others
   Who, though having faults, possess such qualities.
   Rain can damage a manor house,
   But it makes the farmers very pleased.

Those who have been well trained and possess good qualities may also have a few unseemly shortcomings, due to being reborn in cyclic existence with mental delusions and bad karmic imprints. Nonetheless, people who admire good qualities should closely rely on those who have them, because that is the sole source of such attributes. Rains from the heavens can damage a nobleman's mansion, but it makes ordinary farmers happy because it helps the crops in their fields.

238 If people simply look nice but lack good qualities,
   The wise cannot take any interest in them.
   If a champion horse lacks a good gait,
   Even if good tempered, it is of little value.

If one lacks the good spiritual and temporal qualities that are indispensable to those with a precious and rare human body, merely being attractive with fine clothes is insufficient; the wise, accomplished in working for the common good, take no interest in such people at all. As it is said,

> Rather than being first among those with no good qualities
> It is better to be last among the excellent ones.

Excellent horses must have a good gait. Without it they are of little value, even if they have a good disposition, good color, and good conformation.

One should cultivate the good qualities that benefit both present and future lifetimes, but avoid acting as a know-it-all merely to get the food and clothing needed for this life.

239 Among fools, many are rich;
   Among carnivores, many are brave;
   But among the wise who have appeared in this world,
   Rare are the sages who explain things well.

Among fools who are unable to distinguish between good and bad, there are many who are wealthy, mainly creatures such as nāgas. Among carnivorous beasts like tigers and leopards, there are many brave animals who do not hesitate to sacrifice their lives or confront other challenges. But among the numerous wise in this world, those who with pure thought and action give lucid explanations that help everyone are as rare as stars that shine in the daytime.

One should abandon useless activity, work hard to develop the wisdom by which one can discriminate between what is known as Dharma and what is not, and engage in study and contemplation to thoroughly master the extensive treatises that enable one to hold one's head high in the presence of the wise.

240 Whatever qualities people possess
   Are those by which they gain their reputation.
   Wisdom establishes the reputation of the wise,
   And bravery is how heroes acquire their fame.

Anyone with inexhaustible wealth acquires a reputation of being rich. Being highly regarded as wise comes from engaging in activities consistent with the Dharma and avoiding those that are not. Heroes become famous through their unshrinking valor when confronting physical, verbal, or mental difficulties, or ultimately, risk to their lives.

It is essential to apply oneself in acquiring the most important of these reputations—that of being wise.

241 Those honored by the great
   Are scorned by the coarse.
   The moon ornament on mighty Śiva's head
   Is devoured by lesser gods.

Excellent and inferior people possess different inner knowledge, resulting in dissimilar outer behavior. Exceptional, learned individuals find the wise deserving of their respect and honor. Coarse, ignorant people, however, concerned only with external appearances, not only disrespect the wise but abuse them as well. Behold how the radiant white moon, crown ornament of the great god Śiva, is seen as food by the lesser god Rāhu, who takes it into his mouth.[134]

One should disregard others' external behavior, and understand the special qualities of the genuinely wise. In distinguishing between those who are worthy of respect and those who are not, cherish clear-mindedness.

242   Knowledge left behind in books,
        Tantric practices unaccomplished,
        Instructions completely forgotten:
        These often deceive in times of need.

One may know in general how to exercise good judgment and be able to refute others, but if that knowledge remains in one's books during formal debate sessions, nothing comes to mind and thus one has nothing to say. Inept tantric practitioners, having never completed a three-month retreat on a meditational deity, often appear accomplished, but their practices are useless at critical times, such as when evil spirits and hindrances need to be expelled. Also, when it is time to act, those who utterly forget everything in which they have been trained fail to distinguish what to do from what to avoid and so end up doing the exact opposite. When the need is essential and these resources are unavailable, many people are deceived.

Like the old proverb about the traditional summer and winter debate sessions at Ngamring,[135] one must be very careful at the outset of any activity to bear in mind what will follow after.

243   Even though wealthy, if the intelligent are lazy
        It is hard for them to gain high position.
        Though ears emerge first at the time of birth,
        Are the horns not seen to be more prominent?

Intelligent people may have the most magnificent spiritual and temporal wealth, yet be lazy, with no enthusiasm for physical, verbal, and mental activity by which they can better their situation and benefit both themselves and others. It is very difficult for such people to attain high position in the realm of spiritual and temporal affairs. Laziness is like the ears of dzos and elephants: they are present at the time of birth from the mother's womb and stay simply stuck on the head. Enthusiasm is like an animal's horns: though nonexistent at birth, can one not observe that they grow even bigger than the ears that were there from the beginning?

Wise people who have both temporal and spiritual wealth should rid themselves of laziness, put their knowledge to use, and generate enthusiastic perseverance to bring the majesty of their temporal and spiritual experience to full bloom.

244   Gourmet food for dogs and pigs,
       Butter lamps for the blind,
       A meal for those with indigestion,
       And Dharma for fools—of what use are these?

Aromatic, delicious food is not necessary for dogs and pigs who are nourished by such filth as regurgitated garbage. Similarly, sightless people do not need butter lamps to illuminate forms, and rough food should not be fed to those with poor digestion. Lastly, fools who lack positive predispositions derived from previous lifetimes have no wish to improve their knowledge in this life, so it is pointless to give them a lot of explanation on the fundamentals of the Dharma, which benefits this and future lives. But it is important for those deficient in both innate and acquired knowledge to diligently offer prayers of supplication to reliable spiritual teachers and the three supreme jewels of refuge, which are as dependable in future lives as they are in this life.

245   Fine gold, knowledgeable people,
       Heroic warriors, champion horses,
       Skillful doctors, and beautiful jewelry—
       Wherever one goes these are in demand.

People with excellent knowledge derived from the study of general worldly affairs can travel far and wide, and in any country on earth they are well-regarded and considered worthy by all. The same is true for fine gold that comes from excellent sources; for genuine heroes having no regard for their own lives but great loyalty for their country when combating foes on the battlefield; for superb horses with the requisite gait as well as other necessary features like good shape and color; for skilled physicians who are kind and incomparably proficient in any area of medicine, like pulse analysis, urine analysis, and prescribing medicines; and for gorgeous jewelry made from precious diamonds and other rare gems. Wherever one goes these things are sought and cherished.

Those aiming to realize the full potential of their meaningful life as a wholly free and fortunate human being must work hard to develop their knowledge.

246   As for the intelligent and hard-working ones,
       Of course they can achieve their goals!
       It is said that the sons of King Pāṇḍu
       Conquered twelve divisions of the king of Kaurava.

Is there anything that cannot be accomplished by people who have discriminating intelligence and take enthusiastic delight in their work? Legend has it that King Pāṇḍu's wise and persevering sons single-handedly overwhelmed all twelve divisions of Kaurava's army, which was very powerful and difficult to defeat.

Once upon a time when the human life span was eighty thousand years, a period of strife began. There was a great king named Sage Vyāsa who took a wife of royal lineage, and from her an eldest son named Prince Pāṇḍu was born. The king also took a Brahmin wife who gave birth to the youngest son Dhṛtarāṣṭra. Eventually Prince Pāṇḍu came to rule the country.

Prince Dhṛtarāṣṭra had no sons. One day he went to pay respects to his father, Sage Vyāsa, and request his help. His father offered this prayer in response, "May your holy Queen Gandharva have one hundred sons."

Ten months later the queen gave birth to a rounded, stomach-like piece of flesh. Again Dhṛtarāṣṭra pleaded with his father. "Let alone one hundred sons, not even a single son has been born!" he cried.

But his father replied, "There are one hundred sons in that piece of flesh. Cut it into one hundred small pieces, wrap it in a cloth, and hide it away. After seven days, whichever piece is on the top of the pile will be the oldest son. Examine his good and bad qualities carefully."

Dhṛtarāṣṭra and his queen did as they were told. After seven days they looked, and there were one hundred infants. It was prophesied: "If the eldest is not quickly killed, then even though there are one hundred sons, ultimately the lineage will be broken. Therefore, that child must be slain!"

"This child may be an evil omen, but I cannot bear to kill him," grieved the queen. "He is a son of my own flesh!" So she ignored the prediction.

Observing the next child, the minister Pitāmaha said, "He has six moles —one each on his throat and forehead, and two each on the palms of his hands and soles of his feet. Thus he has been born on the day associated with the constellation Pleiades. Until all six of these moles are punctured simultaneously, even if his head is cut off, we shall not be blessed by his death." But the son was not harmed. He was very brave and was named Duryodhana.

In time, since King Pāṇḍu had no sons, he entrusted his kingdom to his younger brother, Dhṛtarāṣṭra, and went off on holiday with his two queens, Devi Kṛṣṇa and Kunti, to the forest for solitude. In the forest was an evil sage emanating in dual form as male and female tame deer. The king happened to be hunting when he saw them and, thinking they were real deer, he shot the male with an arrow.

"It is I, manifesting as this male and female deer," screamed the enraged sage. "Now I am experiencing much pain! You have fatally wounded me and I must depart for the next world. May you die in this manner when you engage in sexual intercourse with your queens!"

Flinging that curse at King Pāṇḍu, the sage's manifestation in the male deer body burst miraculously into flames. His other manifestation as a female deer climbed atop the pyre of her mate. She also pronounced a curse, "Oh, you jealous king! At the time of your death may your queen also die in this manner!" and she jumped into the fire.

King Pāṇḍu, frightened by these maledictions, settled down in one place and turned his back on the pleasures of lowly desires. Queen Kṛṣṇa thought to herself, "In order to keep the king's lineage intact, I must obtain a mantra that will produce a child. I will request a knowledge mantra from the ascetic sage Durvasa." When she told the king of her idea, he was very pleased and gave his permission, so she carried out her plan and obtained the knowledge mantra.

She then offered prayers to Yama, the lord of death. From their union was born the son Yudhiṣthira, who had a very handsome body just like his father. Among his many special quality was that he could not speak a dishonest word even at the risk of his life, and his divine body radiated many rays of light.

Next she offered prayers and joined in union with Indra. To them was born a son called Arjuna. He had the special quality, derived from his father, of being renowned in this world as a highly skilled archer. Because of his fame as a practitioner of Dharma, he set an example for others.

Similarly, from offering prayers and joining in union with the god Brahma, a son named Bhīmasena was born. He was known as the strongest in all the world.

A knowledge mantra was then given to Queen Kunti who, by offering prayers, joined in union with the medicine gods known as the two brothers Pathaka. From this union were born twin brothers, Nakula and Sahadeva. Their special qualities derived from their fathers: the former having very stable clairvoyance and the latter, a most handsome body.

In that way, although the three sons of Queen Kṛṣṇa and two sons of Queen Kunti were actually the sons of gods, in this world they were known as the five sons of King Pāṇḍu.

Since he now had five sons, King Pāṇḍu was freed from concern about the discontinuity of his lineage. He gave his kingdom to Dhṛtarāṣṭra and settled down with his family, without ever engaging in sexual pleasures with his two wives. The day came, however, when he was overcome by the enticement of Kṛṣṇa's body.

"To be unable to enjoy such a desirable wife as this is no different than death!" he lamented and joined in union with Kṛṣṇa. Just as he deposited his sperm in her womb, the curse that the sage had uttered came to fruition. From the heavens a great knowledge mantra arrow shot down and as it struck King Pāṇḍu, his body burst instantaneously into flames.

"Please! Look after my three sons along with the two that are your own," Kṛṣṇa cried to Kunti. With that final wish, she jumped into the fire and died. Kunti and the five sons went to live in the palace, and they were loved by all the people.

Before long, an evil idea came to their uncle Dhṛtarāṣṭra, the wicked king of Kaurava. "If Kunti and her sons grow strong, they will likely take away my kingdom," he thought. "So now while they are weak, I must engage in a bit of treachery and put them to death."

From sealing wax he made a house with a single pillar. He invited Kunti and her sons inside, then quickly locked the door and lit the house on fire. The tongues of flame reached up to the top of the beams.

With his clairvoyance, Nakula could see that beneath the pillar his Uncle Viṣṇu was using a vajra to make a secret underground passageway. He signaled to the others. Bhīmasena then held up the pillar while mother and sons escaped through the tunnel. They arrived in the land of the cannibal demons[136] known as Sengala.

Bhīmasena slayed all the cannibal demons, seized their land, and married a female cannibal demon from whom a son was born. This son had his father's handsome physique, but from his mother's side, he had stiff reddish-golden hair that stood up like a horses mane, so he was given the name of Kumbhakarna.

Eventually the evil King Duryodhana of Kaurava, with his ninety-nine brothers and the twelve divisions of the armies of the world, fought a battle with the five Pāṇḍu brothers, Arjuna's nephew, and Viṣṇu, making a total of seven. The twelve divisions lost the battle and nearly all were killed. On that occasion the gods of the Heavens said in verse:

> Though there were many troops bearing weapons
> In the twelve divisions of Kaurava's army,
> When they faced the supreme archer, Arjuna,
> They performed as weakly as women.

With the one hundred sons of Dhṛtarāṣṭra and practically all their troops thus decimated, Bhīmasena became king of the world, in recognition of his battlefield skill.

One division of troops declared, "It is better for a man to die than to be the subject of one who has killed his older brother!" So two brothers fled to the mountains in the land of Tibet. Tibetan people have descended from them, and that is said to be the reason Tibet and India have such a good and enduring friendship.

247   Usually the conduct of children
        Follows in line with their ancestry.
        There is no way for a cuckoo chick
        To mature into a sparrow hawk.

In this world the conduct of most people's children follows whatever patterns of behavior have been established by their ancestors, although it is possible for there to be in the family one or two bad offspring who delight in unwholesome conduct, as exemplified by the disgraceful individuals in any family history. Generally speaking, however, there is not the slimmest chance for the chick of a large cuckoo to turn out to be a bird-eating hawk.

The essential point young people should understand is that rather than engaging in bad conduct they should treasure the traditions of their ancestral lineage.

248   Mountains and rivers, elephants and horses,
        Wood and light, jewels and stones,
        Men and women—though each is a unique type,
        There are qualitative variations in each.

There are different kinds of mountains: the best ones, like the seven golden mountains and Mount Sumeru, are made of the four precious jewels; middling ones are made of rock, and inferior ones are made of sand and coal. So also there are good rivers, like those having eight special qualities, and poor rivers with saline water. There are good elephants, like the one named Very Steady on the Earth, and ordinary elephants; smart, intuitive horses and ordinary horses; trees like the wish-fulfilling tree and poisonous trees; the light of wisdom and ordinary light; jewels like the King of Great Expansive Thought and ordinary jewels; stones like diamonds and ordinary stones. There are men who turn the Wheel of Dharma and ordinary men; and there are superior women, such as *ḍākinīs*, middling ordinary women, and inferior women, like demonesses.

Things like mountains, rivers, and so on are individual general categories, but within each are large qualitative differences. Recognizing clearly that this is the case for all classes of knowable things, it is fundamental to distinguish accurately between what to accept and what to reject.

249   The lowly endure with difficulty
        Even mere words from virtuous people.
        The ocean king was bound, it is said,
        By mere words from the king of Gauda.

When those with genuine merit energetically apply themselves, they can defi-
nitely achieve objectives and defeat others. But even should they utter merely
one word, lowly people without merit cannot bear it and are rendered help-
less. Consider the famous case of Rāmapāla, king of the southern land of
Gauda. He had acquired a store of merit, and with nothing more than words
he defeated the king of the ocean, leaving him disabled and discouraged.

Once upon a time in the southern land of Gauda, there lived a merit-rich
king named Rāmapāla. In order to subjugate the island territories he summoned
together all his subjects. "Wage war on Gyatso Ching, king of the ocean!" he
ordered. Just hearing this command paralyzed Gyatso Ching with fear.

Later, a woman appeared, wearing fine jewelry. "Release this king of mine
who has been completely bound!" she cried.

"He's not tied up," the king of Gauda replied. "What is binding him?"

"Did you not give the order to attack Gyatso Ching?" she asked.

"Ah," the king of Gauda said, "if that is the case, then may he now be
released!" With nothing but these words, the other king was freed.

Usually one cannot fetter others merely by saying, "Wage war!" or free
them by the words, "Release them!" Only the magnificence of supportive
merit can cause this to happen.

250   One may vigorously strive to complete a task,
        But attainments depend on the power of virtue.
        A jewel that merchants cannot find in the ocean
        Is possessed in the treasure house of the king.

Usually people put forth great effort to accomplish all kinds of worthwhile
things. Ultimately, however, achieving goals and putting them to good use
depends only on the strength and capacity of an individual's supportive merit.
Merchants may thoroughly search the great ocean, but the wish-fulfilling
jewel they fail to find is sitting in the treasure house of the king who has merit.
It is the power and blessing of his merit that enables him to enjoy the jewel.

251   Signs of love and anger in fools are recognizable,
        But in those with guile they can appear differently.
        When dogs bare their fangs, it is a sign they will bite;
        When the Lord of Death smiles, it is a sign he will kill.

Both the benevolent kindness and destructive animosity practiced by fools is bereft of knowledge and ability; thus one can immediately tell from external clues whether their intentions are good or bad. The affection and malice of shrewd, intelligent people, however, might seem to be genuine, but since they have many ways of concealing their real intentions, their behavior could be deceptive if one does not examine the situation carefully. When dogs lower their tails and run at someone with bared fangs, it is obvious they are about to bite. But when the Lord of Death—whose only pleasure is to take life—smiles, that indicates that he will certainly kill. It is important not to be influenced merely by the outward display of someone's anger or kindness. Examine things carefully to avoid later regrets.

252　　The supreme wealth is generosity;
　　　　The supreme happiness is a joyous mind;
　　　　The supreme ornament is learning;
　　　　And the supreme friend is an undeceitful person.[137]

Of all that one can strive for, these are the best. The supreme wealth which gladdens people is generosity that has no expectation of getting anything in return. Such giving not only increases one's prosperity in this lifetime, but is like riches stored away in a treasury that can be effortlessly enjoyed in future lifetimes as well; it is known as "wealth created by generosity." Moreover, being the foremost of the four ways of gathering disciples, it can satisfy the material aspirations of others and complete the perfection of generosity for oneself.

　　Similarly, happiness means completion of the sublime inner and outer collections of merit and wisdom and being freed from all manifest sufferings. The best of these is a happy and supple mind, the opposite of desirous cravings. Nāgārjuna says,

　　　　Among all kinds of happiness, extinction of desire is best.

And,

　　　　You! Please subdue your mind!

Buddha Śākyamuni has well stated:

　　　　The mind is the foundation of Dharma.

And Śāntideva says in *Engaging in the Bodhisattva Deeds,*

　　　　If guarding the mind is not among one's ascetic practices,
　　　　Then of what use are the rest?

The supreme of all adornments, with a natural beauty and radiance, is to acquire wisdom that is learned in the various subjects of Dharma, the most important being the Buddhist sciences. Learning removes ignorance of the good personal qualities that should be perfected, then develops in those who maintain a sense of propriety such qualities as contemplation and meditation. From *The Special Verses Collected by Topic (The Tibetan Dhammapada, ched du brjod pa'i tshoms),*

> Learning is the lamp that dispels ignorance,
> The best gift to offer when meeting the upstanding ones.

From *The Ornament for Sutra,*

> Even if children wear very fine clothing,
> It gets soiled from the transgressions of impropriety.
> But bodhisattvas who are clad with a sense of propriety
> Are free of such defilement even when youthful.

Sakya Pandita says,

> Grasping the handle of the wisdom-sword of learning,
> One completely conquers ignorance, stupidity, and confusion.

Also,

> It is said that to the extent one has a sense of shame,
> To that extent one has the supreme jewel of good qualities.

And from *The Sutra of Individual Liberation (Prātimokṣa Sūtra):*

> Of the learned who abide in the forest
> The mature ones dwell there in peace.

The best close friends are those who in this life speak the truth, are compassionate, and are not deceitful when relied upon for a long time. From *The Ornament for Sutra,*

> The bodhisattva has much learning, sees the truth,
> Speaks skillfully, and is compassionate.
> Such a superior one who has transcended birth
> Is understood to be a great being.

Sakya Pandita says in *A Classification of People,*

> A suitable friend is someone who has
> Long studied the excellent scriptures,
> Does not reveal secrets, is not deceptive,
> And gives abundant food and wealth in time of need.

Having generated certainty about what is observed these days, it is important for everyone—inferior, middling, or superior—to apply himself seriously and single-pointedly to generate these four supreme qualities.

253   Who is there with no worries about wealth?
        Who can sit comfortably all the time?
        All suffering and happiness change,
        Just as summer turns into winter.

What person does not struggle over matters concerning money and property? There is no one! Who can remain seated forever without the slightest discomfort? That person does not exist either! In this regard, Āryadeva says in *The Four Hundred,*

> The great have mental anguish, and
> The lowly have bodily suffering.
> The world is perpetually oppressed
> By these two kinds of misery.

Happiness is simply the nonmanifestation of suffering, while misery torments both body and mind alike. For all sentient beings these change back and forth, one alternating with the other like the changing seasons or the passage of night into day.

Avoid being influenced by concerns about the transient states of wealth or poverty and their accompanying feelings of pride or meekness. Be content knowing that wealth and pride are determined by karma. It is no use to get stirred up about such temporary situations as being pleased by wealth or displeased by impoverishment.

254   Merely by dropping the names of the great,
        The lowly are protected by others.
        It is taught that by using Aṅgulimāla's name
        One is protected from common misleaders.

Lowly individuals lacking wealth and devoid of the power of merit accumulated in former lifetimes surely can achieve what they want by relying on authoritative people who are strong and capable. But they are also protected by simply dropping the names of important individuals who do not harm them, although they have the power to do so. Śāntideva says in *Engaging in the Bodhisattva Deeds*,

> Though one may have committed immense, unbearable
>   wrongdoings,
> By relying on [the awakening mind] one is swiftly liberated,
> Like entrusting oneself to a brave person when afraid.
> Why, then, do the conscientious not devote themselves to this?

Also,

> For example, though some royal officials
> Create trouble for many citizens,
> The farsighted will not retaliate,
> Even if they are able to do so.
> They see those officials not acting alone,
> But backed by the power of the king.

According to an example taught in the tantras, while it is surely true that ordinary people who lead one astray cannot inflict harm and will even offer protection if one cloaks oneself in the support of the allies of Aṅgulimāla, the same end is achieved if one merely mentions his name.

It is important for the lowly to abandon pride and arrogance, and to rely on eminent people of good character who have the ability to give protection.

255   Any relationship between sentient beings
        Takes shape in accord with past karma.
        Notice vultures with marmots on their backs
        And otters making offerings to owls.

Among the relationships found among the various kinds of sentient beings, those known as beneficial function according to the power of karma amassed in previous lifetimes. Observe how some animals help others, like the vulture who loads the marmot on its back and carries it to the far side of the river, or the otter who hears the call of the owl and provides it with fish and tadpoles.

Since it is important from this moment onward to set aside a reserve of good karma that will benefit future lives, one must work hard at this task.

256   If the rich want to increase their wealth,
      Its best insurance is to give it away.
      If you want to add more water to a pond,
      Draw down the pond and it replenishes itself.

One becomes wealthy as a result of having been charitable to others in previous lifetimes. Therefore, those who want to increase their fortune need to purge themselves of greed, give spiritual offerings to the Three Jewels, and provide ordinary charity to all kinds of people. This kind of generosity is the best way to protect and preserve wealth because it is a repository of assets for both this and future lives. If one wants to add a lot more water to a pond, one simply uses up some of the pond water, and it will naturally refill itself with other water. In this fashion, the water is never depleted.

Wealth can be accumulated, but one should recognize that one has no lasting power over it. One's riches, like a bee's honey, can be seized and consumed by others. Therefore, one must exercise freedom of choice to use it meaningfully.

Chapter 7 ~

AN EXAMINATION
of UNSEEMLY TENDENCIES

257   Servants who are very arrogant,
       Ascetics who behave foppishly,[138]
       And kings who act contrary to the Dharma:
       These three engage in unseemly conduct.

Some servants, having become destitute and sold themselves into bondage, need others to provide their food and clothing, yet they act conceited. Some ascetics fail to concentrate on the required practices of austerity, like living in secluded places and making do with deprivations of food and clothing, and instead get preoccupied with elegant dress and mannerisms. Some kings pursue exclusively political objectives without exercising their rule in ways that are consistent with the Dharma. They intently engage in deceitful conduct to improve their weaponry, gain victory for themselves, and defeat others. They do not adhere to King Srongtsan Gampo's *Ten Moral Principles and Sixteen Rules of Public Conduct,* which would bring about happiness for their subjects. These three kinds of individuals epitomize people who are involved solely in improper conduct.

258   Starting work that one lacks time to complete,
       Being hostile to many, arguing with the powerful,
       Trusting shameless spouses, and befriending bad people:
       These five are causes for swift self-destruction.

Those who make many promises and begin things but have insufficient time for completion deceive others and exhaust themselves with trouble. Those who provoke belligerence by being quarrelsome and domineering are ravaged not only by the hatred borne in their own hearts, but even more by the animosity of others. Furthermore, to argue heatedly with powerful and influential people instead of behaving in a humble manner and refraining from criticism; to trust as a spouse a companion who, although learned, cannot adhere to his or her own agreements and is shameless; and to befriend evil people who foster enmity in their hearts but present themselves with smooth talk—these are five examples of circumstances that quickly bring about one's own ruin and, like a murderous butcher, should be avoided at all costs.

259   Lacking wealth, yet desiring the best food and clothing;
        Begging from others, yet being very arrogant;
        Not understanding the treatises, yet wanting to debate:
        These three situations cause others to laugh.

To desire for oneself such luxuries as fine food, drink, silks, and jewelry, yet be without the affluence necessary to enjoy them denies reality. The same is true of people who cannot secure food and clothing for themselves and must rely on others' kindness, but remain nonetheless self-centered and arrogant. Still others wish to engage in vigorous debate amid a group of scholars even though they do not fully comprehend the meaning of the commentarial texts by Tibetan and Indian masters. Those who are wise find such situations ludicrous, because they contradict the actual nature of things.

One should examine one's own mind, abide harmoniously, and avoid unseemly, incongruent situations that are laughable to others. For example, to enjoy fine food and clothing, one should be wealthy with no lack of resources; to take pride in personal ambitions, one should be clever and totally independent of others in all worldly and spiritual matters; to engage in dialectics with scholars, one must teach, debate, and write about the teachings of the Buddha, having first become skilled in study, contemplation, and meditation upon those teachings.

260   Despite the good places to live that exist,
        Bad people stay destitute, attached to bad places.
        Who but a jackal is going to expect
        That the *kiṃśuka* flower[139] is a piece of meat?

Although there are many fine places to live where one can achieve the collection of merit and wisdom that brings happiness in this and future lives, there are those who, deficient in merit, live in perpetually unpleasant places. Bereft of understanding, ability, and wealth, such people are attached to these wretched spots, where they dwell in a state of misery. The jackal thinks to itself, "That red kiṃśuka flower is a piece of meat." But hoping the flower is edible just leaves the jackal deprived, with nothing to experience but the misery of its empty wish.

Those with merit should rid themselves of any affinity with evil places. Always reside in and depend on environments conducive to accumulating merit and wisdom.

261   The close associates of important people
       Can do them more harm than enemies.
       How can the body of a lion be eaten
       By any creature other than its own vermin?

If they are unwise in protecting themselves, graver misfortune will befall officials from their own associates than could possibly arise from external enemies, because their inner circle has intimate knowledge of their activities. Consider the king of beasts. Apart from being afflicted by germs and parasites that thrive in its body, what can endanger a lion? Will it be devoured by tigers and leopards? Impossible! Prominent people need to develop skills in treating all their associates, even the most lowly, with genuine, careful impartiality.

262   When a king inflicts harm on people,
       Who is there to defend the king?
       When a light casts a shadow on some figure,
       There is no way to see it.

It is a bleak situation when one who is supposed to protect the people turns into their enemy. Sometimes kings become remote from their subjects or persuade others to spread rumors betraying their followers, harming them in every conceivable way. Who supports such rulers? Ordinary people say that when leaders become enemies, the citizens need to have a plan to escape. When light sources—the sun, the moon, or lamps—cast concealing shadows, there is no hope of seeing such forms as pillars and vases; they cannot be perceived without light.

263   For Dharma practitioners living peacefully,
       Harmful acts are particularly despicable.
       Who can ever consider brave
       One who kills those seeking protection?

Once people have become practitioners of the Dharma they abide with their body, speech, and mind pacified. Injurious acts like killing other sentient beings are thoroughly loathsome for them, because they contradict the teachings of Buddha. Āryadeva says in *The Four Hundred,*

In brief, tathāgathas explain
Virtue to be nonviolence.

And from the sutras,

To inflict harm on those who are ordained,
And on other people in general, is not virtuous.

If someone kills those who come to him asking for protection, no sensible person would proclaim, "He is a hero who murders lowly people!" One may not be able to work compassionately like wish-fulfilling gems for the sake of others. But by studying the faultless sutras, commentaries, and teachings of great masters, one can strive not to harm others and to become fully capable of discriminating between what should be avoided and what should be undertaken.

264   Bad individuals inflict harm on others
Even when they derive no benefit from it.
Poisonous snakes strike at the wind as food;
Do they not also kill others when they see them?

Evil individuals are either ignorant of the relationship between causes and their effects or, if aware, are contemptuous of it. They torment others—provoke aggravations, thwart ambitions, even threaten lives—although they gain not the slightest advantage in prestige or wealth. Oblivious to the ultimate consequences of their actions, they do these things themselves or engage others to act on their behalf. Regarding those who are satisfied in doing what yields themselves no benefit, Śāntideva says the following in *Engaging in the Bodhisattva Deeds:*

[Even if your enemy suffers as you wish,
Why should that make you happy?]
If you then say, "I am pleased by that!,"
What could be more despicable than that?

When the poisonous *ardzaga*[140] snake spies humans, animals, or other creatures, will it not kill them out of hunger? But it also strikes at the wind as if it were nourishing and fails to get anything to eat.

Inflicting harm on others yet not receiving for oneself even a single hair of advantage for either this or future lives is definitely animal behavior. Realizing this, one should know how to discriminate between what to do and what to avoid so the ultimate consequences of such actions need not be experienced.

265   Although it is believed that desires bring happiness,
        Acting on such impulses brings only misery.
        Those who think drinking beer is happiness
        Assume their intoxication is bliss.

Desires are a cause of self-destruction. Those who misunderstand what precipitates ruin in this and future lives equate their desires with happiness. In fact, beyond the immediate enjoyment of gratification, desires create causes for unbearable misery. Śāntideva says in *Engaging in the Bodhisattva Deeds,*

    In this world as well as the next,
    Desires brings about destruction:
    In this life—killing, bondage, and stabbings;
    While in future lives—rebirth in the unfortunate realms.

People who drink alcohol usually assume drinking and intoxication brings them happiness. But in fact the pleasure they experience is because they are ignorant fools adrift in a crazed, drunken state, bearing neither recollection nor shame. Desires are the basis of disgrace and bring misery in this and future lives; one should turn one's back on them, and instead be adorned with the ornament of conscientiousness.

266   Ordinary people respect those with good qualities;
        Much effort is required to obtain them.
        What is the point of being arrogant toward others,
        Without having perfected one's own good qualities?

Getting angry at others is meaningless without first having put forth the effort to develop good personal qualities. People of excellence have good knowledge of worldly affairs in general and the Buddhist and non-Buddhist sciences in particular. They are especially knowledgeable about the Buddhist scriptures of sutra and tantra that set forth Buddhist philosophy. They are honored with courtesy and offerings from all informed ordinary people (apart from mere ignorant barbarians), who willingly and respectfully follow their wishes.

    Such good qualities are not easy to acquire; they do not simply grow in the ground nor fall from the sky. Their development depends on a potent ability to develop them by exerting great physical, verbal, and mental effort. One must ignore hardships, gamely endure problems, and make sacrifices in food, clothing, and reputation. This can be appreciated by examining biographies of the famous scholars of historical India and Tibet.

Some people realize these precious qualities are important, yet put forth no effort to acquire them. Why then should they be angry and arrogant toward others who have these good qualities and deserve respect? It is of no use at all! Śāntideva says in *Engaging in the Bodhisattva Deeds*,

> Not clinging to that which brings gain,
> Why should I not be angry [at myself]?

A sense of dissatisfaction from lacking good qualities should inspire one to exercise unerring judgment about what to do and what to avoid.

267 See how people pray for long life,
   Yet are fearful of growing old.
   Not wanting to age yet wanting longevity
   Is the perverse notion of a fool.

Desiring a long life but having an aversion to aging is a childish[141] misunderstanding. Usually, ordinary ignorant people want to live a long time, so they pray, "May I live a hundred years!" Yet note how they fear and loathe becoming white-haired and wrinkled! Longevity is synonymous with aging; one should not be pleased about living a long life, yet displeased about getting old—an idea peculiar to childish, idiotic fools.

268 At times when wise people are available,
   Those who learn nothing from them
   Are either affected by demons
   Or suffering the influence of past karma.

There are great scholars learned in the various subjects that the wise study, contemplate, and meditate upon. People with poor supportive karma accumulated in previous lifetimes can have these mentors right in their midst, but lack the faith, respect, and joy to learn from them the knowledge that is so essential. Instead, they sit around carelessly at their leisure without requesting instruction. In manner, they seem to be humans who are able to speak and understand, but actually they have been affected by inner and outer demons like pride, jealously, and competitiveness, or are under the influence of evil and lazy friends. This shows they have been rendered powerless by bad karma, which ultimately will lead them to suffer rebirth in the unfavorable realms.

  Attaining the life of a fully free and fortunate human being is like journeying to a jewel isle from which one must not return empty-handed. Realizing this, one should investigate the life stories of accomplished scholars who relied properly on their spiritual masters. Then, to avoid wasting an excellent human rebirth, one should earnestly request from the wise the teachings of Dharma that benefit both this and future lives.

269   When those who happen to have some wealth
        Fail to use it or give it away,
        Either they are stricken with disease
        Or are appearing as pretas.

It is contemptible when those who have wealth fail to put it to good use. Some people practiced generosity in former lifetimes, the result of which is that in this lifetime they enjoy such riches as gold, silver, and silken garments. Yet they might never use their resources for any worthwhile personal needs or philanthropic purposes, like making spiritual offerings, paying respects to others, or giving charity to beggars. They simply pile up their assets and closely guard them. Internally, this situation is as if they have indigestion and cannot eat. Externally, it seems as if they have been possessed by demons, causing them in this life to manifest as starving creatures utterly bereft of food and drink, and in future lifetimes to take rebirth as pretas. Some great masters have said,

> Contemplate death, have no need of luxury,
> Dine in a measured way without craving,
> Do not be greedy for riches,
> Be charitable to all lowly beggars:
> These are a vault of wealth that benefits future lives.

When the rich do not apply their resources properly, there is no difference between them and the utterly destitute. Strive to be generous and put wealth to good use since this is of value for lifetimes to come.

270   If Dharma is understood but not practiced,
        How could it be of any use?
        A harvest may be bountiful
        But would that delight a carnivore?

Some people know well the general and specific details of how to practice the Dharma through reliance on a wise spiritual teacher, yet fail to apply its meaning to their physical, verbal, and mental activity; nor do they adopt antidotes to their greed, anger, and ignorance. If they do not help others by writing, teaching, and debating, of what possible use is their knowledge? It is just as if they had no understanding of Dharma at all! When the fields of the earth yield abundantly, why would that be of interest to carnivores? Crops serve no purpose for them, so they could not care less.

Those who understand the Dharma need to ensure that all the outer, inner, and secret practices they employ in their daily lives are consistent with the meaning explained in the vinaya, sutras, and tantras, and they should apply themselves correctly.

271   Those who suffer the effects of bad karma
      Cannot enjoy wealth even if they have it.
      Though the crow may be hungry, it hides its food.
      How then can it possibly fill its belly?

Some people are tormented by the exacting imperatives of karma accrued in previous lifetimes. They endure the misery of amassing and protecting wealth, but no matter how much they stingily stash away, they are unable to put it to good use because they worry about coming misfortunes like old age, hunger, and thirst. Even when crows are hungry they often eat only a little, then hide most of their food underground, hoping to eat it later. How do they find it again? They never can!

Rather than behaving like this bird that has "grown a horn for a mouth," one must cleanse oneself of previously accumulated adverse karma by thoroughly applying the four antidotes and working hard at the ways of the noble ones.

272   If wealth neither enjoyed nor given away
      Prompts thoughts of being well off,
      Then imagining a mountain to be gold
      Would be an easy way to get rich.

Wealth improperly used is meaningless. Some people are arrogant because they are rich, but they neither utilize their wealth for their own requirements nor donate to those in need. Preoccupied with their affluence, they think of themselves as beyond the reach of poverty. Such affluence is devoid of the acts that contribute to wealth and is as flawed as having no wealth at all. One might as well envision a mountain that is entirely gold, or the wish-fulfilling tree that satisfies all desires, and think, "This all belongs to me," as if there were no actions required for such a simplistic achievement of wealth other than mere conceit. In fact, one must try hard to accomplish the preconditions for wealth by using resources well and being charitable.

273   Though many are skilled in discussing
        What is Dharma and what is not,
        Those who practice such understanding
        Are extremely rare in this world.

In Tibet and India, many superb scholars have always appeared to speak about what is or is not the Buddha's excellent Dharma and whether or not it accords with tradition. But having acquired such understanding and taught it to others, those who then actually put their understanding into practice properly so that their words and thoughts are consistent with each other—in this world, such people are as rare as stars that shine in the daytime. Some great masters have said,

     By being rid of followers, raucous disciples, and material
        possessions,
     There is no desire for bubble-like words.
     By assimilating golden drops of practice,
     Joy comes to those who realize the examples of the ancient sages.

Ignorance is a source of suffering. The empty talk of those who do not put into practice what they know makes them just as stupid as parrots.

274   Though one may have good ancestry, physique, and youth,
        Without knowledge one lacks beauty.
        Though the peacock's feathers are handsome,
        Are they suitable ornaments for the great ones?

Knowledge is the ornament that beautifies fully free and fortunate human beings. People of fine lineage, who are fit and filled with youthful vitality, look attractive to everyone. However, merely these characteristics, without the praiseworthy, sublime inner knowledge of spiritual and worldly matters, will not beautify the precious human body that is so hard to obtain. Peacocks have gorgeous feathers of all colors of the rainbow, but their beauty comes from a diet of poisonous plants. So can their feathers be considered appropriate adornment for the great ones? Hardly! Some great masters have said,

     Even the prominent quickly become servants, trampled underfoot
        by others;
     Even youthfulness quickly deteriorates, like flowers that bloom
        at autumn's end;
     Even wealth, like the pleasure of borrowed jewelry, dissipates
        as time passes; and

>Even our lives, like flashes of lightning, appear here just for
>   an instant.

Until attaining the state of buddhahood, one should devote oneself to mastering the knowledge that beautifies the human body, principally inner awareness, which never deteriorates.

275   Imitation noses, purchased children,
       Borrowed jewelry, stolen wealth, and
       Knowledge gained without spiritual masters—
       These exist but are not respected by others.

Consider the following examples of things that are pretentious by nature and inappropriate to admire: wearing a fake nose as a substitute for one's own that was either cut off as punishment for bad behavior or was damaged by disease; substitute children for the childless such as those purchased from someone else; wearing fine ornaments and elegant clothing borrowed from others for special occasions because one has none of one's own; and showing off to others riches one has stolen through intimidation, thievery, and swindling. Similarly, some individuals have considerable knowledge, but it demonstrates their stupidity as a perverse form of ignorance that blithely deceives others. They lack the fine understanding imparted to new students of keen intelligence by renowned scholars who have developed thorough proficiency in the subject matter by relying on a spiritual master.

    The altruistic wise do not regard self-taught knowledge as worthy, because it is unrelated to the authority of scriptural lineage and therefore benefits neither the physical, verbal, nor mental activities of oneself or others. Rather, one should apply oneself to mastering that excellent knowledge derived from an unbroken scriptural lineage by employing firm faith, conviction, and care in relying on discerning spiritual teachers who fully comprehend all necessary subjects, especially Buddhist wisdom.

276   Those with no gratitude for kindness
       Harm themselves more than others.
       People who cast malevolent spells
       Suffer the consequences before their enemies do.

Truly good people are forever appreciative of others, wishing to repay such immeasurable benevolence as being cared for physically, being given material aid, or even having others risk their lives for them. But some people discard such good character and forego any acknowledgment of kindness. These thoughtless individuals usually seem at the time to be hurting others, but first and foremost they sabotage themselves since the causes they set in motion and their inevitable results never deteriorate. The great, wise Sakya Pandita says in *A Classification of People,*

> Hold paramount the reliability of cause and effect:
> All that one does must be consistent with this.

Malicious people conjure up evil spells to inflict misfortune on others, but before any harm befalls the intended recipient, it first strikes the perpetrators themselves. Having rid oneself of that great arrogance that feels contempt for the relationship between actions and their effects, one must develop discrimination to align deeds with words by clearly realizing that all actions— good, bad, and neutral—have their consequences.

277   Though one might look forward to becoming wealthy,
       Who would take riches from an unsuitable source?
       By licking the spilled blood of battling rams,
       The fox's head was smashed to pieces.

Nothing should be expected or taken from inappropriate sources. One might anticipate acquiring desired wealth, but its source could be unsuitable, involving risks that exceed the potential advantages to be gained. What intelligent person having analytical skills would try to get rich this way?

Once upon a time there was a fox who had a strong yearning for meat. He went looking for food near a village where two unruly rams had been fighting for some time. Blood was dripping from the tips of their horns, and when the fox saw this he thought, "Here is what I've been looking for!" Carelessly, without considering the circumstances, he darted over to lap up the blood. The two rams charged at one another just as the fox put his head in the exact spot where they butted together. The fox's skull burst like a cotton seed pod.

Get rid of confused behavior, the self-generated problems one must experience due to greed devoid of any careful examination. Analyze things thoroughly, then distinguish between what to do and what to avoid.

278   After ingratiating oneself with some associates,
       Do not opportunistically abandon others;
       Even Indra and his attendants
       Go everywhere together like camphor.

Great people like spiritual teachers and high officials do not forsake their old friends by fawning over other acquaintances, such as relatives or dining and conversational companions, just because some opportunity beckons. In so doing they would fail to achieve their own and others' objectives and develop many shortcomings. Even the great god Indra stands by his friends, just as camphor and its aroma are inseparable. Surely ordinary people should do the same.

Sycophants are thin-eared people, doing and believing whatever their associates tell them. Such zigzag behavior is unacceptable. Be unbiased toward all those in need and strive to treat everyone equally.

279   Do not abandon long-standing friendships
      And then shift loyalties to new companions.
      It is known that by relying on the crow minister
      The king of owls destroyed himself.

If one rejects enduring, dependable friends, then recent acquaintances that one hardly knows will be of little value and should not be indiscriminately trusted. These days it is evident that there is great danger of new relationships being misled by meaningless talk. There is a famous legend about the king of owls who, without inquiry, believed the sweet nonsensical words of a crow and came to ruin.

Once upon a time the king of owls, Suparṇa, and the king of crows, Rāṣṭrapāla, loathed each other utterly. The owl king had an important minister named Suvarṇaksa, and the crow king was loyally served by his minister Balāhaka.

One day Balāhaka summoned all the crows and said, "Things are very difficult because of the intense animosity between us and our enemy, the king of owls. It is agreed that we are unable to fight, so we must deceive him. Therefore, pluck out my feathers, break my limbs, and then flee."

They did as he suggested and disappeared, leaving him in his nest at the top of a *yadrodha* tree.

Not long after, all the owls living on top of Craggy Mountain assembled and set off to wage war on the crows, but they found no one except the lone crow minister crying out pitifully.

"What happened?" they asked.

"We had an understanding and I wanted to stick to it, but they argued with me, and then threw me to the enemy," lamented Balāhaka.

Hearing this the king of the owls declared, "What he says is certainly true. We must take him to our place."

But the owl minister Suvarṇaksa objected, "He is a clever one. I think it best to keep him here and take good care of him."

But the king didn't listen, and the owls carried the injured crow to their home. The suspicious Suvarṇaksa, however, went elsewhere.

The owl king then said to Balāhaka, "You are skillful. Can you make a more comfortable nest than this?"

"Yes, I can do that," Balāhaka replied. He proceeded to construct a snug, protected aerie by piling up ten thousand dried sticks and filling it with powdered dung. The owls were happy then, with the king's nest in the middle and the other nests all around. During the day the crow minister went out to look for food, and at night he stayed and guarded the nests.

One day, though, Balāhaka sought out the other crows. "Tomorrow at noon," he instructed them, "each of you should bring some firewood to the owls' nests." Then he returned and stayed among the owls as usual.

The next day at noon all the owls, unable to see during sunlight hours, were sleeping when the crows arrived. Each nest was set afire and every one of the owls burned to ashes. It is commonly known that all owls these days are descended from the owl minister Suvarṇaksa. Some great masters have said:

> Who is more foolish than the careless ones
> Who plunge into rash and mistaken situations
> Simply because they hear a deceiver's first pleasant word
> And take what is said to be totally true?

Following others without properly investigating what they say causes one to commit impulsive acts that contradict important present and future objectives. One should earnestly try to rid oneself of such imprudent conduct.

280　One tries hard to depend on bad people,
　　　But they do not become trusted allies.
　　　No matter how much water is boiled,
　　　It cannot possibly burst into flames.

One can expend much energy trying to rely on people of despicable character whose bad thoughts and actions show ignorance of inner and outer matters. But besides the harm caused by bad conduct, one will never progress with them as partners, united in thought and deed. No matter how much water is boiled, apart from the heat of the bubbling steam, it is impossible for it to truly become fire and burn. As Sakya Pandita says in *A Classification of People*,

> Those preoccupied with food and drink
> Trouble anyone who relies on them and
> Enjoy going around engaging in mischief;
> Such people are like fleas and must be avoided.

It is important to understand that one should not wholly depend on people who conceal the self-interest in all their pursuits, aspiring only to gratify their personal needs and secure advantage for themselves.

281   Justifiable anger is somewhat acceptable
      And can even be quelled,
      But who knows how to placate
      Anger that lacks tenable cause?

There are advantages to investigating situations in advance. Anger can be provoked by others who are scornful, speak coarsely, thwart one's desires, or bring about what is unwanted. When the underlying reasons for such animosity and cruelty have been analyzed and reflected upon, it can be accepted as having arisen for good reasons. Moreover, one should understand the means of quelling anger and investigate whether there are remedies to get to the root of it. If one's mind is unsettled when others are abusive like that, then one will become as destructive as a mad elephant.

The practitioners of Mahāyāna Buddhism make a special effort to pacify themselves by meditating on topics like the altruistic mind of enlightenment. Some great masters have said,

> Maintain a helpful attitude, abate harmful thoughts,
> Cultivate love, and pacify anger naturally.

Conversely, if there is no understanding of the reasons involved or one has simply believed what was heard from others, how could anybody find a way to soothe anger that is unjustified at the outset? Be very cautious; it is quite apparent that there are many disputes these days because people lack skills in maintaining friendly relationships with each other.

282   Do not abuse even humble enemies,
      Without assessing their capacity.
      Because the little *tadibhala* bird[142] was mistreated,
      The garuḍa destroyed the entire ocean.

Before one has investigated an adversary's capabilities—external or internal, concealed, or visible—one should not oppose them with harsh speech and force just because they seem feeble and ignorant. Appearances may not correspond with inner dispositions, so it is difficult to determine hidden potential. For this reason it is improper to disrespectfully mistreat lowly people.

Once upon a time a certain tadibhala bird lived on the seashore. One day a large wave rolled in and swept away its nest and eggs. The bird summoned others of its kind to ask them for help.

"What can we possibly do to the ocean?" the birds replied. "We must assemble all the various birds and send a cry of distress to the garuḍa."

Everyone agreed and they called out loud and clear to the garuḍa, "Help! Do you not see that the only one who can lay waste the ocean is a bird such as you?"

In response the garuḍa tormented the nāgas who dwelt in the depths, so thoroughly harassing them that they had to return the bird's nest and eggs to the shoreline.

The mark of a complete fool is to bully and contend with others without first scrutinizing their strengths. It is essential to be careful and analyze things with farsightedness.

283   When merit diminishes, evil thoughts arise;
       When lineages decline, bad children are born;
       When wealth runs out, avarice is produced; and
       When life is spent, signs of death appear.

Distinguish carefully among the various indications that foretell the future. Some people develop bad thoughts, like the wish to commit the ten nonvirtuous actions or the five boundless transgressions, which reveals that the merit they once amassed is almost exhausted. When children are born who behave poorly and, contrary to the exemplary conduct of their ancestors, involve themselves in nothing but thievery, dishonesty, and gambling, it is a sign that one's ancestral lineage is in decline. Wealth results from charity and can bring temporary happiness to people; its decline is indicated by the rise of extreme greed and attachment to others' riches. One's lifetime is drawing to a close when the ominous outer, inner, and secret signs of death manifest in one's body, speech, and mind.

Generally, if bad omens arise anywhere in the world, one should carefully study the sutras and commentaries in which these omens are analyzed and apply oneself to alleviating them by performing the associated rituals. Specifically, as there are reasons behind bad omens, one should carefully perform the counteractive practices that enhance one's good qualities and diminish one's deficiencies.

284   If someone does not engage in wrongdoing,
       He cannot be criticized, even by Indra.
       If a spring has not ceased flowing of its own accord,
       How then can it be stopped by covering it with earth?

Whatever unbearable misery one might experience, all undesirable things that happen come from negative karma accumulated in previous lifetimes. Thus if one does not personally engage in any bad behavior, how can one be disparaged? Even the mighty god Indra, to say nothing of ordinary people, will find no fault with this. When a spring runs out of water, it dries up; but if its water is not exhausted, can its flow possibly be stopped by merely covering it with earth? No way!

285   Those who start a hundred different schemes
        Are unable to achieve even one success.
        These crazy-minded individuals are
        Like old dogs always roaming the town.

Promising to do many things that one initiates but then is unable to finish is the mark of a fool. People with lots of ideas but fickle minds get started on various temporal and spiritual tasks and put forth some effort for awhile, yet ultimately there is nothing they can point to and say, "This is a project I completed." Their heads full of notions, they plunge into their work, but end up always wandering around like stray dogs cruising the town, merely looking for things to eat and drink. Some great masters have said,

        One listens to useless stories; it is meaningless.
        One engages in useless work and just gets exhausted.
        One starts many different things; none are completed.
        A lot of hasty ideas is what leads one to trouble.

One should avoid pledging to do things that one has neither the time nor ability to carry out, thereby deceiving both oneself and others. Endeavor to accomplish with a clear mind those things that you know you can do.

286   When led by the force of karma,
        The intelligent go down the wrong path.
        Śiva, the supreme leader of the Tīrthikas,
        Once behaved like a lunatic.

When carried away by the inflexible dictates of karma from previous lives, even those who are intelligent and analytic (to say nothing of the ignorant and small-minded) veer in wrong directions, becoming shameless, powerless, and rightfully ridiculed by all. Even the great Śiva, renowned as supreme leader of the non-Buddhist Tīrthika sect, once acted like a madman.
    Once upon a time Śiva was acclaimed the most eminent in the world, a

spiritual teacher worthy of respect. One day all the gods were gathered togeth-
er for a celestial celebration and were talking about their aspirations. They
waited for Śiva for a long time, but he had not arrived. When at last he did
show up, his body was totally covered. The gods of victory laughed at him,
and he bared his teeth. When some other gods smiled at him, he merely
stared back at them.

"I will explain Śiva's past lives," declared Brahma. He paid honor and
began. Śiva had once been a zombie, he explained, and others were afraid to
be in his company. A demon had cut off his head; Śiva was utterly miserable
that he had been killed, and he wandered everywhere, holding in his hands
a spear and a skull. His arms were adorned with pieces of skull, and his body
draped in an elephant skin embellished with bone ornaments. Many quick-
ly fled when he danced in their presence; others ridiculed his conduct. Viṣṇu's
followers proclaimed,

> He resides in graveyards,
> Happy in the company of evil spirits.
> If the likes of him are considered gods,
> Then what kind of creatures are these flesh-eaters?

Knowing the reasons why the power of karma cannot be reversed, intelligent peo-
ple should try in every way possible to cleanse themselves of the defilements they
have accumulated through the combined actions of body, speech, and mind.

287   Howsoever anyone breaks the law,
       They may win for a while, but eventually they lose.
       Although Valāka gained the entire world,
       Because he violated the law, the Lion killed him.

As vigorously as if trying to move mountains or agitate lakes, some people
employ cunning and deceit to disrespectfully violate the two excellent traditions
of law in spiritual and worldly affairs. Even if they appear to be victorious and
unharmed (solely due to their cleverness, lying, and duplicity), in the end they
definitely will meet with defeat. Sakya Pandita says in *A Classification of People*,

> What they say and what they mean,
> Like seeds and spouts respectively,
> Invariably follow one another—
> [Those people are the honest ones].

The *asura* Valāka, known as the golden-clad one, violated the system of laws acknowledged in the three realms. Consequently, although he had obtained special powers, he was ultimately slain by Viṣṇu, the lion of men, in keeping with the above analogy about the inevitability of seeds and sprouts following each other.

Once upon a time the leader of the asuras, the golden-clad protector of beings, Kāśyapa Valāka, propitiated the mighty god Śiva for a hundred thousand years. At last he attained special wrathful capabilities and Śiva said to him, "I shall grant you supreme powers. Anything you desire I can give to you."

Valāka said, "I desire special force such that I cannot be killed either inside or outside the house, on the ground or in the sky, during the day or the night, by humans or nonhumans, by weapons or nonweapons, or by hand." Śiva granted him this just as he wished.

Many of Valāka's sons grew old and died. One day Valāka summoned one son, still young.

"Praise me if you know how," Valāka growled at him, "and if you do not, I shall kill you. Usually a son's needs are met when the father dies. But I am not going to die, so what can my son do about it?"

The youth listened, but fearing that whatever he said would displease his father, he had not the courage to praise him, so he slipped away. At this time Viṣṇu, having taken the form of an ordinary person, happened to be nearby and the boy went to see him. As Viṣṇu questioned him, the boy related in detail the events that had occurred.

"I can teach you how to honor your father," said Viṣṇu. The boy was delighted and requested that he do so.

Viṣṇu said, "Return to your house just as the sun is going down behind the mountain pass. Build a large throne on the threshold of the door, and seat your father upon it. Take your place before him and hail him in this way:

> In the mountains live the sages;
> In the waters live the water spirits;
> At the crossroads lives Śiva, and
> Śiva is the one who pervades everything.

Having received these instructions, the young boy went before his father and did exactly as directed, putting his father on the throne and honoring him with the verse. But the verse praised the all-pervader and not the father. This made the father very angry.

"If the all-pervader is everywhere," he thundered, "is he even in this place?" and he struck his fist on the threshold. Instantly a crack appeared, from which issued an emanation of Viṣṇu, Narasiṃha, the lion of men. He had a human body, with the head of a lion—antidotes to the special power he had earlier granted Valāka so that he could not be killed by humans or nonhumans. He had hands with steel claws as antidotes to the special powers not to be killed by weapons or nonweapons. Because they were on the threshold, Valāka was neither inside nor outside the house, and as an antidote to not being killed on the ground or in the sky, Viṣṇu pulled Valāka onto his lap. As an antidote to not being killed either during the day or night, and to not be killed by hands, just as the sun was setting Viṣṇu grasped Valāka with his claws and killed him. In this way, all the protective capacities that had earlier been bestowed upon him were overcome.

It is essential to understand that ridding oneself of the ten nonvirtuous actions is the basis of living according to the law. Because the laws of cause and effect are just as reliable as the upper and lower pans of a balance scale, it is very important to act with decorum, upholding the excellent principles of spiritual and worldly affairs as carefully as if one were protecting one's own eyes.

288   When an excess of intelligence
       Makes one too involved, one ruins oneself.
       A king with too many ideas
       Brings much degradation to the land.

There are disadvantages to knowing too much. Some people have an excess of information and an overabundance of ideas gleaned from whatever they have studied. They initiate every conceivable kind of project, believing they can do absolutely anything. But ultimately they achieve nothing at all because, like those who grab wildly at fish and birds, they try to do too many things at once and end up dissipated and ineffective. For example, often in this world certain high officials are seen to wreak havoc in their jurisdictions because they have too many ideas about what needs to be done that stack up one atop the other. As cited in verse 16, some great masters have said,

One must proceed in accordance with the lines on one's forehead.

Similarly, as cited above in verse 285, consider also:

One starts many different things; none are completed.
A lot of hasty ideas is what leads one to trouble.

In general, the later steps to a task cannot be undertaken unless the preliminary steps have been completed. More particularly, one must understand that no matter how great one's wisdom, it is critical to do things by aligning one's ability and power with one's karma and merit.

289   The wealth one has accumulated to excess
       Becomes one's executioner.
       Mostly the rich experience downfall,
       While beggars move about happily.

Amassing extravagant wealth makes one miserable. Some people are obsessed with the indiscriminate and tasteless piling up of assets over the years, paying no attention to bad language, ill deeds, or shamelessness. Ultimately their wealth turns into the executioner that takes away their lives. Generally most of the present and future difficulties that torment people only befall the rich; poor beggars can actually be observed going about free of the three sufferings associated with wealth—first acquiring it, then guarding it, and finally losing it. Some great masters have said,

> The mind is tormented when overly attached to riches;
> Be content, not totally preoccupied with wealth!

These days destitute beggars are cast aside like blades of grass at an intersection, while immoderate riches become the foundation of hardship. The best kind of happiness is to remain content within one's capacities.

290   Becoming excessively powerful
       Is preparation for one's own suicide.
       Death on the battlefield
       Often befalls the mighty.

Even excessive power can be one's own executioner. When with utter disregard for all wrongdoing, the very brave become too powerful and terrorize others, they are literally throwing away their lives, formulating their own suicide as if by drowning, self-immolation, or leaping to their death. Well-known heroes killed in battle are often forceful individuals of great courage.

    Avoid bad conduct that derives from excessive courage, confidently work at ways of clearing away previous wrongdoings, and avoid committing faulty actions in the future. Everyone is subject to the power of karma.

291   Wealth, wisdom, and power
       Are aids to those with virtues.
       But for anyone lacking virtues,
       They all are a cause of ruin.

In this world, such things as power, wealth, and wisdom seem to be positive attributes, and indeed are very helpful for those with merit and good karma, clearly beneficial to themselves and others, now and in the future. Yet if one does not radiate the fortunate karma of previously accumulated merit, even apparently positive things become obstacles. It is clear to everyone that these factors often cause people to degenerate, leading to their own destruction and that of others as well.

Without the critical element of merit, accumulated wealth and intelligence are not generally seen to enable people to achieve their objectives. Thus it seems particularly important to work very hard in any way one can to accumulate merit and supporting karma.

292   No matter what tasks the wise undertake,
       They first check their merit, then act.
       In troubled times splendid merit is rare,
       Even for one person in a hundred.

Although the wise can perform any task large or small, they analyze a situation with regard to their karma and merit before proceeding. Should they undertake any activity with calculating, duplicitous greed, whatever they accomplish is a measure of their foolishness and spawns deception for themselves and others.

In these times of strife, those who have the support of merit and who achieve marvelous things are rare individuals, perhaps not even one or two people out of a hundred. There is no way to fully realize any of one's desires without both confident analysis and having such merit that the outcome seems to arise spontaneously. Thus it is important first to pay attention to a spiritual guide and the Three Jewels of refuge, then to apply oneself to tasks that are consistent with one's merit.

293   If a substandard pond is filled with water
       One of its embankments will surely collapse.
       Likewise, an enduring family line is rare
       For anybody who is rich.

Consummate achievement of good fortune is rare if someone lacks merit. When a pond in poor condition is completely filled, inevitably the water will break through a weakened bank, thus voiding the purpose of the pond. Similarly, some people may have obtained a lot of wealth by one means or another, but they seldom have children to carry on their ancestral lineage, and so must confront the question of adoption.

294   People with children seldom have wealth;
        If they do they are ruined by enemies.
        When good fortune has been fully achieved,
        One usually dies at an early age.

People of good lineage may have children to carry on their family name, but nonetheless they might be plagued by poverty and find it difficult to raise them. Those who do have both children and wealth can be ruined by inner and outer adversaries. When one is fortunate in every respect, enjoying things like money and household servants, it is often noted that family members— perhaps the husband and wife—meet with untimely death. It is critical, therefore, to make every possible effort to avoid negative karmic actions and engage in positive ones. This is the basis of merit.

295   Therefore, the wise accumulate virtues,
        The sole precondition for prosperity.
        Wherever anybody has good fortune,
        That indicates the accrual of virtues.

The disadvantages of having no supportive merit noted above inspire the wise, who correctly understand the nature of causes and their effects, to accumulate the twofold collection of merit and wisdom. This is not mere appearance, like bubbles of empty talk or rainbows of empty meaning, but accords with how things actually are in the world. It is said that genuine merit is the only thing that brings about complete good fortune and fulfills the wishes of those who have it. There are people who need never exert so much as a hair of effort to earn others' respect; nor do they need to employ cunning, deceit, dishonesty, others' influence, or bribes of wealth or food. Everyone regards them as leaders and bestows good fortune upon them, yet still they remain worthy of admiration. This is understood to be a sign that in previous lives they accumulated genuine merit.

296   When one thinks, "I deceived others by lying,"
        One really deceives oneself.
        The telling of a single falsehood
        Prompts mistrust when later one is truthful.

Dishonorable speech has its negative consequences. Without considering the long-range implications, certain shameless people mislead others with duplicity and lies in order to gain some minor short-term objective. When their goal is achieved they think, "Ha, ha! I succeeded in fooling them." In fact, they only fool themselves. Once someone is known to be a liar, even if later they speak the truth, it is suspect. Honor and circumspect speech are very important, while those who lie and deceive are worthless everywhere, so one should conscientiously avoid dishonesty and guile and not lose control of one's tongue. Be careful and do not talk too much.

297   One who gets angry and berates others
      Without carefully checking what is right or wrong
      Is like the pigeon who killed his wife,
      Then agonized over the loss of her companionship.

Some people lack the wisdom to examine things carefully and analyze the distinctions between good and bad. They become irate at the slightest provocation, then with furrowed brow and indignant expression they beat others and humiliate them with foul language directly to their faces. Such people are fated to live in hardship later on because they will end up miserable and all alone. Sakya Pandita says in *A Classification of People*,

The harm that the evil-minded inflict on others
Is the spark that ignites the dry tree trunk.

Once upon a time there was a pigeon who lived with his wife in the forest. When springtime came they sought and gathered some fruits, which they stored at a certain place. Then the husband left his wife to guard their cache. Later when he returned, the pile of fruit had shrunk in size.

"You have eaten all this fruit!" the pigeon exclaimed.

"I did not eat a single one!" his wife protested, but her husband would not listen. Without looking into the matter, he beat her and pecked her with his beak until she died.

The following year at fruiting season the pigeon gathered fruit as he had before and filled his storehouse. Again his pile of fruit appeared to decrease but this time, because he had no one to blame, he investigated the situation. To his dismay, he discovered that the volume had been lost because the fruit had dried and shriveled up.

"Oh my!" he thought to himself, "My wife really was not at fault!" and he was overcome with grief. Now some of the youthful deities of that forest sing,

The pigeon who dwelt in the forest
Had multi-colored wings and red eyes.
Without inquiring into right and wrong
He killed his wife, then lived in misery.

The many advantages of thorough investigation have been presented in earlier verses; here is taught the disadvantage of insufficient investigation. Take care not to be rash, getting angry with people before analyzing the circumstances.

298   Without overanalyzing the future,
       Work hard when the time comes.
       Why take off your shoes
       Before you reach the river?

In accordance with examples set by those who attain their goals, generally one should consider the future and determine at the outset whether some contemplated action is worth doing or not. Then at a suitable time one must stop evaluating, not be lazy, and put great effort into achieving one's purpose. Some great masters have said,

> Do not be preoccupied with desires for the future.
> Obsessed with these ambitions,
> One is like the father of Dawa Drakpa.

When walking down the road one removes one's shoes upon reaching the river, but it would be nonsensical to do so before then.

It is unfitting to strive for some objective without considering the reasons; one should think from the beginning about the future results of a course of action. However, when the time is right it is essential to be diligent in carrying out the task.

299   One should not start things that, though worthy,
       Cannot be completed in the future.
       A food may taste delicious,
       But if indigestible, who will eat it?

Failing to consider whether or not an objective is achievable is a fault; some tasks cannot be completed no matter how they are executed. It is inappropriate to undertake such activities, however worthwhile they may seem. Besides the fruitless effort expended, both time and intellectual energy are wasted. Who would eat food that is very tasty but is indigestible or contaminated with disease-causing bacteria? No intelligent person who can anticipate what the future holds would do that!

Thinking that one's aspirations must be achieved immediately is futile, yet it is important to strive for meaningful goals that do not waste one's life or intelligence.

300   Sitting around and avoiding hard work,
           Nothing is achieved for either this or future lives.
           Even though the fields are excellent,
           Good harvests are not obtained without effort.

Some people are lazy and lack interest in wholesome activities, living a life of leisure by shunning any hard work that would lead to constructive ends. They achieve nothing useful for this life nor any happiness for future lives. Rarely do they secure for themselves so much as simple food and drink, let alone anything of longer-range benefit. Sakya Pandita says,

Even water is remote from the mouths of the lazy.

Without physical or verbal exertion one cannot obtain the benefit of a good harvest, even if one has fine fields inherited from ancestors or awarded by the king. Realizing that effort is what determines whether or not well-being is achieved, never forsake working hard to accomplish present and future objectives.

301   When too subdued in the wrong situation,
           One is taken advantage of by all.
           Cotton is used for mattresses;
           Who would use sticks for a bed?

It is important to know when to be yielding or stern depending on time and circumstances. Practicing physical, verbal, and mental restraint and acting humbly to please others is generally the superior conduct of noble, decent people. However, if at times and in situations where this is inappropriate one is overly timid and unable even to stand up straight, then others assume one is lowly and can be enslaved like a horse or donkey, thus rendering meaningless one's precious human existence. Cotton is very soft, so everybody prefers sleeping on cotton mattresses and treading on them barefoot; no one would stretch out on a mattress made of hard sticks!

302   Foolish are those who commit evil deeds,
           Attempt the impossible, or request others do so.
           Who trusts somebody that buys poisonous potions?
           Who can say, "I will give away everything!"?

If one undertakes evil deeds with no concern about avoiding the ten non-virtues or the five boundless actions, one is a fool who does not know right from wrong and is not considered a Buddhist practitioner. Sometimes people take upon themselves such endeavors and then are unable to persevere, lack the time, or otherwise cannot complete them; yet when they order others to carry out these projects and their instructions are followed, it is another matter entirely. Then they are extremely ignorant fools who do not realize their own limitations. What person who cherishes their life would have confidence in someone who blithely procures a poisonous potion in order to gradually kill themselves? Likewise, would any normal, sensible person declare, "I am giving away everything I own. Come and take anything you want!" Nobody in their right mind would say such a thing!

Prudent people refrain from wrongdoing, take delight in being wholesome, avoid bad activities in which it is inappropriate to be involved, and do not even consider deceiving either themselves or others.

303   Amassing wealth but not putting it to good use
       Is like gathering firewood to incinerate oneself.
       Bees, when they fail to consume their own honey
       And others carry it off, are killing themselves.

If one is unable to use riches properly, it is usually the cause of one's downfall. Some dissatisfied people accumulate assets, shamelessly using every means at their disposal, yet fail to put their efforts to good use, benefiting neither themselves nor others in this or future lives. Such are the riches of deficient merit—an accumulation of nonvirtue that is actually like firewood: during this life, it burns day and night with the flames of misery from first accumulating, then protecting, and finally losing wealth; and in future lives, it burns with the flames of unfortunate states of rebirth. When the lowly honeybee, which gathers lots of nectar-laden honey, neither eats nor enjoys that honey and someone else takes it away, it is as if the bee committed suicide with no regard for its own life. The great masters of old from India and Tibet unanimously declare,

The Buddha, teacher of celestial beings and humans,
Taught that contentment is the supreme of all riches.

Therefore, one should be satisfied with whatever wealth one has obtained in accordance with one's previously accumulated merit, and put it to good use. Moreover, one must take great care that one's wealth is applied in ways that do not lead to faulty, unwholesome actions.

Chapter 8 ~
AN EXAMINATION *of* DEEDS

304   When bright people perform even minor works,
        They always consult others before acting.
        Even unfinished tasks bring them dignity,
        To say nothing of things they complete.

Intelligent people always undertake minor tasks (to say nothing of major ones) by first discussing them in advance with those who are experienced in such matters. Needless to say, whatever they accomplish is done well. But if, when all issues have been fully explored, a task still cannot be completed due to significant problems, they nonetheless retain respect and credibility with others and there are no grounds for ridicule. It should be the intention of good, careful workers to carry out any task through experimentation and deliberating with others.

305   Because people have different inclinations
        It is hard for anyone to please everybody,
        But those with good personal qualities
        Are most likely to make others happy.

One can have harmonious relationships with everybody by developing special virtuous qualities in oneself. In general the habits, ideas, and preferences of beings living in the three realms of the universe differ; in particular, the self-interest and malice of those living during this time of the five degeneracies is extreme. Consequently, it is difficult to find anybody who is known as "the one who pleases everyone." According to Śāntideva in *Engaging in the Bodhisattva Deeds,*

        If even the Buddha cannot satisfy
        The varied wants of sentient beings,

Why even mention a bad person like me?
Thus, I should set aside worldly thoughts.

However, if one aspires to the standards set by the buddhas and bodhisattvas of old and by the accomplished masters and bodhisattva kings and ministers of historical India and Tibet, and if one becomes learned through studying the various Buddhist and non-Buddhist sciences that are rightfully praised by the wise, it is the nature of things that one then comes closest to having cultivated positive attributes that hearten everyone. Therefore, follow also the superb example of the modern approach to progress: waste neither time nor intellect, and work hard in every possible way to develop good personal qualities.

306   Even those who have grown very old
Should continue to improve their knowledge.
The benefit for future lives just from learning
Is even greater than that from charity.

There are advantages that come from learning. Young people should enrich their knowledge while their thinking is precise, their memory good, and their intelligence sharp. But even those who are very old, hollow-looking, and need to walk with a cane should continue to develop their knowledge of the stainless scriptures through integrating study, contemplation, and meditation. The omniscient Shalupa says,

Not being an unlearned meditator (a handless rock-climber),
Nor a logician prone to dry explanations of the Dharma,
Since I alternate learning, contemplation, and meditation,
I delight in following the examples of the masters of old.

With this perspective, consider the benefits that arise from learning that accrue not just in this life but in all future lives as well. How can making charitable gifts of all outer and inner riches possibly be as helpful? Sakya Pandita says,

The intelligent ones who investigate things well
Study for many lifetimes,
Rely upon many wise people, and
Fearlessly master all that should be known.

In brief, it is widely declared,

Learning is the lamp that dispels the darkness of ignorance.

Once upon a time there was an abbot who lived in a temple. "As I see it," he thought to himself, "I am elderly and totally uneducated. What can an ignorant one like me possibly do?"

He decided to seek learning, but when he applied himself to the task, Dharmapāla, the king of the region, shook a dry stick under his nose and said derisively, "When an old man such as you becomes wise through studying hard, this will bear fruit."

Hearing these words made the old abbot even more determined, just as beating a beast with an iron bar makes it run faster. He prayed to the Conqueror Mañjuśrī, who bestowed blessings upon him. In just seven days he became very wise. He went before Dharmapāla and said, "Now take the fruit from your dry stick." The king was astounded. He paid the abbot great honor, and the old abbot became highly respected by everyone.

307   Either rely on those who are fully learned,
       Or enjoy the friendship of common folk.
       Water jugs that are completely full or
       Completely empty are easiest to carry.

It is important to make the effort to seek out and depend upon reputable teachers. Whichever master one commits to, in general their knowledge should be fully developed; in particular, their physical, verbal, and mental conduct should be subdued, their character should be influenced by the altruistic attitude of enlightenment, and they should be impartial and honest. *The Condensed Perfection of Wisdom Sutra (Prajñāpāramitāratnaguṇasaṃcayagāthā)* states,

> Good students who respect spiritual masters
> Must always rely on those wise masters.
> Why? The knowledge of the wise comes from that;
> They instruct in the perfection of wisdom.

On the other hand, if such a spiritual master is not found, one should befriend ordinary people who recite the six-syllable mantra *Oṃ maṇi padme hūṃ* with a good heart, live happily, and are not draped with the defects of having broken their commitments. Water jugs are easily carried if they are either completely full—their intended function—or completely empty.

308   Who could place their confidence
       In those with but little knowledge?

Who would carry upon their head
A jug only half filled with water?

Some individuals may have learned a fraction of what should be known, but
their knowledge has engendered no improvements to their physical, verbal,
or mental conduct and may have made them worse. Who would rely on such
people of corrupt character? Their actions of body, speech, and mind are not
moderated and their pride in possessing a little knowledge merely increases
their attachment. Sakya Pandita says in *Advice I Give to Myself (rang gis rang
la gros 'debs pa)*,[143]

Primarily influenced by nothing but personal interests,
Many ill-mannered people are consumed by anger and attachment,
Which study, contemplation, and meditation only exacerbate—
Translator, contemplate well the true nature of reality.

Who would walk around carrying on their head a jug only half full of water?
The sloshing back and forth makes the task difficult. So work hard at truly
depending on the wise who have subdued their minds.

309   Knowing how to complete a task
        By understanding well the difference
        Between noble and coarse individuals
        Is the foundation of all good fortune.

Before undertaking anything, it is necessary to ascertain the strengths and
weaknesses of others. Trustworthy people with honorable aspirations are the
foundation on which the twofold collection of merit and wisdom for this
and future lives is established. They engage in constructive behavior that pro-
duces helpful results. Coarse people, on the other hand, are the basis of ruin
for oneself and others; their negative actions result in errors and failures. One
should clearly distinguish the difference between these two. Knowing how to
be discriminating in this way—and actually practicing it—is the great foun-
dation of all good fortune, present and future. The Sakya Pandita says in *A
Classification of People*,

Whoever embarks on a task
Having first drawn good conclusions
About future advantages and disadvantages,
Is one who can investigate things.

310   When well cared for by the wise,
        Even coarse people can achieve excellence.
        When trained by one who knows how to teach,
        Even a parrot can learn to talk.

Whoever aspires to greatness needs to depend on honest intelligent people
who have the enlightened attitude to help others. When well protected and
nurtured by such people, even those of poor intelligence (to say nothing of
the bright ones) will eventually become outstanding and earn everyone's
respect. An astute trainer can teach even parrots, the lowest of creatures, not
only human speech but also to recite some words of the sacred Dharma.

311   Even the lowly and weak will succeed
        When they rely on others who are great.
        Not even tiny drops of water dry up
        When mixed together with the sea.

Insignificant people who are utterly powerless in thought and action need to
rely on those of great intelligence. They must not be lazy and think to them-
selves, "I am so weak! For me to get a chance to accomplish the great objec-
tive of present and future happiness is exceedingly difficult, even if I put forth
a lot of effort." Śāntideva says in *Engaging in the Bodhisattva Deeds,*

        Do not be indolent and say,
        "How can I ever achieve enlightenment?"

When lowly people depend on others who are important and powerful, and
work hard to rid themselves of sloth, one day even they will definitely achieve
their desired objectives, provided they do not waste their time and effort. A
drop of water is by nature insignificant and powerless, but if it mingles with
the inexhaustible ocean it will never disappear, so long as the ocean exists.
Therefore, it is clearly important for the weak to rely on the great.

312   When one is lacking in understanding,
        Question well those of great understanding.
        If enemies cannot be killed by hand,
        Are weapons not used against them?

Some people lack both inborn and acquired intelligence and cannot accom-
plish anything at all, or else perform their work with excessive zeal. Were
they to properly question their more perceptive colleagues before making

decisions, all their specific and general undertakings would become mean-
ingful. When bare hands cannot be used to slay an enemy that definitely
needs to be destroyed, are weapons like knives and spears not employed as
means of doing them in? Of course, that is what must be done!

Those deficient in wisdom should not sit around stupidly or persist in fool-
ish behavior. They should strive to personally meet and question the wise
who have been well schooled, as well as distinguished elders who carry on the
traditions of excellence.

313   Though enemies are harmful,
        If one has skill they can be befriended.
        Though strong poison will harm the body,
        It can be medicine if correctly prepared.

An enemy may until now have been harmful in every conceivable way, thwart-
ing one's aspirations or provoking aggravations. Nonetheless, Sakya Pandita
says,

        Appear pleasant to enemies, though anger be in your heart;
        Later an even better method will be available.

If one is well meaning and deft in conduct, has a pleasant demeanor, and is gen-
tle with one's words, it is the nature of personal relationships that eventually
a friendship will develop that is mutually beneficial. Usually strong poison is
seriously life-threatening to the body; but if one knows a skillful way of pro-
cessing the poison, it can be transformed into life-sustaining medicine instead.

Those who are called the friends and enemies of this life are as illusory as
a painting of a butter lamp. Regard them thus, and cultivate the resourceful
and skillful means of greeting others with a smile, without making any dis-
tinction between friend and foe.

314   Accept wealth that has been properly acquired,
        But do not covet others' things; they should not be taken.
        Pick fruit directly from the tree,
        But let what has fallen stay on the ground.

Food, wealth, even ordinary items for daily use—all these should be accept-
ed only if they have been obtained in a correct and harmonious manner. Oth-
ers' wealth should be viewed as poison, and avaricious thoughts toward it are
to be avoided. Being even briefly desirous brings about the ruin of one's
future. To freely enjoy the fruits one wants to eat by taking them from the

tree is fine, but it is improper to use fruit that has fallen on the ground and become covered with dust. Some great masters have said,

> When graced with unattachment to illusory wealth,
> One's necessities are ample without hoarding,
> There is no entrapment in the eight worldly obsessions,
> And joy comes from following the masters of old.

Attachments to this short life bring neither prestige nor riches, and both present and future lives are destroyed. Do not be attached to inappropriate kinds of wealth.

315   Misfortune befalls the wise
        So long as they fail to persevere.
        But when the wise persevere greatly,
        The chances for misfortune are slim.

Knowledgeable people comprehend that actions and their effects are as unfailing as the upper and lower pans of a balance scale, and that should they fail to adhere to their vowed commitments, careless discrimination and poor conduct can cause them all sorts of difficulty. They guard their commitments just as they would protect their own eyes, remembering to examine repeatedly their physical, verbal, and mental conduct. Consequently, chances are slim they will transgress their vows since they are mindful to distinguish between what they should do and what must be avoided. Some great masters have said,

> Realizing that actions and their results are as infallible
> As a balance scale, exercise proper discrimination.

And,

> Properly follow advice that accords with good principles;
> Those who break their commitments are worse than dogs.

One should investigate one's own faults, not delve into those of others. Having focused well on the basic principle of abandoning the ten nonvirtuous actions, abide in practicing the genuine ten virtues.

316   "While strength is partial respect your foes;
        Once you have become fully capable
        Take whatever approach works best."
        Some treatises offer this advice.[144]

Whether enemies should be respected or attacked depends on an assessment of one's own abilities. Some other commentaries assert, "Until one's capacity to combat any foe whatsoever is fully developed, one must respect enemies and please them. However, once one's strength is wholly adequate, one should confront the enemy with any gentle or wrathful means at one's disposal." But in our tradition, as stated in verse 313,

> Though enemies are harmful,
> If one has skill they can be befriended.

Just as strong poison can be transformed into medicine, there are excellent methods that transform enemies into friends. Make effort to apply them.

317   Even when enemies speak sweetly,
        The intelligent do not believe them.
        Herons and cats, by being stealthy,
        Always try to kill other creatures.

Certain enemies exhibit friendly mannerisms—a humble demeanor, a smiling face, pleasant words—but since they may be untrustworthy and inwardly harbor ill will, intelligent people do not trust mere physical and verbal impressions before thoroughly investigating. Creatures like herons and cats concentrate day and night on keeping a peaceful outward appearance to achieve their inner objective of killing the fish and birds they desire. People of these degenerate times lack any sense of shame, so do not trust hateful adversaries before scrutinizing them.

318   Even if the ruler of the land is hostile,
        One should stay on and graciously serve.
        Even if one's leg slips on the ground,
        One still needs the ground for support.

No matter how irascible the leaders of the land become, their subjects must remain close to them, treating them pleasantly, because no one has the right to live in a country without supporting its ruler. When somebody's leg slips on the ground, they still must rely on the ground for support; without it there is no chance to stand anywhere else! Uphold the rulers of the land by behaving properly, not breaking laws, and respecting discipline.

319   By being greedy for desirable things,
        People quickly destroy themselves.

> By being so enticed by meat on a hook,
> Fish are instantly killed.

Being covetous, discontented, and excessively attached to the enjoyment of desirable things makes anyone—from the powerful to the weak—quickly decline and come to ruin. Such people are indeed heard of and seen on this earth. Due to their weakness of being attracted to a bit of bait on a fisherman's iron hook, fish meet with a quick end.

Being attached to great temptation is a fiendish attitude; therefore, some great masters have said,

> Death's hour is uncertain, like a dewdrop on the grass,
> So by all means, give little thought to trivial matters.

Likewise, make every effort simply to remain content. Pay minimal attention to irrelevant things, and recollect the unpredictability of the time of death.

320   Those worthy of honor along with their retinue
       Gather followers because they are always generous.
       All beings from gods to pretas
       Gladly protect those who give tormas.

To derive the essence from illusory wealth it is necessary to be diligent about spiritual offerings and philanthropy. Contentment with what they have causes some people who have a little wealth to be generous with everyone, ranging from those most worthy of spiritual offerings to the lowest, most in need of compassion. Additionally, those who are temporarily servants and others who are well-off gather followers and merit by always giving away such things as food and drink—the best way to assemble people.

The highest recipients of offering are spiritual masters, the tutelary deity, and the Three Precious Jewels. From offering pure, stainless torma cakes to them one receives these blessings: pleasing the celestial beings, completing the collections of merit and wisdom, cleansing the two obscurations, and gaining both the common and supreme attainments. Likewise when one offers torma cakes regularly to the lesser recipients of offering (the guests) and to the lowest recipients (flesh-eating pretas), they all happily and respectfully keep their promises to shelter one from obstacles and to provide for one's needs.

One's primary responsibility is to complete the twofold collection of merit and wisdom for this and future lives. Therefore, one must joyfully make spiritual offerings to those worthy of them and be charitable to those in need.

321   The great rid themselves of attachment
         To frivolity, pleasure, and food.
         As punishment for attachment to desirable things,
         It is said that Rāvaṇa of Lanka was killed.

This verse illustrates the penalty for important people who fail to rid them-
selves of attachment to daydreaming and fleeting pleasures. High ranking
officials accomplished in all temporal and spiritual matters should avoid being
preoccupied day and night with amusements like mahjong or dice, and should
not be attached to the temporary pleasures derived from food, clothing, sil-
ver, and gold. Otherwise, the consequences will be broken spiritual com-
mitments, an impoverished household, failed public enterprises, and
ultimately, loss of the country to the hands of the enemy. Unimaginable
calamities like these are actually heard about and observed, generating regret
that burns like fire. Rāvaṇa, the king of Lanka, was slain by King Rāma and
his army as punishment for attachment to temporary pleasures.

Once upon a time Rāvaṇa was king of the land of Lanka. Even though he
had been propitiating the great god Śiva for a very long time, he had achieved
no results. His failure so tormented him that he cut off his ten heads one by
one and offered them in a fire-ritual ceremony.

This came to Śiva's attention, and he said to his wife Umā, "Go to the king
and give him spiritual attainments."

So she went to the king and told him, "I shall give you whatever you desire."

"But I made my propitiations to the great god Śiva," the king protested.

"I was sent by Śiva," Umā replied.

"I do not want any spiritual attainments from a woman!" bellowed the king.

This so enraged Umā that she cursed him, "In the future may your king-
dom be destroyed by a woman," and departed.

Next Śiva sent his son. When he appeared before the king and said the same
thing as Umā had, the king replied as before. The son was also furious. "In
the future may your kingdom be destroyed by monkey-beings!" he swore, and
then he also departed.

Next, Śiva himself went to the king. "What do you desire?" he asked.

But the king was still angry. "Your compassion is very small!" he snapped,
and continued with his fire offering.

"The reason I have come here now is to give you whatever you want," Śiva
persisted.

"Well then," the king said, "I want the multi-tiered iron fence that offers
threefold protection against being destroyed by the ocean, the fire pit, the
army of cannibal demons, the king of the gods of wealth, or by Aśvinī, the
divine physician with a dog's body."

Śiva could see that what the king really wanted was the spiritual attainment of immortality, so he spoke in a melodic but deceptive way. He told the king that his stated desire for immortality would not be fulfilled should his horse's head be cut off. The king agreed.

Some time later a daughter was born to the king. A Brahmin revealed to him that this was a bad omen, and that it would not be suitable for the girl to stay in the kingdom. Without a moment's hesitation, the king placed his daughter in a copper box and set it in the river.

The box was carried to India, the continent south of Mount Sumeru. It was summer and the farmers were irrigating their fields. They found the box at an irrigation canal field turnout and opened it up. Discovering a little girl inside the box, they named her "The One Who Was Found in a Furrow."

She became a very beautiful young maiden. After some discussion, the farmers decided to offer her to the king of their land. His name was Rāma, and he was pleased with his wife, who became known as Sītā.

After some years Rāma and Sītā wearied of the royal life and wished to devote themselves instead to spiritual practice. Rāma gave his kingdom to his older brother, who was rather interested in worldly matters. But then his brother complained, "If you who are king cannot remain here in the kingdom, how can I be attached to this place? I am going with you to meditate on the Dharma."

So they turned the kingdom over to a younger, third brother named Bharata, and the two brothers and Sītā went into the forest to dwell among the ascetics.

Some time later Rāvaṇa appeared, abducted Sītā (together with the ground she was standing on), and returned with his prize to the land of Lanka.

Now, the forest where Rāma lived was filled throughout with many monkeys. Among them was a tall monkey with three eyes called Hanuman. Rāma sought him out and related what had happened. Hanuman took stock of the situation and with a single leap arrived in the realm of the gods of the wind. With another such leap, he arrived in the land of Lanka. Looking around he saw Sītā, imprisoned in a fruit garden.

"Why is she confined in this way?" Hanuman asked the guards.

"She was put there because she was impolite to the king," the guards replied. "She dared to say to him, 'You are the king of the cannibal demons and I am the noblewoman of the king of men.'"

Hearing that, Hanuman went to Sītā. "Will you believe that I have been sent here by your king?" he asked her.

"No, I don't believe you," she declared.

Hanuman then dug into his pockets and pulled out King Rāma's gold ring. "Look at this," he said.

"I came to this place after being seized by the cannibal demon, and I cannot

escape by myself," responded Sītā desperately. "Take me away from here if
you have the power to do so!"

"First, give me some food," demanded the monkey

"But I have no food," Sītā cried. "All this fruit belongs to the king." Normally
she would refuse to take what had not been given to her, but on this occa-
sion she chose a fruit and held it out to Hanuman, who gobbled it right up.
"You are a very greedy monkey," she observed.

Hanuman ate a little more, then uprooted all the fruit trees in the garden
and thrust them back into the ground upside down.

"A very mischievous monkey is in the orchard!" the cannibal demons
shouted. Gathering together, they surrounded Hanuman and closed in on
him. He tried many times to jump away; finally they threatened to kill him,
and began to debate among themselves how best to carry out the deed.

"I know you follow the laws of the king," Hanuman interrupted, "but I
also have two traditions of killing. I would like to die according to my own
tradition, so please use the most suitable one to kill me."

"Well," snarled the cannibal demons, "what are the two traditions?"

"There is the father system and the mother system," Hanuman answered.
"According to the mother system, I should be put in a pantry, fed all kinds
of delicious food, and ultimately strangled to death. If the father system is
used, my tail should be wrapped in cloth, dunked in butter, then set afire,
and that will kill me."

The cannibal demons discussed these options and decided to use the father
system. But as they wrapped his tail with cloth, it grew longer and longer and
longer. Soon they had used up all the cloth in the kingdom, but Hanuman's tail
still was not completely covered. Determined to proceed, they completely doused
it with oil and set it ablaze. The monkey swished his giant flaming tail and
instantly melted the entire kingdom of the cannibal demons along with all their
palaces. Then he sat down in the ocean and extinguished the fire on his tail.

Without a moment's delay, Hanuman jumped into the air and landed
before Rāma. He reported to Rāma why Sītā could not come. "I must lead
the army into battle!" Rāma proclaimed.

Arriving at the ocean shore, Hanuman gathered together all the ordinary
monkeys to build a bridge spanning the ocean. Then King Rāma and his army
marched across the bridge and summoned Rāvaṇa and his retinue. As they
argued back and forth, Rāma cut off the head of Rāvaṇa's horse, and Rāvaṇa,
in keeping with the modified attainment granted him by Śiva, was dead.

At that time the younger brother of the ten-necked Rāvaṇa named Khum-
bakarna was in one of his six-month sleeping periods and difficult to rouse.
Some of the cannibal demons poured molten bronze in his ear. "What is
going on here?" he bellowed, instantly awake.

They told him the story of his older brother being killed. Enraged, Khumbakarna inhaled mightily with a tremendous rush of wind that tore the flesh off everyone, rendering them nothing but skeletons. Only Rāma and Hanuman withstood the tempest. Khumbakarna, however, was satisfied and went back to sleep.

King Rāma then advised the monkey to fly to the snow mountains to bring back some medicine. At first he returned with the wrong medicine, and was again dispatched on his quest. This time he came back bearing the entire mountain. The medicine was gathered from its slopes, and it brought back to life Rāma's entire army that had been slain by Khumbakarna. Rāma then bid Hanuman to replace the mountain where he had found it.

"That will be very difficult," Hanuman grumbled. Nonetheless he proceeded, and telekinetically hurled the mountain back to its original location. To this day, that mountain's peak leans a little to one side, because as it was sailing through the sky back to where it came from, a small piece broke off and fell to earth in the western Tibetan province of Töd (stod). That is now the famous Mount Kailash.

From then on Rāma and Sītā lived happily in their land. It is said that Rāvaṇa met his fate due to the two curses placed on him by Śiva's wife Umā and her son.

This legend is related here in the abbreviated version heard by Tonpa Jetsun Chenpo from the Hindu guru, Mar.

There are two diametrically opposed ways that those in high-ranking positions can discharge their duties: they can assume responsibility for increasing their own and others' good fortune by honestly determining what is most beneficial for the future, following the ways of the wise who uphold the exemplary traditions and keeping their attention on excellence; or they can destroy themselves and others by considering only immediate obstacles, being influenced by bad examples, paying regard to evil, and plunging into confusion. Clearly, it is vitally important that they conduct themselves carefully, adopting the former and rejecting the latter of these two approaches.

322   In both congenial and contentious matters,
        Deal with great people, never the coarse.
        Regarding matters of buying and selling,
        Deal with valuables, not deadly concoctions.

One can engage with others either by being friendly and holding everyone in high regard, or by being hostile and declaring, "I am so and so! You did such and such!" Whichever approach one takes, interacting with superior individuals who have knowledge, ability, and power will certainly bring about significant results. These results can be good or bad—victory comes from the first approach and defeat from the latter! On the other hand, never be sympathetic or argumentative with base people lacking in knowledge, ability, and power—from that there is little potential for gain or loss. Similarly, if one trades in gold or silver, one might become wealthy or lose a fortune, but there is no advantage to trading in poisonous concoctions; nothing significant is accomplished except the grave wrongdoing of killing, which is ruinous to both this and future lifetimes.

Having a positive outlook is the basis of good personal qualities, so it is best if one can do meditational retreats to cultivate altruism. Otherwise, when engaged in temporal or spiritual affairs, realize that a great wave of potential comes from being involved with exceptional people, irrespective of whether that involvement is on good or bad terms.

323   For adequate revenue, the royal vault is filled
        With small taxes, not excessive ones;
        Little by little, anthills, beehives,
        And the waxing moon become full.

Kings need to levy an appropriate and limited amount of taxes. Since the land is vast and the people are numerous, in order for tax revenues to be adequate the citizenry will not be burdened and the royal treasury will be filled if taxation is conducted by collecting very modest taxes rather than exorbitant ones. It can be seen that anthills, beehives, and the waxing moon fill up incrementally without difficulty.

324   A ruler should collect taxes from the populace
        In a fair manner that does not oppress them.
        If too much of its fragrant resin drips away,
        Then the *sal* tree[145] itself will dry up.

Rulers who treat their subjects kindly can generate dependable revenues by implementing suitable taxation that never encumbers the citizens. In this way both the rulers and their subjects benefit and neither are harmed, as explained above. But if a different approach is taken to raise revenues wherein many new taxes are levied under a variety of different names, people become impoverished. They suffer physically and mentally, leave their country, and live abroad for the rest of their lives. Then the rulers are deprived of their subjects, and the situation becomes utterly pathetic for everybody! The sal tree has resin that is used in making incense. If too much of this resin is drawn off, the tree will eventually dry up and there is no hope it will ever be of any use at all.

325   Rulers especially must be even-tempered;
        It is petty to be angered by trifles.
        Even if a snake had a gem on its head,
        What sensible person would stand before it?

Workers in general and especially the rulers of the land should be honest, kind, and composed. When someone commits a small error, rather than pointing out the fault, they should keep criticisms to themselves and treat the offender kindly. Even if they have gathered many supporters by being generous, irascible rulers cannot depend on their subjects. Ultimately, the people will become so embittered that they will counterattack, perhaps even going so far as assassination. As Śāntideva says in *Engaging in the Bodhisattva Deeds*,

        [As for those who depend on him
        For the kindness of wealth and respect]
        Even they will fight to the death
        The ruler who is possessed by anger.

        That brings his friends and relatives to grief;
        His generosity attracts, but he is not served.
        [In brief, there is no angry person
        Who dwells in happiness.]

A precious wish-fulfilling jewel may rest on the head of a poisonous snake, but the snake's venom would cause one's death before use could be made of such a treasure. Who would linger within striking distance to snatch it away? Certainly no reasonable person would attempt such a thing!

Anger makes it impossible for rulers ever to abide in peace, so it is essential that they have a steady disposition.

326   Anyone who desires prosperity
        Should first and foremost safeguard the Dharma.
        How can mere wealth that debases the Dharma
        Ever endure, even in this life?

Riches lacking the wealth of virtue have no lasting stability. Those who desire to end their impoverishment and get rich should be motivated by altruism, keep the three kinds of ethical practices in high regard, depend on the excellent merit field, and otherwise uphold the preeminence of the Dharma. By protecting their wealth and avoiding greed, they should seek externally to generate great waves of good works for others and internally to develop broad-mindedness. Nāgārjuna's advice is,

> Generosity creates wealth.

On the other hand, some assets can be accumulated by violating the standards of Dharma—by being miserly, aiding coarse-mannered people, denigrating the law of actions and results, and caring not at all for future lives. Can such ill-gotten riches reliably endure, even in this short life? Not a chance!

327 Do not be overly affectionate, even to friends,
   Nor excessively harmful, even to enemies.
   Expectations of friends are the basis of disputes;
   Retaliation is easy for anyone.

One should think fondly of friends, relatives, and, indeed, one's own children and treat them well, but should not care for them with excessive devotion. Nor should one seek out ways of being unduly harmful to one's enemies, such as enacting oppressive laws that threaten their well-being. There are good reasons for this. Extravagant attention lavished on friends and relatives gives rise to expectations that can never be fulfilled, resulting in disputes and violations of tradition. Anyone upon whom harm has been inflicted will readily take revenge. Therefore, some great masters have said,

> Recognizing as one's parents all sentient beings vast as space,
> Meditate continuously on love and compassion.

328 Gentleness will pacify the temperate
   And even quell the uncouth.
   Because gentleness can accomplish anything,
   The wise say, "Gentleness itself is sharp!"

In undertaking any task, strive to utilize gentle, pleasing modes of body, speech, and mind. A mild approach will subdue those whose manner is moderate but whose intentions may be sinister; obstacles are surmounted and one's wishes are achieved. Even coarse-minded, angry people are disarmed because they have no chance to respond. Udbhaṭasiddhasvāmin says in *The Especially Exalted Praise,*

> You will triumph without spears or wheel-shaped weapons
> Because the weapon of love is superior.

All wise people who know how things really are say unanimously, "Since gentleness that accords with the Dharma accomplishes all that is good in both cyclic existence and nirvāṇa, that gentleness itself is a keen edge for achieving one's objectives without deceit."

Leave aside the broad task of meeting one's own and others' goals; one should focus on cultivating a peaceful disposition by completely ridding oneself of the flames of anger that scorch the minds of oneself and others.

329   Even if you are disliked by others,
       Do not announce, "He is my enemy!"
       Or "So and so is unkind to me!"
       Mentioning such things exposes oneself.

It is inappropriate to speak carelessly about those with whom one is on unfriendly terms. Some people say, "This person always harms me and never gives me any help." Others say, "That person doesn't like me at all." However, these feelings should be confidential, not openly discussed. When such matters are indiscreetly publicized, others can see right through you and know all about your private affairs.

Talking openly about whatever comes to mind concerning all the good and bad things one does is an idiotic character trait and should be avoided. Try to keep personal matters private.

330   Do not reside in those kinds of places
       Where people are oblivious to modesty and shame,
       Cannot distinguish between reverence and contempt,
       And desire only wealth and food.

There are three kinds of places where sensible individuals avoid living because the inhabitants are unadorned by good personal qualities. In the first, people are careless and lack any sense of shame in the presence of others. They act disgustingly and are unconcerned about rude behavior. In the second, people misunderstand the difference between what is superior and what is vulgar, erroneously assuming one to be the other. (Superior individuals are honorable and respectable, and hold the celestial beings, spiritual teachers, and Three Jewels as lasting sources of refuge throughout their lifetimes. Coarse individuals are contemptuous and mean, and permanently ruin their present and future lifetimes by committing the ten nonvirtuous actions and the five boundless transgressions.) In the third kind of place, people chase around after mere morsels of food and drink like swine and street dogs, fighting angrily over meaningless issues and having inordinate attachment to wealth.

All these situations propagate lawlessness, vile behavior, and obliviousness to the inevitability of death. Rather than live amid such evil where the degeneration of one's present and future lifetimes is guaranteed, seek out places that have the opposite, auspicious qualities.

331   One should not vacate one's original residence
        Without properly investigating other places first.
        If one's leg is not properly positioned,
        When the second leg is raised, one falls down!

One should never completely abandon one's home and run off after enticements and rumors spread by others. When planning to move elsewhere, first thoroughly investigate the conditions of the new place, like the short- and long-term quality of the land and water. If one relocates and then discovers that the land and water are poor, one has no place to return to and must remain, suffering great regret. If while walking one tries to take another step before one's foot is firmly planted, one may experience the miserable result of having both legs raised at the same time—a broken leg!

In any activity, by paying close attention to what has transpired and what is to come, analyze situations carefully in advance so excessive regret is not encountered later.

332   Strive to keep behavior low-key;
        Being demonstrative usually leads to decline.
        If a monkey did not dance,
        Why else would a rope be tied around its neck?

It is common practice to conceal bad behavior so that others will be unlikely to know about it, but indeed, all one's conduct—physical, verbal, and mental—should be veiled. Even minor good actions should remain hidden and not paraded before others. Most people clearly reveal themselves by showing off their knowledge in an arrogant, self-centered way. Consequently they fall under others' control and become weak with misery, not knowing whether to stay put or to go away. Monkeys climb up and down and dance about in various ways, so monkey handlers capture them and tie them on a leash. Deprived of the freedom to move around or rest as they wish, the monkeys grow wretched and pathetic. But if they had not put on such a show in the first place, would there be any reason to tether them? It would be totally pointless!

Sakya Pandita says, "One may have good qualities, but concealing ambition has long-ranging benefits." If one's conduct is truly good, it is like gold underground that radiates its presence to the heavens. One should seriously focus on ways to rid oneself of egocentric pretensions.

333   Even if someone does witness wrongdoing,
       It should not be discussed with the wrong people.
       Common people swear misfortune befalls those
       Who talk about bad omens they have seen.

Hapless persons of bad character are sometimes directly observed violating the temporal and spiritual laws of the land. One may be tempted to point out their mistakes and to explain the advantages of enhancing their virtues and diminishing their vices. But it is unsuitable to talk about these things with such individuals; they are as ill-tempered as wild elephants. Ordinary people declare, "Those who are corrupt groundlessly accuse good people when misfortune occurs or when they see an inauspicious omen. That is their way of talking! But the result of such shameless words is that misfortune visits those who utter them." According to Sakya Pandita in *Advice I Give to Myself*, the learned say,

       If someone speaks pleasantly, others speak well of them;
       If someone speaks coarsely, a cloud of enemies gather;
       If someone remains silent, the scowls of others dissolve—
       Translator, regard the fruits of your words.

It is necessary to know with whom it is appropriate to discuss matters of right and wrong. One can try to reform badly behaved people in the best possible way, but when that is futile, it is preferable to sit quietly and say nothing. To do otherwise inflames the passions of everyone involved.

334   Of what use are food and riches
       That everyone else despises?
       What wise individual would crave
       The filthy fare of dogs and swine?

Reasonable people are not critical on the basis of unjustifiable things like jealousy. Of what use to them would be food and riches derived from robbery, deception, and butchery? Such serious misconduct arises only from bad acts and deeds whose very nature is abhorred by others. Involvement in such acts out of admiration and desire for such food and riches is no different from flies swarming on rotting things or worms gathered in garbage. What reasonable, wise person would even consider eating the disgusting things that dogs and pigs consume, like excrement and urine? Not one would ever do such a thing! Suffering is unbearable whether it occurs during this short lifetime or in lifetimes far into the future. Therefore, one should always purge oneself of any attraction to the fruits of wrongful conduct.

335   Words that strike to the heart of someone
      Ought not to be spoken, even to foes.
      Just like an echo, the censure of others
      Will immediately return to oneself.

Intentionally harmful strong words that fall directly on target should never be spoken to hateful enemies, to say nothing of one's friends. Sakya Pandita advises,

> Do not be excessively angry with enemies;
> Though one can do so, retribution will follow.

Those who harbor evil thoughts and speak evil words deceive themselves; they will reap the fruits of their acts. Retribution for malicious speech in particular will immediately be experienced, because the consequences of one's actions occur very swiftly in these degenerate times. It is just like an echo that bounces right back at someone who goes out in the forest or mountains and sings, talks, laughs, or cries. Having gained firm understanding of karma and how the ultimate effects of one's deeds come about, one will avoid thoughts and actions that hurt others, even enemies.

336   If one wishes to harm an enemy,
      One must possess good personal qualities.
      They will exasperate the enemy
      And increase one's own stock of merit.

If one wishes to harm one's enemies decisively, first one must be replete with good qualities—learnedness in the Buddhist and non-Buddhist sciences that enables one to prove oneself to others. Such an attribute, absent in one's enemies, will undermine their courage and sear their minds, subjecting them to unbearable suffering. Indeed, this not only destroys the enemies, but increases one's own store of merit, benefiting both present and future. Therefore, concentrate on developing good personal qualities by getting rid of malevolent thoughts that lead ultimately to meaningless, unfortunate consequences.

337 First generate the enlightened attitude,
   Then quell fierce people with harsh measures.
   Those who desire to heal their bodies
   Cure disease by bloodletting and surgery.

Some individuals are violent and cruel because of bad companions and former negative actions. They do not follow the path of excellence even when they are skillfully supported. To tame such persons, spiritual masters and temporal officials internally generate the altruistic enlightened attitude and the twofold contemplation on love (wishing others to be happy) and compassion (wishing that they be free from misery). Externally they employ severe measures, like binding and beating. The tradition of the sages is to use whatever means are deftly appropriate to enhance what is virtuous and diminish what is unwholesome in others. Some people have bodily ailments that cannot effectively be treated by gentle methods, so they must be cured with heat applications, bloodletting, and operations if they desire the benefits of being free of disease. Sakya Pandita says,

   Doting on malicious people,
   Not correcting children and students,
   Not meditating on the wheel of protection,
   And failing to recite wrathful mantra—
   Because these contradict all the tantras
   They are not the supreme form of love.

It is essential to subdue ruthless, brutal people by whatever peaceful or wrathful means are required since kind, even-handed treatment is inappropriate for them.

338 Even minor wrongs, when committed,
   Must be promptly and persuasively rectified.
   Once water starts to flow in a ditch,
   Are not flooding gullies then seen?

Animosity, bad speech, or bad behavior are the foundation of future misfortune. These should be clarified and reconciled at the outset while they are still simple trifles, because later they can turn into enormous, intractable problems. If the flow of water through a small channel is not controlled, a deep ravine will develop and the water will be impossible to stop. This has actually been seen to happen. Sakya Pandita says,

Some people are well cared for with food and clothing,
But their resentment, continuous thievery,
Ill-will toward leaders, and bad attitudes
Lead them to ruin in cyclic existence.

Just as it is necessary to extinguish fires while they are small, strive by all
means to promptly rectify inappropriate wrongful acts. One's efforts should
be neither postponed nor sluggishly applied.

339   The wise do not commit wrongful acts
        Even though they know how to do so.
        Since elephants destroy their enemies,
        See how kings always keep them chained.

The wise use reasoning and scriptural authority to fully understand all tem-
poral and spiritual matters, like how wholesome and unwholesome actions
cause pleasant and unpleasant results respectively. They never engage in
endeavors that would be inappropriate for them, such as commerce, farm-
ing,[146] and other activities wherein friends are favored, enemies destroyed,
and dissension generated. They know how to do these things, but they also
know that such deeds ruin the present and future lives of everyone: them-
selves, their helpers, the important, the lowly, the strong, and the weak. If they
do become thus engaged, they are not putting their knowledge into practice;
therefore they are known as "the wise who carry in their mouths the law of
actions and their effects," but are actually indistinguishable from fools who
discredit this law. Elephants will charge at whatever they think is an enemy,
even strangers who are inappropriate targets. For this reason kings always
keep them tied up, not just to prevent them from doing things they should
not do, but to control their acceptable behavior as well. Just observe how
people are fearful around elephants! There are many legends that reinforce
this example.

     Those who would claim to be wise must never commit wrongful acts, even
if they do nothing else that supports the teachings of the Buddha or helps
other sentient beings.

340   Do not abandon allies even if they are troublesome;
        Do not be nice to enemies even if they are kind.
        Crows may harass each other,
        But if they rely on owls they are ruined.

Do not err in distinguishing friends from foes. An enemy who has long been a dependable antagonist is generally preferable to a friend who is greatly enamored with making new acquaintances at the expense of old ones. True allies, however, should not be abandoned even if they are prone to sudden outbursts of anger, because, as a Tibetan proverb states, "Perhaps they cannot be with us when we're sick, but they don't avoid us at the time of our death." Moreover, one should not delight in affability with someone who is a hostile enemy; although they may seem pleasant at the moment, their hearts are malevolent.

Some crows come to ruin when they abandon their own kind and go off to cultivate friendships with the alien owls. The owl king who was destroyed by trusting the crow minister[147] surely exemplifies the fault of acting contrary to convention. It is crucial to analyze advantages and disadvantages, both short and long term, of whatever is popular in the world so as not to confuse reliable friends with unreliable enemies.

341   No matter what size tasks the wise undertake,
       They always concentrate on what they do.
       The lion is unwaveringly attentive
       Whether killing rabbits or elephants.

Anything worth doing should be done with careful concentration. One can labor at the great purpose of attaining the state of release from cyclic existence —nirvāṇa—that benefits oneself and others, or be busy with some lesser task, achieving a measure of temporary happiness free of discomfort. But capable wise people know that whatever they are doing, it is necessary to stay focused until reaching their goal, and see no difference between small, easy tasks needing little thought, and large, difficult ones demanding their undivided attention. For the king of beasts, killing small rabbits is easy and requires minimal concern, while killing large elephants is hard to do without careful deliberation. Yet lions simply regard elephants and rabbits equally as prey and concentrate on their hunting without making distinctions between the two until their objectives have been achieved.

There are many ways to fail, whether one is carefully concentrating on major tasks or casually doing minor ones, so make a serious effort to conscientiously complete all undertakings.

342   What wise person would reside somewhere
       Where the learned are not respected?
       Is it possible to sell crystals
       In a land where they are used as flints?[148]

Only misguided fools like to dwell in misguided places where no respect is accorded those who are especially gentle, conscientious, and have fully mastered all knowledge of spiritual and temporal matters. Except for those oppressed by karma, would any discerning person choose to live where the perspectives and behavior of the wise and the ignorant are totally at odds? There are lands inhabited by uneducated people who use crystals as flint to light fires. How could merchants possibly sell crystals in a place where the difference between the nature of water and fire is not understood? According to Sakya Pandita in *A Classification of People,*

> Alas! In those imperfect places
> Much fancied by imperfect people,
> The filthy water dogs drink is favored
> To water with the eight special qualities.

343   The wise either explain things to others
> Or meditate in secluded forests.
> Jewels either adorn crown ornaments
> Or remain on remote ocean isles.

The wise undergo great hardship to rely properly on distinguished spiritual teachers. Once they are well trained in the sutras and tantras, they must carry on the teachings of the Buddha in two ways: first, to sustain the precious transmission of scriptural teachings extant in oral and written form, they should explain to aspiring students the full meaning of the different classes of tantra along with the Tripiṭaka; second, to sustain the precious transmission of the insight teachings, they should reside in remote forests and mountains and engage in the practices that quiet discursive thought like anger and attachment, and develop the two stages and three higher trainings, which, when achieved, indicate meditative stabilization. Vasubandhu says in the *Treasury of Knowledge (Abhidharmakośakārikā),*

> The excellent teachings of the Buddha have a twofold nature:
> Scriptural transmission and insight transmission.
> The only ones who uphold this teaching
> Are those who practice it themselves and teach it to others.

And as said in the *Sutra on Individual Liberation,*

> Of the learned who abide in the forest,
> The mature ones dwell there in peace.

Precious wish-fulfilling jewels that satisfy all desires are used in two ways: they are retrieved from the ocean with great hardship and offered as crown ornaments for the top of a victory banner, thereby becoming an adornment of virtue for all lands; or they remain on the jewel islands of the great ocean. Truly wise people (not just in name only) work diligently to uphold the perfect victory banner of these two aspects of the Buddha's teachings from which arise all well-being: the scriptural transmission of teaching others and the insight transmission of spiritual realization in oneself.

344   There are personal advantages to be gained
       From depending on those sages superior to oneself.
       The birds who dwell on the slopes of Mount Sumeru
       Become as radiant as gold.

Anyone whose knowledge is limited should rely intimately on excellent spiritual teachers whose good qualities gained from collecting merit and wisdom are more highly developed than his own. Such personal attributes include knowledge of spiritual and temporal matters, skillful means, the superior intention to free all sentient beings from cyclic existence, integrity, and a sense of shame. By so doing, those of insufficient learning rid themselves of faults, perfect their knowledge, and acquire the nature of someone whose personal qualities are beneficial both in the present and the future. According to Maitreya,

    Rely on spiritual teachers who have renunciation,
    Perfect pacification, superior knowledge, perseverance,
    Scriptural enrichment, realization of emptiness,
    Skillful speech, compassion, and resolve.

The bodhisattva Thogmay Zangpo says in *Thirty-Seven Practices of All Buddha's Sons (rgyal sras lag len so bdun),*

    If one relies on a spiritual teacher, one's faults disappear
    And one's good qualities increase like the waxing moon;
    It is the bodhisattvas' practice to cherish
    Their spiritual teachers more than their own bodies.

It is well known that the birds that live on the slopes of golden Mount Sumeru develop a golden hue due to the power of perfection that pervades their dwelling place. This is true of all birds that live on golden mountains.

Whoever desires to be fully human should avoid behaving like an idiot who knows nothing at all or having pride in just a little bit of understanding.

Rather, one should rely on the sages whose learning surpasses one's own and work hard to enrich oneself with the superior knowledge of spiritual and temporal affairs.

345   One does not achieve greatness oneself
        By serving those who are great but jealous.
        See how the moon wanes
        When it draws near the radiant sun.

Trust those who, as described above, are compassionate, honest, and have the superior intention to free all sentient beings from cyclic existence. Do not rely on jealous people who are great in name only, dominated by carelessness, shamelessness, and superficial learning, and surrounded by a mob of angry, armed followers. Even if one serves them properly, their dearth of good qualities like altruism and the superior intention, and other unseemly faults like jealousy, make it impossible for one ever to attain that noble state of possessing exceptional knowledge of temporal and spiritual matters. During its waxing stage the moon is called the "Guardian of the Night." It is positioned far from the sun and its full mandala shines with great white light. But when the moon has waned, forget about its radiating light, the moon itself does not appear and the sky is empty. Also, when the moon's orb eclipses the sun, see how the moon does not appear at all.

346   Who could possibly associate
        With any friend who was undependable?
        Rainbows in the sky have beautiful colors,
        But wishing them as adornments is a fool's delusion.

These days certain individuals are by nature unreliable and dishonest, influenced by winds of praise from fickle companions who disguise their intentions with hypocrisy and readily strike up new friendships at the expense of old ones. Those who analyze situations carefully would never befriend someone who is erratic, adversarial, and persuaded by the slightest bit of slander. They pay no attention to such people because they cannot be trusted! Some great masters have said,

> These days, because most people are enthralled by new friends,
> There is a danger of being duped by nonsense,
> So do not show your concerns to others without careful inquiry.
> First investigate; when truly confident, commit your innermost
>   heart.

The glorious colors of a rainbow in the sky appear fleetingly due to the power of the four elements. To hope that rainbows could be adornments to beautify people is more ridiculous than the fantasies of an unconscious fool who clings to mere appearances as if they were real. Those who abandon ignorance and investigate things carefully should try to associate with people of highly esteemed character who are as stable as mountains and immutable as gold.

347   Whatever one personally dislikes
        Should never be done to others;
        Think instead of how one feels
        When slightly harmed by others.

One should never inflict on others anything that one experiences as unpleasant or unwanted, such as heat, cold, hunger, thirst, disease, and pain. Others will retaliate since they also seek happiness and dislike suffering. Consider how badly one feels when hurt in some small way, such as having one's own desires thwarted or aggravations provoked. Some great masters have said,

        Considering the example of one's own body,
        One should not subject others to harm.

It is imperative to keep in one's heart a genuine feeling of wanting to help others and to spontaneously quell any malevolent impulses to hurt others that may arise.

348   Whenever people bestow on others
        What they themselves find pleasing,
        Others will treat them nicely in return:
        This is the way to be respectful.

If one gives to others the same things that are agreeable and useful to one's own prestige and welfare, present and future, those who benefit will reciprocate. This way of offering is the very essence of honoring others. *The Ornament for Sutra* gives the example of how clever bodhisattvas achieve their own objectives by working for the sake of others. Śāntideva says in *Engaging in the Bodhisattva Deeds,*

        Whatever happiness there is in the world
        Arises from desiring others to be happy.
        Whatever suffering there is in the world
        Arises from desiring oneself to be happy.[149]

There is no need to say much about this.
The childish act in their own interests,
But the Buddha acts in the interest of others;
Just see the difference between these two!

349   The wise neither befriend nor dispute
Those who are savagely cruel.
Examine and abandon both
Animosity and intimacy.

Those who can neither listen nor comprehend and are oblivious to recollecting the past and predicting the future think it is best to persist in achieving their goals as soon as the thought occurs to them. But wise people who can discern the advantages and disadvantages of present and future situations should neither argue with belligerent individuals nor be amiable and trusting. It is often the case that engaging them in any way brings misfortune upon both oneself and others.

Whether disputing with others or relying on them as intimates, proceed with care by thoroughly analyzing present circumstances and future possibilities. Impulsive action—contentious or affectionate—is inappropriate. The tendencies of people these days seem so strange, as Sakya Pandita says in *A Classification of People,*

Those who are thoroughly steeped
In ignorance, dishonesty, and misery
Are unable to distinguish right from wrong.
These days the habits of fools prevail.

Avoid acting senselessly, and work hard to develop the wisdom to honestly discriminate between right and wrong.

350   Relying on people of excellence,
Asking questions of the wise,
And befriending those of good character:
Whoever does this is always happy.

One should place one's confidence in those who are learned, respectable, refined, and have proper conduct of body, speech, and mind; make contact with and question those who have extensive experience in all temporal and spiritual matters and have mastered subjects one should know such as the Buddhist and non-Buddhist sciences; and lastly, associate with reliable companions who maintain decorum. The fortunate ones who maintain such relationships with others will be continually happy and achieve their ultimate objectives. Conversely, continuous discomfort ensues from those many affiliations with individuals lacking these traits. In general, Sakya Pandita says in *Advice I Give to Myself*,

> Many relationships cause us to be bound: teacher and student,
> Priest and patron, relatives, friends, servants, attendants;
> Mutual interdependence is always troublesome—
> Translator, behold the nature of cyclic existence.

Clearly, it is important at the outset of any activity to investigate carefully the advantages and disadvantages that may arise, rather than acting rashly and later regretting what one has done.

351   Whatever is said at awkward times
       Is held in disdain by all.
       Is it not inferred that someone is mad
       From the fact that they talk too much?

Some people will arrogantly speak out without evaluating whether the time and occasion are fitting to do so. Censured by all who discern the circumstances, their words are considered absurd and they are excluded from discussions. When someone rants on recklessly saying whatever pops into their heads regardless of the situation, are they not deemed insane? Of course! Some great masters have said,

> Excessive talk and crude language is said to be
> The gesture which beckons the enemy.

Sakya Pandita also says,

> One is excluded from discussion groups if one talks too much;
> Therefore, speak sparingly.

Intelligent people avoid being garrulous; one must reflect on what is relevant and then speak up without blathering on about any idea that comes to mind.

352   Modest people presume that everything
       They have to say could be mistaken.
       Thinking this way, they say little;
       Such people get more respect than others.

Polite, unassuming people with noble thoughts and good behavior are concerned that what they say could be in error, unhelpful, or hurtful. With such perception, they are able to limit what they say, keep their ideas to themselves, and do not indulge in senseless chatter. Many trustworthy and honorable people prefer their company to that of talkative, cocky individuals. However, one should not speak so little that one becomes mute! Rather, one should rid oneself of hurtful speech that benefits no one, and when it is necessary to say a few words, always think carefully about their effect. To know how to speak in this manner is essential.

353   When the time and place are appropriate,
      Focus your thoughts and speak sparingly.
      Even good advice, when given to excess,
      Loses its value like unsold merchandise.

Being a person of few words generally has the advantage of winning praise from others. However, when the time and audience are right one should be impartial, attentive, and decisive about the right course of action, and then say a few words that are sure to achieve good results. Failing to take this approach, even if one is offering good advice helpful to both oneself and others, one might unreasonably talk on and on, oblivious to whether the time or the person to whom one is speaking is suitable. Then one's words are as worthless as a merchant's unsold wares, or like songs repeated over and over to which nobody listens.

One should avoid talking excessively on topics about which one lacks the slightest comprehension of good and bad. When the time is right, make a few cogent remarks; then one's intentions will certainly be realized.

354   To see one's own faults as faults
      Is very hard, even for the wise.
      When many say that one has defects,
      It shows what they say may be true.

It is rare for somebody to understand their own shortcomings. Even wise people who are well trained in what needs to be known (to say nothing of the ignorant) find it very difficult to perceive their own physical, verbal, and mental deficiencies. This is because most people do not carefully examine themselves, or they arrogantly believe that they know everything.

When just one or two people remark on some imperfection, it is probably due to jealousy and so forth. But if many people mention that one has certain unseemly characteristics, it likely indicates that one really does indeed have faults needing to be acknowledged and remedied. The bodhisattva Thogmay Zangpo says in *Thirty-Seven Practices of All Buddha's Sons,*

> If one fails to examine one's own errors
> One can even be a phony monk doing worldly work.
> Thus, the bodhisattvas' practice is to eradicate faults,
> Baring them to continuous scrutiny.

Pay careful attention to all physical, verbal, and mental conduct, whether sleeping, sitting, going somewhere, or merely dallying, and strive to be aware of any failings.

355   To know one's faults but not to shed them
        Means one is possessed by demons;
        And those who fail to remedy their faults
        Cannot be considered human.

Some people are aware of their own shortcomings yet do nothing to eliminate the errors that are so destructive to their minds. Like those who deliberately commit suicide through self-immolation, drowning, or throwing themselves from cliffs, it is as if they are possessed by evil spirits. Otherwise normal people of sound intelligence may not be possessed by spirits, yet they still refuse to employ the counteractive measures that could rid them of their weaknesses. Without the precious ability to conduct themselves properly, engaging in constructive acts and avoiding destructive ones, they cannot be considered human beings. Either they are animals who do not know how to judge, or they are barbarians who, in spite of knowing, fail to exercise discrimination between what they should and should not do.

    In order to differentiate your actions from those of animals, strive to be aware of your own faults and rely on corrective practices to transform them.

356   Even those of limited intelligence
        Should analyze their faults and eliminate them.
        By implementing the antidotes in this way
        They increasingly enhance themselves.

Those with deficient intellectual abilities who desire to achieve well-being in this and future lives should avoid being lazy and carefully investigate their physical, verbal, and mental conduct. When they discover weaknesses, they can apply antidotes that either temporarily suppress or completely eliminate inferior tendencies. Whoever practices such suitable measures proceeds to increasingly refined stages of happiness such as high status and definite goodness. Śāntideva says in *Engaging in the Bodhisattva Deeds,*

> By mounting the steed of the enlightened attitude
> That clears away all sadness and troubles,
> One attains higher and higher stages of happiness.
> What sensible person would be lazy about this?

357   Others may be intelligent or compassionate,
      Heed advice or be courageous;
      Even if one cannot do these things,
      One should emulate each one of them.

It is well and good that some people have innate and acquired intelligence, know how to maintain harmonious relationships with people, and have kind hearts that see only the good side of others. Others, like patients listening to a doctor's instructions, conscientiously heed the advice of wise, compassionate, altruistic people on what to do and what to avoid, and they, quite rightly, apply intelligence, boldness, and determination to anything that engages them. But there are others who, although in general they are good, decent people of commendable conduct, may not be able to perform well the excellent deeds that safeguard without contradiction the distinguished traditions of spiritual and temporal affairs. Nonetheless, they should support such practices, follow the example of the wise who know how to do these things, and ignore those who do not.

358   One may have long associated with boorish people,
      But happiness comes when they are abandoned.
      "One may have a fine tooth," the elders say,
      "But if it is always loose, extracting it brings happiness."

Some people maintain long amiable relationships with individuals who are ugly, irascible, and always see faults in others; they should cease being enamored by the fleeting pleasures of such companions and forsake them. Such unsavory characters may seem entertaining for awhile, but in fact they are the worst sort of associates—unpredictable, ignorant of their own capacities, and inclined to foist disagreeable tasks upon others. The elders say, "A tooth that always wiggles back and forth may look very nice, but the slightest bit of hot or cold makes it unbearably painful. Therefore, relief is gained only when it is extracted." Sakya Pandita says in *A Classification of People,*

Careless, fickle, and having poor judgment,
Mean, fault-finding people quarrel with others.
Abandon them; they are similar to crows
With their coarse language and unpleasant visage.

It is best not to associate with offensive people who are shameless, ungrateful, boast of all the good they have done for others, and then talk about others' shortcomings.

359   Pests who always hang around and irritate others
Should be given a little something and sent away.
A finger that has been bitten by a snake
Will take one's life if it cannot be amputated.

Self-inflated, bothersome individuals, commonly not well regarded, might perform some minor service for someone and then hang around bragging about all they have accomplished. They should be given some small token such as food or clothing and skillfully dispatched elsewhere; such presumptuous, unruly people can be extremely destructive. When a poisonous snake bites, one must endure the pain and quickly excise that part of the body that was struck, or the poison will spread throughout one's system. It would be most tragic if in the end one were to die.

360   Upon achieving a position of importance,
Avoid stinginess and give others small gifts.
When one has become ruler of the land,
Why be greedy for material things?

Having realized significant status, one should eschew being miserly and, in keeping with time and circumstances, present modest gifts both to society in general and to specific individuals. Otherwise one becomes guilty of conduct inconsistent with one's prestige. When they become great and consolidate power in a region, do sovereigns not give away precious gems? Of course! Are they parsimonious at such times? Of course not!

Important people are obliged to care for their supporters in any way suitable. By being calm, broad-minded, neither angry nor attached, and treating everyone impartially, they should work hard to rid themselves of miserliness.

361   If the wise desire to accumulate wealth,
The best way to guard it is to give some away.
If one wants to increase the flow from a well,
It is advised to draw off some water.

When wise people who are unconfused about causes and effects want to augment their resources and guard against diminishment of present assets, the best way is to offer a portion of their worth to spiritual teachers and the Three Jewels, and to donate a portion as charity for the poor and destitute. Ārya Nāgārjuna says,

> Generosity creates wealth.

The Venerable Candrakīrti says in his *Supplement to (Nāgārjuna's) "Treatise on the Middle,"*

> Though all beings desire true happiness,
> Without prosperity, there is no human happiness.
> Understanding that wealth ensues from generosity,
> The Buddha first discoursed on being charitable.

Thogmay Zangpo taught,

> Rejoice in whatever wealth you have:
> It can really enable meritorious virtuous deeds.
> Whatever well-being is yours, present and future,
> Is certain to be the fruit of merit.

Should one desire more water to be available for use, it is said that repeatedly drawing water from the well will encourage the flow.

362   Whosoever desires worldly affluence
        Must be engaged in many endeavors.
        But if petty distractions are seen to bring misery,
        Then abandon aspirations for prosperity.

If one wishes to be surrounded by abundant riches that satisfy all one's desires, one must be engaged in many activities that generate wealth, such as business ventures that bring high returns from small investments. Yet the physical and mental fatigue of the petty distractions required to accumulate assets can make one as frustrated and miserable as trying to catch ripples on the water with bare hands. If the energy to get rich is lacking, one must forsake the hope of being prosperous so that others' wealth has no appeal. Then the preoccupations of materialistic entanglements can be cast aside like grass shoots trampled at a busy crossroads, and instead one can aspire to the sublime prosperity of complete liberation through the power of the blessings of the supreme sources of refuge. Some great masters have said,

The power of sublime refuge—the lama and Three Jewels—brings
Joy in a meaningful human life that shuns useless busyness,
No mental distraction over a clutter of mundane entailments, and
Pleasure from following the examples of the masters of old.

363   No matter what task you set out to accomplish,
       Consider both its advantages and disadvantages.
       If a task should be avoided when they are equal,
       What need be said when disadvantages prevail?

In any undertaking, whether for oneself or others, one must consider the disadvantages and advantages that will result from its completion. First, one must generally assess what may or may not be achieved, then analyze the magnitude of the short- and long-term consequences, and reflect at the outset on whether the effects of a particular task were good or bad in the past, and whether they are likely to be good or bad in the future. When a task is being done for others, one must imagine whether the impact of the anticipated results would be favorable or unfavorable if one had personally to experience them.

When one investigates situations in this way and finds that the advantages and disadvantages of carrying out a particular task are about equal, one should abandon the task because one's objectives cannot be met. Needless to say, when the advantages are outweighed by the disadvantages, any endeavor is obviously unnecessary! As previously mentioned, however, a special case exists when even though a task has short-term disadvantages, it should be done if its long-term advantages are significant.

Try by all means to distinguish what should be done from what should be avoided by thinking over any possible outcome of an activity before actually undertaking it. That is the best way of doing things without regret.

364   Rely respectfully on those who are wise and honest;
       But if a wise person is known to be tricky, take care.
       Treat kindly those who are ignorant and honest;
       But if an ignorant person is known to be tricky, leave quickly!

There are wise people who are by nature honest, have mastered what needs to be learned, and whose physical, verbal, and mental behavior accords with the Dharma. With polite words and deeds one should sincerely rely on them, not forsaking them even at the cost of one's life. In *The Condensed Perfection of Wisdom Sutra,* it is taught,

> Good students who respect spiritual masters
> Must always rely on those wise masters.
> Why? The knowledge of the wise comes from that;
> They instruct in the perfection of wisdom.

Yet if it is known that someone who appears wise externally is a fraud within, then by all means be careful of them. Because of the deficient karma and merit of sentient beings in these degenerate times, deceitful people are numerous and are commonly regarded as superior. Sakya Pandita says,

> It appears that merchants who seek wealth from wealth
> Are castigated and called deceptive,
> But the fraudulent who seek wealth from dishonesty
> Are called marvelous and greatly honored.

Likewise, uneducated people with an honest nature should be treated kindly in every way; they have been one's close relatives in limitless former lifetimes. But those who superficially seem like idiots yet are inwardly cunning must be hastily abandoned. Devious fools are like dry kindling, able to ignite chaos for themselves and others.

One must ascertain the individual natures of both the wise and the ignorant as honest or deceitful, then strive to discern unerringly whom to associate with and whom to avoid.

365   Even though one may lack wealth and attendants,
   With intelligent friends one achieves one's goals.
   If this is the case even for animals,
   Needless to say it is so for humans.

One may not enjoy riches and retinue, but with fine, enduring friends who are dependable, straightforward, and have the intelligence to discriminate between right and wrong, one's short- and long-term objectives can be accomplished. As portrayed in verse 311,

> Even the lowly and weak will succeed
> When they rely on others who are great.
> Not even tiny drops of water dry up
> When mixed together with the sea.

If ignorant, mute animals can fulfill a specific purpose when they have good friends, what need to mention that thinking, articulate human beings are likewise able?

Please understand, it is important to associate with truly intelligent friends whether or not one happens to have the good fortune of wealth and attendants.

366   Engage those who know how to do things;
       Do not assign tasks to the inept.
       Chariots cannot run in water;
       How can a boat travel on land?

Temporal or spiritual tasks that need to be done should be given to those able to carry them out with a pure attitude and a clear understanding of what is being asked of them. Devoted and conscientious people are competent at accomplishing both their own and others' goals. However, antagonistic, irresponsible fools who lack both time and ability should not be designated to carry out even a few chores. They deceive both themselves and others, and are a source of distress for all. Some great masters have said,

       Regret occurs when work is assigned to the irresponsible;
       Trouble occurs when advice is given to the disaffected.

Just as chariots are not taken into water because they cannot function there, so boats are not used on land because they are not thus designed.

Analyze in advance whether someone is suited to being entrusted with the responsibilities of a task, then delegate such duties only to the right person at the right time.

367   Even if old spiteful foes are friendly,
       One must never mingle with them.
       Even if water is at full boil,
       Does it not douse fire on contact?

One might have a bitter enemy for many years due to one reason or other, then in time both parties weary of their animosity. One day this person may try to be friendly, but one should not be trusting or discuss secrets the moment he or she seems amiable. All arguments that eventually arise in a relationship usually stem from excessive closeness at the beginning. Boiling water has the same hot nature as fire. But is a fire not extinguished as soon as hot water comes into contact with it? Sakya Pandita says in *A Classification of People,*

> We say, "We are friends with them,"
> And tell them all our secrets.
> Carelessly speaking of such matters publicly
> Is like putting mercury in a leaky container.

Some great masters have said,

> It is revolting when we tell secrets as soon as we are friends,
> Then talk of one another's faults as soon as we are fighting!

There are many who entice others by immediately being friendly and care-free, and then when the time comes, deceive them. Be cautious and exercise self-control.

368   Responsible people with a sense of shame,
      Can be relied on even if enemies.
      Someone once sought refuge from a dependable foe
      Who gave protection even at risk to his own life.

A long-standing, dependable enemy is always preferable to a friend who becomes infatuated with new relationships at the expense of old ones. It is fitting to trust dependable individuals who once were hated enemies, provided they feel personal shame for any wrongful acts they have committed and are sensitive to others' aversion to such acts. There is a legend told of the asura Karma's retinue, who requested sanctuary with the youthful Kartika's honest and trustworthy uncle. They were protected by him, although it cost him his life.

Once upon a time Kartika and the asura Karma had been at war with each other for a thousand years. At last the goddess Umā gave a many-pointed spear to the youthful Kartika, who used it to kill Karma. Karma's followers then sought refuge with the youth's uncle and remained with him.

Then Kartika went before his uncle and declared, "The royal traditions do not specify that the survivors of an enemy are to be spared. Release them from your custody!"

"All the followers of Karma now look to me for protection," the uncle thought to himself. He said to his nephew, if he released them then,

> Just as grass cutters going forth to cut grass
> Mow down every last blade at once—
> Seizing it, cutting it, and flinging it aside—
> There is no doubt what would happen to these humans!

"Well then," said Kartika, "if you will not turn them out, I shall take them by force!" In the battle that ensued the uncle was killed by the sharp spear, but his troops captured the youth and won the battle.

It is appropriate to trust anyone who is honest, fair-minded, and maintains a sense of shame—the supreme ornament of good qualities—whether they be friend, enemy, or stranger. Therefore, it is critical to recognize such distinctions.

369   Although one may have no evil intentions,
       One should not trust just anybody.
       Although deer are always good-hearted,
       Carnivores regard them as food.

People who do not harbor negative, duplicitous thoughts themselves should not naively trust others by being utterly credulous of all the silly things they have to say. One may be ethical oneself, but most people of these degenerate times are shameless and deceitful with their sweet-sounding words. Deer are very refined creatures with kind hearts harboring no malevolence toward others and always abide carefree. But carnivores with long sharp fangs consider deer to be food and try to eat them whenever they can.

The physical, verbal, and mental behavior of sentient beings in these degenerate times changes even more quickly than clouds in the autumn sky. One must be conscientious about placing one's confidence in others.

370   When fools go down the wrong path,
       One can presume they really are fools;
       But when the wise take that path,
       One should look for some other reason.

Fools and wise people take the wrong path for different reasons. Fools are oblivious to the law of actions and their effects whereby happiness and suffering primarily arise from wholesome and unwholesome deeds. When they tread the path of corrupt physical, verbal, and mental conduct, one can assume they are unable to discriminate between what to do and what not to do—the true sign of a fool. Conversely, the wise correctly understand how to discern the nature of actions and their effects because they are well trained in the Buddhist scriptures of sutra and tantra and place their trust in distinguished spiritual teachers. When they take the wrong path, one should seek reasons for their so doing rather than assume that such conduct indicates they are actually fools. Wise individuals having the altruistic enlightened attitude will sometimes take a path normally considered improper in order to take care of their students. They may even defer for awhile certain minor practices of the Dharma if it helps others. Śāntideva says in *Engaging in the Bodhisattva Deeds,*

> The main point to consider is the interests of others.

However, it is seen that learned persons, who themselves understand the law of actions and their effects, sometimes take the wrong path because they have suddenly been influenced by bad companions. The bodhisattva Thogmay Zangpo says in *Thirty-Seven Practices of All Buddha's Sons,*

> The bodhisattva's practice is to avoid bad friendships
> [That would strengthen their three poisonous attitudes,
> Weaken their study, contemplation, and meditation,
> And diminish their love and compassion].

Some great masters state that even if one thoroughly understands the nature of actions and effects, the imperatives of powerful karma still may cause one to knowingly and unalterably enter upon a path of unwholesome activity. They go on to say,

> When they suffer from karma,
> The wise wander among fools.

And,

> When led by the force of karma,
> The wise take the wrong path.

In any case, one should investigate the situation carefully rather than being unfaithful or disrespectful to the wise, or inferring that they are mere fools.

371   The wise live in a land of plenty,
       Where charity is lacking, but no robbery exists;
       In a land of poverty, there may be no robbery,
       But one may be ruined by crafty borrowing.

The wise, who understand time, place, and conditions, reside where the wealth that results from generosity in previous lifetimes is abundant, for example, where barley and silver are plentiful. The people who inhabit a place where wealth has accumulated gradually may not be generous, but neither do they resort to any kind of mild or forceful methods of robbery. On the other hand, in impoverished places, people may not openly steal things, but the wise will find that their wealth declines and they become destitute and destroyed through the gentle means of borrowing, either by giving out new loans or by not having old loans repaid.

One must understand the situation of one's locale, time, and associates, and work diligently to rely on "fine circumstances, fine places, and fine friends," according to *The Ornament for Sutra*.

372   One may know quite well how to do things alone,
       But all tasks should be done through consultation.
       Those who fail to collaborate with others
       Buy expensive regret for themselves.

One may have a thorough understanding of how to carry out certain important responsibilities without needing to consult others for guidance. Nonetheless, all tasks requiring careful execution should be discussed with others of similar views to determine the right approach. By consulting knowledgeable, experienced people of sound judgment and then reaching one's own conclusions, one will achieve good results. Occasionally, in spite of all discussion and suggestions, for some reason it may be difficult to complete a task, but one will have no regrets and other people will not be critical.

There are self-centered people who dislike talking things over with suitable advisors who are senior and experienced. These people are paying a high price in the present to buy regret that they will have to experience in the future.

373   When having delicate discussions,
       Speak not to third parties, even if friendly.
       Evil friends performing *vetāla*[150] rituals
       Will be the first ones to be devoured.

Anytime sensitive and potentially dangerous matters are being discussed with somebody, they must never be talked about with a third individual. No matter how friendly and compatible they are, they can pose a great danger that could threaten one's life. Ordinary people say that when three people band together, eventually one will be ousted. If one is with an evil friend engaged in the practice of invoking zombies, when the zombie appears, it certainly will not perform the four transcendental actions of celestial beings—pacification, expansion, power, and wrathfulness. First it will devour the practitioner, then imperil one's own life.

When deliberating on a sensitive issue, in general it is difficult for anything good to result; specifically, it tends to be provocative and should never be discussed with an unsympathetic third party.

374   Knowing how to obtain things, giving impartially with skill,
        Being subdued, having consideration for others' feelings,
        Being grateful for those who quell one's fears:
        If one aspires to these qualities one achieves the world.

Those who desire to attain temporary objectives must possess the following five special qualities:

◆ knowing how to receive spiritual and worldly things by engaging in lawful activities, and avoiding deceit and other improper ways of earning a livelihood;
◆ feeling neither anger nor attachment toward anyone who wants to acquire something, and having the skill and generosity to give them things with equanimity;
◆ being subdued yet not concealing oneself with fraudulent physical, verbal, and mental behavior;
◆ having as one's witness the Three Jewels of Refuge and the law of actions and effects, and treating everyone amicably by smiling and being pleasant; and
◆ being grateful to others who help us by clearing away harmful and frightening things such as obstacles to wholesome behavior or even threats to our lives.

Those possessing such laudable qualities can prevail over the entire world if they desire, just like highly respected kings.

People who aspire to excellence must strive to avoid attachment, anger, and competitiveness, empathize with others, be willing to take on their burdens, and treat them well.

375   When enemies come seeking refuge,
        Honor them and speak pleasantly.
        Elders of the past say a crow
        Gained happiness by relying on a mouse.

Sometimes those who have long been hateful enemies earnestly come seeking protection for some reason or another. When that happens one should not cruelly throw stones at their heads, clinging to the excuse that they used to be enemies. Instead, one should be congenial and suitably honor them in a respectful manner. The objectives of both oneself and others are achieved by giving kind treatment to conceding enemies. The respected elders of olden times recounted how everyone was made happy when a crow or a pigeon[151] depended on a mouse, sought its protection, and treated it kindly.

Once upon a time in a forest lived two friends, a mouse known as Jeweled One and a pigeon named Beautiful Neck. One day the pigeon and his flock were trapped by a net. They all desperately tried to fly away, but Beautiful Neck said, "You cannot escape that way. What are we to do?" They all huddled there, terribly depressed.

When a hunter arrived, he assumed that all of them were trapped and he released the ties of the net. At that very instant Beautiful Neck and all his flock flew away together, carrying the net, and landed in front of his friend, the mouse. "Oh, excellent Jeweled One," said the pigeon, "come here."

The mouse scurried over and exclaimed, "What misfortune has befallen you? All you birds are tangled up!"

"Please chew through the net," requested the pigeon, and the mouse obligingly gnawed a hole through the mesh.

"Will you come out first?" asked the mouse. "No," replied the pigeon, "first the others, then I shall follow." In that way all of them were freed.

A crow who was secretly lurking nearby observed this event and thought, "That was very good. I shall also befriend this mouse."

He then called out to the mouse, who replied, "What do you want?"

"I want to be your friend," the crow replied.

"No way," answered Jeweled One. "I'm afraid you'll eat me up!"

"No, I won't," insisted the crow, "I like you."

So the two of them pledged to be friends. A deer named Painted Body noticed, and also came to see the mouse. A turtle named Slow Going did likewise. All the animals in the forest did the same thing.

One day the turtle was coming down the path to visit a friend. Suddenly a hunter grabbed him, tied him up tightly with his bowstring, and carried him off. The turtle called out for help and the pigeons heard. Two of them fetched the deer and they all went to see Jeweled One to discuss what to do.

The mouse told them, "You all go lie down on the path in front of the hunter and pretend to be dead. The hunter will set Slow Going down and come toward you. Meanwhile, the crow can free Slow Going from the bowstring. At that instant Painted Body must run away and the pigeons fly off." They did exactly as the mouse instructed and everyone was safe.

The need for like-minded people to talk things over together was discussed earlier in this chapter (verse 304),

> When bright people perform even a minor task,
> They always consult others before acting.

In another text it says,

> Since the way to do things is to consult others,
> One should ask questions of intelligent people.
> This is obviously so if things turn out well,
> But even if things fail, it is still alright!

Kind and impartial treatment of everyone, whether friend, foe, or stranger, is the noble custom of people of great distinction; therefore, one should understand its significance.

376   The wise do not involve themselves with
       Bad friends and bad learning,
       Bad thoughts and bad actions;
       If they did, they would be just like fools.

Truly wise people, unconfused about causes and their effects, do not involve themselves with four things that many excellent spiritual masters throughout the ages have criticized as indications of ignorant fools. First, they do not associate with unwholesome companions who reinforce the disturbing emotions to be avoided, namely, the three poisonous attitudes of greed, anger, and ignorance. Furthermore, such friends ruin their superb accumulation of merit and wisdom, which must be developed to generate present and future happiness. Second, they do not engage in misguided scholarship, studying and contemplating treatises that enhance pride, jealousy, and competitiveness and waste a lot of time and youthful intelligence. Third, they do not occupy their minds with a lot of negative discursive thinking, which leads them and others to ruin in this and future lifetimes. And fourth, they do not involve themselves in shamelessly corrupt activities like the ten nonvirtuous actions and the five boundless transgressions. There are extensive teachings that support these points. As quoted in verse 370, the bodhisattva Thogmay Zangpo says in *Thirty-Seven Practices of All Buddha's Sons,*

> The bodhisattva's practice is to avoid bad friendships
> That would strengthen their three poisonous attitudes,
> Weaken their study, contemplation, and meditation,
> And diminish their love and compassion.

Sakya Pandita says,

> Though of great interest to fools,
> The study and teaching of so-called treatises
> Containing many meaningless, disjointed ideas
> Give the wise no pleasure at all;
> They are a waste of time and intelligence.

Some great masters have said,

> Bad discursive thought is the precursor of misfortune.

And,

> Ignorant discursive thoughts
> Plunge one into the sea of saṃsāra.

And,

> Those who have depraved conduct are more foolish than cattle.

Some who consider themselves wise participate in these four bad actions with the excuse that it is an accepted practice if the time is appropriate. One can only conclude they are no different from uninformed, bovine fools. Instead, one should diligently employ the methods that result in the constant happiness of life as a fully free and fortunate human being—a state so difficult to obtain!

377　　Regarding action taken after careful analysis,
　　　How could things possibly turn out poorly?
　　　For those with good vision who watch where they're going,
　　　How could they ever walk off a cliff?

Prior to undertaking important tasks, one should assess whether they can be completed or not. When executed with careful analysis from the very beginning, it is impossible for projects of any magnitude to become known as failures; most are certain to turn out well. Normal people with good eyesight proceed on their way after investigating which road is correct. Would they happily abandon their route, take the wrong path, and walk right over the edge of a cliff and die? That would never happen! For all activities the most important factor is to undertake the task after confirming it can be completed to one's satisfaction. Because this avoids future regrets, investigate things carefully.

378   When one trains in good qualities that improve
        Both oneself and others, it is the sign of wisdom.
        But certain knowledge, like archery,
        Is destructive to one's family lineage.

Clear-minded people who wish to master worthwhile knowledge study top-
ics that will definitely lead to increased happiness for themselves and others
in this and future lifetimes. This shows they are wise people who understand
the benefits and special qualities of knowledge. But if one studies to achieve
some other kind of proficiency, that knowledge in and of itself can destroy
the continuity of one's bloodline. The ultimate result of developing a skill in
archery, for example, could be one's own and others' demise.

The outcome of training in wisdom differs from that of training in fool-
ishness. With this understanding, try to develop good personal qualities that
benefit both self and others, in keeping with the cultivation of wisdom.

379   If one wants to achieve stature for oneself,
        One must only do that which helps others.
        Do not those who want to clean their faces
        Need first to wipe the mirror clean?

It is imperative for people who truly aspire to achieve authentically high
stature in spiritual and temporal affairs to give short- and long-range assis-
tance to others. In so doing, they are certain to fulfill their own desires. As
quoted in verse 348, Śāntideva says,

> Whatever happiness there is in the world
> Arises from desiring others to be happy.
> Whatever suffering there is in the world
> Arises from desiring oneself to be happy.
>
> There is no need to say much about this.
> The childish act in their own interests,
> But the Buddha acts in the interest of others;
> Just see the difference between these two!

Is it not true that those who wish to clean their faces and look nice first have
to wipe the dust off the mirror? Of course!

380   Those who want to completely subdue another
        Must work hard to develop their own good qualities.

See how those who want to kill a foe
Achieve their goal through force of arms.

If one desires to thoroughly defeat an opponent, one should willingly and joyously exert great effort to acquire the requisite knowledge, namely, cultivating the good qualities of merit and wisdom accrued through temporal and spiritual work. In this way one utterly destroys the adversary and obtains the personal benefits of virtue for this and future lives as well. Observe how those who wish to slay enemies must first strive to become adept in the use of such weapons as bows, arrows, swords, and spears.

Do not wait until tomorrow or the next day to exert great effort in developing good personal qualities, that which attains all peaceful and wrathful objectives in a gentle manner.

381   Since swindlers use deceit in their words,
       The honest must check them out carefully.
       Having once been misled, what then is the use
       Of self-promotion, saying, "I'm honest!"

It is always important to carefully examine the words of deceptive people. By persistently probing into others' affairs and wearing friendly expressions that make them appear trustworthy, some people mislead others by disguising the facts of a situation in a billow of pleasant speech. Individuals of good character should carefully analyze what such frauds have to say, because their words are very clever. Sakya Pandita says in *A Classification of People,*

> Those who deceive with lies and nice smiles,
> Who politely mislead with exhaustive explanation,
> And who always probe and examine others—
> They are the cunning and manipulative ones.

Some people are sincerely honest and clever in what they do, but in the end they are deceived by the broad toothy smiles of others. What then is the point of their praising themselves, saying, "I am honest and swear by the Three Jewels, but others tricked me!"? They have themselves become at fault for not knowing to investigate things carefully.

382   It is said in the accounts of ancient times,
       "What is needed when dealing with others is:
       Deceit with the deceitful, honesty with the honest,
       Stability [with the stable, and instability] with the unstable."

The proper response to the ways that crafty, misleading people act is to be skillfully deceitful in return. Honest people, however, should be dealt with honestly. Moreover, one should be erratic with undependable people yet steady with those who are stable and responsible.

Although this approach is the custom set forth by the elders of long ago, it is not to be interpreted literally. They are but examples of the pervasive nature of the suffering[152] that characterizes cyclic existence. Sakya Pandita says in *Advice I Give to Myself,*

> Excessive honesty is provocative;
> Wide-ranging skill is considered deceptive;
> Even being cool can annoy others—
> Translator, isn't the rat race a hassle?

Try to develop the ability to maintain self-control, and analyze things carefully in advance without being influenced by what others say.

383 It is always good when the wise are kindly,
   Even to those who are enemies.
   It may not promote true reconciliation,
   But it is a sure cure for malice.

Generally speaking there is no one who does not harbor some bad feelings toward hateful people. But the wise inferentially know what brings good or bad results. They avoid sarcastic, irate expressions, not only toward friends and relatives, but also toward those who have long been bitter enemies and, like old friends, they always try to do things for others and act in a kind and peaceable manner. Even if this congenial approach does not bring about true reconciliation, it is commonly recognized as a remedy that overcomes and expels malevolent attitudes.

384 Because it is hopeless in this world
   To achieve one's aims with bad language,
   Though one may have private ambitions,
   Speak agreeably with everyone.

Those who want to fulfill their aspirations cannot possibly do so by reviling other people with coarse, offensive language. Instead, they should converse agreeably with others and maintain a pleasant appearance. Even if one's purpose is entirely personal, one should try to accomplish it by generally helping others, speaking kindly to them, and keeping in mind what is most important in the long run.

385   When working on behalf of oneself and others,
       Rough and gentle means are both valid.
       But the Buddha did not teach deceptiveness
       As a practice of skillful means.

Some people strive to accomplish their own present and future goals, and also to work for the welfare of other sentient beings and the Dharma. They are not restricted to trying to please everyone with physical and verbal docility. Even employing rough measures that seem to be effective, such as attacking someone one moment and then helping them the next, is acceptable. This approach is known as the bodhisattva's practice of skillful means that achieves the aims of others. But among the skillful methods included in these practices, the greatly compassionate conqueror, Buddha Śākyamuni, did not teach the unwholesome act of deception. According to Śāntideva, cited above in verse 370,

> The main point to consider is the interests of others.

The most important aspect of fulfilling one's own and others' objectives is to hold altruism foremost and practice skillful methods that do not contradict the sublime Dharma.

386   The wise place their trust in counsel that is
       Temporarily unpleasant, but ultimately helpful.
       They teach good qualities to an only child
       By voicing disapproval and imposing discipline.

Various opinions hold that, while in general both the short- and long-term value of all activities should be assessed, the most important consideration is what will be of greatest benefit in the end. The wise definitely rely on this kind of advice, even though it may present every sort of difficulty concerning their body and wealth in the short run. Those who discern future advantage counsel parents with only children to object when their sons or daughters misbehave and to discipline them immediately; then, to cultivate in them good qualities that will definitely benefit their eventual well-being.

Think carefully about what will result from following any advice.

387   When one's wealth grows to excess,
       One's downfall is close at hand.
       A pond completely full of water
       Overflows, or even fails.

There are disadvantages to hoarding an excessive amount of wealth. Generally in this world, poor people are discarded by others, just as grass growing on a busy crossroads is trampled and kicked aside. However, when very greedy people amass exorbitant wealth, their undoing is at hand, either through external causes like fire, water, or wind, or by internal factors like kings and thieves. Ultimately though, since improvident affluence brings about a decline in one's wholesome activity, the punishing conditions of the three unfortunate states of rebirth in cyclic existence loom near. A pond filled to capacity with water becomes defective—it can break apart and drain away when the water either ruptures the earthen embankment or overflows and washes it away. Sakya Pandita says in *Advice I Give to Myself*,

> Those who renounce wealth are kicked aside like grass at
>   a crossroads;
> If they hang onto their wealth, they are said to be getting too rich;
> When they live comfortably, they are considered too clever—
> Translator, think about the fundamental nature of the world!

Some great masters have said,

> When graced with unattachment to illusory wealth,
> One's necessities are ample without hoarding;
> There is no entrapment in the eight worldly obsessions,
> And joy comes from following the masters of old.

Make effort to dispel any tendencies to fixate on the mirage of opulence, and by all means avoid falling to the extremes of excessive poverty or excessive wealth.

388   Some are unsuited to engage in deeds
      That are beneficial to others.
      Usually garlic helps nervous tension,[153]
      But for bile ailments is poisonous.

There is no certainty in saying that a particular thing is beneficial or harmful. It does not suit some people with the ten qualities of an enemy of the Dharma to engage in gentle, conducive practices like developing the altruistic enlightened attitude, understanding the law of causes and their effects, or realizing the shortcomings of cyclic existence. A violent personality contradicts the peaceful nature of such pursuits, so these individuals will be helped by any kind of harsh, overpowering treatment motivated by love and compassion. Garlic is often used as a medicine for treating wind disorders. However, in the case of bile disorders, white garlic is not merely benign, it can even be toxic. Since wind and bile disorders are different kinds of ailments, it is necessary to relieve them with different kinds of medicines. A single remedy is not suitable for both.

One must analyze all requirements to understand the essential purpose of what needs doing, then apply oneself single-pointedly to adopting what is helpful and abandoning what is not.

389   Though the weak must always be cared for,
       The great fear decline if they befriend them.
       When melted butter is put in a container,
       Do mice not come and gnaw on it?

Important people whose deeds accord with their words must consistently care for indigent persons of lesser aptitude as if they were children and give them whatever is possible in terms of Dharma teachings and material things. But they must always be careful in these associations, because they risk being harmed by the influence of those among the weak whose behavior is negative. When butter is put in a wooden container, mice will come to nibble, not just on the butter itself, but on the saturated wood as well.

390   Those who depend on bad people
       Are themselves harmed by their bad influence.
       When fish depend on flowing canal water,
       Notice how they get scattered over the field.

If one relies upon people of poor character and bad conduct, the cloak of their negative influence will damage both present and future. Fish that swim into irrigation canals lose their lives when the water is dispersed across the fields and they are stranded.

It is important to avoid getting entangled with evil individuals who are detrimental both in the short and long run. Instead, place confidence in resolute, reliable people who are aware of their own limits.

391   When unreliable pests are about to lean on you
       Give them a little something and send them away.
       When an unlucky sign appears to a family,
       Some resources should be earmarked to counter its effect.

Troublesome, greedy, shameless people lead others to destruction. If one is being maneuvered into a position of support for such a person, the way to deal with the problem is to give them a small amount of food or money befitting their temperament and dismiss them. One gets into trouble mainly due to these unprincipled associates, so it is critical to exercise caution with them. When an inauspicious omen appears to one's family, a portion of one's savings should set aside for employing means to counteract the unlucky sign.

It is important not to be miserly toward depraved people who harm those on whom they depend, yet take firm steps to distance oneself from them.

392   Though noble people may have gone elsewhere,
        They are respected and close relationships maintained.
        If one always worships wish-fulfilling jewels,
        Good fortune prevails and one's work gets done.

Skilled spiritual masters who maintain equanimity toward everyone and whose qualities are praiseworthy are a source of esteemed virtue. They should be respected, not just when they reside nearby, but also when they have moved to other places; one should unwaveringly cultivate one's association with them. As was explained earlier in verse 37,

        Noble people, even when living far away,
        Care for their friends by helping from a distance.

A precious wish-fulfilling jewel is the source from which all needs are met. When it is offered and installed at the tip of the victory banner ornament on a temple roof, good fortune spreads throughout the land. The people enjoy health and longevity, and all concerns of temporary happiness, such as inexhaustible wealth, are effortlessly accomplished.

Beautified by the many good qualities of wisdom, the sages are the basis of the entire collection of merit and wisdom for this and future lives. They should never be considered ordinary individuals whether close at hand or far away; therefore, make every effort to respect them.

393   When coarse people are overly praised,
        They later scorn those who praised them so.
        When filth is tossed up into the sky,
        It falls back down on the tosser's head.

Vulgar, inconsiderate people accept help from others but harm them in return. Shamelessly arrogant and considering themselves terribly clever, when they are overly praised as being industrious or educated, they later vilify the very people who commended them. Sakya Pandita says in *A Classification of People,*

> Those who return harm to the helpful,
> Belittle good deeds, and torment the lowly
> Are bad people of bad character,
> Indistinguishable from swine.

When a thoughtless person throws some disgusting thing up in the air, it will inevitably drop to earth on top of his or her own head.

Refrain from such things as bestowing excessive praise and admiration upon inconsiderate fools who are base, greedy, and swinish. However, one must know the correct way to act when the occasion is appropriate.

394   When wise people are humiliated,
       The fault will rebound on the abusers themselves.
       When torches are held upside down,
       The hands of the brandishers are burned.

Coarse, mean people follow a discredited kind of knowledge that is contrary to essential understanding. When they senselessly degrade and humiliate those who are honorable and intelligent, ultimately they themselves will surely encounter retribution. When ignorant children and the like take a flaming torch in hand and hold it upside down, their hands are seared by the fire, because its nature is to burn upwards.

In *The Ornament for Sutra,* the protector Maitreya teaches that it is best if one bestows praise and honor on exemplary people of exceptional learning, but if that is not possible, there is no fault in simply treating them equitably. This approach produces no unpleasant consequences that must be experienced later.

395   There is a place for everything, and
       Everything should be kept in its place.
       Crown ornaments should not be placed on the feet,
       Nor foot ornaments on the crown of the head.

As previously explained, one must avoid confusing objects of praise with objects of contempt. Intelligent, worthy people should abide where they are honored and well respected for being willing to shoulder the burdens of society; coarse people should dwell where they are deservedly criticized for their ingratitude to others. When this is the case, contrary understanding as described above will not arise. Similarly, crown and foot ornaments differ and so should be placed where each belongs. Knowing this, one should be able to keep distinct things in their respective places.

396   When undertaking important tasks,
        One must firmly rely on good friends.
        When setting a fire to burn a great forest,
        The wind must decidedly be one's aide.

When there is any sort of significant responsibility to fulfill, whether temporal or spiritual, for oneself or others, one must rely on excellent assistants—capable people who can facilitate what must be done by providing enthusiastic and skillful help and removing hindrances. When one wants to burn down a large forest, if one heeds the direction of the wind and lights the fire accordingly, it can indeed be seen that the wind is one's partner!

For any kind of task, not just major ones, depend on friends who are good, competent helpers. Then the work is easily accomplished, with no subsequent regrets.

397   Pleasant words filled with kindness are the best way of
        Achieving things easily, attracting others, and pleasing them.
        Who can satisfy others simply with riches?
        Sacrificing life and limb will not please even half of them.

Fulfilling one's desires depends on affectionate and gracious language. Motivated by love for all beings, wishing happiness for friend, enemy, and stranger, one should speak in ways pleasing to the ear, free of coarseness or offense to others. This is the best way to readily achieve one's aspirations, make others happy, and assemble a group of followers. What person could possibly make everybody content using the approach of giving away money to them? One could make not merely the external sacrifice of wealth, but the internal sacrifice of body and life as well, and still one would never satisfy even half the people.

In pursuing one's own and others' objectives, one must make effort to use polite, agreeable words and to maintain the enlightened attitude, recognizing all sentient beings as one's parents. This entails being practiced at regarding the good side of others.

398   Though impoverished, do not be depressed;
        Though wealthy, do not be gleefully proud.
        Since the effects of karma last a very long time,
        Various pains and pleasures are yet to come.

This eighth chapter concludes by showing that it is improper to be proud of wealth or depressed over privation. Being wealthy is mainly a consequence of having been charitable to others in previous lifetimes. One may lack food and clothing after losing one's wealth and becoming destitute, but that is no cause for depression; impoverishment does not last forever. Likewise, one may have acquired immeasurably fabulous riches and every conceivable good fortune—a good family, house, land, and so on. But one should not allow zealous enjoyment in being rich to cause arrogance; wealth does not last forever.

There are important implications to these considerations. The combined power of good and bad karmic actions accumulated throughout beginningless cyclic existence have enduring effects. Many different aspects of what is known as happiness and misery will occur far into the future, just as one's life transits from youth to old age, spring turns into fall, and the waxing moon becomes a waning moon. Ordinary people say,

> Do not brag about being wealthy;
> Poor, lowly people will feel depressed!
> Happiness and misery, like the phases of the sun and moon,
> Become manifest after circling around the universe.

Placing no trust in any circumstances, rich or poor, try to implement the practice known as "Taking the Path of Riches and Poverty." With regard to "Taking the Path of Poverty," Thogmay Zangpo has taught in *Thirty-Seven Practices of All Buddha's Sons,*

> Whether beings are poor, always scorned by others,
> Seriously ill, or possessed by evil spirits,
> Still the brave bodhisattvas put into practice
> Taking upon themselves the suffering of all.

And, with regard to "Taking the Path of Riches,"

> Whether they are famous, respected by many,
> Or as wealthy as King Vaiśravaṇa,
> Still humble bodhisattvas put into practice
> Seeing worldly riches as having no essence.

Chapter 9 ~
AN EXAMINATION *of the* DHARMA

399   Extending devotion to other teachers
        While the protector of beings, the Buddha, lives,
        Is like digging a brackish well near a river
        Of water with the eight good qualities.

Relying on something bad despite the existence of good alternatives is an inferior act that causes harm and regret. The fully accomplished Buddha is a protector of all sentient beings in the three realms of the universe, a guide for both human and celestial beings, and a great friend with whom one need not even be acquainted to be helped. If one fails to request refuge from the Buddha while he is actually present, yet gives respect to and seeks refuge from other teachers, one brings about one's own and others' downfall in this and future lifetimes, and has much cause for lament. Sometimes, in spite of there being a source of soft and delicious water having the eight special qualities, people will go to the trouble of drilling a well nearby that ends up having saline water and consume it instead. This is a case of their karma being very deficient.

Once upon a time there was a householder named Śrīgupta who was very devoted to a naked ascetic named Nyethung. One day Nyethung said to Śrīgupta, "O, householder! All these newly ordained young monks are incompetent and arrogant. Deprive them of their livelihood, and you will become famous."

But the householder replied, "I cannot do such a thing!"

"Yes, you can!" Nyethung insisted. "Have a large deep pit dug at your front gate. Inside it, make a fire that does not smoke, and cover the hole with thin broom straws. Then prepare a meal of poisonous food at your house. Invite the Buddha, and it will become obvious whether or not he is really omniscient! If not, he will die along with all his disturbing emotions. Should he get past the pit, you can give him the food."

The householder bowed down to the naked ascetic and left. Returning to his residence, he ordered his attendants to do as Nyethung had instructed.

Now, the householder's wife happened to be the daughter of Anāthapiṇḍada, one of the Buddha's most devoted supporters. Observing all the preparations, she asked her husband, "Who is your enemy?"

"The monk, Gautama," replied Śrīgupta.

"You won't be able to harm him," she declared. "He is the incomparable, fully accomplished Buddha."

Śrīgupta thought to himself, "This wife of mine is of the Śākya clan. She will surely reveal my secret plan." So he confined her to the inner rooms of the house.

Then Śrīgupta went to Vulture's Peak where the Buddha was living and extended his invitation. The Buddha understood perfectly well what the householder's intentions were, but he accepted nonetheless. Śrīgupta circumambulated the Buddha three times to acknowledge his consent and departed.

The Buddha then turned to Ānanda and said, "Go tell the other venerable monks not to enter the householder's residence before me."

The next morning, a massive earthquake occurred. Surrounded by great gods like Brahma and those who take joy in the doctrine, the Buddha arrived at Śrīgupta's residence, performing many miracles. As he placed his right foot on the threshold of the doorway, blind people regained their eyesight, the deaf regained their hearing, and insane people recovered their senses.

A person holding lay vows requested the Buddha to relate the significance of these events with regard to the past. "Oh, holder of lay vows," the Buddha replied, "fire was not able to harm me when previously I was born as an animal. What harm can possibly befall me now that I am actually a fully accomplished Buddha?"

The holder of lay vows asked him how that was so. The Buddha explained, "Formerly, I was born as a partridge in the forest of Kaliṅga. You were born as a rabbit, and the god Indra invited a Brahmin…" and he went on to relate this legend from the Jātaka.

Then the Buddha stepped forward, putting his foot on the edge of the flaming pit. Instantly the fire snuffed out and the pit transformed into a garden of lotuses, on which his retinue walked. Everyone cried out in astonishment, and much conversation ensued.

Śrīgupta's wife, sequestered deep inside, heard the uproar. "Oh, my! Has the Buddha died?" she wondered, and ran to see what had happened. Seeing the Buddha alive and well, she praised his magnificent qualities.

Śrīgupta and Nyethung were on the roof of the house, watching all that occurred, and became very frightened. Quickly they bowed to the Buddha and made preparations to receive him. Then the householder confessed, "O, Buddha! I have been under the influence of unvirtuous spiritual teachers and committed wrongful acts."

"Do you understand now what you have done?" the Buddha asked.

"Yes," said Śrīgupta, "I request your forgiveness. I am so ashamed." He

bowed. "Buddha, please sit for a while. All the food is poisoned. I will pre-
pare some more."

"This food will do," replied the Buddha. "You see, even when I was born
as an animal I was not harmed by poison. In a former lifetime I was the queen
of the peacocks, Golden Light, who was given poison by Pemömo, the daugh-
ter of Brahmādatta. Householder, you should recite these verses three times
and then serve the food:

> Attachment, anger, and ignorance
> Are the three worldly poisons.
> The victorious Buddha has no poison;
> The Buddha's truth destroys these poisons.

(Repeat two more times, substituting the words 'Dharma' and 'Sangha' for
'Buddha.')

> Upon the vast poisonous lands
> Are many poisonous creatures.
> All of these come from the poison of attachment;
> This attachment is the worst of all poisons.

(Repeat two more times, substituting the words 'anger' and 'ignorance' for
'attachment.')"

It is said that the householder, while living comfortably, developed the
stainless eye of wisdom, which correctly understands all phenomena.

Those who disregard the Buddha—teacher of the perfect path—and rely
on bad friends are deficient in merit and karma, human beings in name only.
One must strive to be genuinely human by correctly knowing what to follow
and what to avoid.

400   When one is familiar with any kind of task,
> There is no difficulty at all in doing it.
> The sublime Dharma can be mastered as easily
> As one trains to practice the technical crafts.

Anything worthwhile, whatever the magnitude, can be readily achieved if one
makes a willing effort and acquaints oneself with what is involved. Śāntideva
says in *Engaging in the Bodhisattva Deeds,*

> There is nothing whatsoever that is not easy
> When one becomes accustomed to it.

Familiarity and training make any of the modern or traditional crafts like painting or metalwork easy to do, even fine, intricate work. Likewise, if one joyously strives to follow the examples of the spiritual masters of ancient India and Tibet, the vast and profound Dharma can be understood with no difficulty. Without question one can acquire the temporary status of a learned person, and ultimately even the omniscient state of a fully accomplished Buddha.

To achieve such lasting happiness, the ultimate objective of this and future lives, one must develop familiarization and experience with the practice of the sublime Dharma by successively studying, contemplating, and meditating in the correct way.

401   Those who are content with just a few things
        Will never know the depletion of wealth.
        Upon those who are dissatisfied, looking for more,
        A continuous rain of misery falls.

It is inappropriate for intelligent people to be content with the quality of their internal knowledge until achieving the state of an omniscient, fully accomplished Buddha. Yet, their desires are few and small and they are satisfied with whatever external material wealth they have, so for that reason alone their resources do not get depleted. Even the god Indra would have difficulty finding the happiness that comes from such a practice as that. Śāntideva says in *Engaging in the Bodhisattva Deeds,*

        The happiness experienced from being content
        Is difficult for even the powerful to discover.

Yet some people do the exact opposite: no matter how rich they are, their desires are unquenchable and they persist in amassing ever more wealth. The three kinds of suffering shower down upon them and they have no chance to experience happiness, only distress.

Sensible people understand their limitations, curb their desires, and take assiduous care in being content. Such practice is praised by all the buddhas and bodhisattvas.

402   The Buddha taught that the wealth one gets
        Should be given away when needed.
        Accumulated wealth is like honey—
        One day it will be used by others.

To have wealth is to experience the fully actualized results of having once been generous. Accordingly, Buddha Śākyamuni has taught that people should rid themselves of avarice, taking some of their accumulated wealth and using it magnanimously at necessary times to make donations to the poor and offerings to the distinguished field of spiritual masters. As Candrakīrti was quoted in verse 361,

> Though all beings desire happiness,
> Without prosperity, there is no human happiness.
> Understanding that wealth ensues from generosity,
> The Buddha first discoursed on being charitable.

It is essential that one put accumulated wealth to good use while one has the freedom to do so, for some day one will be seized by death, the type of imper manence unique to living beings, and like a hair pulled from butter, wander off to one's future lives utterly alone, powerless to take along so much as a needle and thread. The riches that one so greedily amassed are appropriated without regret by strangers, just as bees spend their entire lives accumulating honey only to have it uncontrollably wrenched away and enjoyed by others.

Intelligent people who, as the result of their generosity, acquire a little wealth, willingly commit themselves before they die to making spiritual offerings and being charitable to the poor, thereby creating the causes for inexhaustible material prosperity and the attainment of enlightenment in the future.

403   In this world there is no certainty
      The loans that one has made will be repaid.
      But just a little charity given to beggars
      Brings a hundredfold results effortlessly.

Some people lend things like grain or money to others in order to increase their assets. However, not only is there no guarantee they will collect any interest, it is also possible that unpaid debts will cause hostile feelings, as previously explained (verse 192). On the other hand, if on special occasions one can employ pure thought and action to be truly charitable to those in need, one will effortlessly purify wrongdoings amassed over ten million eons and multiply the merit of that beneficence a hundred-million-fold. At the very least, if one's generosity is good-hearted, no matter how little one gives, the results later reaped will definitely be a hundred times the original gift. Therefore, the fortunate ones who trust the teachings of the Buddha, the bodhisattvas, and the excellent spiritual masters should, at auspicious times and according to their ability, make spiritual offerings and give generously to the poor.

404   Since it is impossible for the miserly to become rich
       Or the generous to become poor,
       It is as if misers have no interest in wealth
       And generous people are greedy.

Those who insatiably amass excess material riches can never become truly wealthy due to the very fact that they hoard their wealth. On the other hand, those who are unselfish can never become truly impoverished because they give away anything that comes into their hands. Therefore it is taught that it is as if avaricious people who are unable to be charitable have little liking for wealth; their self-interest is demonic. Similarly, it is as if people who primarily give everything away and use nothing for themselves are ravenous for wealth; their concern for the interests of others is the sublime Dharma. According to Śāntideva in *Engaging in the Bodhisattva Deeds,*

> When one says, "If I give it away, what can I use?"
> That self-centered attitude is the way of a fiend.
> When one says, "If I use it, what can I give away?"
> That concern for others is the sublime Dharma.

By knowing the difference between the disadvantages of accumulating wealth and the advantages of giving it away, one avoids the fault of greedily hoarding wealth and becomes skilled in the means by which clever bodhisattvas further their own interests. As previously quoted (see verse 348 above), *The Ornament for Sutra* gives the example of how tricky bodhisattvas achieve their own objectives by working for the sake of others.

405   Fearing generosity will impoverish them,
       The miserly are incapable of charity.
       Knowing greed will surely impoverish them,
       The intelligent donate whatever they have.

Small-minded people are primarily concerned with their own interests. Afraid that giving their wealth to others will result in deprivation, either for themselves in old age or for their heirs, they hoard their wealth and do not practice charity. Thoughtful people, on the other hand, realize that miserliness does not increase their material wealth and, indeed, will definitely render them poor. So when they happen to acquire even a minor amount of wealth, to say nothing of a mother lode, they give it away with no hesitation. As a result they are never able to deplete their riches. As cited above, Nāgārjuna says,

Generosity creates wealth.

Having understood this reasoning, one must strive in every way to apply one-self to the great deeds of astute people.

406   Since assets do not increase if left sitting idle,
        Merchants distribute their wares for sale.
        The wise, like merchants, distribute their wealth
        Since they will not get rich if it is stashed away.

Those who are keen in the ways of commerce know that if they keep their goods stored in a treasure house their wealth will not grow, so they widely distribute their merchandise for sale in order to obtain profits. Similarly, individuals who come into a little wealth and then hoard it will never acquire inexhaustible riches, so those wise in the ways of becoming prosperous and powerful make spiritual offerings to the Three Jewels and widely distribute alms to the poor. By this superb path, one can accomplish the objectives of both oneself and others.

407   It is said by the very learned that
        Those who possess countless treasures
        Yet give not a thing to anyone
        Are the truly impoverished of this world.

Wise scholars learned in the sutras, tantras, and treatises explain: "Although some people possess an inexhaustible amount of wealth—thousands of millions of treasure mines—they gluttonously hoard their riches, neither using it for themselves nor giving it away to anybody else. Needless to say, propelled by their greed these skinflints will take rebirth as pretas in future lives; but even in this life they are in fact indigent since they do not apply their wealth serviceably for either themselves or others."

One must diligently undertake the method that brings freedom from the misery of poverty in this and future lives and leads to the enjoyment of all the wonderful benefits of charity.

408   Fearing their descendants may become destitute,
        The small-minded hoard even trivial things.
        In order for their heirs to gain high status,
        The wise help out others, as if bribing them.

The wise who are generous with their wealth and fools who hoard theirs have different objectives. Ignorant, small-minded people are apprehensive about their heirs becoming destitute, so they tightfistedly stash away whatever they acquire, not only valuables but small coins as well. But the wise who understand the basis for things will impartially give away to others whatever wealth they have as if it were a bribe of a mere blade of grass, in order to further their own practice of Dharma and so that their descendants might attain some kind of high status.

With a definitive understanding of one's own objectives and the manner of attaining what one needs, by all means try to practice charity, the excellent path of the wise.

409   Thinking to make their descendants wealthy,
      Some sacrifice themselves to enrich their children.
      But then the little brats fight with their parents,
      Squandering their wealth and roaming like dogs.

The small-minded not only fail to achieve their objectives but must endure suffering as well. Aiming to make their descendants rich in whatever they desire, some people sell themselves in order to earn money, laboring very hard under the control of others. Without regrets they generously give their hard-earned wealth to their children, whom they cherish with boundless love as if they were the very eyes on their foreheads or the hearts in their chests. Yet the fat whelps just sit around rudely tyrannizing their parents, burdening them with suffering, abusing them verbally and physically. They end up roaming around town like stray dogs, carelessly squandering their parents' money on unwholesome meaningless things like whoring and drinking.

To achieve their objectives is arduous for those of deficient merit; therefore, one must work hard to accrue the merit of generosity, a superior path which definitely brings good results.

410   Children lack the kindness for parents
      That their parents have given to them.
      Children are cared for so long by their parents,
      Then parents age and their children mistreat them.

Parents have great affection for their precious children. They give them all they have achieved through great physical, verbal, and mental effort; they ignore the wrongs committed, and the suffering and bad reputations incurred in caring for them; and they relinquish hope of achieving their own ultimate aspirations. Yet no matter how much devotion parents bestow, providing food, clothing, and even their very names, in return their children willingly neither respect nor obey them, nor fulfill their aspirations. Then when parents grow old and cannot even get up or sit down, their children reward them with depression and regret, not just refusing to help but mistreating them as well.

Parents need to recognize that they must bear personal responsibility for any wrongdoings they have done, yet little can be expected of children deficient in merit. Practicing the admirable path of generosity will fulfill one's ultimate aspirations.

411   Some of the wealthy hoard their money,
        While others give charity where needed.
        For these two types and their descendants,
        Future lifetimes will be quite different.

Some rich people are inwardly grasping and accumulate property they neither use for themselves nor generously give away; others contribute anything they have wherever it is needed in terms of time, place, and circumstance. There may be little contrast in current life conditions for these two types of wealthy people and their heirs, but in future lives their circumstances will be very different. Prosperity does not increase for wealthy people who are avaricious; therefore, they and their descendants will become ever more destitute from the present onward and will have to experience the fully matured negative results of their past miserliness. Conversely, generosity is the profound instruction that enables philanthropists and their heirs to attain high status and enhanced wealth, enabling them to enjoy the benefits of inexhaustible resources.

The duration of future lifetimes is much longer than one's present lifetime, so one should by all means strive to master the practice praised by the sages—generosity.

412   Those who are enslaved by their attachments
        Pursue wealth with no regard for their lives.
        But when the contented obtain some wealth,
        They calmly give it away to others.

Some people, because they are in bondage to an obsessive lust for riches, are not able to abide in tranquility; they commit the folly of ruining their lives by chasing after fortune. Either they have no regard at all for life, or they consider life equal in value to wealth. But contented people with few desires do not pursue affluence. Even if they should gather up a few resources, they have no regrets in calmly giving it all away to others who are in need, thus enjoying the reward of achieving others' objectives as well as their own in this and future lifetimes.

It is wrong to be controlled by attachments. Avoid the tragic fault of wasting your life; do not throw away this precious human existence, which is so difficult to obtain. With diligence, cultivate the good personal qualities of being content and having minimal desires.

413   Some perfect generosity by giving away their possessions;
     Their patience increases if that makes others angry,
     And they feel joyous when others are satisfied.
     Theirs is the supreme practice of generosity.

Generosity is the principal spiritual practice to be mastered by all ordinary and exalted beings. Feeling great faith and delight, some practitioners of Dharma perfect their generosity by freely giving away all their possessions, including the future merit that results from their beneficence. Śāntideva says in *Engaging in the Bodhisattva Deeds,*

     Generosity is said to be perfected
     With the attitude of giving to everyone
     All one's possessions and resulting merit;
     Hence it is simply a state of mind.

When others get angry at people while they are being generous, it simply enhances the aspect of patience that pays no attention to mistreatment.[154] If the recipients of generosity are pleased, the givers themselves rejoice at achieving their own and others' objectives. If a timely act of generosity is characterized as possessing all six perfections in conjunction with steady concentration and the nonconceptual wisdom regarding the three aspects of giving and so on, then such generosity is primary or supreme among the spiritual practices of Dharma that are to be accomplished by all ordinary and exalted beings. Candrakīrti says in his *Supplement to (Nāgārjuna's) "Treatise on the Middle,"*

     For both the compassionate and uncompassionate,
     This advice on generosity is essential.

Entering the practice of making spiritual offerings to the Three Jewels and being generous to the poor becomes a repository of wealth that definitely benefits this and future lifetimes. It is called, "realizing the essence of illusory wealth"; therefore, one should refrain from hollow miserliness and apply oneself in every way to the excellent path of the perfection of generosity.

414   Usually the body is like an enemy,
       An ocean-like receptacle of suffering.
       But when the wise know how to put it to use
       It rightfully serves as a support for merit.

It is important to know how best to utilize the human form, which is exceedingly difficult to obtain. The contaminated body is like the great ocean, immeasurably deep and wide, filled with crocodiles, and hazardous to cross. Because it is a receptacle of inexhaustible woe—birth, hunger, and thirst, old age, sickness, and death—the body is considered as harmful as a real enemy, unsuitable as an object of excessive concern or familiarity. However, when intelligent people understand the body's nature, they can skillfully use it for a worthy purpose and suffering is overcome. Employing the body as a vehicle to generate limitless merit is suitable and definitely benefits future lifetimes. Śāntideva says in *Engaging in the Bodhisattva Deeds,*

       I should think of my body as a boat,
       Merely a means of coming and going,
       And transform it into a wish-fulfilling body
       To accomplish the objectives of all beings.

By relying on this troublesome human form as a prop, one is released from a great river of misery and can utilize the sublime path of perfecting the strategy for transforming one's body into an omniscient wish-fulfilling jewel, which satisfies the interests of sentient beings.

415   Although one's life can be destroyed in an instant,
       Predispositions of virtue carry forward a long time.
       The aroma of sandalwood borne by the wind
       Spreads far and wide, inducing pleasure.

One should engage in wholesome activities that will be truly helpful at the time of death. The virtues of generosity and the other perfections, which are supported by the altruistic enlightened attitude and the determination to be free, are of definite benefit not only in this lifetime but also at the actual moment of death, the type of impermanence unique to living beings, and the consequence of having been born as a composite phenomenon, which helplessly disintegrates moment by moment. Moreover, propensities for virtue are indestructible and carry into the future until one has advanced and achieved the state of a fully accomplished omniscient Buddha. Candrakīrti says in his *Supplement to (Nāgārjuna's) "Treatise on the Middle,"*

When good qualities are nurtured in a field of ethics,
The enjoyment of their fruits is unceasing.

Śāntideva says in *Engaging in the Bodhisattva Deeds,*

The perennial tree of the enlightened attitude
Yields an inexhaustible supply of fruit.

It is like the fragrance of Malaya sandalwood carried by the wind and spread
far and wide in time and space, giving rise to endless delight in all whom it
reaches.

Anyone who is sensible will apply themselves diligently to skillful meth-
ods of creating positive predispositions in order to enjoy the boundless fruit
of wholesome activities.

416 There is immense suffering at being separated
From the happiness one has long enjoyed.
Those who insist their body is permanent
Are devastated when, powerlessly, they must die.

Some people fail to see there is no assurance they will not die, even as imme-
diately as today. They are unaware that all close personal relationships, like
parents and friends, are by nature as fleeting as the composite phenomenon
of summertime mist, no different than brief associations between market-
place visitors who are with each other awhile then go their separate ways.
Having for some time savored the pleasure of parents, friends, and wealth,
finally they are separated from what they most cherish. In powerless anguish
they must go on alone; the experience of such misery far exceeds earlier pleas-
ures. These ignorant, confused people, clinging to the notion of permanence,
make preparations as if that which is impermanent will endure; but in the end
they must die defenseless since all composite phenomena are governed by the
four limits. They discard in ruins the very name and meaning of their human
life of leisure and opportunity, failing to grasp its essence. Sakya Pandita says
in *Advice I Give to Myself,*

One lives a long time but is drawn to wrongdoing;
One achieves human form but does not work for the future;
Death is a certainty and one goes on alone—
Translator, bear in mind impermanence.

Thogmay Zangpo says,

There is no assurance of living beyond today,
But we calmly continue preparing to live forever,
Risking regret at death with hands clasped to chest.
Please bestow blessings for me to keep death in mind.

Rather than patiently readying oneself for a long life, one should make an effort
to leave home, take ordination,[155] and meditate on impermanence—the uncertainty of death's hour—so as not to experience grief and regret when death arrives.

417   Surrounded by all of one's friends and family,
       Frightened, voice quivering, and vision failing,
       There is no way to know where one is headed;
       At such times phony virtues prove destructive.

Some people, alone on their death bed, surrounded by all their beloved friends
and relatives, do not know what will happen. They watch with tearful eyes,
experiencing immeasurable suffering as their vital essence ebbs away. The
compositional factors of this life depart and they are separated from the people who have been most dear to them. In the grip of the fearsome Lord of
Death, they speak but few words with a faint, terrified voice, and their eyesight is weak. Because they have made no preparations at all, they lack confidence and have no familiarity with where they are going. At such times the
only real virtuous acts are those firmly governed by the three excellences: the
excellent altruistic attitude to help others, the excellent realization of suchness, and the excellent dedication of merit. Anything else merely enhances
one's skill, fame, and reputation for this life's activities—superficial practices
that are the foundation for the eight worldly obsessions. It is taught that such
phony virtuous activities are destructive, unhelpful, and self-deceptive. Sakya
Pandita says in *Advice I Give to Myself*,

       When all alone lying down on one's death bed,
       Surrounded on all sides by cherished relatives,
       The ending of one's life inconceivably painful—
       Translator, nothing else helps apart from the Dharma.

Having understood the nature of composite phenomena that appear in this
life, one must strive to accumulate virtues through wholesome acts that will
surely benefit at the time of death. This is accomplished by training in the
six perfections, of which the principal practice must be uncompromisingly
directed by the three excellences, implemented by spiritual masters and celestial beings alike.

418   The maladies of rebirth in miserable realms
      Must be prevented before they occur.
      Like a lightning bolt that strikes one's head,
      What can be done once it has hit?

The three unfortunate states of rebirth are the realms of hell beings, pretas, and animals, wherein conditions are not conducive for the practice of Dharma. One suffers as if in the grip of a serious disease, having to experience various kinds of misery like heat, cold, hunger, and thirst; one is beaten, enslaved, and even killed. Guarding one's ethical conduct before this misfortune can come about is the way to insure against being reborn in and enduring these adverse circumstances. Some great masters have said,

> No matter how much learning one has, without ethical conduct
> One cannot be protected from proceeding to the lower realms.

Also, Candrakīrti says in his *Supplement to (Nāgārjuna's) "Treatise on the Middle,"*

> The cause of high status is nothing other than ethical conduct.

And,

> While having freedom and conducive conditions,
> If one cannot engage in wholesome activities
> But loses control and falls into the abyss,
> How can one possibly rise up from there later?

What can be done once misfortune has struck? Nothing at all! Once there was a caravan leader named Mitra whose daughter, because of her previous unwholesome actions, was struck on the head by a thunderbolt. She had to suffer this calamity; there was nothing that could be done about it! Both wise people and fools know this tale well.

One must not waste this precious human life, nor allow it to become meaningless. With the intent to forsake cyclic existence, try hard to observe ethical conduct by refraining from the ten nonvirtuous actions.

419   While people know they definitely will die,
      Severed from all friends and family,
      Still they peacefully go to sleep;
      What can possibly be in their minds!

Some ignorant fools know that one day they must be parted from relatives of their own flesh and blood and from friends with whom they have long been acquainted; they must set aside even the body with which they were born, absolutely leaving behind all animate and inanimate things. Yet knowing this, still they neglect to engage in wholesome activities and to refrain from wrongful deeds. Lazing about carefree, sleeping unperturbed like animals, giving not the slightest consideration to death—what can these fools possibly be thinking? Either they are under the corrupting influence of evil demons or their ignorance is of bestial proportions. For these people, Śāntideva advises in *Engaging in the Bodhisattva Deeds,*

> Relying on the ship of human form,
> One is freed from the vast river of suffering.
> Since this ship will be hard to find in the future,
> Do not sleep away the time, fool!

420   One may not be able to be diligent,
> But at least do not fall to the lower realms.
> Heroes might not slay their enemies,
> But do they ever kill their allies?

Intelligent people who are born as fully free and fortunate human beings, complete with the eight characteristics of leisure and the ten endowing factors that facilitate the practice of Dharma, should be unfailingly resolute in these ways: they must leave their families to become ordained;[156] become acquainted with the precious teachings of the Buddha by observing pure ethical conduct based on the wish to be free of cyclic existence; enrich their mental continua by cultivating a relationship with eminently wise spiritual teachers and by studying and contemplating the stainless treatises; and, rather than only studying the teachings, always try to put them into practice through meditation, which advances spiritual progress—the temporary result being high status, and the permanent result being definite goodness. Some great masters have said,

> By recollecting that the human rebirth, difficult to obtain
> Yet easily destroyed, can pass away in a fleeting instant,
> Please bestow blessings, that I may enthusiastically engage
> Only in virtuous deeds and remain not a moment in idleness.

Other people may possess in entirety these conducive factors: they have obtained a human form, which is difficult to get; encountered the Buddha's teachings, which are difficult to find; developed a relationship with spiritual guides, who are difficult to meet; are protected by kings who rule the land in accordance with the Dharma; and live in places that are replete with all facilitating factors. Yet due to the imperatives of karmic deeds in their previous lifetimes, they are unable to apply themselves as described above. Nonetheless, they should in any case carefully protect the lay vows, which prohibit killing, stealing, lying, sexual misconduct, and consuming alcohol. Moreover, to avoid falling into unfortunate states of rebirth, they must definitively guard their ethical conduct, which shelters them from fear.

To have all favorable elements yet still commit wrongs is a pitiful thing to do, like going to the land of jewels and returning empty-handed. Usually heroes having the capacity to destroy an enemy will coordinate their strategies to annihilate hostile troops. But even if, with their plans and their power, they are unable to kill the enemy, do they slaughter their own allies? Of course not! There could be nothing more pathetic than that!

Thus, in order to achieve the excellent human form in future lives, one must strive to thoroughly protect one's pure ethical conduct in concert with the determination to be free of cyclic existence, as unanimously praised by the Buddha and wise spiritual masters.

421   Even during temporary discomfort,
       The wise cultivate lasting happiness.
       Curing disease by burning and bloodletting
       Is the tradition of skillful physicians.

When one practices the sublime Dharma by properly listening to the teachings and meditating on their meaning, some minor distress can occur due to interferences created by evil demons and their attendants. One might encounter unpleasantness, or might not attain desirable objectives, or could lack conducive factors for the practice of Dharma. The wise, who are unconfused about how to achieve present and future well-being, until they attain enlightenment will continually cultivate the means to have lasting happiness, because there is but a finite amount of misery involved in the practice of Dharma. However for childish people who have only limited tolerance even for inconsequential, transient discomforts, there are no occasions when they are happy and free of difficulties. People with serious internal illnesses employ external means to remedy their afflictions, such as sharp instruments for bloodletting and fire for heat treatments. By tolerating pain for awhile, their ailments are completely alleviated; such is the method of highly skilled physicians.

Having understood that it is necessary to bear with temporary discomfort in order to achieve future happiness, be discriminating about what to do and what to avoid.

422   When one cannot tolerate
       The good fortune of others,
       One's own good fortune is destroyed,
       Thus, one is just aiming envy at oneself.

Some people find it unbearable when they see others who are either inferior
or of the same background and education acquire exceptionally good fortune
such as abundant wealth or the knowledge and capacity for success in tem-
poral and spiritual affairs. They get very angry and jealous. But such hostility
eradicates all the merit they themselves have accrued over a hundred thousand
eons, together with the beneficial results that merit would have yielded.

Thus their envy, though intended to sabotage another's good fortune, only
undermines their own by failing to safeguard the mind, which needs protec-
tion. In *Engaging in the Bodhisattva Deeds*, Śāntideva says,

> Not only do you feel no sorrow
> Over your own acts of wrongdoing,
> Do you not even wish to compete
> With others who act meritoriously?

423   If one wants to destroy foes because they give harm,
       One need only destroy one's own anger.
       In cyclic existence, since time immemorial,
       Our anger has given us endless trouble.

On occasion, under the influence of anger one wishes to destroy intractable
outer enemies because they are injurious to others. But the crushing of one's
enemies will never happen at such times; rather, one must eradicate only the
internal enemy of one's own antagonistic feelings. Throughout beginningless
cyclic existence until now, anger has caused immeasurable harm, as in the suf-
ferings of taking rebirth in the hell realms. Śāntideva says in *Engaging in the
Bodhisattva Deeds,*

> One will never be able to annihilate entirely
> All unruly sentient beings, as vast as space.
> But simply to abolish one's angry feelings
> Is the same as decimating all enemies.

And,

> Thus, why do I not give up anger,
> The cause of distress in the hells?

424   Though one may desire to destroy every enemy,
        How could they all be abolished by killing?
        Simply by conquering one's own anger
        One simultaneously slays all enemies.

When hot-tempered people want to completely annihilate all their unruly enemies, how can they possibly do so by trying to kill every one of them? Rather than getting rid of them all, there will be more! However, a means equivalent to killing all one's enemies is to vanquish that single internal enemy, one's own anger. This is just like obliterating all external enemies at once; likewise, one also permanently eliminates doing harm. Thogmay Zang-po says in *Thirty-Seven Practices of All Buddha's Sons,*

        If one fails to subdue one's own enemy-like anger,
        One may best other enemies, but they keep reappearing.
        Thus the bodhisattva's practice is to quell one's own mind
        With the armed forces of love and compassion.

This is like the analogy posed by Śāntideva in *Engaging in the Bodhisattva Deeds,*

        How would it ever be possible
        To cover the whole planet with leather?
        Simply covering the soles of one's shoes
        Is the same as covering the entire earth.

        Likewise, it is impossible for me
        To drive away all outer adversaries.
        Were I simply to quell my own mind,
        What need would there be to repel others?

By employing love, compassion, and the superb enlightened attitude, one should specifically apply oneself to the strategy of taming one's own angry feelings, principal of all enemies.

425   If one gets angry at the rash but mighty,
        It is oneself who is especially harmed.
        Whatever could there be to make one angry
        At fine people who are totally at peace?

If one gets angry at presumptuous people who have a great deal of power and act impulsively, careful analysis of the situation would reveal that it is oneself in particular who will suffer harm. Moreover, how could there possibly be circumstances that would necessitate getting angry at noble, conscientious individuals who are utterly undisturbed physically, verbally, and mentally? If there is no reason, be patient and refrain from anger as it senselessly destroys one's present and future happiness and leads to misery. Candrakīrti says in his *Supplement to (Nāgārjuna's) "Treatise on the Middle,"*

> There is no wrongdoing worse than impatience.

And,

> Impatience quickly throws one into unfortunate rebirths.

Śāntideva says in *Engaging in the Bodhisattva Deeds,*

> In brief, nobody at all
> Lives peacefully with anger.

Having rid oneself of anger—the basis of all faults in life—one should unceasingly strive to practice the perfection of patience, for which all exalted beings are consonant in their praise.

426   Grass leaves growing from a single stalk
        Are strewn everywhere by the wind;
        Those born together in a single family
        Are parted from each other by karma.

Sensible people should be diligent about understanding the impermanence of friends and relatives. Just as the various parts of a tree like branches, leaves, and so forth grow together from a single trunk during the summer, then are forcefully scattered to the ten directions by the autumn wind, so individuals who are born of the same parents in the same household live with each other for a short while, but eventually are forcefully parted from each other by the force of karma. Śāntideva says in *Engaging in the Bodhisattva Deeds,*

> Though this body arose as a single thing,
> If the flesh and blood with which it is made
> Break apart into separate elements,
> What need be said about friends and relatives?

Friends and relatives are like visitors shopping in the market place with whom one is briefly together, then all go their separate ways. With this understanding, one should with every moment generate enthusiastic perseverance to eschew short-sighted thinking and discriminate between what to adopt and what to avoid.

427   We cling to those who once were strangers;
       After that, they again go elsewhere.
       Why do we and they get connected?
       They die, and then we grieve over them.

It is meaningless to lament that people eventually part and go their individual ways. Persons we have never seen nor heard of before suddenly become our friends, we embrace them and take good care of them for awhile. Yet later, having no autonomy due to the power of karma, we become separate wanderers in other worlds. On what grounds do we come together? If at first we form a relationship for no apparent reason, then it is useless to mourn on account of the final parting of death. Both the gathering and the dispersal are merely arbitrary. Āryadeva says in *The Four Hundred*,

       When someone has become your son
       Without having asked permission,
       It is not unreasonable
       If he leaves without asking.

There is nothing definite or reliable about so-called close friends and relatives, individuals who come together at birth and separate at death. One must recognize such relationships are as devoid of essence as a dewdrop on a blade of grass and strive to practice the sublime Dharma, which is definitely beneficial.

428   If one strongly wants to achieve private aims,
       One first must work for the interests of others.
       By working solely for personal concerns,
       It will be impossible to achieve them.

Those wanting to achieve present and future happiness for themselves through industrious effort should first and foremost work for the welfare of others. By so doing, they will amply meet their own needs as well. Conversely, it is impossible for those who work solely out of self-interest to gain mere temporary happiness, leave alone to accomplish their long-range goals. As noted earlier (verses 348 and 379), self-interest causes childish people of coarse thought and behavior to be constantly oppressed by the misery of cyclic existence. Some great masters have said,

Lessen your own desires and work hard for others' interests.

Specifically, one must assiduously endeavor to work purely on behalf of others by implementing the expansive thought and action of the excellent path of the Buddha and bodhisattvas.

429   Those who work mainly for the welfare of others
        Are like clever people furthering their own interests;
        But those who work only for their own interests
        Are like honest people working to help others get ahead.

Achievements motivated by self-interest are entirely different from those that derive from concern for others. By working primarily with others' benefit as their objective, intelligent people usually achieve all of their own goals concurrently. However, because they appear to be working purely on behalf of others, their approach is like impostors who are really out for their own ends. On the other hand, there are ignorant people concerned only with their own advantage, which they fail to gain and end up spending their time in misery. Their way of behaving is like honest people who earnestly toil to enable others to get ahead. In *The Ornament for Sutra* Maitreya says,

     The ignorant labor only for their own interests;
     They never achieve them and are perpetually miserable.
     Those who steadily strive always to work for others
     Reach their own and others' goals and attain nirvāṇa.

Having realized that the distinctive achievement of one's own and others' goals results from employing good ideas and actions to benefit others, work with enthusiasm to do things honorably.

430   Even when the wise work for goals of this life,
        They succeed by doing so following the Dharma.
        See the difference in wealth and good fortune
        Between good people and ordinary thieves.

Since there even are differences in how happiness associated with only this lifetime is achieved, one must be discriminating about what to do and what to avoid. As explained above, generally the main objective of intelligent people is to work solely for the happiness of future lives. But should some temporary condition induce them to pursue a bit of pleasure that seems of this life only, if they conduct themselves according to the Dharma, avoiding

things, like deceit, that harm others, they will have adhered to the incon-
ceivably reliable law of actions and their effects and will achieve what they
seek. Good fortune acquired by people of excellence arises from the benefit
of their practicing Dharma with whole-hearted resolve to lead others to
enlightenment. Its nature is excellent and can be enjoyed in a relaxed man-
ner. On the other hand, there are thieves who steal the belongings of others—
silk clothing, gold, and silver. Needless to say they will have to experience the
fully mature consequences of their wrongdoing: punishment now in the rul-
ing court and later in the court of the Lord of Death. Even if they do pro-
cure some fleeting good fortune, its nature is impure. They will have to live
with a troubled mind and be unable to lightheartedly enjoy their wealth.

One must understand that karma, the law of cause and effect, is totally accu-
rate, just as whatever seeds are planted determine the type of sprouts that will grow.

431   One half of the short human life span
        Is spent sleeping at night as if dead,
        And the other half also lacks joy
        Due to ills of sickness and aging.

It is important to avoid attachment to the appearances of things since in this brief
life there is little rewarding happiness. Nowadays, because the five degeneracies
are prevalent, human beings have short life spans. Of that, half the time is passed
in sleep when one is like a corpse, so happiness has no value. One begins with
birth, and as an infant cannot speak or understand a thing. Later on, disturban-
ces arise in one's four elements, which causes sickness. Then gradual degen-
eration of the four elements over time leads to old age. Sometimes people do
not get what they want; at other times, what they do not want suddenly
befalls them. These various sufferings give rise to much distress, so even during
the half of their life span that people are awake they cannot enjoy happiness.

Indeed, everyone undergoes this experience, so by all means make this
momentary life meaningful. Some great masters have said,

        This short life has little worthwhile joy or woe
        And is key to gaining lasting future peace,
        Do not be engrossed in this life's fantasies—
        The only certainty is that all will die.

To avoid preoccupation with capricious notions, one must recognize that
there is no happiness or misery that amounts to much in this short lifetime.
To gain lasting happiness in future lives it is most essential always to perse-
vere enthusiastically in wholesome physical, verbal, and mental activities.

432   When one actually sees the Lord of Death,
        Who is sitting right next to everybody,
        One cannot remember to finish eating,
        To say nothing of doing other tasks.

Death will come swiftly. Therefore, it is necessary to practice the Dharma, which will definitely help at that time.

Death, the type of impermanence unique to living beings, sits beside all beings in the three realms of cyclic existence from the moment of birth, watching them and blocking all their escape routes. Nonetheless, they absent-mindedly fritter away their time day and night, just eating and sleeping, like a water buffalo in the presence of a butcher. Then one day they are lying on their death bed and actually behold the Lord of Death; breath can no longer flow through their bodies and they utter a woeful cry. Needless to say, they do not remember then to care for their friends or subdue their enemies; indeed, they cannot even remember to finish uneaten food in the bowl before them. Even if one tries, it is meaningless at that time to give up laziness; the timing is wrong. Śāntideva says in *Engaging in the Bodhisattva Deeds,*

> Having cut off all your escape routes,
> The Lord of Death sits there watching you.
> How can you go about enjoying your food?
> How can you sleep in comfort?

And Sakya Pandita says in *Advice I Give to Myself,*

> When death comes, as one lies in bed for the last time,
> The breath stops flowing through one's body,
> A rasping sound is emitted inside one's throat—
> Translator, then nothing helps but the Dharma.

Though death itself is certain, the actual time of death is uncertain. Seeing clearly that at that moment one's only support is the Dharma, one must from now on ardently persevere in accumulating the twofold collection of merit and wisdom that truly helps at death's hour.

433   The Lord of Death does not sit waiting,
        Nor ask, "Have you finished your work yet?"
        So if you have things that must be done,
        Begin immediately.

Some people live as lavishly as gods of the desire realm, oblivious to death yet all the while in its grip. But when the merciless Lord of Death actually comes, he doesn't first ask, "Do you have any important things that must be completed? If so I can wait for awhile." Instead of idly standing by while they finish what they are doing, he immediately destroys them.

This has important implications for those born as humans of good station in life rather than as idiots who are as ignorant as animals. Whatever definitely needs to be done, such as engaging in good deeds and avoiding wrongful ones, must be vigorously pursued during this short lifetime when one can recognize the full nature of what will be of benefit or harm for both present and future. It is advised that these things be undertaken with enthusiastic perseverance from today onward, not postponing them until tomorrow or the next day. Śāntideva says in *Engaging in the Bodhisattva Deeds,*

> Think to yourself, "this is not done,
> This is started, this is half done;
> Then the Lord of Death suddenly arrives
> Alas! I am ruined!"

In order not to be tormented by distress due to regret and the recollection of wrongful deeds when one is suddenly overcome by the unpredictable Lord of Death, one must begin at once to engage and joyously persist in worthwhile activities. Like the sun shining through a break in the clouds, there is still a little time remaining of this life.

434   Though choked with tears, and pleading,
        "I haven't finished what I am doing!
        Could you please wait for a little while today?"
        How can the Lord of Death's mind be changed?

Some people may think that by petitioning the Lord of Death, they will be able to change his mind. But when he arrives, he does not ask if they are ready to leave and then just hang around. They might not have accomplished the work of discriminating between what to do and what to avoid, a task that benefits this and future lifetimes, so they become choked with tears and mournfully cry, pleading helplessly with the Lord of Death, "Please wait for just a little while today!" One might try to deter him by various means such as powerful force, great wealth, brave armies, beautiful bodies, skillful talk, or deception, but how could it be possible to dissuade the ruthless Lord of Death? At such times there is no difference between monastic officials on golden thrones and child beggars who sleep in doorways; therefore, one must put the Lord of Death to shame with joyful determination to develop the superb twofold collection of merit and wisdom. Candrakīrti says in his *Supplement to (Nāgārjuna's) "Treatise on the Middle,"*

> All good qualities follow upon enthusiastic perseverance,
> The cause of the twofold collection of merit and wisdom.

Śāntideva says in *Engaging in the Bodhisattva Deeds,*

> Having thus practiced patience, develop enthusiastic perseverance;
> Enlightenment dwells only in those who exert themselves.
> Just as things do not move when there is no wind,
> Merit does not arise without enthusiastic perseverance.

Since there is no way of dissuading the Lord of Death, there is no certainty about when death will occur. When one sees clearly that this is so, one avoids the three kinds of laziness: attraction to wrong activities, belittling oneself, and plain indolence. Henceforth, discriminate carefully between what should be done and what must be avoided by applying interested, continuous, and enthusiastic effort, the source of all good qualities.

435   Shun the hectic life and be happy;
       If impossible, mix with good people.
       Why bother rearing a deadly snake?
       If you must, take care to recite spells.

Intelligent individuals rid themselves of frenzied involvements in worldly affairs. Associating with childish people is the source of all failings—arrogance, jealousy, competitiveness and so forth; no such relationships means one can happily enjoy life with the freedom of a spacious mind, having no attachments nor the need to protect anything. Being physically and mentally disengaged from temporal pursuits, one can abide in equanimity without distraction. Those who are not able to live unfettered by the clamor of daily life ought to associate with good spiritual masters who guide them away from mistaken paths, remove all their faults, and develop in them the good qualities of being helpful to others as well as themselves. From these masters they gain the benefit of expanding the good side of their character and diminishing the negative. How could it be proper to foster a poisonous snake? They are a source of misfortune, even of such calamity as losing one's life! However, if one does take care of a snake in any way, for the action to be suitable, one must at the outset assiduously recite magical secret tantric incantations so the snake's poison will be helpful to others and not harm oneself, thereby achieving everyone's objectives.

To cultivate meditative stabilization primarily means to avoid becoming absorbed in worldly diversions and the misfortunes they generate. Knowing this, make effort to develop concentration, which means one must keep far away from childish individuals!

436   When the mind is in a state of distraction,
       Practicing the sublime Dharma is hopeless.
       But when the mind is completely pacified,
       It is very close to being serviceable.

For those whose minds are captivated by thoughts of past, present, or future, or by objects that are good, bad, or neutral, there is no chance at all to practice the perfect sublime Dharma, which benefits both present and future lives. They may appear to be doing so, but if they are distracted by greed, anger, ignorance, and so forth, their efforts really are meaningless. Śāntideva says in *Engaging in the Bodhisattva Deeds,*

> The person whose mind is distracted
> Abides twixt the fangs of delusions.

And,

> The one who knows reality has taught it is useless
> To take action when the mind is wandering elsewhere.

Moreover, by totally pacifying all such discursive thought, the mind becomes exceptionally able to be focused on itself without distraction and to be placed in meditation on the enlightened attitude and so forth. In this way one develops the causes for obtaining the good qualities of both cyclic existence and nirvāṇa. Śāntideva also says in *Engaging in the Bodhisattva Deeds,*

> Completely pacify discursive thoughts and
> Cultivate the enlightened attitude.

Sakya Pandita says,

> In the midst of distractions caused by external objects
> It is difficult for the mind to be serviceable.
> Thus, pay attention to the focal object
> And achieve pacification of the mind.

Some great masters have said,

> Students! Watch your own minds and never be distracted.
> View cyclic existence and nirvāṇa as theatrical shows.

Harmful, discursive thoughts are like a wind that scatters meditative stabilization, but since meditative stabilization is what makes the mind serviceable, one must make diligent effort in its practice.

437 One greatly skilled with all meditative objects,
     Mentally subdued through meditative stabilization,
     And well trained in the exalted Dharma
     Is a vast field of all good qualities.

People with the power of special concentration have three qualities. First, they are highly adept at turning their minds to all objects of meditation; they can contract or expand the scope of, or abide in, their field of concentration, thus achieving the path of liberation. Second, they place their attention single-pointedly on subduing their minds, renouncing distractive signs during meditative stabilization, and thereby counteract the disturbing emotions that arise from conceptual thought. Third, they are proficiently schooled in the Dharma through having studied and contemplated its subjects such as the factors concordant with enlightenment. Ultimately, these individuals are vast fields of support for the development of all special features of buddhahood, such as fearlessness and the ten powers. Śāntideva says in *Engaging in the Bodhisattva Deeds,*

> Having understood all disturbing emotions are destroyed
> By special insight with a calmly abiding mind,
> First seek to achieve calm abiding, which is actualized
> By one who delights in detachment from worldly matters.

Make a serious effort to cultivate meditative stabilization, the concentration praised by the exalted ones. It is the direct cause of all good qualities in general, particularly the special insight that constitutes the wisdom that realizes selflessness. This is the indispensable antidote to ignorance, which is the main thing that must be eradicated.

438 Fools are astounded by those who study,
     But the wise are amazed by those who do not.
     Therefore, even when the wise get elderly
     They continue learning to aid future lives.

Childish fools oblivious to the workings of causes and their effects do not personally study what needs to be known and are astonished at those who do. This attitude toward study is the fault of ignorance concerning what naturally results from different kinds of actions. On the other hand, the wise who understand the nature of actions and their results are dumbfounded by lazy so-called Dharma practitioners who lie in the sun, their bellies full, not studying what they need to learn, and wasting their flawless free and fortunate human rebirth because they are suffering from their past actions. For that reason the wise who comprehend the situation with regard to cause and effect, namely, what arises in dependence on what, will always, even in their old age, pursue their learning in the Buddhist sciences to benefit present and future lifetimes. As explained earlier, the benefits are incomparable because one can then master generosity and the other perfections.

The good and bad ways of thinking of the wise and fools respectively are different in their causes and effects. Understand this well, and try in every way to train in the knowledge that is definitely advantageous both now and in the future.

439   Apparently, since fools lack wisdom,
       They have failed to learn anything useful!
       Examining themselves and seeing their ignorance
       Should prompt them to study especially hard.

There are different reasons why some people are wise and others are fools. Those lacking inborn and acquired wisdom find it hard to develop their knowledge even if they study. Fools use this as their excuse, and apparently do not and will not acquire good qualities. Such a pretext saddens the heart. If fools just examined their situation honestly they would conclude that because of their ignorance they need to study much harder than the wise. One must apply oneself to study and investigate things with an open mind, realizing that those who lack wisdom need to make special efforts.

440   Having seen that one is a fool in this life
       Due to neglect of study in previous lives,
       Fearing birth as a fool in future lives,
       One studies hard in this life, even if difficult.

Since results do not arise without causes, some people, because they made no effort in previous lives to learn what needs to be known, see that in this life they are like cattle who know nothing at all. In future lives again they can only be born as ignorant fools, since causes always accord with their effects. Those who fear such a fate must study the Dharma very diligently in this life in order to develop their knowledge no matter what hardships and weariness arise. Śāntideva says in *Engaging in the Bodhisattva Deeds,*

> If one does nothing useful in this life,
> How can one gain good fortune later?

Fools who, based on the evidence of their present life, fear they must again be born ignorant in future lifetimes should endeavor to develop the wisdom that comes through study.

441   Fools with very limited intelligence say,
      "If one meditates, there is no need to study."
      Without study, mere meditation, even if assiduous,
      Is the way animals achieve things.

Regarding the circumstances of this lifetime, it is generally said that hard work is necessary to develop wisdom that comes through study. However, certain ignorant fools of very limited intelligence say,

> Applying oneself solely to meditational practice is what is most important. Apart from that, in this life when time is short and there are many things to do, it is unnecessary to engage in dry-headed study, which lacks the moisture of compassion and the meat of calm abiding meditation and higher insight.

Others might say that, although generally one should endeavor to dispel doubts through studying and contemplating the meaning of what is to be meditated upon, ultimately it is sufficient simply to receive the oral transmission of the teachings without any attempt on one's own part to generate analytical wisdom. But effort merely in the practice of meditation is in fact the method animals use to accomplish things. In *Advice to the Great Meditators of Tibet* (*gangs can gyi sgom chen rnams la gdams pa*), Sakya Pandita says,

> Gripped by mental lassitude during calm abiding meditation
> Without cutting through fabrications using the advice of
>   the excellent,
> With stupidity and mental darkness ever increasing—
> Such a "great meditator" is a hibernating marmot.

Since the customary path and principal meaning of scriptural teachings is the need to develop wisdom through study and contemplation prior to meditation, one must by all means apply oneself accordingly.

442   The reliability of the law of cause and effect
Is the special instruction of the Omniscient One.
If one can become omniscient without studying,
How can the law of cause and effect be true?

It is necessary to study what needs to be known because there is nothing deceptive about the law of cause and effect. Some teachers propound such erroneous notions as results arising from no causes at all, or incomplete causes. In contrast, the unique feature of a fully enlightened buddha is to know all phenomena exactly as they are, just as one sees a myrobalan fruit placed in the palm of one's hand. Only such a buddha knows how such effects as pleasure and pain or sweet and sour seedlings issue invariably from their respective causes with no confusion or waste. By practicing meditation after dispelling doubts through studying and thinking about all phenomena (the path phase), the Buddha became incomparably omniscient (the result phase).

Some ignorant individuals seem to be conferring praise when they state that one who never trained at the path phase is an untrained omniscient at the result phase, but this is an insult. How can such a person be omniscient? If one could become omniscient without studying, then how could the law of cause and effect be true? As everyone including fools can clearly can see for themselves, being satiated without first eating, or arriving without first leaving are clearly contradictory. Based on that Sakya Pandita says,

> Those who study in many lifetimes
> And rely on many who are wise
> Attain fearlessness regarding all that should be known
> Through an intelligence that thoroughly analyzes things.

Having gained confidence in the undeceiving ways of the law of cause and effect, if one aspires to become omniscient one must industriously acquaint oneself with all Buddhist and non-Buddhist subjects that will bring about that result.

443   Meditating without first studying may temporarily
Bring achievements, but these quickly vanish.
Even if gold and silver are thoroughly melted,
When heat is removed they harden again.

Wisdom developed through study and contemplation analyzes what constitutes the path and what does not. Meditation practice lacking this wisdom is unreliable; it may temporarily act to suppress what one needs to discard, so although it may seem to accomplish the aims of freeing one from disturbing emotions and pacifying discursive thoughts, these achievements quickly disintegrate and vanish because the actual antidote—the wisdom of selflessness—is absent. For example, even if gold and silver have been properly melted by fire, once separated from heat they again solidify. As quoted in verse 306, the omniscient Shalupa says,

> Not being an unlearned meditator (a handless rock-climber),
> Nor a logician prone to dry explanations of the Dharma,
> Since I alternate learning, contemplation, and meditation,
> I delight in following the examples of the masters of old.

The stability of one's meditational practice ultimately depends on whether or not one has first correctly studied and thought about the meditational topic. Therefore, one ought to do as learned masters have: leave home, endure hardships in search of learning, and definitely develop the wisdom that comes through study.

444   Meditation is the discarding of faults and their causes
        Through the use of wisdom to analyze the profound.
        Meditation alone may achieve something for awhile,
        But like washing the unclean body, the results do not last.

Suchness is understood by those who use wisdom derived from the study and contemplation of stainless texts to intensively investigate that which is difficult to fathom. Only by cultivating meditative stabilization combined with the wisdom that understands suchness will they rid themselves of the delusive and cognitive obscurations along with their principal cause, ignorance. Śāntideva says in *Engaging in the Bodhisattva Deeds*,

> As for those wishing to quickly gain omniscience,
> How can they avoid meditating on emptiness,
> The counteracting force that dispels the darkness
> Of the two obscurations—delusive and cognitive?

Those who do otherwise, practicing meditative stabilization devoid of the wisdom that realizes suchness, may achieve some temporary objective as explained earlier. However, because they have not developed the counteracting forces that completely eradicate faults, after a while the achievements vanish and, as usual, the disturbing emotions will arise again. It is similar to washing one's grubby body with soap and water: it is temporarily clean, but again becomes soiled because there is no force that can make it totally pure.

Those who recognize the deficiency of mere meditation without study and contemplation should make effort to unite their practice of meditative stabilization with wisdom.

445   If causes and effects are incomplete in any way,
       Selflessness may be realized, but not buddhahood.
       Those unpracticed in supreme methods
       Are foe destroyers who only see the truth [of selflessness].

It is necessary to practice skillful means, since that is what primarily gives rise to omniscience. Through the union of method and wisdom, motivated by love, compassion, and the enlightened attitude, one creates the complete cause from which comes the complete result: achievement of the state of a fully omniscient buddha. Without such completion of cause and effect, even if one understands the selfless nature of all phenomena, one will not actually become a complete buddha. Those whose spiritual achievements are not accomplished by supreme skillful means, even if they directly realize the truth of selflessness, are merely foe destroyers who have eradicated their disturbing emotions. In *An Explanation of the Three Vows,* Sakya Pandita says,

> If one does not train in method,
> It is impossible to know all phenomena
> Or act in the interests of others.
> As a tapestry's warp is generally uniform
> And variations in weft determine the quality of its weave,
> So emptiness is generally the same for all practitioners
> And method determines the quality of their achievements.
> With the view of emptiness one attains nirvāṇa;
> But when proficient in method, one attains complete buddhahood.
> Therefore, if one desires to realize buddhahood,
> One must carefully cultivate skillful means.

Therefore, intelligent people who wish to attain the state of a fully omniscient buddha should strive to properly accomplish the six perfections, the consummation of method and wisdom.

446   Therefore, having comprehended well all phenomena
       And placed one's mind in meditative stabilization,
       All faults and their predispositions are eradicated
       And one becomes a fully completed buddha.

In general, only the path that combines method and wisdom brings about omniscience. Because one does not achieve omniscience without having the complete causes and effects for doing so, intelligent people first maintain perfect ethical conduct, the foundation of all good qualities. Then they dispel their doubts about the various Buddhist and non-Buddhist sciences through study and contemplation, and mastering systematically the six perfections. Next, they develop proper realization of the ultimate mode of existence of all phenomena and combine that realization with single-pointed meditative stabilization on that which has been understood, primarily suchness. Whoever uses this method of practice thoroughly eradicates the faults of cyclic existence along with their subtlest predispositions and becomes a fully accomplished buddha. Vasubandhu says,

> One who properly engages in study and contemplation
> Is best prepared to practice meditation.

Sakya Pandita says in *Advice I Give to Myself,*

> First, understand all phenomena by thorough study,
> Next, analyze everything with detailed contemplation,
> Then, come to realizations with meditative stabilization—
> Translator, practice the two stages this way.

Mahāyāna practitioners should be resolute in their effort to master the distinctive path that inseparably combines method and wisdom contained within the six perfections.

447   If one lacks intelligence, how could one grasp
       The treatises, even though they are excellent?
       How could cattle appreciate golden jewelry
       Inset with gems, even though it is lovely?

One may act in the interest of all sentient beings by engaging in such practices as the six perfections. However, giving extensive discourses on various subjects serves to benefit others only when, at the outset, the people present are intelligent enough to comprehend the explanations. If not, then even though the words and meaning of the treatises are excellent, who will listen and take them in? No one will understand their significance! No matter how beautiful golden earrings inset with many precious jewels may be, ignorant cattle will pay not the slightest attention.

While the treatises provide excellent explanations, one should not be negligent in one's efforts to elucidate them for intelligent people who are capable of understanding and can accomplish their own and others' objectives.

448   If the wise fail to put into practice
        The meaning of all good advice they've received,
        Yet all along know it to be quite true,
        What use is their knowledge of the treatises?

As explained above, wise people first engage in study and contemplation in order to understand the importance of knowing what to accept and what to reject. They may consider what is presented in the flawless treatises concerning conventional and ultimate truth, superbly explained by the great Indian and Tibetan masters of the past according to their students' mental capacities, to be entirely valid. But insofar as they fail to practice the significance of what they have understood, they continue to act contrary to the Dharma through attachment, anger, and partiality. Even if they pretend to follow the three kinds of trainings and understand the treatises having the two features of protecting one from the suffering of bad rebirths and worldly existence, what good is that? Besides being useless, it acts as a cause for bad rebirth!

By inwardly examining the meaning of what one has understood from discourse and study on the stainless sutras and treatises, one should apply them to one's physical, verbal, and mental conduct as much as possible. Introspection is necessary to determine whether one has become disciplined (an indication of study) and whether disturbing emotions have been eliminated (an indication of meditation). Having realized the importance of this, one must make every effort to do this practice.

449   Each day one should take to heart a few words
        Of the scriptural advice that one needs;
        Before very long one will become wise,
        Just as ant hills are built or honey is made.

The wise who trust in the Dharma do not distract themselves with the meaningless affairs of this life and say they will put off their practice of Dharma until tomorrow or the next day. Instead they strive with steady diligence to study the sutras and treatises, which are sure to benefit them now and in the future. At the very least, every day they memorize one line; then, during the day they mainly fathom it, and at night they mainly contemplate its meaning and put it into practice. By never being parted from the Dharma, day or night, in time they become sagacious and prominent among those who uphold the doctrine. Weak little ants can build large dwellings with many small pieces of earth. So also, bees gather many bits of pollen and make a large hive of honey. Sakya Pandita says,

> During the day melodiously recite the scriptures;
> At night contemplate their oceanic meaning.
> This always accords with the tradition of Dharma;
> Thus it characterizes its foremost upholders.

Sensible people know there is no chance for their suffering to end unless they stop postponing Dharma practice, which is vital for their interests, and apply themselves to it continuously day and night. We also should try to do this.

450　　When there arises desire to behave wrongly,
　　　 Quell the impulse, whatever the cost.
　　　 Bear every hardship, even at risk of life,
　　　 To safeguard the mind as scriptures prescribe.

Whenever weak-minded people feel drawn to engage in wrongful actions deprecated again and again by the excellent buddhas and bodhisattvas, they should deflect such improper notions and not allow themselves to be influenced by them. With a willingness always to tolerate adversity, one should value and adhere well to what is written in the perfect scriptures, even at the cost of one's life. Briefly summarizing this way of protecting one's mind, Śāntideva says in *Engaging in the Bodhisattva Deeds,*

> "I am constantly abiding in the presence
> Of all the buddhas and bodhisattvas
> Who are always endowed
> With unobstructed vision."
> Thinking thus, I shall bear in mind
> A sense of decency, respect, and fear.

And,

> O you who wish to guard your minds,
> With folded palms I appeal to you,

> Make every effort to safeguard both
> Mindfulness and mental alertness.

And,

> If, mind, you should not do
> Exactly as I have advised,
> You will simply be demolished
> Because all faults depend on you.

Having recognized the long-range importance of this life as a time when we correctly comprehend the differences between what is beneficial and what is dangerous, one will work hard and even risk one's life to eradicate erroneous and destructive behavior.

451   If by such effort one can practice antidotes
      Exactly as the scriptures advise,
      Because the wise do not tell falsehoods
      One will see the benefits later!

As explained earlier, with effort dim-witted, error-prone people can correctly discern what to discard and what to cultivate by being motivated by a sense of shame, respect, and apprehension and by applying the antidotes of recollection and mental alertness, just as described in the stainless treatises. If this is so, then since the buddhas and the wise bodhisattvas do not speak untruths, it is clear that applying the antidote of discarding shortcomings during this lifetime gives rise to the benefits of discernment that accrue in future lives.

As for the assertion that the wise do not tell falsehoods, it means that their scriptural citations are credible. Śāntideva says in *Engaging in the Bodhisattva Deeds,*

> Because the Buddha's statements are undeceptive,
> Their special qualities will be seen later.

Concerning the ability to practice, he says,

> When one gets familiar with something
> There is nothing that is not easy.

Concerning the benefits of practice, he says,

If you had performed
These activities earlier,
A condition like this would not have occurred,
Which is not the bliss and perfection of the Buddha.

Concerning the possibility of practice, it is said in Dharmakīrti's *Commentary on (Dignāga's) Compilation of Prime Cognition (Pramāṇavārttikakārikā)*,

Cultivate such attitudes as love;
Eventually these come naturally to mind.

Concerning the benefits of practice, it says,

Elimination of the causes [of suffering] and possession of
The three features is [the state of] having gone to bliss,
Which comes about through familiarity with seeing selflessness.
It is an excellent state because it is not a basis for suffering.

Sensible individuals should accept such trustworthy scriptural statements as reliable and seriously focus on implementing those teachings as advised.

452   Note how such practitioners of the past have flourished,
        And practitioners of today as well.
        By means of this excellent rationale,
        Those in the future will also prosper.

The possibility of spiritual practice and the benefits of spiritual accomplishments are established not only by trustworthy scriptural statements but also through reasoning. Intelligent people who in previous lives, in accordance with the advice of the faultless Buddhist scriptures, engaged in the practices of cultivating constructive behavior and eliminating destructive actions, now enjoy the good results that derive from concordantly good causes in that their good activities increase and they live in comfort and happiness. Indeed, one can clearly see how even at present since they acted that way earlier in this life their wishes are fulfilled. Thus, using the past and the present as proof and the good results as a reason, if one continues to act positively as one did in the past, one will be sure to attain the wished for prosperity in the future because the cause has preceded. Some great masters have said,

Look at your present body to see what you did in the past;
Look at your present deeds to see where you later will go.

As described in the scriptures on the pure threefold analysis, one can actually verify by logic such things as the benefits of spiritual practice and those from the application of the counteractive forces. Therefore, those who desire good for themselves and are capable of analysis should endeavor to master these superb methods to guarantee that they will not waste the propitious circumstances they have attained in this life as a free and fortunate human being.

453   Even if the intelligent are learned in their own systems,
They study with interest the textual systems of the wise.
Even if a precious gemstone is very fine,
Until it is cut and polished, it is worth little.

Innately intelligent people study and contemplate their own textual sources, reading the commentaries and examining them in detail. Yet no matter how learned they are in their own systems, they will study with interest the unbiased textual sources of Indian and Tibetan scholars, first examining them carefully and analyzing them honestly. Those they find correct, even if they are of a textual system different from their own, are then accepted as aids to their own development. Those scriptures with which they disagree that are not in general very harmful they treat with equanimity. Those found harmful, in general and in particular, are repudiated as teachings to be refuted.

In this way, one becomes truly learned, whether carrying out the Dharma activities of study, contemplation, and meditation, or pursuing the scholar's activities of explanation, debate, and composition. Even though such precious stones as diamonds may be regarded as very fine quality, they must be properly cut and polished by skilled gem cutters; until that is done they are of little value to others. In *An Explanation of the Three Vows* Sakya Pandita says,

Through studying language and logic,
I became knowledgeable in composition.

And,

Moreover, with effort I have listened well
To most of the famous scholars
Who are found today in India and Tibet.
My training has not been superficial;
I have heard most teachings
And thus am not biased.
Therefore, the intelligent should uphold
This honest analysis.

Through study and contemplation that is impartial, respectful, and joyous, one should clarify one's understanding of the textual systems of India and Tibet, both those to which one personally subscribes as well as others, differentiating between what is constructive and what is not, and striving to enrich the mind with knowledge.

454   Even though there are many forests,
       The special places where sandalwood grows are few.
       Likewise, although there are many scholars,
       Those who explain things well are very hard to find.

Although there are many forests with trees of juniper, aloe, and so forth thriving on this earth, the particular soil in which sandalwood grows is rare, so there are few sandalwood trees. Similarly, on this earth there is a multitude of those reputed to be scholars, a status that derives from one's ability to thoroughly elucidate the good explanations in the sutras and treatises, and to debate based on one's investigation of those texts for contradictions and connections. But since most have not first studied, those who actually deserve this recognition are few.

When one is young and has good intelligence, one should take interest and delight in mental enrichment through study and reflection on the general and specific treatises, and work hard at the fine ways of becoming a genuinely wise scholar with no regrets upon reaching old age.

455   A good horse is known when ridden,
       Gold or silver are known when melted,
       An elephant is known in battle, and
       Scholars are known when they write good advice.

Horses are recognized as good or bad by the quality of their gait when they are ridden. When gold or silver is melted, one can easily tell if it is of superior or inferior quality. An elephant's bravery when it is sent into battle with others determines whether it is praiseworthy or not. The quality of things is recognized by observing whether or not the respective necessary attributes are present.

Reputable scholars in general and others who do not have much confidence in public, such as reclusive yogis, fear that careless activities and much commotion will cause their commitments to degenerate, so they take no great pleasure in giving oral explanations in debate. However, as in the examples above, one can discover whether or not they are true scholars when they write exegeses on the excellent explanatory texts, using logical analyses and summarizing the general meaning.

One definitely should understand that those lacking proficiency in the three erudite pursuits of explanation, debate, and composition are incompetent as scholars and cannot claim a place among the wise who understand the collection of scriptures. With this important point in mind, having committed oneself in advance to endeavors that will achieve genuinely meaningful results, one must make great effort.

456   Those who want to be recognized
       As exemplars by all in the world
       Should investigate this treatise well
       And strive to develop antidotes.

If intelligent people want to be regarded by others in the world—lay or ordained, of high, low, or middling status—as reliable, good individuals who serve in every way as examples to all in temporal and spiritual matters, they should properly examine and investigate with an open mind what is explicitly, implicitly, and indirectly described in this text, which is a good explanation fulfilling all wishes. Once the meaning has been clearly established by way of scriptural citations and reasoning, and what is to be cultivated and discarded has been ascertained, then, in accordance with this extensive presentation, they should strive to develop the antidotes that get rid of what is to be discarded.

Inquiring people who desire their own well-being, by treasuring this text, which differentiates between what is proper and what is not, will definitely develop their knowledge.

457   Those who know how to perform worldly tasks well
       Are adept in the ways of sublime Dharma.
       Therefore the practice of the ways of Dharma
       Is the way of life of the bodhisattvas.

The conclusion to this chapter shows that treating temporal and spiritual affairs as complementary to each other is exemplified in the lives of noble people.

Intelligent people who know how to work for happiness follow not the example of fools who create confusion by vilifying the law of causality, but rather of those who preserve the teachings of the wise masters of the past. In this way they are able to discriminate fully between beneficial and detrimental worldly activities that leads to the excellent results in this and future lives, namely, achievement of the well-being of humans and celestial beings. Those who can put this into practice honestly and keep their words consistent with their deeds also accomplish perfectly the practice of the ten wholesome actions and other disciplines of the sublime Dharma that bring about the three forms of enlightenment. To safeguard harmony between the secular and the spiritual in this manner is the excellent way of superior people. For that reason, this superb approach of being equally involved in the ways of the world and of the Dharma is the incomparable way of life of the bodhisattvas who accomplish their own and others' objectives. This accords with the meaning of an earlier citation:

> Logical analysis does not contradict the ways of the Dharma.

One should not be involved in worldly affairs for the sake of a self-interested pursuit of wrong livelihood. Rather, it is of value to practice, seriously and honorably, a combination of these two indispensable methods, in order to achieve complete enlightenment for others' benefit.

THE MANNER IN WHICH
THE TEXT WAS COMPOSED

> As the physician Kumāra Jīvaka cured the seriously ill
> By persuading them to think medicine was food,
> So I have taught this sublime Dharma
> Through reference to the ways of the world.[157]

The wise physician Kumāra Jīvaka used skillful means to treat the grievously ill, who are extremely difficult to cure. He enticed his patients to believe the medicine he gave was food that would dispel their hunger and thirst. This enabled him to administer excellent remedies. Likewise, the Venerable Sakya Pandita says, employing skillful means, my approach has been to talk about the various characteristics of the foolish and the wise. In fact, this great treatise I have taught, *A Jewel Treasury of Good Advice*, provides for the needs of students according to the level of their mental abilities; it is the sublime Dharma whereby one can attain the state of high status (the happiness of gods and humans) and definite goodness (the state of enlightenment).

Once upon a time there was a lustful woman who, finding no men nearby, coupled with a scorpion. A son was born from this union and grew up to be king. His name was Tumpo Pradyota. Pradyota means "Great Illumination," and this appellation was given to the king by his followers who mistakenly attributed a brilliant light seen shining across the earth at that time to the king's birth. In fact, the light was due to the living presence of the Buddha.

It is said that scorpions are afraid of grease or oil. Apparently King Pradyota had inherited this trait from his father, because he was so very terrified of fats that he became agitated and confused at the mere utterance of the word "butter." But there came a time when the king could not sleep; he was suffering from nervous tension, the treatment for which, in Tibetan medicine, is to eat small amounts of fats. The doctor was summoned.

The King of Physicians, Kumāra Jīvaka, arrived and examined the king.

"Make ready the king's fastest camel," he instructed the ministers. "Feed the slow elephant named Damburi parched rice, but don't give him any water. And fill an animal stomach full of urine from a female elephant."

Next, Kumāra Jīvaka added a little refined butter to some excellent chang and fed it to the king, who went right to sleep. Then, riding the camel and carrying with him the bag of female elephant urine, the doctor fled to the town of Śrāvastī.

Later the king awoke with a belch and instantly recognized the taste of butter in his mouth. "That doctor fed me butter!" he exclaimed. "Kill him! From now on, if that trickster gives anybody anything to eat, they must refuse it!"

One of the ministers mounted the slow elephant Damburi and went off in pursuit of Kumāra Jīvaka. Just as he was closing in, he came upon a water hole. Damburi halted and would go no further until he had quenched his thirst. Meanwhile the doctor hurried on, increasing the distance between them.

When the minister again began to overtake him, the doctor threw the bag of female elephant urine on the ground. This made Damburi very aroused, and again he stopped and stubbornly would not proceed until he had thoroughly smelled it. The doctor raced ahead and arrived in the pleasure grove of Śrāvastī.

A while later the minister reached the garden and grabbed Kumāra Jīvaka.

"It is good that you have come," the doctor said. "I'll go with you to the king, but there is no hurry. Let us rest here in this nice garden for awhile and eat a piece of fruit."

"I cannot eat anything taken from you," the minister replied. "The king has ordered it."

But the doctor persisted. "Here, eat this," he said, offering half of a small myrobalan fruit to the minister as he ate the other half himself.

Seeing that the doctor had eaten his portion, the minister assumed the fruit was safe and ate it. But Kumāra Jīvaka had concealed under his left thumbnail a small amount of potion that would cause diarrhea, which he inserted into the piece he gave to the minister. Immediately the minister was seized by a violent case of diarrhea. The doctor treated him with good food and medicines and the minister began to get better. In fact, the treatment was so effective that it even cured a case of leprosy that had been troubling him. In the meantime, Kumāra Jīvaka once again disappeared, so when the minister was completely recovered, he had to return by himself to the king.

"Where is the doctor?" demanded the king.

"He has escaped," the minister replied. "If I had caught him, what would you have done?"

"He would be put to death!"

"But that would not be right," said the minister. "He has completely healed both of us."

"What should I do, then?" asked the king.

"You should reward him," the minister declared.

So the king summoned Kumāra Jīvaka and asked him what he would like as a reward.

"I myself need nothing," the doctor said, "but if you want to bestow favor it should be for another younger doctor in your kingdom. That doctor originally informed me of the circumstances surrounding your illness and how he thought you could best be treated. I followed this advice with success, so he should be presented with a large reward."

The king expressed his appreciation to Kumāra Jīvaka by giving him two rolls of precious fabric. The doctor, in turn, gave the cloth to the Buddha, who sewed it into a set of monk's robes. The remainder was stitched into robes by Ānanda.

This story comes from accounts given in the vinaya sutras concerning the matter of discipline with regard to monk's robes.

Similar to the approach used by the skilled physician for the king (who otherwise would not have taken the butter that helped him), this great bodhisattva, Sakya Pandita, guides others, referring to accounts of the ways of the world, while what is really being explained here should be understood as the Dharma practiced by the sages.

> This glorious *Jewel Treasury of Good Advice*
> Arose splendidly from an island in the ocean of learning,
> Held by the nāga king, who is wise.

This verse formulates through example the manner in which to ponder this advice.

Because the logicians cannot fathom its full extent, the bodhisattva Sakya Pandita's knowledge is likened to the great depths of the ocean; what wondrously arises from an island in that ocean is a "jewel treasury of good advice." This counsel is comparable to jewels because both have the same five special qualities: rarity, flawlessness, power, supreme immutability, and service as worldly ornamentation.

Similarly, regarding the owner of such jewels, it is said that just as rubies, emeralds, and so forth are held tight in the grasp of the nāga king, so also this treasury of advice is firmly held by the "nāga king," wisdom. What distinguishes this wisdom is its perfection above all else in the world, and its acquirement by all students who are attracted to it. It is said in this example that Sakya Pandita's wisdom is the nāga king because it holds the treasury of matchless jewels. Therefore, the splendid *Jewel Treasury of Good Advice* is so named.

Just as all jewels come from the king of the nāgas residing in the ocean, so the bodhisattva Sakya Pandita arose as a spiritual teacher who is a great ocean of Dharma and a boundless treasury that provides for the needs of all students. The jewels of flawless good advice that come from him have never been known to become depleted in any time or situation. Therefore the metaphor "jewel treasury" is used. Other metaphors that make this point, such as "the treasury of waters—the great ocean," are taught elsewhere.

> The treasury of wisdom is filled with clear understanding
> In order to fulfill all desires of the wise.

These lines show that the composition of this treatise is related to temporary needs.

Jewels that come from the ocean fill up the treasure houses of kings and such. Those who possess these jewels can satisfy all their desires and have the power to dispel darkness and spread light wherever they live. Likewise, the jewels of good counsel that come from the shores of the ocean of wisdom are free of irrelevant meanings and do not include the cheap trinkets of partiality. These jewels fill up the wisdom treasure house of those who aspire to achieve clear understanding and enthusiastic perseverance.

Wishing that the flawless details of his teachings should present new and unfamiliar material (such as the clear analogy about jewel ornaments) to scholars learned in the scriptural systems, Sakya Pandita perfected a style of exposition and composition. To distinguish his system from the teachings of others, he set forth a detailed classification of what to do and what to avoid. One should work hard to meet one's temporary needs by relying on this good counsel.

> The Venerable Śākya Bhikṣu Kunga Gyaltsen,
> Having examined things well with a virtuous mind,
> Revealed this good advice to eradicate ignorance everywhere.

Here are shown the three superb qualities of the author of this treatise.

First is the distinguished quality of the author's name, which is not obscured because he has used "Venerable Śākya Bhikṣu" (a designation of the Buddha). The Buddha himself is known definitively as the Venerable Flawless Buddha, the Tathāgatha, Our Leader Beyond Comparison in the Three Realms of Cyclic Existence. Were all the meaningful names of Buddha Śākyamuni enumerated, they would be countless: The One Who Spreads the Radiance of His Thought Everywhere in All Mandalas of Knowable Things, and The One Who Communicates in Excellent Places of Practice are examples. But these epithets are not presented here. Rather, Sakya Pandita simply uses "Venerable Śākya Bhikṣu Kunga Gyaltsen" to spread peace and happiness with a kindly name that is familiar to everyone.

Second is the distinguished quality of his motivation, which is wholly virtuous because he is devoid of attachment, anger, and ignorance and has the attitude of helping others. His excellent investigation is like the threefold analysis applied to ascertaining the purity of gold (by melting and so on); therefore he writes, "Having examined things well with a virtuous mind...."

Third is the distinguished quality of the reason the author composed the text. To elucidate from every perspective all the various aspects of phenomena that are knowable but not clearly seen, and to classify them in a definitive way, Sakya Pandita has provided *A Jewel Treasury of Good Advice*. It is said that by doing so he has clarified everything.

One must cherish this well-explained treatise and make effort to accomplish what is necessary.

> May the flawless virtues that arise from this composition
> Shine brightly, like cool radiant moonlight,
> Dispelling darkness from the hearts of sentient beings and
> Causing the water lily of their wisdom to blossom widely.

Here Sakya Pandita dedicates to others' well-being the virtues generated from composing this text.

The crystal-jewel moon of autumn, unobscured by dust, clouds, or fog, dissipates the night's darkness with its white light. Its cooling radiance shines impartially, giving relief to all tormented by heat. Simultaneously, the white water lily flourishes far and wide as the moonlight causes the petals of its splendid blossoms to open. Swarms of buzzing bees draw forth honey nectar, hovering delightedly about these flowers as they would their hives.

Similarly, with impeccable motivation to benefit others, Sakya Pandita has superbly composed this treatise, *A Jewel Treasury of Good Advice*, in order to promote clear thinking and to refine others with the threefold analysis. From this effort a swarm of stainless virtues has risen, and positive energy as white as a conch shell, a water lily, or the moon. May these clear away all the darkness of ignorance in the hearts of sentient beings and simultaneously spread far and wide the illumination of the threefold faith wherein reside all sentient beings of clear intelligence and correct aspirations. May these also engender fearless courage for mastering all spheres of knowledge by means of engaged, continuous, and enthusiastic effort.

The sages say that in concluding one's practice, the dedication is of vital importance.

> Because the state of omniscience is attained
> Through comprehensive study of all that should be known,
> May this text I have composed enable everyone to achieve
> The state of a fully accomplished buddha.

Intelligent people who wish to realize the fully completed state of buddha-hood, omniscient in all knowable phenomena, should study, contemplate, and meditate on every subject said to be necessary to achieve that objective. While one is perfectly engaged in this way, the binding knot of disturbing emotions is loosened and one attains omniscience. Therefore, the author says here, "I have composed this text, *A Jewel Treasury of Good Advice*, that all sentient beings in need of discipline might obtain the final objective of fully accomplished buddhahood." In *The Ornament for Sutra*, Venerable Maitreya says,

> Not even the great āryas will become omniscient
> If they do not train in the five major Buddhist sciences.
> Therefore, they apply themselves to debating others
> And to philosophical examination of the nature of the self.

Śāntideva says in *Engaging in the Bodhisattva Deeds,*

> Just as there is nothing whatsoever
> As that which bodhisattvas do not study;
> So for those skilled in living that way
> There is nothing that is unmeritorious.

Summarizing the significance of all these citations, Sakya Pandita says,

> Without studying everything that should be known,
> The edge of the heaven of omniscience is remote.
> With that consideration, it is said,
> The buddhas and bodhisattvas study all things well.

Causeless results being a contradiction in terms, prior training in all important subjects is necessary for the subsequent result of obtaining omniscience. Having developed through reasoning and scriptural citation a thorough understanding of the causes needed to attain omniscience, one must take responsibility for engaging in continuous study.

Part III: The Conclusion:

AN EXPRESSION *of* GRATITUDE
to the AUTHOR

SAKYA PANDITA LIVED IN TIBET, the Land of Snows, in the grand Sakya temple in Latoh Drompa (la stod grom pa) in the district of Tsang (gtsang). This is several hundred miles north of where the Buddha attained enlightenment in Bodh Gayā, India, the Land of Transcendent Ones.

The special qualities of Sakya Pandita's knowledge are thus: light rays emanating from Mañjuśrī's heart released a little pollen from the lotus blossom of wisdom, enabling Sakya Pandita to master completely grammar, logic, poetry, metrical composition, and the use of conjunctive particles by studying and understanding most of the well-known scriptures of the tathāgathas. In this way, he attained illuminating intelligence and was unmistaken concerning key points of scriptural citation, reasoning, and quintessential special instructions.

Secure in his abilities at explanation, debate, and composition, this superb author is fully named the Excellent Well-Spoken Śākya Bhikṣu, Venerable Kunga Gyaltsen. The place where he composed the text was the grand Sakya temple. This concludes what I have to say at this point.

SAKYA KHENPO SANGYAY TENZIN'S CONCLUDING PRAYER

> Bestower of everyone's rightful share of happiness;
> A wish-fulfilling tree providing ready satisfaction
> With the immortal nectar of well-being, vast and profound—
> O Buddha Śākyamuni, foremost refuge, a sun-like friend.

> Residing on the Snow Mountain Sakar Tenpa,
> Soaring freely in the heavens of all knowable phenomena,
> Venerable guardian of students, destroyer of the harmful—
> O Mañjuśrī, the ever-victorious Lion of Speech.

Known as the powerful sun of guidance, which
Spreads far and wide the flawless teachings of Buddha,
You carry the "Victory Banner of Pervasive Joy"[158] and
Speak sweet words of poetry, generating bounteous impartiality.

Alas, of the people who pass for wise these days,
The so-called "radicals," most seek happiness in this life,
But even if everyone were to accept and appreciate this text,
Some critics, confused of mind, would look for faults.

Others, who cannot bear being led down a false path,
Have long requested me with honest sincerity [to teach]
The perfect dual tradition of temporal and spiritual matters.
Therefore, I thought I would try contributing to the ocean
    of wisdom.

Sown with seeds of actions and their effects in soil of the dual
    tradition
And watered with good rain of the treatises of the wise,
This garden of new plants of discriminating thought
Is a dwelling for bees of the fortunate ones' clear wisdom.

Having properly examined all that is true and untrue,
If one puts into practice only what is by nature true,
One is led by the messenger of truthful words, and
Surely only truth will come into one's hands.

May this advice, rich with all excellence,
This jewel treasury, a source of all excellence, and
This meaning commentary, a rain of sublime excellence,
Spread everywhere auspicious signs of sublime excellence.

Accordingly, this meaning commentary on *A Jewel Treasury of Good Advice* is called *A Hive of Bees of Clear Understanding*. These days it is included in the curricula of many different kinds of schools.

Because of the expressed wishes of many people in many places far and wide, there is keen interest that for years has urged me to write this commentary. Until now I have been unable to do so. The main reasons I postponed this task were my lack of ability and being under the influence of distracting laziness. But others have insisted yet again that I undertake this work, so this time I simply could not refuse.

It is stated in Ngawang Tenpa Dorje's (ngag dbang bstan pa'i rdo rje) composition entitled *In Praise of the Master of Dharma* [Sakya Pandita] *(chos rje'i bstod pa),*

It is said, "When I attain full buddhahood, [reality is as obvious as]
A myrobalan fruit resting in the palm of one's hand.
Likewise, those with spiritual teachers do not meet with ruin,
So cultivate joy in spiritual relationships."
I sincerely pledge to act in this way.

So also I hold this master of Dharma, Sakya Pandita Kunga Gyaltsen, as my refuge for this and future lifetimes and pray that later I may be reborn in his presence.

I have consulted many new texts and other printed materials from Kham (khams) and central Tibet, and have edited the basic text by Sakya Pandita to eliminate transcription and printing errors. For matters needing further clarification from earlier works I examined the well-known commentary composed by Marton Chögyay. Apart from that, whatever I have written here accords with the instructions of earlier nonsectarian masters of India and Tibet and with other teachings of Sakya Pandita. There is really nothing here I have fabricated myself.

For contemporary readers I have used examples that will assist them to comprehend certain points. Yet there are always some scholars who find faults in works such as this, claiming that the chosen examples and their meanings are disproportionate and do not match. However, such criticisms are extreme and unfair. An example and the point it illustrates need to fit together like a lock and key; the result can be as elegant as this citation from Venerable Śāntideva's *Engaging in the Bodhisattva Deeds,* found above in verse 119:

Herons, cats, and robbers
Clearly attain their objectives
By moving silently and stealthily;
That is how the Buddha always functions.

If it can be shown that these three examples encourage the followers of Buddha Śākyamuni to be subdued, peaceful, and careful, then that is acceptable. When an example and the point it illustrates are congruent in all respects, it is a gross mistake for critics to assert that Buddha Śākyamuni—the one who possesses all good qualities, has eliminated all bad qualities, and remains unrivaled in the three worlds—is being likened to a robber or an animal by use of this citation. Therefore, I fold my palms together at my heart and earnestly request these skeptics not to get snarled up in the literal designation of words.

The author of this treatise, an adherent of the great Sakya tradition of Tibetan Buddhism, named Śākya Bhikṣu Maitri Buddha Shasanadhara (Sakya Khenpo Sangyay Tenzin), completed work on the main body of the text on an auspicious Sunday, the first day of the ninth Tibetan month. This date was exactly seven hundred and twenty years after the venerable guru, Sakya Pandita, the great Kunga Gyaltsen's ascent into *parinirvāṇa*, and seven hundred and ninety years following his birth in the grand Sakya temple. A short while later the entire text was completed on the fourteenth day of the ninth Tibetan month (October 21, 1972) in Darjeeling, India, in the Sakya monastery in Ghoom called Dongak Norbu Ling (mdo sngag nor bu'i gling). This day is also a special holiday commemorating the ascent to the blissful abode of Sukhāvatī of the great Kunga Nyingpo (Sakya Pandita's grandfather), a manifestation of Avalokiteshvara.

May this work serve as a sublime cause for all sentient beings to be unmistaken about that which they should do and that which they ought to avoid.

May there be virtue!
May there be virtue!
May there be virtue!

NOTES

....

1 Josef Kolmas, "The Aphorisms *(legs-bshad)* of Sa-ska Pandita" in *Proceedings of the Csoma de Körös Memorial Symposium,* held at Mátrafüred, Hungary, 24–30 September 1976, L. Ligeti, editor (Budapest: Akadémiai Kiadó, 1978), 191, footnote 9.

2 Sa skya mkhan po sangs rgyas bstan 'dzin (Śākya Bhikṣu Maitri Buddha Shasanadhara), *Legs par bshad pa rin po che'i gter don gyi 'grel blo gsal bung pa'i bsti gnas (Sa legs 'grel pa)* (Dharamsala: Tibetan Cultural Printing Press, 1988).

3 Dmar ston chos rgyal, *Legs par bshad pa rin po che'i gter dang 'grel pa* (Lhasa: Bod ljongs mi dmangs dpe skrun khang, 1990).

4 Dbyangs can dga' ba'i blo gros (A kya yongs 'dzin), *Sa skya legs bshad sogs kyi brda don 'ga' zhig dgrol ba,* in *The Collected Works of A kya yongs 'dzin* 2 (New Delhi: Lama Guru Deva, 1971), folios 374–82.

5 Kolmas (1976), 192–94.

6 W. D. Shakabpa, *Tibet: A Political History* (New York: Potala Publications, 1984), 54.

7 C. W. Cassinelli and Robert B. Eckvall, *A Tibetan Principality: The Political System of Sa skya* (Ithaca: Cornell University Press, 1969), 5.

8 The following account of the history of Sakya is from Cassinelli and Eckvall (1969), 6–13, and George N. Roerich, *The Blue Annals* (Delhi: Motilal Banarsidass, 1979), 210–13.

9 This connection between the Khon and Tibetan royalty is disputed by David Snellgrove and Hugh Richardson in *A Cultural History of Tibet* (Boston: Shambhala, 1986), 132.

10 From a review of various Tibetan biographies of Sakya Pandita found in David Paul Jackson, *Sa-skya Pandita on Indian and Tibetan Traditions of*

Philosophical Debate: The Mkhas pa rnams 'jug pa'i sgo, Section III (Ph.D. diss., University of Washington, 1985), 30–31.

11   Leonard W. J. van der Kuijp, "Marginalia to Sa-skya Pandita's Oeuvre" in *Journal of the International Association of Buddhist Studies* 7.1 (1984): 46.

12   Snellgrove and Richardson (1986), 145–47.

13   Jackson (1985), 33–34, and Leonard W. J. van der Kuijp, *Contributions to the Development of Tibetan Buddhist Epistemology* (Weisbaden: Franz Steiner, 1983), 100–101.

14   Jackson (1985), 71–75.

15   van der Kuijp (1983), 101.

16   van der Kuijp (1984), 48.

17   van der Kuijp (1983), 99.

18   Shakabpa (1984), 61–64.

19   One source claims the Tibetans chose Sakya Pandita as their negotiator, Giuseppe Tucci, *Tibetan Painted Scrolls* (Kyoto: Rinsen Book Company, 1980), 9; another source claims otherwise, Warren Smith, *Tibetan Nation* (Boulder: Westview Press, 1996), 83.

20   Sarat Chandra Das, "Contributions on Tibet" in *Journal of the Asiatic Society of Bengal* 1 (1882): 66; for a translation of the letter see Shakabpa (1986), 61–62.

21   Smith (1996), 86.

22   Tucci (1980), 9–12.

23   For a detailed examination of this topic see Smith (1996), 93–100.

24   Hugh Meridith Flick, Jr., *Carrying Enemies on Your Shoulder: Indian Folk Wisdom in Tibet* (Delhi: Sri Sat Guru Publications, 1996), 1.

25   Ludwik Sternbach, *The Spreading of Cānakya's Aphorisms Over "Greater India"* (Calcutta: Calcutta Oriental Book Agency, 1969), 13.

26   Flick (1996), 3–4.

27   Sir Monier Monier-Williams, *Sanskrit-English Dictionary* (New Delhi: Munshiram Manoharlal Publishers Pvt. Ltd., second reprint, 1981), 565.

28   Ludwik Sternbach, "Subhāṣita-saṃgrahas, A Forgotten Chapter in the Histories of Sanskrit Literature," in *Indologica Taurensia* (1973): 170.

29 Monier-Williams, (1981), 1229.

30 Flick (1996), 5–7, and Ludwik Sternbach, *Subhāṣita, Gnomic, and Didactic Literature* (Weisbaden: Otto Harrassowitz, 1974), 44–65.

31 The Jātaka stories exist in a long and a short version. The English translations consulted were: the longer version of 537 stories translated from Pali by E. B. Cowell, editor, *The Jātaka* (New Delhi: Munshiram Manoharlal Publishers, vol. I–IV, 1990); and a shorter version of 34 stories attributed to Āryaśūra translated from the Sanskrit by J. S. Speyer, *The Jātakamālā* (Delhi: Motilal Banarsidass, 1982).

32 Arthur W. Ryder, translator, *The Pañchatantra* (Chicago: Phoenix Books, The University of Chicago, 1967).

33 Edward C. Dimock, *The Literatures of India: An Introduction* (Chicago: The University of Chicago Press, 1974), 199.

34 A. Berriedale Keith, *A History of Sanskrit Literature* (Oxford: Clarendon Press, 1928), 242.

35 Dimock (1974), 200.

36 V. Balasubrahmanyan, *The Hitopadeśa* (Pondicherry: M. P. Birla Foundation, All India Press, 1989), 2–47.

37 Sternbach (1974), 4.

38 Suniti Kumar Pathak, *The Indian Nītiśāstras in Tibet* (Delhi: Motilal Banarsidass, 1974), xiv.

39 Pathak (1974), 31; these texts are located in Daisetz T. Suzuki, editor, *The Tibetan Tripitaka, Peking Edition* (Tibetan Tripitaka Research Institute, 1957), vol. 144, nos. 5820–27, folios 140b–191b.

40 Pathak (1974), 34–38.

41 Sternbach (1969), 19–20, and Pathak (1974), 33.

42 Sternbach (1974), 103.

43 G. Bethlenfalvy, "Three *Pañchatantra* Tales in an Unedited Commentary to the Tibetan *Subhāṣita-ratna-nidhi*," in *Acta Orientalia Academiae Scientiarum Hungaricae*, vol. 18 (1965): 317–18; and Ludwig Sternbach, "Note on the Identification of Some of the Sayings in Sa Skya Pandita's Subhāṣita-ratna-nidhi," in *Acta Orientalia Academiae Scientiarum Hungaricae*, vol. 34 (1980): 249–62.

44 Zhang rgyal ba dpal bzang po, *Dpal ldan sa skya pandita chen po'i rnam par thar pa*, in *The Complete Works of Pandita Kun dga' rgyal mtshan*, compiled by Bsod nams rgya mtsho, vol. 5, Bibliotheca Tibetica 1–5 (Tokyo: Tokyo Bunko, 1968), 433–38.

45 Jackson (1985), 34.

46 van der Kuijp (1983), 303, footnote 289.

47 Tshe ring dbang rgyal, *The Tale of the Incomparable Prince*, translated by Beth Newman (New York: HarperCollins, 1987).

48 Kolmas (1976).

49 Sarat Chandra Das, *An Introduction to the Grammar of the Tibetan Language*, Appendix II (Delhi: Motilal Banarsidass, 1983), 2.

50 James E. Bosson, *A Treasury of Aphoristic Jewels: The Subhāṣitaratnanidhi of Sa Skya Pandita in Tibetan and Mongolian* (Ph.D. diss., University of Washington, 1965), 1.

51 Nāgārjuna, *A Drop of Nourishment for People, and Its Commentary, The Jewel Ornament,* translated by Stanley Frye (Dharamsala: Library of Tibetan Works and Archives, 1981).

52 *Bshad mdzod*, treasury of exposition.

53 Constance Hoog, *Prince Jiṅ-gim's Textbook of Tibetan Buddhism* (Leiden: E. J. Brill, 1983), 1–10.

54 Paṇ chen bsod nams grags pa, *Mkhas pa dang blun po brtag pa'i bstan bcos dge ldan legs bshad pad ma dkar po'i chun po zhes bya ba bzhugs so*, in *The Collected Works (Gsuṅ 'bum) of Paṇ chen bsod nams grags pa* 11 (Mundgod: Drepung Loseling Library Society, 1988), folios 389–410.

55 All verses from the *Sakya Legshe* used in this chapter are taken from the main body of the text of the present work, which follows this introduction.

56 Paṇ chen bsod nams grags pa (1988), folio 406/3–5.

57 Dbyangs can dga' ba'i blo gros (A kya yongs 'dzin), *Mkhas pa dang blun po brtag pa'i bstan bcos dge ldan legs bshad pad ma dkar po'i chun po'i 'grel pa nyi ma'i 'od zer* (Xining: Mtsho sngon mi rigs dpe skrun khang, 1995; and Dharamsala: Imperial Printing Press, 1970).

58 Gung thang dkon mchog bstan pa'i sgron me. The *Chu shing bstan bcos* consists of two works: *Legs par bshad pa shing gi bstan bcos lugs gnyis yal 'dab brgya ldan*, and *Legs par bshad pa chu'i bstan bcos lugs gnyis rlabs phreng brgya*

ldan, in *The Collected Works of Gung thang dkon mchog bstan pa'i sgron me* 9, compiled by Ngawang Gelek Demo (New Delhi: 1979), folios 146–74.

59 Gung thang dkon mchog bstan pa'i sgron me (1979), folio 162/4–5.

60 Ibid., folio 159/4–5.

61 Dze smad sprul sku blo bzang dpal ldan, *Legs par bshad pa shing gi bstan bcos kyi 'grel ba lugs zung blang dor 'char ba'i me long* (Mundgod: Drepung Loseling Printing Press, 1980).

62 Ibid., p. 2.

63 Gung thang dkon mchog bstan pa'i sgron me (commentary author unknown), *Chu dang shing gi bstan bcos* (Thimphu: Text Book Division, The Department of Education, Royal Government of Bhutan, 1984).

64 Gung thang dkon mchog bstan pa'i sgron me, *Chu shing bstan bcos* (Dharamsala: Tibetan Cultural Printing Press, 1984; and the first of many editions printed in Tibet is: Lhasa: Bod ljongs mi dmangs dpe skrun khang: Bod ljongs Shin hwa dpe tshon khang nas bkram, 1981).

65 Sixth Panchen Lama, Blo bzang thub bstan chos kyi nyi ma, *Legs par bshad pa sa'i bstan bcos lugs gnyis 'od rgya 'bar ba'i dbyig gi 'phreng ba* and *Legs par bshad pa chu'i bstan bcos lugs gnyis blang dor kun gsal* in *The Collected Works of the Sixth Panchen Lama Blo bzang thub bstan chos kyi nyi ma*, 1 (New Delhi: Lham khar Yons 'dzin Bstan pa rgyal mtshan, 1973), folios 548–82.

66 'Ju mi-pham rgya-mtsho, *Rgyal po'i lugs kyi bstan bcos sa gzhi skyong ba'i rgyan* (Delhi: Gelong Jamyang, Ladakh Institute of Higher Studies, 1968).

67 Lauran Hartley, *A Socio-Historical Study of the Kingdom of Sde-dge (Derge, Khams) in the late Nineteenth Century: Ris-med Views of Alliance and Authority* (master's thesis, University of Indiana, 1997).

68 Fifth Dalai Lama, *Mchog dman bar ba rnams la lugs zung dang 'brel ba'i bslab bya gsal bar ston pa'i rim pa zla ba 'bum phrag 'char ba'i rdzing bu* in *The Collected Works (Gsuṅ 'bum) of the Fifth Dalai Lama, Ngag-dbang blo-bzang rgya-mtsho* (reproduced from the Lhasa edition (Xylograph preserved in SRIT)), vol. 19 (Gangtok: Sikkim Research Institute of Tibetology, 1993): 271–350.

69 Fifth Dalai Lama, Ngag dbang blo bzang rgya mtsho, *Lugs zung dang 'brel ba'i bslab bya mu thi la'i 'phreng ba* (Kalimpong: Tibet Mirror Press, 1960) [the second half of this work (pp. 13–24) is entitled *Skyes bu'i rnam 'byed gzhon nu'i mgul rgyan*, a text attributed to Sakya Pandita (see note 110 below)].

70 Ibid., p. 22.

71 Cowell (1990), vol. III, story no. 322, 49–52. That this story does not appear in the *Jātakamālā* suggests that Sakya Pandita either had access to the longer version, or that the story was a well-known folk tale in Tibet as indicated by the footnote to this story in Cowell, p. 49.

72 Gung thang dkon mchog bstan pa'i sgron me (1979), folio 161/6–162/1.

73 Fifth Dalai Lama, Ngag dbang blo bzang rgya mtsho, (1993).

74 Ibid., folio 4b/5–5a/1.

75 Ryder (1967), 81–88.

76 Suzuki (1957), vol. 144, no. 5821, folio 148b/6–7.

77 Paṇ chen bsod nams grags pa (1988), folio 393/6–394/1.

78 Gung thang dkon mchog bstan pa'i sgron me (1979), folio 165/2.

79 Ryder (1967), 122; *TSW* in Suzuki (1957), vol. 144, no. 5821, folio 147a/2–3; *TDNB* in Suzuki (1957), vol. 144, no. 5822, folio 157b/6–7; *SL* 64; Paṇ chen bsod nams grags pa (1988), *VEC* 39, folio 396/5–6.

80 Cowell (1990), vol. IV, story no. 484, 161–66; *SL* verse 182; Paṇ chen bsod nams grags pa (1988), *VEC* 18, folio 392/5; 'Ju mi-pham rgya-mtsho (1968), 88–89.

81 *SL* 328, Sakya Pandita, *Legs par bshad pa rin po che'i gter*, in *The Complete Works of Pandita kun dga' rgyal mtshan* 5, compiled by Bsod nams rgya mtsho (Tokyo: Tokyo Bunko, 1968), Bibliotheca Tibetica 1–5, 58, folio 2/5 ['jam pos 'jam po 'joms byed cing/ 'jams pos rtsub po'ang 'joms par byed/ 'jams pos kun 'grub de yi phyir/ 'jams nyid rno zhes mkhas rnams smra]; *ATTA*, 6.15, Flick (1996) 95, and Suzuki (1957), vol. 144, no. 5827, folio 190a/4–5 [mnyen pas mi mnyen 'jig pa ste/ 'jam pos rtsub pa 'jig par byed/ mnyen pas mi 'dul cung zad med/ de bas mnyen pa shin tu rno].

82 Flick (1996), 52, and Suzuki (1957), vol. 144, no. 5827, folio 187a/4–5.

83 Paṇ chen bsod nams grags pa (1988), folio 394/3–4 and 400/1–2, respectively.

84 Ibid., p. 66.

85 Suzuki (1957), vol. 144, no. 5821, folio 146a/7–8.

86 Theodore Duka, *The Life and Works of Alexander Csoma de Körös* (New Delhi: Mañjuśri, 1972), Bibliotheca Himalayica, series II, vol. 2.

87 Alexander Csoma de Körös, No. XIV, "A brief notice of the *Subhāṣita-ratna-nidhi* of Saskya Pandita, with extracts and translations," *Journal of the Asiatic Society of Bengal* XXIV (1855), 141–65 and XXV (1856), 257–94, reprinted in *Tibetan Studies: Being a Reprint of the Articles Contributed to the Journal of the Asiatic Society of Bengal,* edited by E. D. Ross (Calcutta: Asiatic Society of Bengal, 1911), 93–172.

88 Bosson (1965).

89 Kolmas (1976), 191.

90 Nāgārjuna and Sakya Pandita, *Elegant Sayings* (Berkeley: Dharma Publishing, 1977).

91 Lu-trub (Nāgārjuna), *She-rab dong-bu, or Prajnya Danda,* edited and translated by Major W. L. Campbell (Calcutta: Calcutta University, 1919).

92 Brian Beresford, a book review of *Elegant Sayings,* by Nāgārjuna and Sakya Pandita (Berkeley: Dharma Publishing, 1977) in *The Tibet Journal* 3.2 (summer 1978): 62–64.

93 Losang Thonden and John T. Davenport, "Extracts from the *Sakya Legshe,*" in *Chö-Yang (chos dbyangs): The Voice of Tibetan Religion and Culture* (Dharamsala: Council for Religious and Cultural Affairs, Gangchen Kyishong, 1991), 74–76.

94 This story is using a play on the word "field" in the conversation between Sumagadhā and her husband. The latter is referring to ordinary fields while Sumagadhā is talking about the Buddha and his retinue as a "field of merit." This is a common Buddhist usage of the term denoting objects of devotion, which when cultivated, yield a crop of merit to the devotee as an ordinary field yields a crop of grain to the farmer.

95 This stick *(tshul zing),* traditionally made from a branch of the tamarisk tree, is used by the discipline masters in monasteries to discipline monks. *The Great Tibetan-Chinese Dictionary (Bod rgya tshig mdzod chen mo)* (Beijing: Mi rigs dpe skrun khang, 1984), 2280.

96 The term "pheasants" is *gong ma sa* in Tibetan. I suspect this should read *gong ma sreg* (pheasant). I am indebted to Mr. Lobsang Lhalungpa of Santa Fe, New Mexico, for pointing out this spelling inaccuracy.

97 The Wheel of Life scroll painting *(thangka)* is always located near the entrance of a Tibetan Buddhist temple. This painting depicts beings in the six realms of cyclic existence, the process by which beings are trapped in the

cycle, and indicates a way out of the process. In the center a cock, a snake, and a pig chase each other, symbolizing greed, anger, and ignorance, the three main disturbing emotions that are the basis of the cycle. Radiating outwards from the center are the six realms—gods, demigods, humans, animals, pretas, and hell beings. The rim of the wheel is divided into the twelve links of interdependent origination that describe the entrapment process, and the whole wheel is in the mouth of the Lord of Death. A bodhisattva outside the wheel shows the way out of the cycle leading to enlightenment. The ignorant cowherd in the story is pointing to buffalo he notices in a part of the animal realm segment of the painting.

98   *Gnod sbyin,* a *yakśa,* or malevolent demon

99   Dbyangs can dga' ba'i blo gros (A kya yongs 'dzin) (1971), folio 377/1, suggests that the term "char sdod byi'u" (or "char 'dod byi'u") refers to several possible birds, perhaps here a swallow, or a cuckoo, as Sakya Khenpo Sangyay Tenzin uses below.

100   This expression states a Tibetan belief that one's past record of merit is imprinted on one's forehead as psychic lines, not ordinary visible wrinkles.

101   A cross between a yak and a cow.

102   The text has the term *bal pos se'u,* which is an incorrect spelling. It should be *bal po'i se'u.* Sakya Pandita, *Legs par bshad pa rin po che'i gter* (1968) 51/1/3. This is a common name for "crab apple" in some dialects according to personal communication from Lobsang Lhalungpa.

103   Shakabpa (1984), 25 *(lha chos dge ba'i bcu dang mi chos gtsang ma bcu drug).* According to Tashi Tsering of the Library of Tibetan Works and Archives in Dharamsala, India, it is dubious whether these principles actually originated with Srongtsan Gampo.

104   This flower *(sna ma'i me tog, dza ti)* may also be of the nutmeg tree, Dbyangs can dga' ba'i blo gros (A kya yongs 'dzin) (1971), folio 377/5–6.

105   This metaphor derives from a well-known Tibetan proverb, "even though gold is beneath the earth, it shines in the sky" *(gser sa 'og la yod kyang nam mkha' la khyab),* Sangye T. Naga and Tsepak Rigzin, *Tibetan Quadrisyllabics, Phrases and Idioms (Bod dbyin shan sbyar gyi tshig tshogs dang gtam dpe)* (Dharamsala: Library of Tibetan Works and Archives, 1994), 247.

106   *(Skyu ru ra, āmalaka);* there is some variation in the Latin taxonomical designation for this plant: *Phyllanthus emblica L.,* according to Karma chos 'phel, *Bdud rtsi gyi 'khrungs dpe legs bshad nor bu'i phreng mdzes* (Lhasa: Bod

ljongs mi dmangs dpe skrun khang, 1993), 27; *Emblica officinalis,* Vaidya Bhagwan Dash, *Tibetan Medicine: With Special Reference to Yoga Śataka* (Dharamsala: Library of Tibetan Works and Archives, 1980), 277; Liberty Hyde Bailey and Ethel Hyde Bailey, *Hortus Third: A Concise Dictionary of Plants Cultivated in the United States and Canada,* revised and expanded by the staff of the Liberty Hyde Bailey Hortorium, Cornell University (New York: MacMillan, 1976), 865–66, lists PHYLLANTHUS L. Emblica L. EMBLIC, MYROBALAN. Deciduous tree, to 50 feet, native to tropical Asia, with flaking bark, oblong ½–¾ inch leaves, clustered yellow flowers, and lobed 1-inch diameter fruit; Monier-Williams (1981), 146, defines āmalaka as the fruit of Emblic Myrobalan, Emblica Officinalis Gærtn.

107 Name of a mountain range on the west of Malabar (the modern state of Kerala), the western Ghāts (abounding in sandal trees), Monier-Williams (1981), 792.

108 The "predictive signs" refers to their respective names: "Subhartha" means "decent intent;" "Papartha" means "evil intent."

109 *Sa lu,* a kind of plant described in Alexander Csoma de Körös, No. V, "Origin of the Shakya Race translated from the *la,* or the 26th volume of the *mDo* class in the Kangyur commencing on the 161st leaf," in *Journal of the Asiatic Society of Bengal* II (1833): 385, reprinted in *Collected Works of Alexander Csoma de Körös,* edited by J. Terjek (Budapest: Akadémiai Kiadó, 1984), 30.

110 In conformity with the Sakya tradition of Tibetan Buddhism, the author attributes this quotation to "Chos rjes nyid," an appellation for Sakya Pandita in the context of this text. David Jackson questions this attribution (Jackson (1985), 106–7 and 119–20). The verse as quoted in the commentary reads, *rang bzhin brling la shes rgya chel nyi ma lta bur kun la snyoms/ nye ring med par 'khor 'dab skyongs/ de dag skyes bu chen po yin.* The text title, *Skyes bu rnam 'byed,* is not found in the list of Sakya Pandita's works in vol. 5 of the *Sa skya bka' 'bum.* However, such a title is included as the second half of a book by the Fifth Dalai Lama containing his short didactic work entitled *Lugs zung dang 'brel ba'i bslab bya mu thi la'i 'phreng ba* (1960). Here a nearly identical verse is found on p. 17 that reads, *rang bzhin rling la shes rgya chel nye ring med par 'khor 'dab skyongs/ rtag tu gzhan la sems brtse ba/ de dag skyes bu chen po yin* (Persons of serene character and extensive wisdom,/ Who care for their subjects impartially,/ And who are always compassionate to others:/ These are the truly great ones). [Several other verses from this work are noted below.]

111 The inclusion of eating garlic with wrongdoing refers to the belief that certain strong foods such as garlic and onions create interferences to the pro-

cess of mental development in the practice of meditation. Some ordained Buddhist practitioners refrain from eating these foods, as do others engaged in the stricter meditation practices, especially during periods of retreat.

112   *Ce spyang,* a crossbreed between a jackal and a wild dog or wolf, or occasionally a fox, Dbyangs can dga' ba'i blo gros (A kya yongs 'dzin) (1971), folio 378/1.

113   The Tibetan calendar is lunar-based, with the full moon always occurring on the fifteenth of the month and the new moon always on the thirtieth.

114   *Ya so,* "upper teeth," according to Geshe Sopa of Deer Park Buddhist Center in Wisdonsin, refers to the canine teeth that humans and other carnivores possess but are lacking in herbivores like cattles.

115   The term here is *chö-yön (mchod yon),* a contraction of *mchod gnas* (those who are worthy of honor) and *yon bdag* (those who extend such honor). See the introduction above for a discussion of Sakya Pandita's time in Mongolia, which first established the chö-yön relationship between Buddhist clerics of Tibet and temporal rulers of Mongolia, and later, China.

116   *Jasminum zambac,* Monier-Williams (1981), 793.

117   From the author's perspective as a Buddhist monk, a wise person who best understood the laws of actions and their effects and avoided wrongdoing would most likely be a monk or nun living according to ordination vows. For such a person neither business nor farming would be suitable livelihood. Farming, for example, would entail cultivating the land, which would injure and kill many insects and other creatures who live in the soil, thus violating the vow against killing sentient beings. Business can entail competitiveness, misleading others, not telling the truth, and other wrongdoing. This is not to say that farmers and business people could not be good Buddhists, but that their good actions are partially offset by negative ones, an inevitable compromise of their livelihood.

118   As occidental folklore sees "a man in the moon," so in Asia there is "a rabbit in the moon," which is the imagery being referred to in this story.

119   The individual work assignments delegated at taxation time would be referring in part to corvée labor, which was an important component of the government of Tibet's way of administering the country. Landowners were obliged to provide transportation and horses to those holding permits, such as government officials. They were also obliged to pay taxes in the form of grain to the government. The people who actually had to donate their time and effort to satisfy these policies were the laborers connected to the lands in question.

120 This bird *(chu skyar)* is defined as "a kind of waterfowl that eats fish," *The Great Tibetan-Chinese Dictionary (bod rgya tshig mdzod chen mo)* (1984), 796; Mr. Lobsang Lhalungpa calls it a duck.

121 The white water lily (*ku mu da,* also *ut pa la dkar po*), Dbyangs can dga' ba'i blo gros (A kya yongs 'dzin) (1971), folio 378/6; it has been variously interpreted as: *Nymphæa esculenta,* Sarat Chandra Das, *A Tibetan-English Dictionary* (Kyoto: Rinsen Book Company, 1979), 1350; *Nelumbo nucifera,* Dash (1980), 347; *Nymphæa cærula,* Monier-Williams (1981), 180.

122 There are minor differences between the wording of this citation as given in the commentary and its source in the Peking Bstan 'gyur (Suzuki (1957), vol. 144, no. 5827, folios 189b/8–190a/1). The translation here follows the Peking Bstan 'gyur version.

123 Perhaps the black walnut tree, *tin tu ka,* according to *The Great Tibetan-Chinese Dictionary (Bod rgya tshig mdzod chen mo)* (1984), 1029.

124 The text Sakya Khenpo Sangyay Tenzin used has for line three *'chi ba ji ltar gsos gyur kyang,* where the subject matter is "death" *('chi ba),* which is elaborated on in the commentary. However, this is probably a mistake as other texts read, *mchil pa ji ltar gsos gyur kyang,* where the subject matter is "sparrow" *(mchil pa),* in which case the last two lines would read, "No matter how one rears a sparrow/ It is impossible for it to be fearless." The texts that have "sparrow" are: Sakya Pandita, *Legs par bshad pa rin po che'i gter* (1968), 54, folio 4/3; Dmar ston chos rgyal (1990), 37; and Dbyangs can dga' ba'i blo gros (A kya yongs 'dzin) (1971), folio 379/2.

125 This term, "'chi ba (death) mi rtag pa (impermanence)," is often rendered "death and impermanence," but it more accurately means "death, the type of impermanence unique to living beings." I am indebted to Venerable Yangsi Rinpoche of the Deer Park Buddhist Center for this clarification.

126 The sage "Ahtrotala" could not be identified; the translation for this and the following two verses follows the version of the *Nītiśāstra* by Masūrākṣa found in Suzuki (1957), vol. 144, no. 5827, folio 187a/3–5.

127 The translation for this third line follows the *Nītiśāstra* by Masūrakṣa; it reads slightly differently in Sakya Khenpo Sangyay Tenzin's commentary: *de bzhin g.yul du phyin pa na* (Then later when fighting with him).

128 Ibid., folio 187a/4; line 4 in Sakya Khenpo Sangyay Tenzin's commentary reads slightly differently: *rngan can gnod pa byed pa gzhom* (Destroy those harmful bullies).

129 Sakya Pandita seems here to be paraphrasing a verse from the *Nītiśāstra* by Masūrākṣa (Suzuki (1957), vol. 144, no. 5827, folio 187a/3–4); see also the commentary to verse 185 above.

130 It is unclear which nītiśāstra Sakya Pandita is referring to here. This verse is not found in the *Cānakyarājanītiśāstra* that appears in the Tibetan Bstan 'gyur. Sternbach attempted to reconstruct the original lost Sanskrit version, but in so doing ended up referring to approximately one hundred *Cānakya-rājanīti* texts, Ludwik Sternbach, *Cānakya-rāja-nīti: Maxims on* Rāja-nīti *Compiled from Various Collections of Maxims Attributed to Cānakya* (Madras: Adyar Library and Research Centre, 1963), 42.

131 Some marine gastropod mollusks are known to be highly poisonous.

132 The sun's rays struck the tip of the mountain in the west before the sun rose in the east.

133 In India the springtime is a dry season that precedes the summer monsoon.

134 This is referring to a lunar eclipse. Rāhu is one of the heavenly bodies of Indian cosmology and is responsible for eclipses. Originally a demon who tried to capture the sun and moon, Rāhu was later subdued and is now said to be one of the planets.

135 The proverb referred to here states: *[gsang bu dbyar chos la mi 'dug zer na bdag shi ba 'bad red/ ljang dgun chos la 'dug zer na bdag smyo ba 'bad]* "If I am absent at the summer session at Sangbu, then I have died./ If I am present at the winter session at Jang, then I am crazy." According to Shes rab rdo rje, *Mkhas dang grub pa'i 'byung gnas byang ngam ring chos sde chen po'i chos 'byung rna ba'i bdud rtsi'i snying po* (Lhasa: Bod ljongs mi dmangs dpe skrun khang, 1994), 10 Geluk and 15 Sakya monasteries used to meet for summer and winter debate at Ngamring (Ngam ring) and that if one wished to be excused from one of these sessions, one had to present a silver coin and a white offering scarf in advance—this is why it was necessary to think about it beforehand. I am indebted to Geshe Sonam Rinchen and Ruth Sonam of the Library of Tibetan Works and Archives in Dharamsala, who researched this proverb for me and provided this reference.

136 *Srin po* or *rākṣa*, cannibal demons in Indian and Tibetan mythology.

137 The commentary to this verse follows closely that of Dmar ston chos rgyal (1990), 180 (not located at verse 252 itself, but inexplicably added to the commentary for verse 249).

138 The term *chas gzob*, rendered here as "foppish" (spelled *ches gzob* in the commentary), means "to be preoccupied with adorning oneself with fine clothing and jewelry and being fastidiously attentive to other meaningless matters," Gung thang dkon mchog bstan pa'i sgron me (1984), folio 380/2–3.

139 The flower of the flame-of-the-forest tree, *Butea frondosa (rgya skegs, lākshā)*, upon which the lac insect feeds, Gung thang dkon mchog bstan pa'i sgron me (1984), folio 380/3–4; Vaidya Bhagwan Dash, *Tibetan Medicine: With Special Reference to Yoga Śataka* (Dharamsala: Library of Tibetan Works and Archives, 1980), 287; Monier-Williams (1981), 899; Cornell University (1976), 191.

140 Possibly a misspelling of a kind of serpent called the *urāga*; Monier-Williams (1981), 217.

141 *Byis pa* literally means "child" or "childish individual," and is used several times in this text. Geshe Sopa of Deer Park Buddhist Center in Wisconsin explains that this term refers to those who are "spiritually immature" in comparison to ārya beings (see glossary).

142 Gung thang describes this bird as pale gray in color and the size of a pigeon, known in his native Amdo dialect of the late eighteenth century as *'bya dru dru'*; Gung thang dkon mchog bstan pa'i sgron me (1984), folio 380/6.

143 With this citation (and several more that follow), Sa skya mkhan po sangs rgyas bstan 'dzin is drawing from a short work of Sakya Pandita entitled *Advice I Give to Myself (Rang gis rang la gros 'debs pa)*, where most verses contain at their conclusion the term "lo tsa ba," or "translator." In other words, he is addressing himself as "translator" in keeping with his well-known status as a translator of Sanskrit. Jackson (1985), 77, claims Sakya Pandita never wrote this text.

144 Sakya Pandita seems here to be paraphrasing a verse from the *Nītiśāstra* by Masūrākṣa (Suzuki (1957), vol. 144, no. 5827, folio 187a/3–4); see also the commentary to verse 185 above.

145 *Shorea robusta*, a common tree found in the foothills and Terai of northern India, valuable for wood, fodder, and incense, which is made from its resin.

146 See note 117 above.

147 See verse 279.

148 Crystals are said to have a cool, water-like nature while flints have the

nature of fire. In Tibet flints are so common they need not be bought and sold. Anyone in need of a flint can either find one on the ground or get it for free from someone.

149 The commentary interchanged the first two lines with the last two lines of this verse; this translation corrects that mistake, though the meaning is the same read either way.

150 *Ro langs,* a kind of demon or spirit that occupies dead bodies, a zombie or corpse-raising spirit.

151 The commentary is confusing at this point because it refers to a "crow or a pigeon" (Sakya Pandita's verse mentions only a crow) then goes on to talk mostly about the pigeon with the crow entering at the end in passing. The original story in the *Pañchatantra,* where both the crow and the pigeon clearly benefit from relying on the wise mouse, is longer and more convoluted than the abbreviated version here taken from Dmar ston chos rgyal's commentary; Ryder (1967), 213–88, Dmar ston chos rgyal (1990), 197–98.

152 See "three kinds of suffering" in the glossary.

153 This malady is known as *lung (rlung nad)* in Tibetan, a disorder of the wind element.

154 See "three types of patience" in glossary.

155 The exhortation to become ordained must be understood as ideally the most efficient way to focus one's full attention on the practices that are conducive to spiritual progress; however, as with any action one must carefully consider the consequences. In Tibet, young men or women often felt drawn to monastic life before they had committed themselves to lay life, and those who felt compelled later would usually be part of an extended family in which responsibilities and support systems were broadly based. In a Western context, to abandon familial and other responsibilities for the sake of ordination may be more self-serving than meritorious, so one should be extremely conscientious about making such a decision.

156 See note 155 above.

157 The commentary to this verse has been given additional details by referring to a more extensive account of the story of Kumāra Jīvaka found in "'Tsho byed gzhon nus sman spel tshul," Sde srid sangs rgyas rgya mtshos, *Gso rig sman gyi khog 'bugs* (Lanzhou: Kan su'u mi rigs dpe skrun khang, 1982), 90–120.

158 A literal translation of Sakya Pandita's name, Kun dga' rgyal mtshan.

GLOSSARY

Aṅgulimāla
    a bandit who made a necklace of the thumbs of his first nine hundred and ninety-nine victims, but was converted by the Buddha, his intended one thousandth victim

antidotes (gnyen po)
    positive acts that counteract negative acts; patience, for example, being an antidote to anger

ārya ('phags pa)
    one who has achieved liberation but not omniscience

asura (lha ma yin)
    demi-gods, one of the six realms of cyclic existence

Avalokiteshvara
    the manifestation of the Buddha's compassion

bhikṣu
    Sanskrit term for monk

bodhisattva (byang chub sems dpa')
    Buddhist practitioner who has resolved to attain enlightenment for the sake of all sentient beings

Brahmin
    high priestly caste of India

Buddhist sciences (rig gnas bcu)
    five major (arts and crafts, medicine, grammar, logic, and philosophy) and five minor (poetry, synonyms, lexicography, astrology, and dance and drama)

calm abiding (zhi gnas)
    an advanced level of concentration, in which attention is focused upon an internal object of observation and the mind is settled, alert, and free from distraction

chang
> a fermented liquor consumed in Tibet

cognitive obscurations (see obstacles to omniscience)

collection of merit and wisdom (tshogs gnyis)
> another way of describing the practice of the Buddhist path, namely, the steady accrual of merit and wisdom through engaging in virtuous activity and developing insight

commitments (dam tshig)
> vows taken at different points on the Buddhist spiritual path, such as the five precepts to refrain from killing, lying, stealing, sexual misconduct, and intoxication

concentration (bsam gtan)
> generally, any focusing of mind; in advanced practice, a state of mind that is free of delusions and able to focus on an object without distraction

cyclic existence (srid pa, 'khor ba)
> the six realms of cyclic existence through which all sentient beings migrate from lifetime to lifetime according to the law of karma until enlightenment is achieved (three higher realms—humans, upper celestial, and lower celestial; and three lower realms—animals, pretas, and hells)

definite goodness (nges legs)
> complete liberation from cyclic existence and the attainment of a buddha's omniscience, or full enlightenment

degenerate times (see five degeneracies)

delusions (nyon mongs)
> negative states of mind such as anger, pride, shamelessness, pretense, avarice, laziness, and so on that produce turmoil and confusion, thus disturbing one's mental peace

determination to be free (nges 'byung, sometimes translated "renunciation")
> the wish to be completely free of the misery of cyclic existence

Dharma (chos)
> the teachings of the Buddha

Dharma king (chos rgyal)
> cakravartin; a ruler who governs according to Buddhist principles; two famous examples are considered to have been King Aśoka of India (B.C.E. 269–232) and U Nu, the first leader of independent Burma in the 1950s

discarding and cultivating (spang blang, or blang dor)
> discarding negative states of mind and cultivating positive ones

discursive thought (rnam rtog)
> conceptual cognition, ideas, imagination

disturbing emotions (see delusions)

dzo (mdzo)
>   a cross between a yak and a cow

eight worldly obsessions ('jig rten chos brgyad)
>   preoccupation of ordinary people with gain and loss, good and bad reputation, praise and blame, and pleasure and misery

emptiness (stong pa nyid)
>   the absence of independently or permanently existing phenomena, i.e., things do not exist in and of themselves as we imagine, but in fact are produced and disappear depending on causes and conditions; the highest view of the nature of reality in Buddhist philosophy

enlightened attitude (byang chub kyi sems)
>   the altruistic thought to attain enlightenment oneself in order to most efficiently assist other sentient beings to attain enlightenment

enlightenment (byang chub)
>   the final attainment of the Buddhist path (buddhahood) where all negative states of mind have been thoroughly eradicated and all positive states of mind are fully realized

five boundless transgressions (mtshams med lnga)
>   patricide, matricide, killing a foe destroyer, drawing blood from the body of a buddha with evil intent, causing a schism within the Sangha

five degeneracies (snyigs ma lnga)
>   a decrease in average life span, the spread of delusions, an increase in perverse views, depravity of people, degenerate times

foe destroyer (dgra bcom pa)
>   an arhat, a spiritual practitioner who has attained nirvana

four antidotes (gnyen po'i stobs bzhi)
>   the means of counteracting the effect of negative actions: strong remorse for the act; firm intention not to commit such an act again; taking refuge in the Three Jewels and developing the enlightened attitude; and firm determination to overcome negative acts by engaging in wholesome acts

four elements ('byung ba bzhi)
>   earth, water, fire, wind

four ends (mtha' bzhi)
>   death as the end of birth, separation as the end of meeting, exhaustion as the end of accumulation, and downfall as the end of high position

four noble truths (bden pa bzhi)
>   the first teaching of the Buddha: 1) that cyclic existence is pervaded with misery (the truth of suffering); 2) that misery arises dependent upon causes (the truth of the origin of suffering); 3) those causes can be removed

(the truth of cessation); 4) the means of removing those causes is the Buddhist path (the truth of the path)

four ways of gathering disciples (bsdu ba'i dngos po bzhi)
   giving students whatever material things and Dharma teachings they desire, speaking pleasantly to them, acting according to their wishes, helping them complete their activities

fully free and fortunate human being (dal 'byor)
   one who possesses the eight freedoms or leisures (dal ba brgyad) and the ten endowments ('byor ba bcu). The eight freedoms include the four freedoms from being born as a nonhuman in the hell, preta, animal, or celestial realms; and the four freedoms from having been born as a human in a barbaric land, in a place where the Buddha has not appeared, as a mute or fool, or as one who holds wrong views. The ten endowments include the five personal endowments of being born as a human, in a time and place where the Dharma flourishes, with one's sense faculties intact, having not committed the five boundless transgressions, and having faith in the Dharma; and the five circumstantial endowments, that the Buddha appeared in the present era, that he taught the Dharma, that his teachings continue to flourish, that there are others who follow his teachings, and that there are loving and compassionate teachers to help in the practice of Dharma.

garuḍa
   a large mythical divine eagle
Gauda
   an ancient kingdom in modern-day Bengal
gods (lha)
   one of the six realms of cyclic existence
good personal qualities, or good qualities (yon tan)
   see Translators' Preface for a discussion of this term
guests (mgron pa)
   objects of invocation in tantric meditation practices

hearer (nyan thos)
   originally, the disciples who personally listened to the teachings of Buddha Śākyamuni and then propagated them; later, an advanced class of Buddhist practitioners whose study and practice concentrates on the four noble truths and the law of cause and effect
Heaven of Thirty Three (sum cu rtsa gsum)
   celestial abode of the gods of the desire realm
high status (mngon mtho)

attainment of rebirth as a human or a celestial being

illusory wealth (sgyu ma'i nor)
> wealth is a transient phenomenon to which we ascribe properties that we assume are real (such as permanence), but in fact are imaginary, as when we are fooled by the illusions of a conjurer's performance

insight transmission of spiritual realization in oneself (rtogs pa'i bstan pa)
> transmission of the Buddha's teachings through putting them into practice and gaining insights and realizations

Kālidāsa
> preeminent poet and dramatist who lived during the Gupta Empire (320–550 C.E.)

karma (las)
> the relationship between physical and mental actions and the effects they generate in either this or future lifetimes for the actor

lama (bla ma)
> a guru or spiritual teacher

liberation (thar pa)
> freedom from being propelled by karma in the cycle of death and rebirth, but lacking the omniscience of full enlightenment

logician (rtog ge pa)
> a non-Buddhist religious sect in ancient India

Maghada
> a kingdom of ancient India located in present day West Bengal

Mahāyāna
> the bodhisattva path of Buddhism

Malaya
> name of a mountain range on the west of Malabar (the modern state of Kerala), the western Ghāts (abounding in sandal trees)

Mañjuśrī
> a manifestation of the Buddha's wisdom

Maudgalyāyana
> with Śāriputra, one of the two foremost disciples of the Buddha

meditative stabilization (ting nge 'dzin)
> the union of special insight with calm abiding required to progress to all higher levels on the Buddhist path; the meditator is able to focus single-pointedly on emptiness without distraction for as long as desired

merit (bsod nams)

virtues; positive energy generated by engaging in wholesome mental and
physical actions

merit field (zhing dam pa)

the buddhas and bodhisattvas in the Buddhist pantheon who, when ven-
erated, enable one to acquire merit

method (thabs)

all virtuous actions categorized under the first five of the six perfections

method and wisdom

virtuous action and development of insight, which together are the causes
that produce enlightenment

Mount Sumeru

the mythical center of the universe of ancient Indian cosmology

nāgas (klu)

serpent-like creatures believed to dwell in subterranean realms and to
control rain, ponds, rivers, and soil productivity

nirvāṇa (mya ngan las 'das pa)

the state of peace arising from eradicating the obstacles to liberation

obscurations to liberation (nyon sgribs)

twenty-six major and minor delusions that must be eliminated before
liberation from cyclic existence can be attained

obscurations to omniscience (shes sgribs)

delusions and wrong views that obstruct the attainment of omniscience

omniscience (thams cad mkhyen pa)

the wisdom consciousness that realizes emptiness, developed through the
practice of the six perfections on the sutra path or through special med-
itation techniques on the tantra path

perfection of generosity (see six perfections)

predispositions (bag chags)

mental habituation implanted on one's mental continuum stemming
from any kind of action one engages in; these dispose one to behaving
in certain ways in the future

pretas (yi dvag)

pretas, one of the six realms of cyclic existence

Rāhu

in Indian astrology, a malevolent planet that has a detrimental influence
over mankind and is responsible for creating eclipses by swallowing the
moon or the sun

Rāhula
> the son of the Buddha

Sakya (sa skya)
> name of the town in Tsang Province of Tibet where the great Sakya
> Monastery is located and where Sakya Pandita lived

Śākya
> name of a tribe that lived in the Himalayan foothills (in modern-day
> Nepal) into which Buddha Śākyamuni was born

saṃsāra (see cyclic existence)

saṅgha (dge 'dun)
> the community of followers of Buddhism, originally considered to be
> ordained monks and nuns, but now thought of as lay practitioners as well

Śāriputra
> with Maudgalyāyana, one of the two foremost disciples of the Buddha

scriptural transmission of teaching others (lung gi bstan pa)
> oral and written transmission of the extant teachings of the Buddha

selflessness (bdag med)
> the lack of inherent existence of persons and other phenomena

seven precious possessions of a universal monarch (rin po che sna bdun)
> ruby, sapphire, lapis lazuli, emerald, diamond, pearl, and coral

Śiva
> a major deity in the Hindu pantheon

six perfections (pha rol tu phyin pa'i drug)
> the perfections of generosity, ethical conduct, patience, enthusiastic per-
> severance, concentration, and wisdom

skillful means (see method)

solitary realizer (rang sangs rgyas)
> a class of Buddhist practitioners who do not rely on spiritual teachers

special insight (lhag mthong)
> an analytical consciousness that investigates the emptiness of phenomena;
> cultivated by repeatedly applying calm abiding on emptiness

Śrāvastī
> a major city of fifth century B.C.E. Buddhist India

Srongtsen Gampo (617–49 C.E.)
> the first great king of Tibet, considered the father of the nation, who
> unified the country and was responsible for its military superiority, the
> introduction of Buddhism, and Tibet's written language

suchness (de kho na nyid)
> the true nature of something as opposed to its apparent reality; a Bud-
> dhist philosophical term referring to ultimate reality, the emptiness or

absence of all misconception

superior intention (lhag bsam)

the wish to assume personal responsibility for liberating all sentient beings from the suffering of cyclic existence

sutra (mdo)

the classification of Buddhist teachings presenting a gradual path to enlightenment

tantra (rgyud)

the esoteric classification of Buddhist teachings presenting a speedier method of attaining enlightenment

tathāgatha (de bzhin gshegs pa)

another term for a buddha

Ten Moral Principles and Sixteen Rules of Public Conduct

a code of law attributed to King Srongtsen Gampo; the ten moral principles (lha chos dge ba bcu) abandoning the acts of (a) killing, (b) stealing, (c) indulging in sexual misconduct, (d) telling lies, (e) slandering, (f) using harsh words, (g) indulging in idle gossip, (h) being covetous, (i) harming others, and (j) upholding wrong views or philosophies; and the sixteen rules of public conduct (mi chos gtsang ma bcu drug) (a) respecting the Three Jewels, (b) practicing the sublime Dharma, (c) honoring one's parents, (d) honoring the learned scholars, (e) honoring the elders and those of good lineage, (f) being helpful to one's neighbors, (g) being honest and humble, (h) being loyal to one's friends, (i) following and being true to decent people, (j) being modest about food and wealth, (k) repaying the kindness of the generous, (l) not being deceptive in business, (m) not being jealous to anyone, (n) maintaining self-control, uninfluenced by bad talk, (o) being soft-spoken and saying little, and (p) being courageous and broad-minded in great duties

ten nonvirtuous actions (mi dge ba bcu)

killing, stealing, sexual misconduct, lying, slander, harsh speech, idle gossip, covetousness, malice, wrong view

ten powers (stobs bcu)

the powers of knowing: right from wrong, the consequences of actions, the various mental inclinations, mental faculties, and degrees of intelligence of others, the paths to all goals, the ever-afflicted and purified phenomena, past lives, death and birth, the exhaustion of contaminations

ten qualities of an enemy of the Dharma (zhing bcu tshang ba'i bstan dgra)

according to the tantras, someone with all the following qualities can rightfully be killed: destroying the teachings, belittling the Three Jewels, robbing the saṅgha, ridiculing the Mahāyāna path, threatening the life of a lama, criticizing another tantric path practitioner, making obstacles to spiritual attainments, having no love or compassion whatsoever, breaking spiritual commitments, holding views contrary to the law of cause and effect

three aspects of giving (sbyin pa'i 'khor gsum)
the giver, the recipient, and the act of giving

three excellences (dam pa gsum)
the excellent altruistic attitude to help others, the excellent understanding of suchness, and the excellent dedication of merit

Three Jewels (dkon mchog gsum)
the Buddha, the Dharma, and the Saṅgha

three kinds of ethical practice (lag len dam pa gsum, or tshul khrims rnam gsum)
(a) refraining from misconduct, (b) accumulating virtues, and (c) acting on behalf of other sentient beings; alternatively, (a) giving protection from fear, (b) admiring virtues, and (c) seeking liberation from cyclic existence
[it is unclear which is referred to in verse 326]

three kinds of knowledge (rig pa gsum)
extrasensory abilities developed at an advanced stage of the Buddhist path

three kinds of suffering (sdug bsngal gsum)
the suffering of pain, the suffering of change, and pervasive suffering (cyclic existence itself is of the nature of suffering)

three kinds of wisdom (shes rab gsum)
wisdom understanding (a) conventional phenomena, (b) ultimate phenomena, and (c) the welfare of sentient beings; alternatively, wisdom acquired through (a) hearing or study, (b) contemplation, and (c) meditation

three poisonous attitudes or delusions (dug gsum)
attachment, anger, and ignorance

three realms of cyclic existence (khams gsum)
desire realm, form realm, and formless realm

three trainings (bslab pa gsum)
the trainings in ethical conduct, meditative stabilization, and wisdom

three types of patience (bzod pa rnam gsum)
patience that pays no attention to mistreatment (gnod pa la ji snyam pa'i bzod pa), patience of voluntarily undergoing suffering (sdug bsngal dang len gyi bzod pa), patience of discriminating awareness of the Dharma

(chos la nges shes kyi bzod pa)
threefold analysis (dpyad pa gsum)
> the threefold criteria for validating a phenomenon: obvious things are not contradicted by valid bare perception, slightly obscure things are not contradicted by valid inference based on the force of evidence, extremely obscure things are not contradicted by valid inference based on scriptural authority; alternatively, thorough examination of something as one would assay the purity of gold by melting, cutting, and rubbing

threefold faith (dad pa gsum)
> sincere faith of body, convincing faith of speech, and aspiring faith of mind

Tīrthikas (mu stegs pa)
> a non-Buddhist religious sect of ancient India

Tripiṭaka (sde snod gsum)
> the three general divisions of Buddhist teachings: vinaya, emphasizing training in ethics, sutra, emphasizing training in concentration, and abhidharma, emphasizing training in wisdom

truth of suffering (sdug bsngal bden pa)
> the first of the four noble truths

tutelary deities (yi dam)
> tantric deities whose meditation rituals are followed by practitioners who have received the appropriate initiations and have a special bond or relationship with those deities

twelve special qualities of learning (sbyangs pa'i yon tan bcu gnyis)
> this refers to twelve ascetic practices: wearing robes of rags, wearing the three Dharma robes, wearing robes only of wool, eating one's food in one sitting, subsisting on alms, not accepting food after having risen from one's seat, dwelling in a hermitage, dwelling in a forest, dwelling in an open and unsheltered place, dwelling in cemeteries, remaining in the sitting posture, sleeping wherever one may happen to be

two obstacles (sgrib pa gnyis)
> the delusive obstacles to liberation and to omniscience

two stages (rim pa gnyis)
> the generation and completion stages of tantric practice

universal monarch (see Dharma King)

victory banner (rgyal mtshan)
> symbolic representation of the victory of Buddhism, portrayed as cylindrical multi-colored cloth banner on a pole, or as gold ornament on a temple roof

vinaya ('dul ba)

teachings on ethical conduct
Viṣṇu
    a major deity in the Hindu pantheon

water with the eight special qualities (chu yan lag brgyad ldan)
    water that is cool, refreshing, tasty, smooth, clear, has a good smell, is soothing to the throat, and harmless to the stomach
wisdom (shes rab, blo gros, mkhas pa, mdzangs, ye shes)
    in the first eight chapters these terms are used more or less interchangeably referring to ordinary notions of wisdom, good sense, and intelligence; in the ninth chapter wisdom takes on a more precise meaning in Buddhist philosophy, referring to emptiness or the true nature of phenomena

These definitions are adapted from *The Great Tibetan-Chinese Dictionary (bod rgya tshig mdzod chen mo)* published in Beijing by the Mi rigs dpe skrun khang, 1986; Gyurme, Dorji, and Matthew Kapstein, *The Nyingma School Of Tibetan Buddhism: Its Fundamentals and History*, Volume Two: Reference Material (Boston: Wisdom Publications, 1991), pp. 105–87; and Rigzin, Tsepak, *Tibetan-English Dictionary of Buddhist Terminology* (Dharamsala: the Library of Tibetan Works and Archives, 1993).

BIBLIOGRAPHY

Bailey, L.H. *Hortus Third: A Concise Dictionary of Plants Cultivated in the United States and Canada.* Initially compiled by Liberty Hyde Bailey and Ethel Zoe Baily; revised and expanded by the staff of the Liberty Hyde Bailey Hortorium, Cornell University. New York: MacMillan (1976).

Balasubrahmanyan, V. *The Hitopadeśa.* Pondicherry: M. P. Birla Foundation, All India Press (1989).

Beresford, Brian. Review of *Elegant Sayings,* by Nāgārjuna and Sakya Pandita. *The Tibet Journal* 3.2 (summer 1978): 62–64.

Bethlenfalvy, G. "Three *Pañchatantra* Tales in an Unedited Commentary to the Tibetan *Subhāṣita-ratna-nidhi.*" *Acta Orientalia Academiae Scientiarum Hungaricae,* vol. 18 (1965).

Bod rgya tshig mdzod chen mo (The Great Tibetan-Chinese Dictionary). Beijing: Mi rigs dpe skrun khang (1984).

Bosson, James E. *A Treasury of Aphoristic Jewels: The Subhāṣitaratnanidhi of Sa Skya Pandita in Tibetan and Mongolian.* Ph.D. diss., University of Washington, 1965.

————. *A Treasury of Aphoristic Jewels: The Subhāṣitaratnanidhi of Sa Skya Pandita in Tibetan and Mongolian.* Bloomington: Indiana University Publications (1969), Uralic and Altaic Series, 92.

Cassinelli, C. W., and Robert B. Ekvall. *A Tibetan Principality: The Political System of Sa skya.* Ithaca: Cornell University Press (1969).

Cowell, E. B., editor. *The Jātaka.* New Delhi: Munshiram Manoharlal Publishers I–IV (1990).

Das, Sarat Chandra. *An Introduction to the Grammar of the Tibetan Language.* Delhi: Motilal Banarsidass (1983).

————. "Contributions on Tibet." *Journal of the Asiatic Society of Bengal* 1 (1882).

————. *A Tibetan-English Dictionary.* Kyoto: Rinsen Book Company (1979).

Dash, Vaidya Bhagwan. *Tibetan Medicine: with Special Reference to Yoga Śataka.* Dharamsala: Library of Tibetan Works and Archives (1980).

Dbyangs can dga' ba'i blo gros (A kya yongs 'dzin). *mkhas pa dang blun po brtag pa'i bstan bcos dge ldan legs bshad pad ma dkar po'i chun po'i 'grel pa nyi ma'i 'od zer.* Lhasa: Bod ljongs mi dmangs dpe skrun khang (1995); and Dharamsala: Imperial Printing Press (1970).

————. *Sa skya legs bshad sogs kyi brda don 'ga' zhig dgrol ba* in *The Collected Works of A kya yongs 'dzin* 2, New Delhi: Lama Guru Deva (1971), folios 374–82.

Dimock, Edward C. *The Literatures of India: An Introduction.* Chicago: The University of Chicago Press (1974).

Dmar ston chos rgyal. *Legs par bshad pa rin po che'i gter dang 'grel pa.* Xining: Bod ljongs mi dmangs dpe skrun khang (1990), and Dharamsala: Tibetan Cultural Printing Press (1982).

Duka, Theodore. *The Life and Works of Alexander Csoma de Körös.* New Delhi: Mañjuśrī (1972). Bibliotheca Himalayica, series II, volume 2.

Dze smad sprul sku blo bzang dpal ldan. *Legs par bshad pa shing gi bstan bcos kyi 'grel ba lugs zung blang dor 'char ba'i me long.* Mundgod: Drepung Loseling Printing Press (1980).

Fifth Dalai Lama, Ngag dbang blo bzang rgya mtsho. *Gong sa lnga pa chen po mchog gis mdzad pa'i lugs zung dang 'brel ba'i bslab bya mu thi la'i 'phreng ba.* Kalimpong: Tibet Mirror Press (1960) [the second half of this work (pp. 13–24) is entitled *Skyes bu rnam 'byed gzhon nu'i mgul rgyan*, a text attributed to Sakya Pandita].

————. *Mchog dman bar ba rnams la lugs zung dang 'brel ba'i bslab bya gsal bar ston pa'i rim pa zla ba 'bum phrag 'char ba'i rdzing bu.* In *The Collected Works (Gsuṅ 'bum) of the Fifth Dalai Lama, Ngag-dbang blo-bzang rgya-mtsho* (reproduced from the Lhasa edition (Xylograph preserved in SRIT)). Volume 19. Gangtok: Sikkim Research Institute of Tibetology (1993) 271–350.

Flick, Hugh Meridith, Jr. *Carrying Enemies on Your Shoulder: Indian Folk Wisdom in Tibet.* Delhi: Sri Satguru Publications (1996).

Gung thang dkon mchog bstan pa'i sgron me (commentary author unknown). *Chu dang shing gi bstan bcos.* Thimphu: Text Book Division, The Department of Education, Royal Government of Bhutan (1984).

———. *Chu shing bstan bcos.* This consists of two works: *Legs par bshad pa shing gi bstan bcos lugs gnyis yal 'dabs brgya ldan* and *Legs par bshad pa chu'i bstan bcos lugs gnyis rlabs phreng brgya ldan.* In Ngawang Gelek Demo, compiler, *The Collected Works of Gung thang dkon mchog bstan pa'i sgron me* 9 (1979).

———. *Chu shing bstan bcos.* Dharamsala: Tibetan Cultural Printing Press (1984).

———. *A Hundred Waves of Elegant Sayings.* Translated and edited by Yeshi Tashi. The Dalai Lama Tibeto-Indological Series-X. Sarnath: Central Institute of Higher Tibetan Studies (1991).

Gyurme, Dorji, and Matthew Kapstein. *The Nyingma School of Tibetan Buddhism: Its Fundamentals and History.* Volume 2: Reference Material. Boston: Wisdom Publications (1991).

Hartley, Lauran. *A Socio-Historical Study of the Kingdom of Sde-dge (Derge, Khams) in the late Nineteenth Century: Ris-med Views of Alliance and Authority.* Master's thesis, University of Indian, 1997.

Hoog, Constance. *Prince Jin-gim's Textbook of Tibetan Buddhism.* Leiden: E. J. Brill (1983).

Jackson, David. *Sa-skya Pandita on Indian and Tibetan Traditions of Philosophical Debate: The Mkhas pa rnams 'jug pa'i sgo, Section III.* Ph.D. diss., University of Washington, 1985.

'Ju mi-pham rgya-mtsho. *Rgyal po'i lugs kyi bstan bcos sa gzhi skyong ba'i rgyan.* Delhi: Gelong Jamyang, Ladakh Institute of Higher Studies (1968).

Karma chos 'phel. *Bdud rtsi gyi 'khrungs dpe legs bshad nor bu'i phreng mdzes.* Lhasa: Bod ljongs mi dmangs dpe skrun khang (1993).

Keith, A. Berriedale. *A History of Sanskrit Literature.* Oxford: Clarendon Press (1928).

Kolmas, Josef. "The Aphorisms *(legs-bshad)* of Sa-ska Pandita." *Proceedings of the Csoma de Körös Memorial Symposium.* Budapest: held at Mátrafüred, Hungary, 24–30 September 1976, Ligeti, L., editor, Akadémiai Kiadó (1978): 189–203.

de Körös, Alexander Csoma. No. XIV, "A brief notice of the *Subhāṣitu-ratna-*

nidhi of Saskya Pandita, with extracts and translations." *Journal of the Asiatic Society of Bengal* XXIV (1855): 141–65 and XXV (1856): 257–94. Reprinted in *Tibetan Studies: Being a Reprint of the Articles Contributed to the Journal of the Asiatic Society of Bengal,* edited by E. D. Ross. Calcutta: The Asiatic Society of Bengal (1911) 93–172.

————. No. V, "Origin of the Shakya Race translated from the *la,* or the 26th volume of the *mDo* class in the Kangyur commencing on the 161st leaf." *Journal of the Asiatic Society of Bengal* II (1833): 385. Reprinted in *Collected Works of Alexander Csoma de Körös,* edited by J. Terjek. Budapest: Akadémiai Kiadó (1984).

Kuijp, Leonard W. J. van der. *Contributions to the Development of Tibetan Buddhist Epistemology.* Weisbaden: Franz Steiner (1983).

Lu-trub (Nāgārjuna). *She-rab dong-bu, or Prajnya Danda.* Edited and translated by Major W. L. Campbell. Calcutta: Calcutta University (1919).

Monier-Williams, Sir Monier. *Sanskrit-English Dictionary.* New Delhi: Munshiram Manoharlal Publishers (1981).

Naga, Sangye T., and Tsepak Rigzin. *Tibetan Quadrisyllabics, Phrases and Idioms (Bod dbyin shan sbyar gyi tshig tshogs dang gtam dpe).* Dharamsala: Library of Tibetan Works and Archives (1994).

Nāgārjuna. *A Drop of Nourishment for People, and Its Commentary, The Jewel Ornament.* Translated by Stanley Frye. Dharamsala: Library of Tibetan Works and Archives (1981).

Nāgārjuna and Sakya Pandita. *Elegant Sayings.* Berkeley: Dharma Publishing (1977).

Paṇ chen bsod nams grags pa. *Mkhas pa dang blun po brtag pa'i bstan bcos dge ldan legs bshad pad ma dkar po'i chun po.* In *The Collected Works (Gsuṅ 'bum) of Paṇ chen bsod nams grags pa* II. Mundgod: Drepung Loseling Library Society (1988).

Pathak, Suniti Kumar. *The Indian Nītiśāstras in Tibet.* Delhi: Motilal Banarsidass (1974).

Rigzin, Tsepak. *Tibetan-English Dictionary of Buddhist Terminology.* Dharamsala: Library of Tibetan Works and Archives (1993).

Roerich, George N. *The Blue Annals.* Delhi: Motilal Banarsidass (1979).

Ryder, Arthur W., translator. *The Pañchatantra.* Chicago: Phoenix Books, The University of Chicago (1967).

Sakya Pandita. Excerpts from "A Precious Treasury of Elegant Sayings (Legs-bshad rin-po-che'i gter)." In *Elegant Sayings,* by Nāgārjuna and Sakya Pandita, pp. 63–71. Berkeley: Dharma Publishing (1977).

——. *Legs par bshad pa rin po che'i gter.* In *The Complete Works of Pandita kun dga' rgyal mtshan* 5, compiled by Bsod nams rgya mtsho, pp. 50–61. Tokyo: Tokyo Bunko (1968). Bibliotheca Tibetica 1–5.

——. *Rang gis rang la gros 'debs pa.* In *The Complete Works of Pandita Kun dga' rgyal mtshan,* 5, compiled by Bsod nams rgya mtsho, pp. 427–28. Tokyo: Tokyo Bunko (1968). Bibliotheca Tibetica 1–5.

——. *Skyes bu rnam 'byed gzhon nu'i mkhul rgyan.* Included as the second half of a book entitled *Gong sa lnga pa chen po mchog gis mdzad pa'i lugs zung dang 'brel ba'i bslab bya mu thi li'i 'phreng ba.* Kalimpong: Tibet Mirror Press (1960).

Sa skya mkhan po sangs rgyas bstan 'dzin (Śākya Bhikṣu Maitri Buddha Shasanadhara). *Legs par bshad pa rin po che'i gter gyi don 'grel blo gsal bung ba'i bsti gnas (sa legs 'grel pa).* Dharamsala: Tibetan Cultural Printing Press (1988).

Sde srid sangs rgyas rgya mtshos. "'Tsho byed gzhon nus sman spel tshul." In *Gso rig sman gyi khog 'bugs.* Lanzhou: Kan su'u mi rigs dpe skrun khang (1982): 90–121.

Shakabpa, W. D. *Tibet: A Political History.* New York: Potala Publications (1984).

Shes rab rdo rje. *Mkhas dang grub pa'i 'byung gnas byang ngam ring chos sde chen po'i chos 'byung rna ba'i bdud rtsi'i snying po.* Lhasa: Bod ljongs mi dmangs dpe skrun khang (1994).

Sixth Panchen Lama Blo bzang thub bstan chos kyi nyi ma. *Legs par bshad pa sa'i bstan bcos lugs gnyis 'od rgya 'bar ba'i dbyig gi 'phreng ba* and *Legs par bshad pa chu'i bstan bcos lugs gnyis blang dor kun gsal.* In *The Collected Works of the Sixth Panchen Lama Blo bzang thub bstan chos kyi nyi ma,* 1. New Delhi: Lham khar Yons 'dzin Bstan pa rgyal mtshan (1973), folios 548–82.

Smith, Warren, W. Jr. *Tibetan Nation.* Boulder: Westview Press (1996).

Snellgrove, David, and Hugh Richardson. *A Cultural History of Tibet.* Boston: Shambhala (1986).

Speyer, J. S., translator. *The Jātakamāla* by Āryaśūra. Delhi: Motilal Banarsidass (1982).

Sternbach, Ludwik. *Cānakya-rāja-nīti: Maxims on* Rāja-nīti *Compiled from Various Collections of Maxims Attributed to* Cānakya. Madras: Adyar Library and Research Centre (1963).

———. "Indian Wisdom and Its Spread Beyond India." *Journal of the American Oriental Society* 101.1 (1981): 97–131.

———. "Note on the Identification of Some of the Sayings in Sa Skya Pandita's *Subhāṣita-ratna-nidhi.*" *Acta Orientalia Academiae Scientarium Hungaricae,* vol. XXXIV (1–3) (1980): 249–62.

———. *Subhāṣita, Gnomic, and Didactic Literature.* Weisbaden: Otto Harrassowitz (1974).

———. *The Spreading of Cānakya's Aphorisms Over "Greater India."* Calcutta: Calcutta Oriental Book Agency (1969).

———. "*Subhāṣita-saṃgrahas,* A Forgotten Chapter in the Histories of Sanskrit Literature." *Indologica Taurinensia,* 1 (1973): 168–219.

Suzuki, Daisetz T., editor. *The Tibetan Tripitaka, Peking Edition.* Tokyo: Tibetan Tripitaka Research Institute, 144 (1957), 5820–27, folios 140b–191b.

Thonden, Losang, and John T Davenport. "Extracts from the *Sakya Legshe.*" In *Chö-Yang (chos dbyangs): The Voice of Tibetan Religion and Culture* pp. 74–76. Dharamsala: Council for Religious and Cultural Affairs, Gangchen Kyishong (1991).

Trichen, Chogay. *The History of the Sakya Tradition.* Bristol: Ganesh Press (1983).

Tshe ring dbang rgyal. *The Tale of the Incomparable Prince.* Translated by Beth Newman. New York: HarperCollins (1997).

Tucci, Giuseppe. *Tibetan Painted Scrolls.* Kyoto: Rinsen Book Company (1980).

Zhang rgyal ba dpal bzang po. *Dpal ldan sa skya pandita chen po'i rnam par thar pa.* In *The Complete Works of Pandita kun dga' rgyal mtshan,* 5, compiled by Bsod nams rgya mtsho, pp. 433–38. Tokyo: Tokyo Bunko (1968). Bibliotheca Tibetica 1–5,

SUBJECT INDEX
(located by verse number)

ALSO FROM WISDOM PUBLICATIONS

~Available in April 2000!
HERMIT OF GO CLIFFS
Timeless Instructions of a Tibetan Mystic
Translated and Introduced by Cyrus Stearns
Paper: 224 pages, 0-86171-164-5, $19.95

The great Tibetan meditation master Gyalwa Godrakpa (1170–1249) practiced and taught a nonsectarian approach to realization. *Hermit of Go Cliffs* is the first English translation of *The Collected Songs of Godrakpa*, presented here with the original Tibetan text and with Cyrus Stearns' comprehensive introduction to Godrakpa's life, legacy, and poetry.

Like the songs of Tibet's great saint Milarepa, Godrakpa's songs are uniquely beautiful and accessible: sometimes stern and sharp, sometimes lyrical and filled with allusions to the natural world. These songs express what Godrakpa emphasized in his life—a no-nonsense approach to the practice of meditation.

THE FULFILLMENT OF ALL HOPES
Guru Devotion in Tibetan Buddhism
Tsongkhapa
Translated by Gareth Sparham
Paper: 160 pages, 0-86171-153-X, $15.95

Why is it important to have a spiritual teacher? How does one enter into such a relationship intelligently? Devoting oneself to a spiritual teacher is a practice much misunderstood in the West, yet fundamental to the tantric Buddhism of Tibet. *The Fulfillment of All Hopes* is an explanation of this core practice by Tsongkhapa, one of Tibet's most revered scholar-practitioners. Presented here is a complete translation of Tsongkhapa's commentary on the well-known *Fifty Stanzas on the Guru* accompanied by the original Tibetan text.

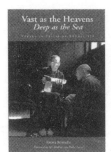

INTRODUCTION TO TANTRA
A Vision of Totality
Lama Thubten Yeshe
Paper: 176 pages, 0-86171-021-5, $15.95

What is tantra? Who is qualified to practice it? How should it be practiced? What are the results? According to Buddhism, every human being has the potential to achieve profound and lasting happiness. And according to the tantric teachings of Buddhism, this remarkable transformation can be realized very quickly if we utilize all aspects of our human energy—especially the energy of our desires.

Introduction to Tantra is the best available clarification of a subject that is often misunderstood. In this book, Lama Yeshe, who was a fully realized tantric meditator, scholar, and yogi, outlines the entire tantric path.

"No one has summarized the essence of tantra as well as Thubten Yeshe does here."
—Religious Studies Review

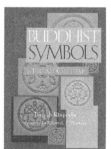

BUDDHIST SYMBOLS IN TIBETAN CULTURE
An Investigation of the Nine Best-Known Groups of Symbols
Dagyab Rinpoche
Foreword by Robert A.F. Thurman
Paper: 168 pages, 0-86171-047-9, $15.95

"…an excellent summary of symbols used in Tibetan culture. Dagyab Rinpoche goes beyond just presenting a beautiful compendium of symbols and generously tries to convey some of the power and magic that formed the culture of Tibet."
—Shambhala Sun

"…interesting for both the specialist and any interested reader."
—Himalayan Research Bulletin

ABOUT WISDOM

WISDOM PUBLICATIONS, a not-for-profit publisher, is dedicated to making available authentic Buddhist works for the benefit of all. We publish translations of the sutras and tantras, commentaries and teachings of past and contemporary Buddhist masters, and original works by the world's leading Buddhist scholars. We publish our titles with the appreciation of Buddhism as a living philosophy and with the special commitment to preserve and transmit important works from all the major Buddhist traditions.

If you would like more information or a copy of our mail-order catalog, please contact us at:

Wisdom Publications
199 Elm Street
Somerville, Massachusetts 02144 USA
Telephone: (617) 776-7416 • Fax: (617) 776-7841
Email: info@wisdompubs.org • www.wisdompubs.org

THE WISDOM TRUST

As a not-for-profit publisher, Wisdom Publications is dedicated to the publication of fine Dharma books for the benefit of all sentient beings and dependent upon the kindness and generosity of sponsors in order to do so. If you would like to make a donation to Wisdom, please do so through our Somerville office. If you would like to sponsor the publication of a book, please write or e-mail us for more information.

Thank you.

Wisdom Publications is a non-profit, charitable 501(c)(3) organization and a part of the Foundation for the Preservation of the Mahayana Tradition (FPMT).